CliffsAP®

Psychology

CliffsAP®

Psychology

An American BookWorks Corporation Project

Text by:

Lori A. Harris, PhD
Department of Psychology
Murray State University
Murray, KY 42071

Tests by:

Kevin T. Ball, BA
Indiana University
Bloomington, IN

Deborah Grayson Riegel, MA
President, Elevated Training Inc.

Lisa S. Taubenblat, CSW
Partnership with Children,
Brooklyn, NY

WILEY

Wiley Publishing, Inc.

Editorial

Project Editor: Marcia Larkin and Kelly D. Henthorne

Acquisitions Editor: Greg Tubach

Copy Editor: Kathleen M. Robinson

Technical Editor(s): Jeff Kellogg

Composition

Proofreader: Debbye Butler

Wiley Indianapolis Composition Services

CliffsAP® Psychology

Published by:
Wiley Publishing, Inc.
111 River Street
Hoboken, NJ 07030-5774
www.wiley.com

Copyright © 2005 Wiley, Hoboken, NJ

Published by Wiley, Hoboken, NJ
Published simultaneously in Canada

Library of Congress Cataloging-in-Publication Data

Grayson, Fred N.
  CliffsAP psychology : an American BookWorks Corporation project / written by Fred Grayson.
     p. cm.
  Includes bibliographical references and index.
  ISBN-13: 978-0-7645-7316-3 (pbk. : alk. paper)
  ISBN-10: 0-7645-7316-0 (alk. paper)
  1. Psychology--Examinations, questions, etc. 2. Psychology--Examinations--Study guides. 3. Advanced
placement programs (Education) I. American BookWorks Corporation. II. Title.
  BF78.G72 2005
  150'.76--dc22

                              2005017384

Printed in the United States of America

10 9 8 7 6 5 4

1B/RV/QV/QY/IN

Table of Contents

PART I: SUBJECT AREA REVIEW

Introduction

About the Test

Welcome to the AP Psychology test review. In this book you will learn how to improve your score on the final test. How can we say that? Studies have proven throughout the years that the more practice you have taking sample tests, the better your score is when you finally take the actual exam. It makes sense, doesn't it? The more you study, the better you do.

And of course, it helps to know something about the test that you'll be taking. The test is a two-hour exam and has two parts. The first part is a 70-minute multiple-choice section. The second part is a 50-minute free-response section. The following is a list of the major content areas covered by the AP Psychology exam, including the *approximate* percentage of multiple-choice questions devoted to each area.

    I. History and Approaches (2%–4%)

    II. Research Methods (6%–8%)

    III. Biological Bases of Behavior (8%–10%)

    IV. Sensation and Perception (7%–9%)

    V. States of Consciousness (2%–4%)

    VI. Learning (7%–9%)

    VII. Cognition (8%–10%)

    VIII. Motivation and Emotion (7%–9%)

    IX. Developmental Psychology (7%–9%)

    X. Personality (6%–8%)

    XI. Testing and Individual Differences (5%–7%)

    XII. Abnormal Psychology (7%–9%)

    XIII. Treatment of Psychological Disorders (5%–7%)

    XIV. Social Psychology (7%–9%)

A good part of the test involves a knowledge of vocabulary, so it's best to create your own list of words that are important. As you review the material in this book, start keeping a list of those words that are important, or those that you aren't sure of. If you begin to practice and memorize these words early in the study process, you'll be well armed when the test begins. You should be able to develop a list of 100–200 words and/or terms. If you know those, it will make your test taking much easier.

Multiple-Choice Questions

The questions that are covered in the multiple-choice section of the test are selected from the 14 areas of scientific psychology, listed previously. For the most part, the questions are evenly distributed throughout the test. Some of the questions test your knowledge and understanding of psychological terms. Other questions ask you to apply concepts derived from a specific psychological theory. Other questions assess your ability to demonstrate understanding of a specific theoretical framework or measure your knowledge of specific research studies.

The key to doing well on this part of the examination is understanding *how* to answer multiple-choice questions.

Most of the standardized tests that you've probably taken throughout your educational career have contained multiple-choice questions. For some reason, these types of questions give a large percentage of test takers a difficult time. If you approach these questions carefully, they should be easier than you think.

Let's analyze the concept of the multiple-choice question. Keep in mind that these questions are created to test your ability to recognize the correct answer from five choices. This makes it a little more difficult than those with only four choices.

Questions are composed of three parts:

1. The question stem
2. The correct choice
3. Distracters

Test-item writers normally include the following:

- One choice that is absolutely correct
- One or two choices that are absolutely incorrect (distracters)
- One or two choices that might be similar to the correct answer, but contain some information that is not quite accurate or on target, or choices that do not answer the specific question (distracters)

How do you approach these questions? Read the question, and see whether you know the answer. If you know it automatically, you can look at the choices and select the correct one. Let's look at a basic example:

---

1. The _____ demands that we behave morally at all times.
   - **A.** id
   - **B.** ideal self
   - **C.** superego
   - **D.** ego
   - **E.** real self

If you have a basic understanding of Freudian psychology, this question should be easy for you. It requires, of course, knowledge of the different terms. Let's analyze each of the choices:

A. The id operates according to the pleasure principle, seeking immediate gratification of all impulses at all times.

B. The ideal self and the real self are concepts proposed by Carl Rogers. They represent our current self and the self we would like to become.

C. The superego demands that we behave morally at all times. It operates according to the morality principle and demands perfection and adherence to rules and standards at all times.

D. The ego operates according to the reality principle, seeking a balance between the impulses of the id and the desire for moral behavior from the superego.

E. See the previous explanation for choice **B.**

The choice can only be **C,** superego. How did you do? Were you able to analyze the question in terms of the answer? You could have eliminated both ideal self and real self from the choices because they are not Freudian concepts, and neither one has to do with behaving morally—which is what the question asks. This is the time-honored approach of *process of elimination.*

You start by eliminating choices that do not seem logical, or those that you know immediately are incorrect. As we said, you can eliminate choices **B** and **E.** This leaves only three choices. You've reduced your odds of selecting the correct answer from one out of five (20%) to one out of three (33 1/3%), which is a lot better.

When you've eliminated those two choices, move to the next choice. What about the id? If you know that the id functions according to the pleasure principle, it is not likely that morality is involved, so you can eliminate choice **A.** Now you have only two choices, and you've increased your odds to one out of two (50%).

Now, unless you know the correct answer, you can guess. In the AP Psychology test, random guessing can count against you because 1/4 of a point is deducted for incorrect answers. However, you have to answer four questions incorrectly to lose one point, so if you have some knowledge of the question and have used the process of elimination, you should take a chance on answering the question. At the same time, you don't lose anything by not answering a question. Unless you have no idea of the answer and no concept of which choices to eliminate, it's probably better to try getting points by taking a chance.

Also, pay attention to words like *always*, *never*, and *not*. Most things in the world are not *always* or *never* anything, and you should be careful if a question asks you to decide which of the choices is *not* something! Also watch the wording on questions that state, "All are correct *except*. . ."

It might be helpful to go through the entire multiple-choice section as quickly as possible, answering all the questions you can answer easily. Then go back and work on those that cause you more difficulty.

Free-Response Questions

The free-response section of the AP Psychology test includes two in-depth questions and is worth one-third (1/3) of your score on the overall test. You have 50 minutes to write both essays, and it's important to understand what they are looking for in the questions. You are asked to incorporate concepts from a number of individual domains, and the material on which you are tested can be derived from any of the 14 topics presented in this book. It might be helpful to consult previous free-response questions that have been released by the College Board as well as work on those presented in this book. Time yourself as you write so that you develop an instinct for how long it takes to write each essay. Keep in mind that you have only 25 minutes for each one.

Here are some tips that might be helpful. Keep in mind that points are *not* deducted for grammar and/or usage, so don't waste time trying to write the perfect essay. It is important, however, to write neatly. If you print more clearly than using script, by all means, do so. Remember that the readers of your responses can only grade what they can read clearly.

Because the free-response questions have multiple parts, make sure that you answer each section. Above all, try to indicate which part of each question you are answering. As you write, it is helpful to give examples that are related to the topic. This helps the reader know that you truly understand the topic. If you aren't familiar with a particular section or are confused by it, just write something, even if it's a list of relevant terms and definitions. You might salvage an extra point.

What if you are working on the second response and suddenly something comes to you that should be included in the first response? If you did not leave enough room to add this material, don't despair. Just include it at the end of the second response, but indicate at the end of the first response that more follows at the end of the second. This is important because each essay might be read by a different person, and if you do not indicate additional information, the reader of the first response has no way of knowing what to look for.

Using This Book

As you go through this book, take your time with the questions and answers. Try to analyze the items you answer incorrectly, and learn from the answers. Identify those questions where you are able to use the process of elimination. Check how well you do on those. How many do you just know and are able to answer? Don't just worry about how well or poorly you do; take the time to do an analysis of your results.

You will note that in the free-response questions, we do not provide actual essays. Instead, we give an outline of what should be included in *your* essay. This is a good way for you to understand how to answer these types of questions—to organize your thoughts, outline them in your head, and then make sure you've covered all the points before beginning to write.

There are no secrets to being a successful test taker. Obviously, you must be armed with an education and have the knowledge and skills to be able to take the test. You also have a better chance if you practice the techniques of answering multiple-choice questions that we've presented here. The real key to success is to practice as much as possible. The more you practice, the better you will do on the test. After reviewing all the chapters in the book, take the practice exams. They are simulated exams, and it is helpful if you time yourself. Take them in a quiet place, away from outside distractions. Use a stopwatch, and you'll find that as you move from test to test, you improve your ability to analyze and answer the questions.

When you've completed each exam, take a break, and then check your answers. We've tried to provide clear explanations for each question so that you learn something as you go along. If you have more questions, go back to the chapters or ask your AP teacher for help. By the time you finish this book, you'll be ready for the actual exam.

Good luck!

PART I

SUBJECT AREA REVIEW

History and Approaches

Psychology is the scientific study of the mind, behavior and the relationship between them. As such it is both a *natural* science and a *social* science. As a natural science, psychology involves the study of the laws of nature. As a social science, psychology involves the study of thoughts, feelings and behaviors of people.

The roots of modern-day psychology can be traced to ancient Greece. In fact, the word *psychology* itself is derived from the Greek word *psyche,* meaning the soul or breath of life. But not until the late 1800s did psychology develop as a formal, scientific discipline. When the first formal psychological laboratory was founded in 1879 by Wilhelm Wundt, a psychologist and philosopher at the University of Leipzip in Germany, the seeds of modern-day psychology were planted.

Since its inception, the field of psychology has included people with different ideas about what to study and how to study it. Today's psychologists work from a variety of theoretical models as they attempt to unravel the mysteries of the mind. And though the field has changed and expanded dramatically since its ancient Greek beginnings, many of the original ideas form the basis of psychological inquiry today.

This chapter provides an overview of the history of psychology and a summary of the seven theoretical approaches to psychological study. Together, these form the pillars of modern-day psychology providing a strong foundation for exploring contemporary psychological ideas as they continue to evolve.

Logic, Philosophy and History of Science

The field of psychology has been shaped by a diverse list of people and ideas throughout history. Each historical phase has left its mark on modern-day psychological studies.

The roots of psychology can be traced back to both philosophy and physiology. *Philosophy* is the study of seeking knowledge and wisdom in understanding the nature of the universe through self-examination and experiences. *Physiology* is the scientific study of living organisms primarily through observation. Both fields had a direct influence on ancient Greek discussions about the nature of human thoughts and behavior.

The Greek physician **Hippocrates** (ca 460–377 B.C.) is commonly known as the father of medicine. However, he was also a respected philosopher who was one of the first to impose empirical observations to the study of medicine. In his research, Hippocrates sought to discover the source of the mind. To him, the mind was a separate, distinct entity that controlled the body. This philosophical belief that the mind is different from the body is called **mind-body dualism.** Proponents of dualism believe that the body is composed of physical substances, but the mind is ethereal and not composed of physical substance. These mental and physical phenomena are considered to be separate in the eyes of dualists.

Two other famous Greek philosophers, **Plato** (ca 428–348 B.C.) and **Aristotle** (ca 384–322 B.C.) also influenced our modern-day psychology studies. Plato is considered a **rationalist** because of his assertion that knowledge is most effectively acquired through rational methods by using philosophical analysis to understand the world and the people in it. Aristotle, Plato's student, is called an **empiricist** because of his belief that we acquire knowledge through empirical methods, obtaining evidence through experience, observation and experimentation. He is often credited with the development of a systematic approach to the physical world, an approach that is at the core of the modern **scientific method.** Today, psychologists rely on the scientific method to conduct research in an orderly, standardized way.

Almost 2,000 years later, a French philosopher named **Rene Descartes** (1596–1650) renewed interest in the mind-body problem. To answer the question of how the mind is related to the body, Descartes developed a concept known as **interactionsism** in which he proposed that the mind affects the body and the body affects the mind. He believed that this interaction occurs in the **pineal gland,** a small gland located in the lower center of the brain. According to Descartes, the dualistic nature of humans is what separates humans from animals. For humans, the mind is essential. *Cogito ergo sum* (Latin for *I think, therefore I am*) is perhaps Descartes' most famous quotation.

Thomas Hobbes (1588–1679), a seventeenth-century English philosopher, furthered the idea of **monism** (the idea that human experiences are physical processes emanating from the brain). According to monism, the mind does not exist in its own right. Instead, our thoughts are by-products of anatomical and physiological activity. As a result, Hobbes believed that we can understand the mind only by understanding the body.

The British empiricist and philosopher **John Locke** (1632–1704) believed that the interaction between the mind and body is a symmetrical relationship. He rejected Descartes's notion that physical and mental phenomena are distinct. He perpetuated the idea that the mind is dependent on the body for all its information and that the body is dependent on the mind to store experiences for later use. Locke also espoused the idea that humans are born without any knowledge, and have to seek knowledge through empirical observation. His belief that a newborn child is a blank slate, or tabula rasa in Latin, means that all knowledge is acquired through experiences over an entire lifetime.

German philosopher **Immanuel Kant** (1724–1804) redefined the mind-body question by asking how the mind and body are related instead of asking which is in control. He proposed that a set of faculties, or mental powers, provides a link between mind and body, integrating the two. These faculties (senses, understanding and reason) were believed to work together, and Kant used both rationalism and empiricism in his quest for understanding the relationship between the mind and body. Kant's philosophical contributions combined with nineteenth-century scientific exploration of the body to influence the eventual establishment of psychology as a discipline.

Charles Darwin (1809–1882) had a significant impact on the evolution of psychology as a science. Before Darwin, human beings considered themselves separate from all other animals and, as such, above the laws of nature. Darwin's *Origin of Species*, published in 1859, introduced the ideas of **natural selection** and **evolution.** Although Darwin was not the first person to propose a theory of evolution, his explanation of how evolution occurs offered a unique perspective. Natural selection promotes the survival and reproduction of individuals who are most able to adapt to their particular environment. Darwin's principles still serve as a cornerstone of all contemporary life sciences, and Darwin's explanation of the mechanism by which evolution worked is essential to the evolutionary approach.

The first psychological laboratory was founded in 1879 by **Wilhelm Wundt** (1832–1920), a physiologist and philosopher at the University of Leipzig in Germany. Wundt's work focused on perception and conscientiousness. He believed that psychology should deal with conscious experiences. This means evaluating the contents of consciousness to find the most fundamental elements of thought. He worked with his students to refine the art of **objective introspection,** the process of recording their thoughts, feelings and sensory experiences in great detail.

One of Wundt's students, **Edward Titchener** (1867–1927), wrote that psychology "is the science of consciousness." He broke consciousness down into three basic elements: physical sensations (what we see), feelings (such as liking or disliking something) and images (memories of things). Titchener believed that even the most complex thoughts can be reduced to these simple elements, and that the role of psychology is to identify these elements and show how they can be combined and integrated. His ideas were similar to Wundt's, as they both subscribed to a school of thought known as **structuralism,** which emphasizes the analysis of consciousness into its basic components through introspection.

William James (1842–1910) was the first American-born psychologist. With an academic interest in both physiology and philosophy, James gravitated toward psychology as a way to link his two passions. As a Harvard professor, he rejected the notion of structuralism, arguing that perceptions, emotions and images cannot be separated. Instead, he believed that consciousness flows in a continuous stream. As a result of his work, he was a leader in the **functionalism** movement. Functionalism goes beyond sensation and perception in an attempt to explore how an individual learns to function in an environment. Influenced by Darwin's theory of evolution, functionalism developed the idea of learning through adapting to the environment.

Modern Psychological Perspectives

Psychological perspectives that emerged in the twentieth century were built on some of the ideas developed throughout history. In fact, some of the central themes found in these perspectives were first examined by the ancient Greeks. While the twentieth-century ideas are more sophisticated than their Greek counterparts, many of the principles are familiar.

The AP Psychology exam focuses on seven approaches: biological, behavioral, cognitive, humanistic, psychodynamic, sociocultural and evolutionary/sociobiological. Historically, psychologists have clashed over the merits of the various approaches to psychology, advocating one theoretical perspective over another. Today's psychologists tend to see the different approaches as complementary, with each contributing in its own way to our overall understanding of human behavior.

Biological Approach

Biological psychology attempts to understand behavior through the study of anatomy and physiology, especially of the brain. Firmly rooted in the work of Hippocrates, biological psychology, or *psychobiology*, assumes that the mind and body are interrelated. And, as such, both nature and nurture can influence personality traits and disorders. Through the years, a biological approach to psychology has helped shed light on the possible treatments of psychological disorders as well as the neural activity related to normal functioning. By using modern-day medical devices such as CAT scans, PET scans, MRIs and EEGs to study the biological functions of the brain, researchers are able to pinpoint regions of the brain that are responsible for specific behaviors.

The view that all psychological disorders have a biochemical or physiological basis has helped researchers discover links between genetic factors and mental disorders, leading to new treatment options.

Behavioral Approach

Originating in the United States during the early twentieth century, **behaviorism** emphasizes the idea that psychology should be completely objective, focusing only on observable behavior and corresponding stimuli. Rejecting the principles of functionalism and structuralism, American **John B. Watson** (1878–1958) is usually acknowledged as the founder of behaviorism. Watson's view states that any behavior can be shaped and controlled. In the most extreme case, he believed that he could take a healthy infant and raise him to become anything he wanted him to be. This idea is reminiscent of John Locke's tabula rasa concept.

Watson's view of psychology was based on experiments conducted by the Russian physiologist, **Ivan Pavlov** (1849–1936). Pavlov used the dogs in his laboratory to test whether a reflex such as salivation could be shaped by learning. By pairing the sound of a bell with the presence of food, and then later ringing the bell without introducing any food, Pavlov concluded that all behavior is a learned response to some stimulus in the environment. Known as **classical conditioning,** this stimulus-response technique was employed by Watson on humans in an attempt to induce specific learned behaviors.

B.F. Skinner (1904–1990) was another radical behaviorist who, like Watson, believed that psychologists should study only observable and measurable behaviors. He was also interested in changing behavior through conditioning, but through a new element: reinforcement. Skinner's work is built around the idea of **operant conditioning**, which rewards subjects for behaving in a specific way. According to Skinner, an external stimulus does not directly elicit a response. Instead, the presence of a reinforcer (a positive consequence that follows a behavior) increases the likelihood that the operant behavior will occur again under similar circumstances. This approach makes the subject an active participant in their own conditioning.

Cognitive Approach

Cognitive psychology emphasizes the importance of cognition—or how people think—as the basis for understanding human behavior. Emerging during the 1960s in response to behaviorism, cognitive psychology states that mental processes must be studied scientifically. By observing quantifiable behavior, cognitive psychologists believe that they can make inferences about the underlying cognitive processes at work.

Early cognitivists tended to emphasize **serial processing,** or step-by-step processing, of information. Today, many cognitivists also include **parallel processing,** in which multiple mental processes occur all at once, in their research.

Drawing from many different disciplines, cognitive psychology fuses together efforts in linguistics, philosophy, neurology, and computer science. Research using computer metaphors and computer programs to simulate human thought processes and behavior is common in this field of study. Artificial intelligence models are used frequently to illustrate how human thought might work, providing insight into specific cognitive processes.

Humanistic Approach

The **humanistic approach** dates back to the ancient Greeks and centers on a holistic perspective that emphasizes the potential for individual growth and change. Humanistic psychologists focus on the impact of self-awareness and free will, emphasizing the role of conscious rather than unconscious experience. They also disregard the view that psychological research can only include measurable behavior.

Notable humanist **Carl Rogers** (1902–1987) is known for his person-centered approach that focuses on how an individual defines reality and personality rather than an external, objective view of these things. This self-concept comprises all the aspects of the self as perceived by an individual. And, according to Rogers, every individual strives to achieve self-actualization, or the fulfillment of their human potential. As an outgrowth of his theories, Rogers developed client-centered therapy in which a patient is given unconditional positive regard by the therapist in an attempt to help the patient develop a sense of congruence between who they are (self concept) and who they aspire to be (ideal self).

Abraham Maslow (1908–1970), a humanistic psychologist best known for his hierarchy of needs, also subscribed to the idea of self-actualization. According to Maslow, five levels of human needs make up the hierarchy. Starting from the bottom with the most basic needs, he believed that people progress through physiological needs, safety and security needs, belongingness and love needs, esteem needs, and finally the need for self-actualization.

Psychodynamic Approach

Psychodynamic (or **psychoanalytical**) **psychology** is based on the idea that unconscious thought is often in conflict with conscious behavior. **Sigmund Freud** (1856–1939) is considered the founder of the psychodynamic approach. His theories propose two levels of reality: conscious and unconscious. The conscious is composed of mental states such as memories, of which we are aware. The unconscious is composed of mental states of which we are unaware or to which we do not normally have access. According to Freud, the conscious and unconscious minds are often in conflict, giving way to a unique school of thought and a treatment methodology known as **psychoanalysis.** Psychoanalysis takes place when an experienced analyst uses techniques such as free association and dream analysis to probe a patient's true motivations.

Psychodynamic theory has been expanded and revised by Freud's colleagues and successors. **C.G. Jung** contributed the idea that the unconscious is made up of various layers, such as the personal unconscious and the collective unconscious. **Alfred Adler** originated the notion of the inferiority complex. And **Karen Horney** focused on the importance of basic anxiety in creating a feeling of isolation.

While the psychodynamic approach laid the foundation for the study of personality and psychological disorders, it has also been criticized due to a lack of empirical support.

Sociocultural Approach

Sociocultural approaches to learning and development are based on the concept that human activities take place in cultural contexts. Psychologists who subscribe to this approach believe that an individual cannot be understood outside of the culture in which they exist. They study the implications of cross-cultural phenomena, looking for unique perspectives and universal themes. The basic ideas of sociocultural psychology were introduced and applied by Russian theorist **L. S. Vygotsky** (1896–1934) and his collaborators. Vygotsky attempted to explain consciousness as the end product of socialization. Many of Vygotsky's ideas have had an impact not only on modern-day psychologists, but also on educators.

Evolutionary/Sociobiological Approach

Evolutionary psychology focuses on the evolutionary origins of behavior patterns and mental processes. Inspired by the work of **Charles Darwin,** it seeks to apply his ideas of natural selection to the mind. Evolutionary psychologists explore how human beings got to be the way that they are and attempts to explain behavior in terms of evolved adaptations. The basic underlying principle of evolutionary psychology is the concept of **reproductive success,** meaning that all species are genetically programmed to produce offspring who can successfully reproduce themselves.

Evolutionary psychologists have recently applied Darwin's theory to explain how the human mind evolved to benefit the individual. From this point of view, complex aspects of human behavior and experience (such as language, memory and consciousness) all evolved because of their adaptive fitness. In one way or another, these features promote survival and propagation of the human species.

Review Questions

1. The belief that the mind is separate from the body is known as:

   A. behaviorism
   B. mind-body dualism
   C. mind-body monism
   D. Darwinism
   E. structuralism

2. Which philosopher introduced the idea of tabula rasa?

   A. Wilhelm Wundt
   B. Rene Descartes
   C. Abraham Maslow
   D. John Locke
   E. Plato

3. American psychologist William James is associated with which movement?

   A. functionalism
   B. structuralism
   C. empiricism
   D. rationalism
   E. Darwinism

4. Which philosopher emphasized mind over body when he said, *"Cogito ergo sum"?*

   A. Sigmund Freud
   B. Rene Descartes
   C. John Watson
   D. Thomas Hobbes
   E. John Locke

5. Which psychological approach has helped researchers discover links between genetic factors and mental disorders?

   A. sociocultural
   B. evolutionary
   C. cognitive
   D. behaviorism
   E. biological

6. The idea of self-actualization was subscribed to by which humanistic psychologists?

    A. Darwin and Freud

    B. Watson and Skinner

    C. Pavlov and Vygotsky

    D. Rogers and Maslow

    E. Plato and Aristotle

7. Which profession has been directly impacted by many of Vygotsky's sociocultural ideas?

    A. neuroscience

    B. law

    C. education

    D. the arts

    E. technology

8. Which psychological approach makes use of computer models to simulate and study human thought and behavior?

    A. cognitive

    B. psychodynamic

    C. humanistic

    D. behavioral

    E. evolutionary/sociobiological

9. What is the biggest difference between classical and operant conditioning?

    A. Classical uses a reward system; operant does not.

    B. Operant uses a reward system; classical does not.

    C. Classical works on animals; operant works on humans.

    D. Operant works on animals; classical works on humans.

    E. Classical relies on serial processing; operant relies on parallel processing.

10. According to Sigmund Freud, the conscious and the unconscious are often _____.

    A. working together

    B. in conflict with each other

    C. misunderstood

    D. the same as dualism and monism

    E. the same as the ego and the superego

Answers

1. B. The philosophical belief that the mind is different from the body is called mind-body dualism. Proponents of dualism believe that the body is composed of physical substances, but the mind is ethereal and not composed of physical substance. These mental and physical phenomena are considered separate in the eyes of dualists.

2. D. John Locke espoused the idea that humans are born without any knowledge, and therefore have to seek knowledge through empirical observation. His belief that a newborn child is a tabula rasa means that all mental knowledge is acquired through experiences over a lifetime.

3. A. William James rejected the notion of structuralism, arguing that perceptions, emotions and images cannot be separated. Instead, he believed that consciousness flows in a continuous stream. As a result of his work, he was a leader in the functionalism movement. Functionalism goes beyond sensation and perception in an attempt to explore how an individual learns to function in an environment.

4. **B.** Descartes developed a concept known as interactionsism in which he proposed that the mind affects the body and the body affects the mind. He believed that this interaction occurs in the pineal gland, a small gland located in the lower center of the brain. According to Descartes, the dualistic nature of humans is what separates humans from animals. For humans, the mind is essential. *"Cogito ergo sum"* is perhaps Descartes's most famous quotation.

5. **E.** The view that all psychological disorders have a biochemical or physiological basis has helped researchers discover links between genetic factors and mental disorders, leading to new treatment options.

6. **D.** According to Rogers, every individual strives to achieve self-actualization, or the fulfillment of their human potential. According to Maslow, five levels of human needs make up a hierarchy of needs: physiological needs, safety and security needs, belongingness and love needs, esteem needs, and finally the need for self-actualization.

7. **C.** The basic ideas of sociocultural psychology were introduced and applied by Russian theorist L. S. Vygotsky (1896–1934) and his collaborators. Vygotsky attempted to explain consciousness as the end product of socialization. Many of Vygotsky's ideas have had an impact not only on modern-day psychologists, but also on educators.

8. **A.** Research using computer metaphors and computer programs to simulate human thought processes and behavior is common in this field of study. Artificial intelligence models are used frequently to illustrate how human thought might work, providing insight into specific cognitive processes.

9. **B.** Classical conditioning is a stimulus-response technique used by Ivan Pavlov to shape learning. Operant conditioning rewards subjects for behaving in a specific way. Both fall under a behaviorism approach.

10. **B.** Freud's theories propose two levels of reality: conscious and unconscious. The conscious is composed of mental states such as memories, of which we are aware. The unconscious is composed of mental states of which we are unaware or to which we do not normally have access. According to Freud, the conscious and unconscious minds are often in conflict, giving way to a unique school of thought and a treatment methodology known as psychoanalysis.

Research Methods

The four primary goals of all scientific research are **description** (*what happens?*), **explanation** (*why does it happen?*), **prediction** (*what will happen next?*) and **control** (*how can behavior be influenced?*). To answer these questions, psychologists rely on three key types of research. Experimental, correlational and clinical research are all used to collect data systematically and objectively. Each method has advantages and disadvantages. **Experimental** research involves the deliberate manipulation of selected isolated variables and the measurement of the effects of those manipulations. **Correlational** research involves the measurement of the naturally occurring relationship between two or more variables. **Descriptive research** involves a variety of approaches designed to describe behavior including observational approaches, the use of surveys, and intensive case studies of individuals.

This chapter provides an overview the primary research methods used today. In addition, the role of statistics in psychological research is covered, and the importance of ethics in both scientific research and the practice of psychology is discussed.

Experimental Research

Experiments are designed to test a specific theory. In psychology, theories are used to predict behavior. A **hypothesis** is a generalization derived or deduced from a theory. It provides a tentative and testable explanation of the relationship between two or more specific variables. To test a psychological hypothesis, an experiment is designed and conducted to identify cause-and-effect relationships through the manipulation of variables in a controlled environment.

A **variable** is defined as an attribute or characteristic of a specific situation, person or phenomenon. Basically, two types of variables exist in any experiment. **Independent variables** are those that are manipulated by the experimenter. These are the variables of interest during the experiment. **Dependent variables** are those that are measured to see how they have changed because of the independent variable during the experiment. These variables are dependent on the independent variable. For example, if a psychologist wants to discover the relationship between test scores and hours of sleep the night before a test, they might use two groups of subjects—one that sleeps eight hours and one that sleeps only four hours. Here, amount of sleep is the independent variable, and test score results are the dependent variable. By having both groups take the same test, the experimenter can determine whether any relationship exists between these two variables.

Subjects or **participants** are the individuals whose reactions or responses are observed during an experiment. For practical purposes, most experiments are conducted using a **sample** of subjects selected from a larger population that is the focus of the study. When a **random sample** is selected, all members of the population have an equal and independent chance of being included. When a **representative sample** is selected, a subset of the population is carefully chosen to represent the proportionate diversity of the population as a whole. Some portions of the test population are more readily accessible than others; these **samples of convenience** are often selected because they are immediately available to the experimenter.

When selected, the sample subjects must be divided into at least two separate groups. The **control group** comprises participants who are *not* subjected to a change in the independent variable. The **experimental group** consists of participants who *are* subjected to a change in the independent variable. The control group results are used for comparison with the experimental group. They provide a baseline against which the experimental group's results can be compared.

To avoid biased results, subjects do not typically know whether they are part of the control group or the experimental group. In addition, experimenters might not know which subjects are in which group. When neither the subject nor the experimenter is aware of which group the subject is in, an experiment is known as **double-blind.** The double-blind technique is often used in drug research to ensure that the results are not influenced in any way by the expectations of either subjects or experimenters.

The primary advantages and disadvantages of experimental research are noted in the following chart.

Experimental Research	
Advantages	*Disadvantages*
Precise control of independent variables.	Artificial lab setting might influence subjects' behavior.
Can be repeated by another experimenter with the proper equipment.	Unexpected and uncontrolled variables might confound results.
Usually, large numbers of participants allow results to be generalized.	Many variables cannot be controlled or manipulated.
Allows for the identification of cause-and-effect relationships.	Usually, less intensive study of individuals.

Correlational Research

Correlation methods are used to assess the degree of relationship between two or more variables or attributes as they occur naturally in the group being studied. In these methods researchers do not directly manipulate variables or assign participants to groups. Instead, they observe subjects in naturally existing groups within a specific setting.

When two variables or attributes show some degree of statistical relationship, they are **correlated.** The nature of this relationship is represented by a **correlation coefficient.** A correlation coefficient tells us two things: (1) *the strength of the relationship between the two variables* and (2) *the nature of the relationship between the two variables*. The strength of the association between the two variables is indicated by the absolute value of the correlation coefficient. A coefficient near 1.00 or –1.00 indicates a strong relationship; a coefficient near zero indicates a weak relationship. The nature of the relationship between the two variables is indicated by the sign that precedes the number. A **negative correlation** is represented by a number between –1 and 0, with –1 indicating a perfect negative correlation (in which one variable increases in direct proportion to a decrease in another variable; for example, as one's level of optimism increases, frequency of illnesses decreases). A **positive correlation** is represented by a number between 0 and +1, with +1 indicating a perfect positive correlation (in which one variable increases [or decreases] in direct proportion to an increase [or decrease] in another variable; for example, as attendance increases, exam scores also increase). A correlation equal to 0 indicates no relationship between two variables.

Using methods such as naturalistic observation and surveys, psychologists try to make predictions from correlated attributes. **Naturalistic observation** occurs when animal or human behaviors are systemically studied in natural settings rather than in a laboratory setting. Behavior observed in everyday life is likely to be more natural and spontaneous than behavior that occurs in a laboratory. This method can fall victim to **observer bias,** an influence on expectations or outcomes by the observer's interpretations. To combat observer bias, many observational studies use videotape to record events that can be viewed and scored by multiple researchers who are not aware of the study's intent. Often, this type of research provides new ideas, new theories and new hypotheses, which can be studied and tested more systematically in a laboratory environment.

Surveys rely on questions being answered by a selected group of people. A set of predetermined questions is posed, and participants provide their answers in either face-to-face interviews or on questionnaires. Survey research can generate a large amount of data quickly and inexpensively, but to be accurate, the survey questions must be clearly worded and the people surveyed must be willing to provide honest answers.

Correlational research (such as naturalistic observation and surveys) can provide a lot of raw data to describe behaviors, beliefs, opinions and attitudes. But these methods should not be used to determine the causes of behavior.

Correlational Research	
Advantages	*Disadvantages*
Useful for identifying relationships between variables.	Not useful for establishing causal direction of a relationship.
Behaviors are spontaneous outside a lab setting.	Potential for researcher interference (for example, observer bias).
Often provide new ideas, new theories and new hypotheses.	Time-consuming.

In a **case study** a single individual or group of individuals is examined intensely to study a problem or issue. Procedures such as collecting biological data, administering psychological tests and conducting interviews with subjects may be used to gather information for a case study. The information gained from a case study is then used to draw general conclusions about the behavior of the group being studied or a larger population. An advantage of clinical case studies is that they provide very detailed information about a specific individual or group and the circumstances for their behavior. A potential disadvantage of this method is that the sample size is typically small, making it difficult for researchers to apply their results to the general population.

Statistics

A **statistic** is a numerical value obtained by analyzing data about a representative sample population. **Statistics** is the discipline that deals with the collection, analysis, interpretation and presentation of the numerical data. In psychology, statistics provide a tool for exploring issues, answering questions, solving problems and making decisions.

The two types of statistics are descriptive and inferential. **Descriptive statistics** are numerical analyses that summarize and organize quantitative information about a population. They are used, as the name implies, to describe data, situations and observations. **Inferential statistics** attempt to generalize from the actual observations of a small group to the general population. Inferential statistics are used by researchers to determine the likelihood that a given set of findings is the result of systemic, not random, events.

To organize the data collected during research, several key statistical concepts must be understood. A **frequency distribution** is used to organize data in a list of all possible scores and the frequency with which they occur.

Frequency Distribution		
Score	*Relative Frequency*	*Cumulative Frequency*
10	4	15
9	2	11
8	5	9
7	1	4
6	3	3

Using this distribution, two kinds of numbers can be obtained. The **relative frequency** represents the number of subjects with a specific score or range of scores. The **cumulative frequency** represents the total number of instances of values up to a certain level, including all values below this level.

This data can also be charted graphically using a **histogram** to depict the frequency distribution with a series of rectangles. The location of each rectangle on the x-axis of the histogram indicates the score; the height of the rectangle indicates how often that score occurs.

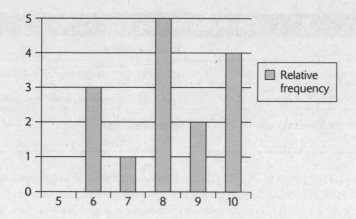

A **measure of central tendency** can be used to summarize an entire distribution with a single score. The typical value, or central tendency, of a set of data is expressed in three primary ways: the mode, the median and the mean.

The **mode** is the score that occurs most frequently within a distribution of values. In the preceding example, the mode is 8. This number occurs five times. Although it is a rough estimate, the mode provides a quick index of central tendency. This measurement is useful when at least some repeated values exist. If no repeated values occur, there is no mode. If two values appear the same number of times, the data has two modes, or is **bimodal.** If two or more values appear the same number of times, the data is **multimodal.** Because the mode takes into account the least information in the distribution, it is the least used way to measure central tendency.

The **median** is the point that divides the distribution data into two equal halves, the 50th percentile. After arranging the scores in increasing or decreasing order, the median is the middle score in the list. Using the scores from the preceding example, the median is 8.

6, 6, 6, 7, 8, 8, 8, **8**, 8, 9, 9, 10, 10, 10, 10

Because the number of values in the list is odd, the median is the number right in the middle. When an even number of values exists, there is no middle number. In this case, the median is the number halfway between the two middle numbers.

The **mean** is the average score within a distribution of values, computed by adding all the scores together and dividing by the number of scores. The mean is represented by M, and the number of scores is represented by N in this mathematical formula:

$$M = \frac{\text{sum of scores}}{N}$$

Using the example data, the mean is 281 (the sum of all scores) divided by 15, or 18.733.

The median and the mean differ most in the degree to which they are affected by extreme scores. When the highest or lowest score changes, the median remains unaffected but the mean might change drastically.

To measure the **variability** (or dispersion of scores in a data set), the **range, standard deviation** and **variance** are calculated. If the scores in the distribution are all the same, no variability exists. But if the scores in the distribution are spread out, there is variability and the degree of variability will depend on the degree of spread (with a greater spread indicating greater variability).

The **range** is calculated by subtracting the lowest score from the highest score. In our example, the range is 4 (10 – 6). A disadvantage of the range as a measure of variability is that it reflects the values of only two scores from an entire sample. Other measures of variability take more information into account.

Standard deviation is a statistical measurement of the variability of scores in a group. It provides a measure of the typical distance of scores from the mean. This measurement is considered more advantageous than the range because the standard deviation takes the full distribution of scores into account. To calculate the standard deviation, follow these steps:

1. Compute the difference between each value in the distribution and the mean.
2. Square the difference between each value and the mean.
3. Add the values of the squared differences.
4. Calculate the average of the sum of squared differences.
5. Calculate the square root of this average.

If all the values in a distribution are equal to the mean, the standard deviation is zero. If all the values in a distribution are spread out, the standard deviation is half the value of the range.

The **variance** is the degree to which a set of values varies from its mean. It is calculated by squaring the standard deviation. Variances are used in many statistical calculations, but are not as easily interpreted as standard deviations.

Normal distribution is a distribution of scores or values in which most values congregate around the median, and the measurement values quickly and evenly decline in number on either side of the median. When plotted on a frequency histogram, this distribution creates a symmetrical, bell-shaped curve known as a **normal curve.**

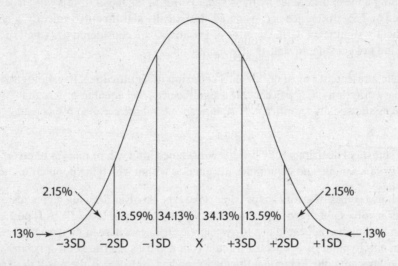

In a completely normal distribution, the median (the middle value), the mean (the average value) and the mode (the most frequent value) are exactly the same. Most distributions are approximately normal. But not all distributions are normal. A distribution can be **skewed,** or lopsided, which indicates how far the mode is above or below the mean and median values. In a negatively skewed distribution, the values of the median and the mode are greater than the value of the mean. In a positively skewed distribution, the value of the mean is greater than the values of the mode and the median.

To help researchers interpret statistical data, standard and percentile scores can be used. The **standard score** is a statistic that can be used for any distribution to equate the scores for that distribution to scores for other distributions. Also called z-scores, standard scores are arbitrarily defined to have a mean of 0 and a standard deviation of 1. When the distribution of scores is normal, approximately 68% of the scores are between –1 and +1, approximately 96% of all scores are between –2 and +2, and 4% of scores fall beyond 2 standard deviations. Standard scores make scores that are on different scales comparable. Standard scores are calculated by subtracting the mean raw score from the raw score of interest, and then dividing the difference by the standard deviation of the distribution of raw scores.

The **percentile score** refers to the proportion of subjects or scores falling at or below a given value. For example, if a score falls into the 80th percentile, 80% of scores are at or below that score.

The measure of statistical association between two sets of paired scores is called the **correlation coefficient.** This number expresses the strength and the direction of the correlation, ranging from –1 (showing a perfect inverse relationship) to +1 (showing a perfect positive relationship). A correlation coefficient of 0 occurs when no relationship exists between scores.

When two variables have a **positive correlation,** a change in one variable's value is likely to be associated with a change in the same direction of the other variable's value. When two variables have a **negative correlation,** a change in one variable's value is likely to be associated with a change in the opposite direction of the other variable's value. A correlation does not mean that a cause-and-effect relationship exists. In other words, correlation does *not* imply causation.

To determine when correlations and other indices are statistically meaningful, researchers turn to **inferential statistics.** These statistics attempt to generalize from the actual observations of a small group to the general population and are used by researchers to determine the likelihood that a given set of findings is the result of systemic, not random, events.

To draw conclusions about a general population based on studying a sample population, researchers turn to significance testing. **Statistical significance** is the probability that a given result will be obtained through pure chance. A result is statistically significant when the result is more likely due to systemic, rather than random, factors.

A **null hypothesis** is a hypothesis which states that the independent variable has no effect on the dependent variable. A **research** or **alternative hypothesis** is a hypothesis which states that the null hypothesis is false. **Experimental hypotheses** are proven by disproving null hypotheses.

By expressing the research data as a standard score (or z-score) a **critical ratio** is used to test null hypotheses. This ratio is obtained by dividing a mean difference by the standard error of the mean. If this ratio is large enough, a given null hypothesis is rejected and the difference is considered **statistically significant.** Typically, a critical ratio of 2 or more is said to be statistically significant. Critical ratios of less than 2 are considered too small to allow the rejection of a null hypothesis and are not considered statistically significant.

Before collecting any data, a researcher must decide on a **criterion of significance.** Psychologists typically use a 5% benchmark as their primary criterion of significance. If a significance level equal to or less than 5% is achieved, the results tend to be viewed as statistically significant. A significance level greater than 5% is usually seen as not being statistically significant.

Another way of making statistical decisions is by using a **confidence interval,** or margin of error. This is based on the variability of the scores from a sample and determines the interval within which the population mean likely fails.

In psychological research, two types of errors are possible. One type involves drawing a conclusion when you should not (type I), and the other involves not drawing a conclusion when you should (type II). A **type I** error occurs when a researcher believes that a finding has appeared due to systematic changes when, in fact, it is the result of random fluctuation. In other words, a null hypothesis is rejected when it is in fact true. A **type II** error occurs when a researcher believes that a finding has appeared due to random fluctuations when, in fact, it is the result of systematic changes. In other words, a null hypothesis is not rejected when it is in fact false.

Ethics in Research

Psychologists, like all scientists, must address questions of ethics. But psychological research involving human and animal subjects hasn't always been viewed from an ethical perspective. Over the years many experiments have used unethical—and unsafe—methods to test various hypotheses. For example, in 1963 Stanley Milgrim's experiments used lies and electric shocks to study obedience in human subjects. As a result of the public uproar over Milgrim's methods, the American Psychological Association (APA) revised its ethical guidelines. This new code outlines the ethical principles that guide psychological research and patient therapy.

In addition to the APA's guidelines, psychological testing must also follow the government's Code of Federal Regulations. These regulations include extensive rules to protect human subjects in all types of research.

Research institutions have standard practices and policies that require **informed consent** by all human subjects before research begins and **debriefing** after research concludes. Informed consent requires that subjects be told about the kinds of tasks they will be asked to perform and types of situations they might encounter. During the debriefing subjects are told the exact nature of the experiment and any deceptions are revealed. Throughout all phases of research, most psychology studies are conducted anonymously. (The subject's data is not associated with their name.) Most institutions also have review boards that must approve any proposed research.

For animal research the issues are slightly different. When animal subjects (such as rats, pigeons, rabbits or dogs) are used in psychological research, they cannot sign consent forms or be debriefed. However, most institutions try to ensure that the mental and physical health of all animal subjects is protected. Before any animal research is conducted, the review board must weigh the potential benefits of the research against the potential harm to the animals. Historically, many important psychological discoveries have been made during research in which animals were sacrificed to further our understanding of human health and behavior.

Review Questions

1. In a true normal distribution:

    A. The mean and median are the same, but the mode is higher.
    B. The median and mode are the same, but the mean is higher.
    C. The median and mode are the same, but the mean is lower.
    D. The median is in the middle, the mean is the highest number, and the mode is the lowest number.
    E. The mean, median and mode are all the same.

2. Which number expresses the strongest positive correlation?

    A. −.89
    B. 0
    C. +1.26
    D. +.34
    E. −.20

3. Which of the following is an example of a null hypothesis?

    A. Listening to music has no effect on a person's ability to concentrate on a test.
    B. Listening to music increases a person's ability to concentrate on a test.
    C. Listening to music decreases a person's ability to concentrate on a test.
    D. The effect of listening to music on concentration depends on the volume.
    E. Music is related to concentration.

4. Which type of research design is capable of determining a cause-and-effect relationship?

    A. naturalistic observation
    B. survey
    C. experiment
    D. correlation
    E. case study

5. Consider the following hypothesis: Students who listen to music while studying perform worse on memory tests than students who do not listen to music while studying. In this hypothesis music is the _____, and performance on memory tests is the _____.

    A. confounding variable; independent variable
    B. independent variable; dependent variable
    C. independent variable; confounding variable
    D. dependent variable; independent variable
    E. sample; variable

6. When neither the participant nor the experimenter knows which group the participant is in, the technique being used is called _____.

   A. control group
   B. random sample
   C. sample of convenience
   D. double-blind
   E. confound

7. _____ occurs when the expectations of an examiner cause him to interpret behavior in a particular way.

   A. observer bias
   B. naturalistic observation
   C. negative correlation
   D. double-blind technique
   E. a representative sample

8. If a score is in the 28th percentile, it means:

   A. Twenty-eight participants got that score.
   B. Twenty-eight percent of the participants scored above that score.
   C. Twenty-eight percent of the participants got that score.
   D. Twenty-eight percent of the participants scored at or below that score.
   E. Twenty-eight percent of the participants scored below that score.

Answers

1. **E.** A true normal distribution has a mean, median and mode that are the exact same number. When the mean is higher than the median and mode, it is called a positively skewed distribution. When the mean is lower than the median and mode, it is called a negatively skewed distribution.

2. **D.** The strongest positive correlation is +.34. A strong negative correlation is indicated by −.89. No relationship is indicated by 0.0. The number +1.26 is not a correlation coefficient because it falls outside the −1.00 to +1.00 boundary. A negative correlation is indicated by −.20, which is weaker than −.89.

3. **A.** A null hypothesis supposes that no relationship exists between the independent variable and the dependent variable. The other options are examples of either a research or alternative hypothesis.

4. **C.** Experiments can be set up to determine cause and effect because an experimenter has more control. Naturalistic observation occurs when an experimenter watches a participant in their natural surroundings, and it is a form of correlational research. Surveys are interviews or questionnaires and are also a form of correlational research. Correlations (and correlational research) can help determine whether relationships exist between variables, but cannot determine cause and effect. Case studies are a form of clinical research and can be helpful in studying details about a case, but cannot determine cause and effect.

5. **B.** Music is the independent variable because it is manipulated by the experimenter; performance on the memory test is the dependent variable because it is what the experimenter is measuring, and it depends on the music. A theory is a prediction of behavior that a hypothesis attempts to explain. A subject or participant is an individual whose responses are observed in an experiment. A sample is a group of subjects selected from a larger population. A variable is an attribute or a characteristic of a situation, person or phenomenon.

6. **D.** Double-blind is the term used to describe this technique, which ensures that results are not influenced by expectations. The control group is the group of participants who do not receive a change in the independent variable. They are compared with the experimental group. A random sample is a group of participants selected

from a population, in which all the members of the population have an equal chance of being chosen. A sample of convenience is a group of participants who are immediately available to the experimenter. A confound occurs when unexpected or uncontrolled variables influence results.

7. **A.** Observer bias occurs when the expectations of an observer/examiner cause them to interpret behavior in a particular way (usually in support of the hypothesis). Naturalistic observation is watching participants in their natural settings. Negative correlations describe relationships between variables where one variable moves in one direction, and the other variable moves in the opposite direction. Double-blind experiments are experiments in which neither the participants nor the experimenter know which group the participants are in. Representative samples are proportionate to the diversity of the population.

8. **D.** Scores in the 28th percentile are scores that fall at or below that score. In other words, 28% of the participants got that score or lower, and 72% of the participants scored higher.

Biological Bases of Behavior

Underlying all thought, behavior, and emotion is the highly complex and integrated functioning of cells within the body. Awareness of sights and sounds and the ability to walk, talk, remember, and make decisions are all made possible through the functioning of cells within the nervous system. At the core of every human is a biological system that underlies every thought, behavior, and feeling.

This chapter focuses on the biological bases of behavior, thought, and emotion. In this chapter, we first review techniques used to study and learn about the brain and the functioning of cells within the brain. We will then review the structure and function of the nervous system and how communication occurs within the nervous system. Finally, we will review the structure and function of the endocrine system and the role that genes play in human behavior, thought and emotion.

Physiological Techniques

How do we learn about the brain and how it works? Traditionally, we relied exclusively on **clinical case studies** in which researchers observe people with brain damage resulting from tumors, head injuries, or diseases to understand the functions of different regions of the brain. For example, consider the classic case of Phineas Gage, the railroad worker who had the misfortune of having an iron rod shot through his head, significantly damaging his frontal lobe. After the accident, Phineas could walk, talk and engage in most daily activities. However, he showed marked changes in his personality. Prior to the accident, Phineas was a pleasant and reliable worker. Following the accident, he was irritable, impulsive, unreliable and moody. The Phineas Gage case provided our first clues into the importance of the frontal lobes in personality and mood.

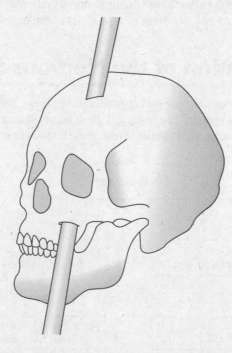

Today, we no longer have to rely solely on clinical case studies to learn about the functions of the brain. Today, a number of physiological techniques exist that allow us to monitor and sometimes view the functioning of the brain and body while at work. In 1929, German psychiatrist Hans Berger invented a machine that could detect, amplify and record activity of the brain through tiny metal electrodes pasted to the surface of the scalp. The machine, called an **electro-encephalograph (EEG),** provides information in the form of line tracings called brain waves. Using EEG recordings, we learned a great deal about the functioning of the brain while a person is relaxed, excited, drowsy, and even asleep and also how brain function is affected by strokes, epilepsy, tumors and the use of various psychotropic drugs.

With recent advances in technology, several brain imaging techniques allow us to look into the brain while it is functioning and understand how the brain operates. The following sections cover three of the most common brain imaging techniques.

Computerized Tomography

Computerized tomography (used in CT scans) uses X-rays to take pictures of the brain at various angles, and then combines these pictures into a single image of the skull and surrounding brain tissue using computer technology. The images produced by CT scans are sharper and more detailed than ordinary X-rays. CT scans are particularly helpful in identifying tumors, tissue degeneration and skull fractures.

Positron Emission Tomography

Positron emission tomography (used in PET scans) allows one to actually monitor activity in the brain. PET scans involve the injection of radioactive dye into the bloodstream that can be traced and detected to monitor blood flow to various regions of the brain (increased blood flow to a region indicates greater activity in that region). The computer then turns these signals into colored pictures indicating where the action is in the brain. This technique allows neuro-psychologists to look at activity while the brain is at rest, sleeping, or engaging in a variety of tasks such as listening to words, reading words and so on by tracking levels of the radioactive dye in various regions of the brain. PET scans are also useful for investigating abnormal brain activity that might occur during epileptic seizures, following strokes, when using drugs and more.

Magnetic Resonance Imaging

Magnetic resonance imaging (MRI) records radio waves given off by brain tissue while individuals lie in a powerful magnetic field. A computer then converts the signals into highly detailed images of tissue and structures in the brain. MRIs are useful for examining brain tissue and structural abnormalities in the brain.

Functional Organization of the Nervous System

The nervous system is a network of neurons that runs throughout the entire body. It can be divided into the **central nervous system** and the **peripheral nervous system.** The brain and the spinal cord make up the central nervous system. The remaining network of nerve fibers that extend throughout the rest of the body makes up the peripheral nervous system.

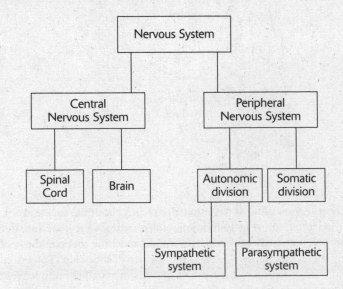

Central Nervous System

The **central nervous system** includes the brain and spinal cord and has two main responsibilities: (1) to process and analyze all information from the external world and the body, and (2) to determine and guide all behavioral, cognitive and emotional responses. The central nervous system is encased in bone, with the brain housed within the skull and the spinal cord housed within the spinal column. The spinal cord receives signals from the senses and relays these signals to the brain through nerve fibers that extend through the spinal column to the brain. Additional nerve fibers in the spinal column carry signals downward from the brain to the muscles and organs in the body. The spinal cord can also direct some behaviors without instruction from the brain. These simple, automatic behaviors, called **reflexes,** occur very quickly and are considered involuntary behaviors because they do not require specific processing or instruction from the brain.

Peripheral Nervous System

The **peripheral nervous system** connects the central nervous system to the external world through the sensory systems and also connects the central nervous system to all muscles and internal organs in the body. The peripheral nervous system can be further divided into two subdivisions: the somatic division and the autonomic division.

The **somatic division** of the peripheral nervous system connects the brain to the sensory systems and to every muscle in the body through afferent and efferent nerves. **Afferent nerves,** also known as sensory nerves, run from the sensory systems to the spinal cord and the brain and carry information to the brain from each of the sensory systems. **Efferent nerves,** also known as motor nerves, run from the brain or spinal cord to all the muscles in the body and carry information about motor responses from the brain or spinal cord to muscles in the body. Without efferent nerves, commands from the brain or spinal cord would not reach the muscles, causing paralysis. Damage to the efferent nerves could lead to poor muscle control, twitching, uncontrollable movement, or no movement at all.

The **autonomic division** of the peripheral nervous system consists of nerve fibers that connect the central nervous system to all internal glands and organs. The autonomic division allows the brain to monitor and guide all bodily processes from breathing to heartbeat to digestion. The functioning of this system is automatic and operates largely outside of our conscious awareness. It can be further broken down into two subdivisions: the sympathetic division and the parasympathetic division. These two systems act in opposition to one another.

The **sympathetic division** of the autonomic division mobilizes the body in times of stress, danger or intense emotional arousal. Activation of the sympathetic division results in a number of physiological changes in the body (including dilation of pupils, increased heart rate, rapid breathing, increased perspiration and heightened physiological arousal). Together, these changes are often referred to as the fight-or-flight response. The **parasympathetic division** of the autonomic division returns the body to a normal state after a sympathetic response.

Specific Brain Structures

The brain is the most vital organ in the body. It controls and directs all bodily activities from thinking to feeling to breathing. The brain is generally subdivided into three broad regions: the brainstem, the limbic system and the cerebral cortex.

The Brainstem

The **brainstem** is the most primitive region of the brain and is the lowest region of the brain that connects to the spinal cord. As a whole, the brainstem is responsible for basic bodily processes, attention and arousal levels. Some important structures within the brainstem are the medulla, pons, reticular activating system and thalamus.

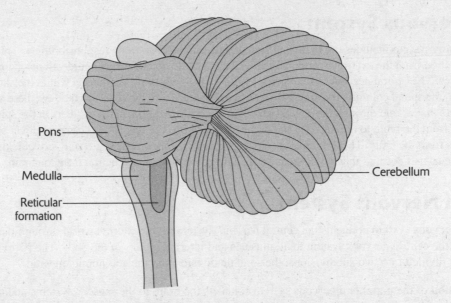

- **Medulla:** Regulates automatic/involuntary bodily functions such as breathing and heart rate
- **Pons:** Monitors and regulates brain activity during sleep
- **Reticular Activating System:** Regulates arousal, alertness and consciousness
- **Thalamus:** Serves as a sensory relay station by channeling all incoming sensory information to appropriate regions of the cortex for processing and back to appropriate muscles and organs in the body
- **Cerebellum:** Attached to the back of the brainstem, this structure resembles a small brain and plays an integral role in balance and coordination of muscle movements

The Limbic System

Sitting atop the brainstem, but surrounded by the cerebral cortex, the **limbic system** comprises a number of connected structures that together play an important role in memory processes and initial emotional responses to events (including fear, anxiety, anger, ecstasy and despair). Structures found within the limbic system are the hippocampus, amygdala and hypothalamus.

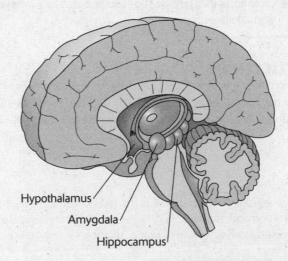

- **Hippocampus:** Involved in processing new information and storing new memories, the hippocampus plays an integral role in learning.
- **Amygdala:** Governs initial emotional reactions to events, particularly fear and aggression. Stimulation of the amygdala typically leads to arousal and/or aggressive responses, whereas damage to the amygdala typically has a calming effect on individuals.

- **Hypothalamus:** Controls bodily activities (heart rate, temperature), motivated behaviors and arousal (sleep, sexual behavior) through its effects on the endocrine system. The hypothalamus also houses reward circuits that, when activated, produce feelings of pleasure and euphoria.

The Cerebral Cortex

The **cerebral cortex** is the largest and outermost part of the brain that surrounds and covers the limbic system much like a helmet. The cerebral cortex is the part of the brain where all abilities unique to humans reside. It is the cerebral cortex that allows for higher-order information processing (including analyzing, integrating, reasoning and thinking). The cerebral cortex can be divided into a number of highly specialized regions that perform specific functions. First, the cerebral cortex is divided into four main lobes:

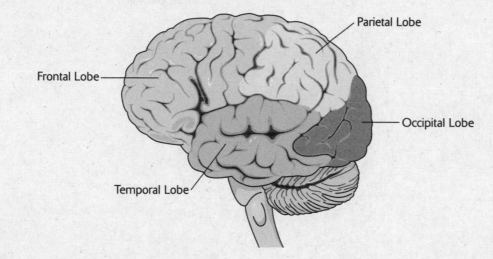

- **Occipital lobe:** Responsible for visual processing
- **Temporal lobe:** Responsible for auditory processing; also plays a role in long-term memory (when damaged, some long-term memory impairment occurs)
- **Parietal lobe:** Responsible for processing body sensations and all skin senses (touch, pressure, temperature and pain)
- **Frontal lobe:** Responsible for controlling behavior, thought, and emotion and for higher-order cognitive processes (such as reasoning, problem-solving and decision-making)

Other important regions of the cerebral cortex include:

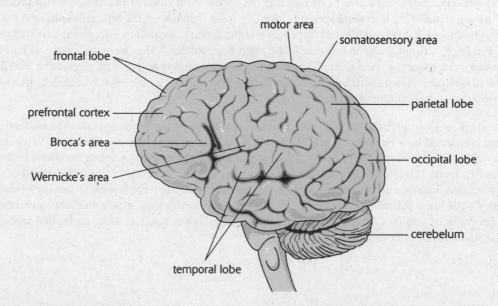

- **Prefrontal cortex:** The most frontal region of the frontal lobe, it is involved in higher-order cognitive processes (planning, decision-making, emotional control).

- **Motor cortex:** A strip of the frontal lobe specialized for controlling voluntary actions of muscles.

- **Somatosensory cortex:** A strip of the parietal lobe specialized for processing sensations of touch and for integrating various sensations.

- **Broca's area:** A portion of the motor cortex found only in the left hemisphere and involved specifically in coordinating the muscles used in speech.

- **Wernicke's area:** A portion of the temporal lobe found only in the left hemisphere and involved specifically in processing and understanding speech.

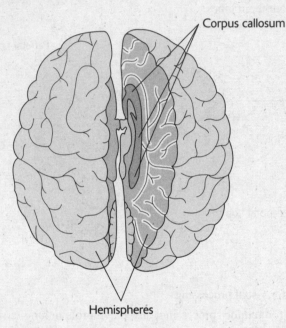

Corpus callosum

Hemispheres

The Brain's Two Hemispheres

The brain can be split down the middle lengthwise to create two symmetrical halves. Each half of the brain is called a cerebral hemisphere. Each hemisphere controls and receives information from the opposite side of the body (called contralateral conduction). Each hemisphere is also specialized for different kinds of functions and for processing different kinds of information (called hemispheric specialization). In most individuals, the **left hemisphere** is the rational, logical half of the brain and is involved in tasks that require logic, order, critical thinking or analysis (such as processing speech and language, writing, math and science). The **right hemisphere** is the emotional, intuitive half of the brain. It is involved in tasks that require artistic or creative skills (such as processing and analyzing pictures, and drawing and completing tasks that require visual spatial skills). Research has also shown that the right hemisphere plays a particularly important role in the recognition of faces.

Though each hemisphere is specialized for particular types of processing, they do not operate independently of one another. They are connected by a bundle of nerve fibers called the **corpus callosum** that allows the two hemispheres to communicate what each one is doing and the information that is being processed by each hemisphere. Individuals who suffer from severe epileptic seizures sometimes have their corpus callosum severed to reduce the spread of neuronal activation during a seizure. Individuals who have had such a procedure performed are referred to as **split-brain patients.** Following surgery, split-brain patients appear normal—their perceptual, cognitive, motor and intellectual skills remain intact, and their personality and mood are unaffected by the surgery. However, under more controlled procedures, some unusual effects of the surgery are evident.

In a series of studies conducted by Roger Sperry and Michael Gazzaniga, it was discovered that when information is presented to only one hemisphere and each hemisphere is tested on what it knows individually, the disconnection between the two hemispheres is evident. For example, when the image of a cup is projected only to the right hemisphere, the patient cannot say what they see. However, when allowed to feel a variety of objects with their left hand, the patient selects a cup. In this instance, it appears that the right hemisphere knows it sees a cup, but has no way of revealing this information in speech because the left hemisphere is required for language. However, when the patient is allowed to use their left hand (which is controlled by the right hemisphere), the right hemisphere is able to command the left hand to choose the correct object.

Neural Transmission

The brain is made up of billions of specialized nerve cells called **neurons.** When we speak of brain regions such as the hippocampus or the prefrontal cortex, we are actually talking about a group of neurons that reside in a particular region of the brain and carry out very specialized functions. Individual neurons transmit and receive information throughout the nervous system through the conduction of electrical and chemical impulses. Electrical impulses allow for transmission of information within a neuron, whereas chemical impulses allow for transmission of information between neurons.

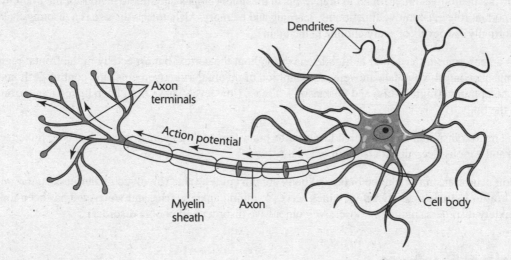

Neural Anatomy

Each neuron is made up of a cell body, an axon, and up to several hundred or several thousand dendrites. The **cell body** or soma is the rounded portion of a cell that serves as the control center of the neuron, directing all cell activities, including the nucleus. Two types of fibers extend from each end of the soma. **Dendrites** are branches that reach out from the cell body and receive signals from surrounding neurons. The **axon** is a much larger branch (with branching ends) that carries signals away from the cell body to surrounding neurons. Within the branches of the axon are small vesicles (tiny sacs) that contain molecules of chemicals known as **neurotransmitters.** Many axons are covered in a myelin sheath, a fatty substance that serves to insulate the axon and to speed the conduction of neural impulses. Axons of one neuron do not directly touch dendrites of surrounding neurons. They are separated by tiny gaps called **synapses.**

Neural Impulses

Impulses are conducted within neurons by means of electrical impulses and between neurons by means of a chemical process. When dendrites receive signals of sufficient strength, the membrane gives way to a surge of positively charged sodium ions that rush in and alter the charge of the neuron in such a way that an electrical impulse known as an **action potential** is created. This action potential moves down the axon by jumping from one gap between the myelin sheath to another as it moves away from the cell body to the axonal branches where the tiny vesicles containing neurotransmitter molecules fuse with the membrane wall, releasing neurotransmitter molecules into the synaptic gap between the axonal branches and the dendrites of surrounding neurons. The neurotransmitters connect to receptors on the dendrites of surrounding neurons, either stimulating or inhibiting the subsequent action of each neuron. The change that occurs in the membrane of the receiving cell is called a **postsynaptic potential.** When the postsynaptic potential stimulates the neuron, it is called an **excitatory postsynaptic potential.** When the postsynaptic potential inhibits the neuron, it is called an **inhibitory postsynaptic potential.** In many instances, a single excitatory postsynaptic potential will not cause a neuron to fire. Rather, it is the combination of incoming potentials (inhibitory and excitatory) from other neurons that determines whether or not the postsynaptic cell fires and how rapidly it fires.

Neurotransmitters

The brain and body contain many neurotransmitters. Some are found in particularly high levels in certain regions of the brain and body and are involved in particular bodily and neurological functions and processes. Just as certain keys only fit certain locks, a neurotransmitter can bind only to receptors designed to receive that specific neurotransmitter and not to other receptors. A few examples of neurotransmitters and their primary functions within the brain are outlined below.

Acetylcholine is a neurotransmitter found in high levels in the hippocampus and limbic regions of the brain. It is believed to play an important role in cognitive functioning, learning and memory. Alzheimer's disease is a disorder that has been linked to abnormally low levels of acetylcholine in the brain.

Dopamine is a neurotransmitter found in high levels throughout the cortex, but especially in the frontal regions. It is involved in muscle control, voluntary movement, inhibition of involuntary movements, and control of thoughts and emotions. Schizophrenia (high levels) and Parkinson's disease (low levels) have both been linked to abnormal levels of dopamine in the body.

Serotonin is a neurotransmitter found in high levels in the brainstem and limbic regions and has been linked to depression (high or low) and various sleep disorders (high or low).

Other common neurotransmitters in the brain and body are **norepinephrine** (involved in alertness, agitation and mania) and **gamma amino byturic acid (GABA),** which serves to inhibit anxiety, fear, and worry and has been linked to a number of anxiety disorders (including obsessive-compulsive disorder and phobic disorder).

Endocrine System

The **endocrine system** is a collection of glands which secrete hormones into the bloodstream that target and exert effects on specific organs in the body. This system, in conjunction with the autonomic nervous system, allows for communication between the brain and specific organs in the body. Communication within the endocrine system is slower than communication in the nervous system because hormones must travel through the bloodstream to reach their target destinations.

The endocrine system is under the control of the hypothalamus, a brain structure located in the limbic region of the brain. The hypothalamus sends out commands concerning the release of hormones, which serve to regulate a number of physiological functions in the body (including growth, metabolism, reproduction and behavior). Some of the major glands are illustrated in the following figure:

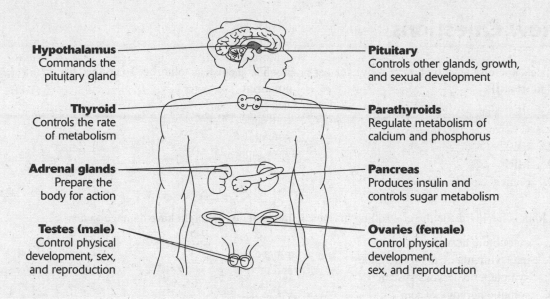

Hypothalamus
Commands the
pituitary gland

Pituitary
Controls other glands, growth,
and sexual development

Thyroid
Controls the rate
of metabolism

Parathyroids
Regulate metabolism of
calcium and phosphorus

Adrenal glands
Prepare the
body for action

Pancreas
Produces insulin and
controls sugar metabolism

Testes (male)
Control physical
development, sex,
and reproduction

Ovaries (female)
Control physical
development,
sex, and reproduction

Genetics

Behavioral genetics is a field of psychology that focuses on the link between heredity and behavior. At the moment of conception, we inherit 23 chromosomes from each of our parents, yielding a set of 46 (23 pairs) chromosomes. These chromosomes carry thousands of genes that form our genetic makeup.

One's specific genetic makeup is referred to as their **genotype.** The influence of genes manifests in various physical, cognitive and psychological characteristics that we call **traits.** One's observable and describable traits and characteristics are referred to as one's **phenotype.** One's phenotype is thus shaped by one's genetic makeup in addition to experiences throughout life.

A great deal of research points to the importance of genetic influences on human thought, behavior, and emotion and there is no doubt today that a number of mental illnesses (including depression and schizophrenia) have at least some genetic origin. In addition, a number of genetic disorders have been identified over the years, including **Down syndrome** (caused by an extra 21st chromosome), **Huntington's disease** (a genetic disorder that does not manifest until middle age, but leads to significant mental retardation after the age of 40), **phenylketonuria** (a genetic disorder that leads to mental retardation) and more.

Questions remain concerning the extent to which genes influence human behavior. One of the most fundamental questions of psychology concerns the issue of nature versus nurture. The **nature-nurture debate** is a classic and heated issue within the field of psychology. A strict nature position holds that individuals are predisposed to behave and develop in certain ways (for example, to be shy, depressed, anxious). In contrast, an extreme nurture position argues that behavior and development are shaped by life experiences. Though the debate continues today about the relative importance of nature and nurture, most individuals choose to take an **interactionist approach** in which they view human behavior as the result of a complex interaction between nature (genetic) and nurture (environmental) influences.

Review Questions

1. Alice's doctor wants to observe activity in her brain while she listens to music. To do this, her doctor needs to conduct a(n):

   A. PET scan
   B. CT scan
   C. EEG
   D. MRI
   E. clinical case study

2. If John is having difficulty controlling his muscle movements, he might have damage to his:

   A. autonomic nervous system
   B. parasympathetic nervous system
   C. sympathetic nervous system
   D. somatic nervous system
   E. reticular activating system

3. When one is startled or under stress, the _____ is likely to be activated.

   A. reticular activating system
   B. parasympathetic nervous system
   C. sympathetic nervous system
   D. somatic nervous system
   E. efferent nervous system

4. Which region of the brain is responsible for basic survival tasks such as breathing and heartbeat?

   A. limbic system
   B. frontal lobe
   C. somatosensory cortex
   D. brainstem
   E. cerebellum

5. After suffering a head injury, Lisa is having difficulty understanding and producing speech. Lisa likely suffered damage to her:

   A. reticular activating system
   B. hypothalamus
   C. left hemisphere
   D. right hemisphere
   E. frontal lobe

6. An individual is injected with a drug that stimulates the release and functioning of dopamine in the brain. This increase in dopamine is most likely to lead to:

   A. difficulties with muscle control
   B. a feeling of drowsiness and fatigue
   C. an increased sense of fear and doom
   D. an inability to remember recently occurring events
   E. a sense of sadness and depression

7. Damage to the hippocampus is most likely to affect:

    A. muscle coordination and movement

    B. learning and memory

    C. mood and emotion

    D. breathing and heartbeat

    E. speech production and comprehension

8. Dr. Jones states that the manner in which parents treat their children is a key influence on the later behavior and personality of those children. This view is most consistent with:

    A. a biological view of behavior

    B. an interactionist view of behavior

    C. the nature side of the nature-nurture debate

    D. the nurture side of the nature-nurture debate

    E. a belief in hereditary influences on behavior

Answers

1. **A.** PET scans are one of the few procedures capable of monitoring brain activity. PET scans indicate which areas of the brain are active by detecting levels of blood flow to different regions of the brain. CT scans use X-rays to take still pictures of the skull and brain tissue. MRIs use magnetic waves to create detailed photographs of the brain and structures within the brain. EEGs monitor brain waves through electrodes placed on the scalp.

2. **D.** The somatic division of the peripheral nervous system is responsible for muscle control and movement. The autonomic division controls more automatic and involuntary functions such as breathing, digestion and so on. The sympathetic system controls fight-or-flight responses, while the parasympathetic system serves to calm the body and return it to a normal level of functioning following a fight-or-flight response. The reticular activating system is an area of the brain responsible for alertness, arousal and consciousness.

3. **C.** The sympathetic nervous system responds in stressful situations by heightening arousal and preparing the body to react to stressors. The reticular activating system is the part of the brainstem responsible for basic alertness and arousal levels. The parasympathetic system returns the body to a resting state after a stress response by the sympathetic nervous system. The somatic nervous system plays an important role in sensing external stimuli and in controlling muscle movement. Efferent nerves are nerves in the somatic nervous system that allow the brain to communicate and direct all muscles in the body.

4. **D.** The brainstem contains the medulla, pons and reticular activating system. Together, these structures are responsible for basic survival tasks (such as breathing, heartbeat and more). The limbic system contains a number of structures involved in learning, memory and emotion. The frontal lobes are involved in higher-order cognitive processes (such as problem-solving and decision-making). The somatosensory cortex processes and integrates sensations of touch. The cerebellum is a structure located at the back of the brain that plays an integral role in balance and coordination.

5. **C.** The left hemisphere is vital to speech production and comprehension. The reticular activating system controls alertness and arousal levels. The hypothalamus controls the endocrine system and is involved in motivated behaviors such as sex, hunger and thirst. It also contains reward circuits that, when activated, produce sensations of elation. The right hemisphere is the artistic and creative half of the brain involved in tasks that involve music, art and visual spatial skills. The frontal lobes are involved in higher-order cognitive processes (such as problem-solving and decision-making) and control and regulation of thought and emotion.

6. **A.** Dopamine is a neurotransmitter that plays an important role in muscle control and voluntary movement. Drowsiness, fatigue, sadness and depression are influenced primarily by serotonin. Feelings of fear and doom are associated with lower levels of GABA, another neurotransmitter found throughout the brain. Poor memory is associated with decreased levels of acetylcholine.

7. **B.** The hippocampus is instrumental in learning and memory. Muscle coordination is most affected by damage to the cerebellum. Mood and emotion are most affected by damage to the limbic system or the frontal lobes. Breathing and heartbeat are most affected by damage to the brainstem region. Speech production and comprehension are most affected by damage to the left hemisphere of the brain or to Broca's or Wernicke's area within the left hemisphere.

8. **D.** The nurture side of the nature-nurture debate argues that environmental conditions and experiences are the key influences on behavior and personality. A biological view of behavior, the nature side of the nature-nurture debate and a belief in hereditary influence on behavior all represent the nature side of the classic debate. The interactionist views behavior and personality as the result of the constant interaction between nature and nurture.

Sensation and Perception

The brain is not directly connected to the external world. It is through our senses—sight, hearing, smell, touch and taste—that we come to experience, know and understand the world around us. Sensation and perception are terms used to describe the processes by which we take in information from the external world, process this information, and interpret and make decisions about the information. **Sensation** refers to the process of actually receiving or detecting information from the environment and transmitting that information to higher biological centers. **Perception** refers to the process of analyzing, recognizing, interpreting and organizing incoming sensory information.

This chapter provides an overview of the processes involved in sensation and perception. It begins with a review of the various sensory systems and sensory mechanisms that operate to allow us to detect information from the external environment. It then reviews attentional processes and the role of attention in sensation and perception. Finally, perceptual processes and the factors that influence our perceptions of the world around us are discussed.

The Sensory Systems

The body has several distinct sensory systems: visual, auditory, tactile, olfactory, gustatory, kinesthetic and vestibular. Each system is associated with specific sensory organs, sensory receptors (cells specialized for detecting specific kinds of stimulus energy) and sensory nerve fibers that transmit information to the brain for further processing. Each sensory system detects a particular type of energy from the external environment. The following table details each of the sensory systems and the organs, receptors, and type of energy associated with each system.

Sensory Systems			
Sense	*Sensory Organs*	*Energy Detected*	*Receptors*
Visual	Eyes	Light waves	Rods and cones in the retina
Auditory	Ears	Sound waves (vibrations)	Hair cells lining the cochlea in the inner ear
Olfactory	Nose	Odor molecules	Hair cells lining the upper nose
Gastatory	Tongue	Taste molecules	Taste buds (papillae) along the tongue
Tactile	Skin	Touch, pressure, temperature and pain	Nerve endings in the skin
Kinesthetic	Muscles, tendons and joints	Limb position and movement	Cells in the muscles, tendons and joints
Vestibular	Semicircular canals in inner ear	Head position and movement	Hair cells lining the semicircular canals in the inner ear

Sensory Mechanisms

The underlying sensory processes are the same in all senses:

1. **Detection:** Energy is detected from the environment.
2. **Conversion (Transduction):** Detected energy is converted to a neural impulse.
3. **Conduction:** The neural impulse is sent to the brain via sensory nerve fibers for further processing.

Vision

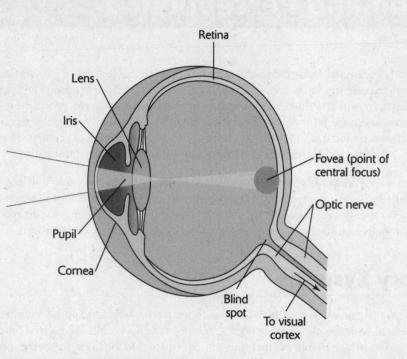

The process of vision begins when light energy stimulates the eye. Light rays enter the eye through the **cornea,** a transparent, protective covering over the eye. After passing through the cornea, light rays enter the **pupil,** a dark hole in the center of the **iris,** the colored part of the eye. Light then passes through the pupil to the **lens,** which changes its shape to focus or reflect the light rays onto the **retina.** The retina sits at the back of the eye and is covered with two types of receptor cells: **rods** that detect black and white light rays, and **cones** that detect color rays. The greatest number of cones is found on the fovea region or macula of the retina.

As the light rays hit the receptors, the process of **conversion,** in which the energy is converted to a neural impulse, begins. Within the visual sense, visual inputs vary widely. For example, visual input varies in brightness, intensity, hue, saturation, shape, movement and more. How are these different visual inputs interpreted by the eye? They are interpreted differently based on the rate and regularity of receptor firing. The specific qualities of the information lead to differences in the rate and regularity of receptor firing.

When converted, the information is sent to the brain for further processing and interpretation via the **optic nerve.** The ultimate processing of visual information occurs in the **visual cortex** (the occipital region) of the brain. In the visual cortex, specialized cells process visual information, including **feature detectors**—cells activated only by very specific types of information such as slanted lines, specific shapes, movement and so on.

Trichromatic theory, previously known as the Young-Helmholtz theory, argues that three types of color receptors exist in the eye (those that respond to blue-violet colors, those that respond to green colors and those that respond to yellow-red colors). Our perception of color is determined by the varying degrees of activation of these three color receptors.

Opponent-Process theory argues that the receptor cells in the eye function as antagonists, with red opposing green, blue opposing yellow and black opposing white. When red receptors activate, green receptors are inhibited; and when blue receptors activate, yellow receptors are inhibited. Opponent-Process theory can explain the phenomenon of afterimages. Afterimages occur after an individual looks at a stimulus for a period of time, and then shifts their gaze away from the stimulus, only to see an afterimage of that stimulus in a different color. We know from research that afterimages produce an image in the color opposing the original color of the stimulus. Thus, if you stare at a green stimulus, and then shift your gaze to a blank white sheet of paper, you see an afterimage of that stimulus in red. If the initial image is blue, the afterimage is yellow.

Both theories are correct to some extent and together can explain color vision quite well. With respect to trichromatic theory, three types of cones respond to different wavelengths of light (blue, red, and green) and the sensation of different colors results when the three types of cones are stimulated to varying degrees. However, information from the cones is fed into specialized cells within the eye that respond to opponent colors and inhibit each other when activated, as suggested by opponent-process theory. Thus, trichromatic theory explains the functioning of the receptors (cones) within the eye, but opponent-process theory explains the functioning of cells that process information from the receptors.

Hearing

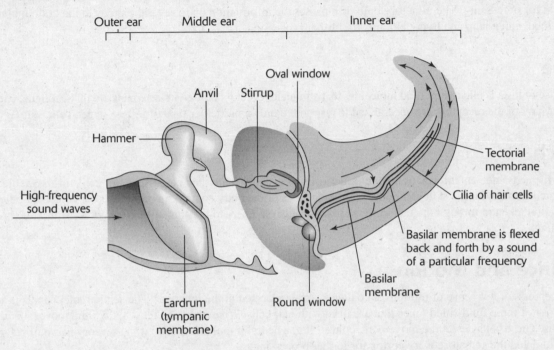

The process of hearing begins when sound waves (vibrations) are picked up by the **outer ear** and channeled into the **auditory canal,** a tube-like passage that leads to the eardrum. The **eardrum** is a tiny structure within the outer ear that vibrates when hit by sound waves. The vibrations are then transferred to the **middle ear,** a chamber that contains three tiny bones: the **hammer,** the **anvil** and the **stirrup.** Together, these three bones operate to transfer the vibrations to the **oval window,** a membrane that leads to the inner ear. The **inner ear** is where the process of conversion actually occurs. Sound waves are transferred from the oval window to the **cochlea,** a fluid-filled tube within the inner ear. The **basilar membrane** runs through the cochlea and is lined with tiny **hair cells.** When vibrations enter the cochlea, the hair cells bend, sending information to the receptors linked to the hair cells. This information is then converted to a neural impulse that is sent to the brain for further processing via the cochlear or **auditory nerve,** which then transmits the sensations to the auditory projection area of the temporal lobe.

How are we able to sort out wavelengths of different intensities and frequencies? The **place theory of hearing** argues that different areas of the basilar membrane are affected by sound waves of varying frequencies. Areas nearest to the inner end of the cochlea are most sensitive to low-frequency sounds. In contrast, **frequency theory** suggests that the entire basilar membrane vibrates in response to sound waves and that the frequency of the sound waves is represented by the number of nerve impulses that are transmitted to the brain. The greater the frequency of the sound, the greater the number of nerve impulses sent to the brain. Today, psychologists recognize that the nervous system relies on both place theory and frequency theory to code different frequencies of sounds. Low sound frequencies are coded by frequency matching in which the rate of firing is matched to the frequency of the sound. High frequencies are coded by the place at which the wave peaks on the basilar membrane. Moderate frequencies are coded by a combination of place and matching.

Similar to vision, neurons in the auditory cortex (the temporal region) of the brain respond to specific types of sounds. Some respond to very specific sound features such as whistles or clicks; some respond to the location of the sound; and some respond to specific patterns of sounds.

Smell

Our sense of smell is elicited by air molecules that enter the nasal passages and stimulate olfactory receptors. There are thousands of types of olfactory receptors—many specialized to respond to very specific odor molecules. As the cells are stimulated, the information is converted to a neural impulse that is sent via the olfactory nerve to the olfactory bulb in the brain for processing. The olfactory bulb then passes the information on to several regions in the brain including the frontal lobe, amygdala, and hypothalamus for further processing.

Taste

Our sense of taste is elicited by food molecules that stimulate receptors housed in taste buds along the tongue, cheek and throat. Many of the receptors are specialized to respond to only a particular type of taste—sweet, sour, salty or bitter.

Touch

Our tactile sense detects information about touch, pressure, temperature and pain. Receptor cells for the tactile sense are located throughout the skin and body, with some areas of the body containing more receptor cells than others. Information taken in through the tactile sense is sent via nerve fibers to the somatosensory cortex within the brain for processing.

Balance and Motion

The receptors for our sense of motion and balance are also located in the inner ear. The semicircular canals of the inner ear consist of three fluid-filled tubes that are lined with hair cells. When the head moves, the fluid moves, bending the hair cells. These cells detect the movement, convert it to a neural impulse and send it via sensory nerve fibers to the cerebellum and the somatosensory cortex for further processing.

Sensory Thresholds

Every receptor in every sense has a threshold level dictating the amount of energy necessary for the receptor to respond. The receptor only activates in response to stimulus energy that exceeds that threshold. The two kinds of thresholds in the sensory systems are an absolute sensory threshold and a difference threshold. The **absolute sensory threshold** refers to the smallest amount of energy needed to detect a stimulus at least 50% of the time. According to the absolute sensory threshold view, my voice must exceed your absolute sensory threshold for you to detect it. If it does not, you cannot detect the sound. The **difference threshold,** or **just noticeable difference (JND),** refers to the smallest amount of stimulus change required before one senses or detects a change in the stimulus. According to Max Weber, the JND is a constant proportion of the stimulus. Thus, as stimulus intensity increases, the amount of stimulus change needed to detect a difference also increases. This is referred to as Weber's Law and explains why at low weights, it is very easy to notice even a slight increase or decrease in the weight of an object. But with heavy objects, slight changes in weight are not easily detected.

According to the **absolute sensory threshold view,** the stimulus alone determines whether it is detected by individuals. If stimulus energy is below the sensory threshold, you cannot detect the stimulus, whereas if stimulus energy is above the sensory threshold, the stimulus can be detected. **Signal detection theory** argues that detection involves more than the characteristics of the stimulus. According to signal detection theory, whether a stimulus is actually detected depends on characteristics of the respondent in addition to characteristics of the stimulus. Sensation and perception are dependent on a judgment process by the individual in which they ask themselves, "Did I see anything?" or "Did I hear anything?" Our readiness to report detection of a stimulus when we are uncertain of its presence is called **response bias.**

Some individuals are biased toward reporting detection when they are unsure of its presence (called positive response bias); others are biased toward not reporting detection when uncertain of the presence of a stimulus (called negative response bias). Thus, in a detection experiment in which sounds are presented randomly at different times and participants are asked to report whether a stimulus is detected, four outcomes are possible on each trial:

- **Hit:** A signal is present, and the participant reports detection.
- **Correct rejection:** A signal is absent, and the participant does not report detecting it.
- **Miss** or **false negative:** A signal is present, but the participant does not detect it.
- **False alarm** or **false positive:** A signal is absent, but the participant reports detecting it.

Response bias is influenced by a number of factors including motivation, expectancies, wants and desires, and arousal level. Consider some instances in which response biases could influence important decisions in everyday life: You are a physician analyzing a brain scan and are not sure whether the little spot you see is a tumor. You think you see something, but you are not sure. What's your final answer: tumor or no tumor? You are a witness to a crime and have been asked to identify the suspect. You think the person might be the perpetrator, but you are not sure. Do you identify the person as the perpetrator?

Sensory Adaptation

Sensory adaptation occurs when sensory receptors reduce their responsiveness to a stimulus after repeated or continuous exposure. Sensory receptors are designed to detect changes in stimuli rather than sameness. Receptors fire off more electrical activity when they are first activated. But when they are accustomed to a situation, they fire or respond less, making us less aware of a stimulus to which we are constantly exposed. Sensory adaptation helps us deal with the hundreds of stimuli constantly bombarding our senses. The fact that you do not constantly feel the touch of your clothes on your body is a result of sensory adaptation. The fact that you no longer notice an aroma after spending a few minutes in a room is also the result of sensory adaptation. The smell itself is not likely gone. Rather, sensory adaptation has occurred.

Attention

Attention refers to the process of focusing awareness and thought. It is guided by both external stimulation and internal goals and motivation. David Broadbent (1958) likened attention to a filtering process. According to Broadbent, attention serves as a filter between the intake of sensory information and the processing of that information. If a stimulus is attended to, it passes through the filter to be further processed and analyzed. Broadbent also suggested that attention is an all-or-nothing process such that if we are currently attending to one stimulus or piece of information, we are unable to attend to anything else. More recent research suggests this is not the case.

Though individuals are able to focus on particular stimuli while tuning out other stimuli, it is also true that we are able to process more than one piece of information at a time. Cognitive psychologists have long recognized the phenomena of **parallel processing,** in which the brain engages in multiple types of processing at any given moment, and of **divided attention,** in which individuals split their attention between two different stimuli or tasks. **Dichotic listening tasks** are the most common methods used to study divided attention. Dichotic listening tasks involve presenting two different pieces of information simultaneously (one to each ear) through special headphones. Typically, subjects are instructed to attend only to information presented to one ear by repeating aloud what they hear in that ear. This technique is called **shadowing.**

Are individuals any good at shadowing and dichotic listening tasks? Research finds that they are. Most individuals are capable of attending to the information in one ear while ignoring the information presented to the other ear. More importantly, research finds that even when participants state no recollection of information presented in the unattended ear, performance on subsequent tasks suggests that the information was processed to some degree. For example, on a task in which subjects are asked to state a person's name, those who heard "John" in the unattended ear are more likely to say "John" than control subjects who had not heard "John" in a dichotic listening task prior to the test.

Perceptual Processes

Regardless of the specific type of information coming in from the senses, perception begins as the information coming in is analyzed, interpreted and pieced back together in a meaningful perceptual experience. The two general processes that the brain uses to interpret information are bottom-up processing and top-down processing. **Bottom-up processing** involves the processing of specific information coming in from the sensory organs. **Top-down processing** occurs when information already stored in the brain is used to help interpret incoming information. As information comes in from the senses, the brain compares the incoming data to information already stored in the brain. It also relies on memories and knowledge already stored in the brain to help interpret the information. The following example demonstrates how top-down processing assists in the processing and interpretation of information.

> Tihs stnecene can stlil be raed eevn thuogh the ltteres are scmrblaed as a rueslt of tpo-dwon prcessonig.

Perception is also influenced by our expectations. Often what we see or hear is what we are expecting to see or hear, or what we want to see or hear. Our readiness to detect a particular stimulus as a result of expectations is referred to as a **perceptual set.** Consider the heading for the following picture: Loch Ness Monster Spotted in Lake. Did you see the Loch Ness monster when you looked at the picture? If so, you were influenced by a perceptual set. The picture is actually a log floating in the water.

We can also expect certain information as a result of the context in which we experience the information. Thus, perception can also be set by the context. If you look at the following note, you probably read "Left at 4:13. Be back in one hour." Although the *B* and the *13* are identical, you likely perceived them as different because of the context.

> **LEFT AT 4:13 – 13E BACK IN ONE HOUR**

Perceptual Organization

Gestalt psychology focuses on the way in which humans construct meaningful perceptions from sensory data. Based on the idea that the whole is greater than the sum of its parts, Gestalt psychologists argue that perception of stimuli goes beyond the mere piecing together of the individual elements that we sense. Rather, perception is a constructive process in which the ultimate perception is quite different from the sum of the individual elements. A number of Gestalt laws or principles have been proposed that speak to the tendency of the brain to organize individual sensory elements into meaningful percepts.

The **figure-ground principle** states that the brain automatically sorts sensory information into a figure and a ground. The figure is the aspect of the sensory experience that stands out and is the center of attention; the ground is the field against which the figure stands out. It is possible in various instances for the background to become the figure, depending on where we focus our attention, and sometimes the figure and ground can be completely reversed, as in the famous face-vase example.

The **principle of similarity** refers to the tendency of the brain to group similar sensory elements together (to see them as a unit). In the following example, individuals tend to report seeing rows of *X*'s and *O*'s rather than several columns of alternating *X*'s and *O*'s.

X X X X X X X X
O O O O O O O O
X X X X X X X X
O O O O O O O O

The **principle of proximity** refers to the tendency of the brain to perceive objects that are close to each other as meaningful units. In the following example, we tend to see the stimuli as pairs of *X*'s and *O*'s, rather than a column of *X*'s next to a column of *O*'s with a space, and then another column of *X*'s next to a column of *O*'s, and so on.

XO XO XO XO XO XO XO XO
XO XO XO XO XO XO XO XO
XO XO XO XO XO XO XO XO
XO XO XO XO XO XO XO XO

The **principle of continuity** refers to the tendency of the brain to perceive fluid or continuous forms rather than jagged or irregular ones. In the following example, we tend to see two intersecting lines (one from points 1 to 2 to 3 to 4 to 5 and one from points 6 to 7 to 8 to 9 to 10).

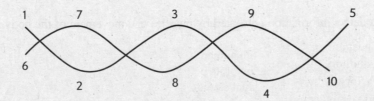

The **principle of closure** refers to the tendency of the brain to close up or complete sensory experiences that are not complete. (If an element is missing, we still perceive the experience as a whole.) In the following example, we tend to see two lines rather than eight separate lines.

The **principle of simplicity,** also known as the **law of pragnanz,** refers to the fact that when multiple interpretations are possible, we tend to create the simplest perception.

Perceptual Constancies

Perceptual constancies refer to the ability of our brains to perceive consistencies in the shape, size and color of certain objects despite differences or changes in the actual image portrayed on the retina. The brain recognizes that certain stimuli remain the same shape, size and color despite changes in the actual retinal images portrayed by the stimuli from different angles. Shape constancy, size constancy and color constancy allow for stable and consistent perceptions of objects and keep us from being fooled by our senses when looking at objects from different angles.

Review Questions

1. When your ears detect a sound from far away _____ has taken place. When you recognize that what you hear is a siren approaching _____ has taken place.

   A. conversion; detection
   B. sensation; perception
   C. detection; conversion
   D. detection; conduction
   E. conduction; conversion

2. Which of the following accurately depicts the order of sensory and perceptual processes?

   A. stimulation, detection, conversion, conduction
   B. stimulation, conduction, detection, conversion
   C. conduction, detection, conversion, stimulation
   D. detection, conversion, conduction, stimulation
   E. stimulation, conversion, detection, conduction

3. If an individual experiences problems with the sensory receptors known as cones, they are likely to:

   A. experience problems hearing high-pitched sounds
   B. experience problems seeing in color
   C. have difficulty seeing at night
   D. feel no pain
   E. experience chronic and persistent pain

4. The two senses that detect information generated by muscles and movement of the body are the:

   A. olfactory and gustatory
   B. gustatory and auditory
   C. visual and olfactory
   D. kinesthetic and vestibular
   E. vestibular and gustatory

5. The phenomenon of afterimages appearing in colors different from the original image viewed can be explained by:

   A. the figure-ground principle
   B. Trichromatic theory
   C. Opponent-Process theory
   D. Place theory
   E. feature detectors

6. You have just lifted a very heavy box and carried it into the living room. You now go to lift a box that you know is heavier, but as you lift it, it doesn't feel any heavier. This phenomenon illustrates:

   A. the absolute sensory threshold
   B. the Gestalt principle of continuity
   C. Weber's Law
   D. Young-Helmholtz theory
   E. the process of sensory adaptation

7. In a signal detection experiment, an individual consistently makes false positive identifications. This means that they:

   A. do not report the stimulus when it is present
   B. accurately report the stimulus when it is present
   C. do not recognize the difference between the stimulus and another different stimulus
   D. report the stimulus when it is not present
   E. do not report the stimulus when it is not present

8. The ability to piece together what someone has said to you even when a loud noise drowns out part of their sentence is possible as a result of:

   A. bottom-up processing
   B. feature detection
   C. shadowing
   D. dichotic listening
   E. top-down processing

Answers

1. **B.** Sensation is the process of detecting information from the environment and converting this information to a format that can be processed by the nervous system. Perception is the process of analyzing and interpreting the information. Detection is the specific process of detecting information and occurs at the receptor level when the receptors are activated by stimulus energy. Conversion is the process of converting stimulus energy to the form of a neural impulse. Conduction occurs when the impulse is transmitted to the brain for further processing.

2. **A.** Sensation and perception are two intertwined processes that begin with stimulation (stimulus energy is received by sensory receptors in each of the sensory organs). The remaining steps involve detection (the sensory receptors respond to the stimulus energy and activate), conversion (the receptors convert the stimulus energy to a neural impulse that can be processed by the nervous system) and conduction (the impulse is sent to the brain for further analysis and interpretation).

3. **B.** Cones are specific receptors found along the retina in the eye that are sensitive to color rays. Difficulty hearing high-pitched sounds suggests a problem in the auditory sense. Difficulty seeing at night indicates a potential problem with receptor cells in the eye known as rods that detect black and white rays. Feeling no pain or experiencing chronic pain involves problems in the tactile sense.

4. **D.** The kinesthetic and vestibular senses detect information from within the body. Specifically, the kinesthetic sense detects information concerning body position and limb movement. The vestibular sense detects information concerning head position, balance and movement. The other senses all receive information from the external environment. The olfactory sense detects odor molecules from the environment. The gustatory sense detects food molecules. The auditory sense detects sound energy. The visual sense detects light energy.

5. **C.** Opponent-Process theory proposes that receptor cells are antagonistic such that red opposes green and blue opposes yellow. When one of the opponent cells is activated, the opposing cell is inhibited. When an opponent cell is deactivated (after being activated for a period of time), the opposing cell undergoes a brief activation period creating an afterimage of a visual stimulus in the color opposing the original color of the stimulus. Trichromatic theory is a different theory of color vision that cannot explain the phenomenon of afterimages. Place theory refers to hearing and how it is that we detect different types of sound energy. Feature detectors are cells in the occipital lobe designed to process very specific types of stimulus information. The figure-ground principle refers to how the brain organizes visual stimuli into a figure (the focus of attention) and ground (the remaining background).

6. **C.** Weber's Law states that as stimulus energy increases, the amount of additional energy required to detect a change in the stimulus also increases. The absolute sensory threshold refers to the minimal amount of energy needed to detect a stimulus. Sensory adaptation occurs when receptors reduce their responsiveness to a stimulus that is repeatedly presented. The Gestalt principle of continuity states that the brain tends to perceive continuous forms rather than discontinuous ones when organizing visual stimuli. The Young-Helmholtz theory is a theory specific to color vision and says nothing about how we detect differences in stimuli.

7. **D.** False positives occur when individuals report detection of a stimulus when the stimulus is not present. False negatives occur when an individual fails to report detection of a stimulus when the stimulus is present. A hit refers to the correct identification of a stimulus when it is present. A correct rejection occurs when an individual correctly states that a stimulus is not present.

8. **E.** Top-down processing occurs when previously stored information is used to help process and interpret incoming sensory information. Bottom-up processing refers to processing based on specific incoming sensory information. Dichotic listening and shadowing are procedures used to test selected and divided attention.

States of Consciousness

Consciousness refers to what you are aware of at any given moment. Information about what is happening around you is continuously entering your brain. Some processing occurs automatically and completely outside of our conscious awareness, such as the monitoring and regulation of automatic bodily functions. This type of processing is generally referred to as **nonconscious** or **automatic processing.** Our brains also register external information that is below our level of conscious awareness. We might or might not become aware of this information, depending on our level and direction of attention. This information is said to be in our **subconscious.** A host of information exists within our brains that we are not always consciously aware of, but can be if we direct our attention to it. This information is said to be in our **preconscious.** Finally, psychoanalysts speak of the **unconscious**—a part of the mind that houses threatening and anxiety-provoking thoughts, feelings and desires. When we speak of altered states of consciousness, we are talking about a condition in which we see significant changes in mental processes and psychological and behavioral functioning.

This chapter provides an overview of various states of consciousness and altered states of consciousness. It first reviews sleep and dreaming with a focus on brain function and awareness during the various stages of sleep. The chapter also addresses the effects of hypnosis and psychotropic drugs on conscious awareness.

Biological and Circadian Rhythms

As biological organisms, we are all sensitive to certain environmental changes, including seasonal changes and the 24-hour day cycle. **Biological rhythms** refer to regular fluctuations in level of activity and alertness within an organism. An internal clock that is particularly important from a psychological standpoint is the 24-hour sleep-wake cycle, also called **circadian rhythm.** Circadian rhythm influences our level of consciousness throughout the day and plays a role in our state of mind, activity level, mood, behavior, performance and physiological processes.

Sleep and Dreaming

Even while asleep, our bodies continue to cycle through different activity levels. As we sleep, we cycle repeatedly through five distinct stages in which body and brain activity varies. In the typical adult, each cycle lasts approximately 90 minutes, and we complete about four to six cycles per night. The sleep cycle begins as we start to feel drowsy. Our decreased level of arousal and alertness is a result of several processes—including signals from the retina to the hypothalamus concerning light levels, signals from the hypothalamus to the pineal gland to release a hormone called melatonin into the bloodstream to induce drowsiness and the reticular activating system decreasing its level of activity.

Stage 1 of sleep is a transitional phase in which we move from an awake, alert state to a relaxed, **hypnogogic** state. While awake and attending to information, our brains emit **beta waves** (short, quick, high-frequency electrical impulses). As we begin to relax, our brains begin to emit **alpha waves** (less intense, but still very quick electrical impulses). Across stage 1 of sleep, the level of activity in the brain and body decreases, alertness decreases, muscles relax, breathing slows, and body temperature begins to drop. During this stage, the brain is likely to continue to register stimuli from the environment (it has not yet shut itself off to external stimulation), but an individual is not likely to wake up and respond.

During **stage 2** of sleep, body and brain activities continue to slow. In this stage, **theta waves** are emitted by the brain (slower, less intense waves), but we still see brief bursts of electrical activity called **sleep spindles.** At this point, the brain might still register external stimuli, but it is not at all likely to respond to the stimulation.

During **stage 3,** brain and body activities slow even more. During this time, the brain emits large, slow waves of electrical activity called **delta waves.**

Stage 4 is the deepest and most relaxed stage of sleep. Heart rate, breathing and brain activities slow considerably, and the brain closes itself off to external stimulation. During this stage, the brain is not likely to register information. (Though important information might still penetrate consciousness and be processed.) Individuals are very difficult to awaken during this stage of sleep, and if awakened directly from this stage, they are likely to be dazed and confused. Following some time in stage 4 sleep, individuals begin to cycle backward through the stages, first regressing into stage 3, then to stage 2, during which time brain and body activities slowly increase. Following a period of time in stage 2 sleep, individuals enter a new stage of sleep called REM sleep.

REM sleep is the stage of sleep in which dreaming occurs. When individuals are awakened during REM sleep, they tend to report vivid, detailed, story-like thoughts and events. REM stands for rapid eye movement, one of the key characteristics of this stage of sleep. EEGs indicate short, high-frequency brain waves similar to those seen when an individual is awake. During REM sleep, body and brain activities increase significantly. This stage of sleep is often referred to as **paradoxical sleep** because of the paradoxical nature of brain and body activities during this stage. Although brain and body activities increase during this stage, muscle control is inhibited to the point that individuals are said to be in a state of **partial sleep paralysis.** In each successive cycle of sleep, we spend increasing amounts of time in REM sleep and less time in stage 4 sleep.

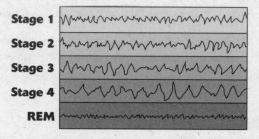

Meaning and Function of Dreams

What do dreams mean, and why do we have them? A number of theories have been proposed concerning the meaning and function of dreams. Sigmund Freud hypothesized that dreams are an expression of thoughts and feelings housed in our unconscious. But unconscious processes are not expressed openly in dreams. Rather the unconscious is represented in symbols. According to Freud, dreams have both a manifest and a latent content. The **manifest content** refers to the actual content of a dream (what we recollect about the dream). The **latent content** is a dream's underlying meaning (what the dream *really* means). Freud believed that a lot of sexual impulses are implied in dreams and a great deal of anxiety-provoking material manifests in the content of dreams.

A more biological perspective on dreams is **Activation-Synthesis theory.** According to this theory, dreams are an end result of random firing of neurons in the lower brain during sleep. Activity in the brainstem during sleep reaches the cortical regions. The cortex attempts to make sense of the neuronal firing from the brainstem region with the end result being a dream that appears story-like and meaningful, but often somewhat bizarre.

In recent years, cognitive and neuropsychologists have discovered that performance on recently learned tasks is impaired if an individual is deprived of REM sleep during the night. In addition, recent research finds that neural activity during REM sleep mirrors neural activity during the learning process, suggesting that dreaming may play a role in the consolidation of memories.

Though psychologists and neurologists are not exactly sure why we dream or whether dreams serve any purpose, we know one thing for sure: If deprived of REM sleep for a night, a person is likely to feel irritable and tired the next day; perform worse on tests of concentration, attention and memory; and spend more time in REM sleep on subsequent nights.

Sleep Disorders

What about disorders of sleep? A number of people experience problems either falling asleep, staying asleep or staying awake. **Insomnia** occurs when one has difficulty either falling asleep or staying asleep at night. **Sleep apnea** is a disorder in which individuals have difficulty breathing while asleep. When oxygen levels drop below a certain level, the individual awakens. This problem results in repeated awakenings throughout the night (some people awaken more than 500 times in one night), often without the awareness of having awakened. Most individuals who suffer from sleep apnea complain of fatigue throughout the day. Sleep apnea might also play a role in sudden infant death syndrome (SIDS), a disorder in which apparently normal infants die in their sleep. **Narcolepsy** is a disorder in which individuals experience short periods of uncontrollable sleep while in the middle of a waking activity (including driving and having a conversation). In fact, narcoleptic attacks involve a sudden shift from an awake state directly into a REM state of sleep. The cause of narcolepsy is unknown. **Nightmares** are frightening dreams that occur during REM sleep. In contrast, **night terrors** occur during stage 4 (NREM) sleep and involve awakening in a state of panic, fear and extreme physiological arousal. Night terrors are more frequent in children, although they can occur in adults. **Somnambulism** refers to sleep-walking and/or sleep talking and also occurs during stage 4 (NREM) sleep. **REM behavior disorder** occurs when the partial sleep paralysis that normally occurs during REM sleep does not occur. In such instances, individuals are able to act out their dreams.

Hypnosis

Hypnosis refers to a trance-like state of mind in which individuals are highly susceptible to the suggestions of others. Whether hypnosis actually represents an altered state of consciousness is a heated and controversial issue. Some argue that the changes in behavior and electrical activity in the brain during hypnosis support the view of hypnosis as an altered state of consciousness. Others argue that this is not sufficient evidence to conclude that hypnosis is an altered state of consciousness.

Contrary to popular myth, people cannot be hypnotized against their will. In fact, about 5%–20% of individuals cannot be hypnotized at all. Those who are easily hypnotized tend to become absorbed in activities such as reading or listening to music, spend more time than others daydreaming and readily become unaware of their surroundings when absorbed in an activity.

Some believe that when in a hypnotic state, individuals are able to recall memories of childhood events that they might not recall when in a normal, waking state. However, no clear support exists for this belief. Still, hypnosis is used to treat a number of practical problems—including reducing smoking, controlling pain and improving athletic performance.

Psychoactive Drug Effects

Psychoactive drugs are drugs capable of crossing the blood-brain barrier and altering brain function. Most psychoactive drugs exert their effects at the neurotransmitter level by altering the functioning or activity of neurotransmitters. Some are structurally similar to neurotransmitters and mimic their effects. Other drugs delay the breakdown of neurotransmitters, leaving them to exert their effects for longer periods of time. Some drugs inhibit the production of neurotransmitters, reducing the amount of neurotransmitters released at the synapses. Some cause neurotransmitters to be broken down quicker following release, reducing the amount of time they spend in synapses exerting their effects.

A number of psychoactive drugs are available today—from illegal drugs (such as cocaine, LSD and heroin) to a number of prescription and legal drugs (such as caffeine, alcohol, Prozac and Haldol). The many psychoactive drugs available can be grouped into four classifications based on their general effects on the nervous system: depressants, stimulants, opiates and hallucinogens.

Depressants inhibit central nervous system activity. At low doses, they relieve anxiety and have a calming effect. At high doses, they impair reflexes, movement, coordination and judgment. The three major types of depressant drugs are alcohol, barbiturates (sedatives) and benzodiazepines (tranquilizers). At low doses, **alcohol** reduces inhibition and relaxes individuals. At high doses, alcohol impairs reflexes, balance and coordination of muscles. At extremely high doses, alcohol can result in unconsciousness and even death.

Barbiturates, also known as sedatives, induce drowsiness and reduce insomnia. Because barbiturates exert their effects on the brainstem, at high doses barbiturates impair life-sustaining functions and can be lethal. In addition, barbiturates (though they induce drowsiness and assist individuals in sleeping), disrupt REM sleep and leave individuals feeling tired even after a regular night of sleep.

Benzodiazapenes, also known as tranquilizers, produce a calming effect and reduce anxiety (without sedation). They produce their effects primarily by acting on GABA pathways in the limbic system (decreasing fear, anxiety and nervousness). Xanax, Valium and Ativan are all examples of benzodiazapenes.

Stimulants increase central nervous system and peripheral nervous system activity, thus increasing alertness and arousal levels. In addition, stimulants exert strong effects on the reward circuits in the limbic system, making many stimulants addictive when used regularly. Cocaine, caffeine and nicotine are all examples of drugs that fall under the classification of stimulants.

The main effect of **opiates** is to suppress or reduce pain. Opiates are psychoactive drugs that are chemically similar to naturally occurring painkillers in the body called endorphins. They are used as analgesics during surgery and to treat pain following surgery. Their use must be carefully monitored due to their highly addictive nature. Morphine, codeine and heroin are all examples of drugs that fall under the classification of opiates.

Hallucinogens are drugs that alter thoughts, sensations and perceptions. Their use can produce sensory and perceptual experiences that are not real, and dissociative reactions in which one feels separated from their own body. Many hallucinogens are chemically similar to serotonin and mimic serotonin in the brain. Mescaline (found in cactuses and mushrooms), PCP (angel dust or phenylcyclidine), LSD (a synthetic compound) and marijuana (found in plant leaves) are all examples of hallucinogenic drugs.

Review Questions

1. Throughout the night, individuals cycle through _____ stages of sleep.

   A. 2
   B. 3
   C. 4
   D. 5
   E. 6

2. Sleep spindles, brief bursts of electrical activity, are found during _____ sleep.

   A. stage 1
   B. stage 2
   C. stage 3
   D. REM
   E. stage 5

3. A hypnogogic state is most common during _____ sleep.

   A. stage 1
   B. stage 2
   C. REM
   D. stage 3
   E. stage 4

4. Dreaming is most common during _____ sleep.

   A. stage 1
   B. stage 2
   C. REM
   D. stage 3
   E. stage 4

5. According to Activation-Synthesis theory, dreams:

    A. can reveal important unconscious desires
    B. are replays of daily events
    C. represent hopes and fears about the future
    D. have no hidden meaning or significance
    E. reflect problems we are having difficulty solving

6. Jason suddenly falls asleep in class right in the middle of taking notes. Jason is likely suffering from:

    A. insomnia
    B. somnambulism
    C. hypersomnia
    D. sleep apnea
    E. narcolepsy

7. Which of the following pairs of drugs falls under the class of drugs known as depressants?

    A. alcohol and nicotine
    B. cocaine and heroin
    C. sedatives and benzodiazapenes
    D. sedatives and heroin
    E. LSD and marijuana

8. The primary effect of opiates is to:

    A. induce drowsiness
    B. elevate well-being
    C. reduce pain
    D. inhibit fear and anxiety
    E. alter perception of time

Answers

1. D. Throughout the night, individuals cycle through five stages of sleep. Stage 1 is a transitional phase in which the brain and body begin to relax. In stage 2, relaxation continues, and the brain emits theta waves and sleep spindles. Stages 3 and 4 are marked by increased relaxation, slow brain waves and deep sleep. The fifth stage, REM sleep, is the stage in which brain and body activities increase and dreaming occurs.

2. B. Stage 2 is marked by theta waves and sleep spindles. Sleep spindles are brief electrical impulses emitted by the brain. During stage 2, our brains still register stimuli, but we are unlikely to respond to the stimulation.

3. A. A hypnogogic state is most common during stage 1 of sleep as the individual transitions from an awake, alert state to a drowsy, inactive state. The hypnogogic state is a state experienced as the individual shifts from alertness to relaxation. It is usually associated with alpha waves (less intense, but still relatively quick electrical impulses).

4. C. Dreaming is most likely to occur during REM sleep. REM stands for rapid eye movement, which is common during dreaming. This stage is also marked by an increase in brain and body activities, but a decrease in muscular activity (to the point of partial sleep paralysis).

5. D. Activation-Synthesis theory states that dreams are the result of the brain trying to make sense of electrical activity in the brainstem. Freud believed that dreams reflect unconscious desires and can be analyzed for their underlying latent content.

6. E. Narcolepsy is a disorder in which sufferers fall asleep uncontrollably in the middle of waking activity. Insomnia occurs when an individual has difficulty falling asleep. Somnambulism refers to sleepwalking and sleep talking. Sleep apnea occurs when individuals stop breathing while sleeping and must awaken to trigger the breathing process.

7. C. Sedatives and benzodiazepines are two types of depressants. Sedatives, also known as barbiturates, are sleep aids that induce drowsiness and reduce insomnia. Benzodiazapenes are tranquilizers or anti-anxiety drugs that reduce anxiety and produce a calming effect in individuals. Alcohol is also a depressant that inhibits activity throughout the cerebral cortex and cerebellum. Nicotine and cocaine are both stimulants. Heroin is an opiate. LSD and marijuana are both hallucinogens.

8. C. The primary effect of opiates is to reduce pain. Opiates are a class of drugs that include morphine, codeine and heroin. Opiates are often used an analgesics during surgery and to treat pain following surgery. They are highly addictive drugs, and their use must be carefully monitored by physicians. Sedatives are drugs that induce drowsiness. Benzodiazapenes inhibit fear and anxiety. Hallucinogens alter perception of time.

Learning

From a psychological perspective, the term learning refers to more than the acquisition of knowledge through formal instruction. According to psychologists, **learning** refers to any relatively permanent change in behavior potential resulting from experience with the environment. This change in behavior can be subtle such as changes in simple motor responses or more dramatic such as changes in emotional reactions, thought processes and more.

In this chapter, we look at some of the basic forms of learning identified by psychologists. This chapter begins with a review of classical conditioning and the elements and processes involved in classical conditioning. It then turns to operant conditioning and the basic elements and processes involved in operant conditioning. It ends with a discussion of social learning as proposed by **Albert Bandura** and a brief review of the cognitive processes important in the learning process.

Classical Conditioning

Classical conditioning is a form of learning in which we learn to associate two environmental stimuli with each other and, as a result, change our response to one stimulus based on its association with the other stimulus. Consider the following example: For young children, a loud scream usually elicits a fear or startle response. Now, say a young child encounters a snake while walking with Mom. The child doesn't know what the snake is, but Mom screams, causing a fear/startle response in the child. Later, they encounter another snake and again Mom screams, causing a startle response in the child. Eventually, the child comes to associate the snake with fear and changes their own response to the snake—they now startle and show a fear response to the snake, even in the absence of Mom's scream.

Classical conditioning was discovered by **Ivan Pavlov,** a Russian physiologist, while he was trying to study the digestive processes in dogs. To study salivation, Pavlov had to initiate the salivation process by feeding the dogs. However, as his study proceeded, he encountered a problem. After several feedings with a meat powder, the dogs began salivating before the meat powder was in their mouth. What had happened to cause the salivation process to occur earlier than it should? Pavlov hypothesized that the dogs had come to associate the sight of the researcher or the sounds of the researcher approaching with being fed, thus leading the salivation process to begin long before the food was actually in their mouths. As a result of the association, the dogs learned to salivate at the mere sight of a researcher—something they had never done before. The dogs changed their behavior as a result of experience.

Elements of Classical Conditioning

Several elements are involved in classical conditioning. A stimulus that elicits a natural reflexive response is called an **unconditioned stimulus.** In the preceding example, the meat powder is an unconditioned stimulus because the meat powder naturally elicits a salivation response in the dogs. In the case of the young child who is startled by his mother's scream, the mother's scream is the unconditioned stimulus. (It automatically elicits a fear/startle response in the child.) The **unconditioned response** refers to the actual reflexive response made to an unconditioned stimulus (for example, salivating, startling). A **neutral stimulus** is any stimulus in the environment that does not elicit any particular response. For example, many people do not have any particular response to a pencil or a chair, and dogs do not typically salivate at the mere sight of a researcher. However, if a neutral stimulus is continuously paired with an unconditioned stimulus (a stimulus that elicits an automatic reflexive response), we might begin to make the same automatic response to the neutral stimulus that we previously only made to the unconditioned stimulus, such as when Pavlov's dogs began to salivate at the mere sight of the researcher.

The process of actually coming to associate a neutral stimulus with an unconditioned stimulus and changing one's behavior as a result of the association is called **acquisition.** Acquisition occurs as a result of repeated pairings of a neutral stimulus and an unconditioned stimulus. When acquisition has occurred and the individual alters their response to the neutral stimulus, the neutral stimulus becomes the **conditioned stimulus.** The neutral stimulus is now called a conditioned stimulus because the individual has been *conditioned* (or has *learned*) to respond to it in a particular way. The response made to the conditioned stimulus is now called the **conditioned response** because the individual has *learned* to make the response.

When a response has been learned through classical conditioning, is it always present? Not necessarily. It is possible for a response to be changed through a process called **extinction.** Extinction can be accomplished by presenting the conditioned stimulus without the unconditioned stimulus repeatedly over several trials. Over time, the learned response diminishes. Still, the response might reappear at a later time, a phenomenon known as **spontaneous recovery** in classical conditioning terms.

Classical Conditioning Applied to Humans

John Watson later demonstrated that humans can be conditioned in the same way that Pavlov's dogs were conditioned. John Watson and his assistant conditioned a young boy named Albert to fear a white rat through the process of classical conditioning. Initially, Albert showed no particular response to white rats. However, after repeated pairings of a white rat with a loud noise (which elicited an reflexive startle response), little Albert began to show a conditioned response of fear to the rat. Incidentally, Watson and **Raynor** found that little Albert feared more than just the white rat. He also feared stimuli that looked similar to the rat. For example, when Albert was presented with other white, furry objects (for example, a Santa Claus mask, cotton balls), he showed the same fear response. He had generalized his newly learned behavior to similar objects, a process known as **stimulus generalization.** But, can people learn to distinguish between stimuli so that they don't fear all white furry objects? Yes; **stimulus discrimination** refers to the process by which individuals learn to discriminate stimuli and only show a response to a specific stimulus. Stimulus discrimination can be accomplished by pairing only the target stimulus with the unconditioned stimulus and presenting those stimuli to which you do not want a particular response without the unconditioned stimulus, a process called discrimination training.

Can individuals overcome fears established through classical conditioning? Many can, and, in fact, a process of counterconditioning is often effective in reducing many fears learned through classical conditioning. In **counterconditioning,** a feared stimulus is repeatedly paired with a positive stimulus in an attempt to associate it with a pleasant stimulus rather than a feared stimulus. Today, a clinical procedure called systematic desensitization is used to treat phobic disorders (disorders characterized by irrational fears of objects). Similar to counterconditioning, **systematic desensitization** involves pairing a feared stimulus with feelings of relaxation over several trials. The individual is first trained in relaxation techniques, then instructed to utilize the relaxation techniques while in the presence of the feared stimulus. The key in systematic desensitization is that exposure to the feared stimulus is increased on each trial. For example, if one has an intense fear of flying, the therapist might first have the individual simply think about flying while utilizing relaxation techniques. When the individual is able to do this, the therapist exposes them to a new level of the feared stimulus, such as having the individual visit an airport or look at a real plane. This process continues until ultimately the individual is flying on a plane while feeling relaxed.

Taste-Aversive Learning

Yet another phenomenon found in humans related to classical conditioning is that of **taste-aversive learning.** It is not uncommon for humans and all other mammals as well to associate nausea and sickness with any food eaten prior to becoming sick (rather than with other stimuli in the environment) and, as a result, to develop an aversion for that food. Taste-aversive learning is considered a form of conditioning because the aversion is *learned* or *acquired* as the result of an association between the food and the nausea. However, it is different from basic classical conditioning in two important ways. First, taste-aversive conditioning does not require repeated pairings of the food with the nausea, but can occur after just one pairing. Second, with taste-aversive conditioning, an association can (and is most likely) when a long delay occurs between the presentation of the food and the onset of sickness. In fact, research is now showing that a long delay is necessary for the development of a taste aversion; if the nausea onsets too soon after ingestion, a taste aversion is not acquired.

Operant Conditioning

Operant conditioning is a form of learning in which we learn to associate a particular behavioral response with the outcome that follows (either good or bad) and change the frequency of the behavior as a result of this association. If we associate a particular behavior with a positive outcome, we are likely to continue to engage in that behavior to receive that outcome in the future. If we associate a particular behavior with a negative outcome, we are likely to decrease that behavior in the future to avoid the negative consequence. Thus, we are changing our behavior as a result of the consequences that follow. **Edward Thorndike** first summarized the relationships between stimulus and consequences in the **Law of Effect** stating that behaviors that lead to positive or satisfying consequences are more likely to be repeated, and vice versa; those behaviors that lead to negative outcomes or no positive outcomes are less likely to be repeated. Thorndike went on to argue that over time and with enough experience, organisms automatically make the connection between stimulus and response.

Using Thorndike's Law of Effect as a foundation, **B. F. Skinner** trained animals (originally pigeons) to make certain behavioral responses by providing them with positive consequences. In his work, Skinner designed an operant chamber (sometimes called a Skinner box), which he programmed to deliver rewards (food pellets) based on an animal's behavior. The operant chamber was later used with other animals to study the effects of reward and penalty, and forms the foundation of what is known today as operant conditioning.

As already noted, the focus of operant conditioning is on the consequences that follow behaviors. These consequences can come as either reinforcers or punishers, and each can be further divided into positive and negative reinforcers or punishers. **Reinforcement** involves the use of consequences to increase the likelihood of a behavior occurring again. Two types of reinforcement can be used: positive reinforcement and negative reinforcement. **Positive reinforcement** involves presenting something desirable following a behavior (praise, a good grade, money, a favorite food or anything positive to the individual). **Negative reinforcement** involves taking away or removing an undesirable stimulus following a desired behavior (ceasing to yell or nag, relieving tension or pain). **Punishment** is always aimed at reducing the frequency or repetition of a behavior. Two types of punishment can be used: positive punishment and negative punishment. **Positive punishment** involves the presentation of an aversive or unpleasant stimulus (for example, yelling, assigning extra chores) to decrease the frequency of a behavior. **Negative punishment** involves the removal of a positive stimulus following a behavior to reduce the likelihood of the behavior occurring again. For example, if parents take car privileges (something desired) away from an adolescent who comes home past curfew, they are using negative punishment.

Schedules of Reinforcement

One of the most basic questions of operant conditioning involves the schedule by which to administer reinforcement and punishment. Punishers and reinforcers can be administered on a **continuous schedule** (following each occurrence of the behavior) or on a **partial schedule** (following only some instances of the behavior). While punishment has been found to be most effective when a continuous schedule is used, reinforcement is more effective at maintaining a behavior when a partial schedule of reinforcement is implemented. In addition, behavior has been found to be more resistant to extinction when partial schedules of reinforcement are used compared to continuous schedules of reinforcement.

Partial or intermittent schedules of reinforcement can be further broken down into various types of intermittent schedules. **Ratio schedules** reinforce a behavior based on frequency of the behavioral response. **Fixed ratio schedules** provide reinforcement after a fixed number of behavioral responses (for example, giving reinforcement whenever a subject engages in the desired behavior five times). **Variable ratio schedules** provide reinforcement after a random number of responses (for example, giving reinforcement after a subject engages in the behavior four times, but next time not giving reinforcement until the subject engages in the behavior six times).

Interval schedules can be either fixed or variable, and provide reinforcement after a certain time interval has elapsed, given that the individual has been engaging in the behavior across the time interval. **Fixed interval schedules** provide reinforcement for the first response that occurs after a fixed time period has elapsed (for example, giving reinforcement every 10 minutes). **Variable interval schedules** provide reinforcement for the first response that occurs after random time periods have elapsed (for example, giving reinforcement after 5 minutes, then after 20 minutes, then after 10 minutes).

Applications of Operant Conditioning

Behavior modification is the use of operant conditioning principles to deal with problematic behavior. It relies on the use of reinforcement and punishment to reduce negative inappropriate behaviors and to increase engagement in appropriate behaviors. Over the years, variants of operant conditioning have been developed for specific applications. One such variant is a process called **shaping.** Unlike strict operant conditioning, which reinforces or punishes already existing behaviors, shaping involves the use of operant conditioning principles, particularly reinforcement, to bring about altogether new behaviors that would not occur by chance. For example, parents who wish to potty train their young toddler might utilize the process of shaping to accomplish their goal. With shaping, one begins with a target behavior, and then reinforces behaviors similar to or involved in the behavior of interest. In trying to potty train a toddler, the parents might first reinforce the child for indicating that they have to potty, even if the child doesn't make it to the bathroom. As this behavior continues, the parents increase their expectations, reinforcing only those behaviors that more closely approximate the target behavior. Thus, the parents stop reinforcing the child for indicating that they have to potty, and instead only reinforce the child for sitting on the toilet. The parents continue to increase their expectations until finally they only reinforce the child when the child goes to the bathroom on their own.

Token economies are a form of operant conditioning in which an individual is given tokens (reinforcers that, in and of themselves, have no value). The reinforcing value of the tokens lies in the fact that the individual can later exchange the tokens for a reward. For example, 5 tokens might be exchanged for a candy bar; 20 tokens might be exchanged for a new toy.

Social Learning

Social learning refers to changes in behavior that occur simply as a result of watching others. The leading proponent of Social Learning theory is **Albert Bandura,** who proposed that individuals can learn without actively participating in a behavior and without being directly reinforced or punished for it. He believed that humans learn a great deal by watching and imitating. Bandura outlined a number of prerequisites for observational learning to occur:

- **Attention:** The subject must pay attention to the actions of another.
- **Retention:** The subject must remember what they observe.
- **Reproduction:** The subject must reproduce/actually perform the behavior.
- **Motivation:** The subject must be motivated to perform the behavior.

In addition to the preceding prerequisites, imitation is influenced by the consequences observed when the model performs the observed behavior. Individuals are more likely to imitate a behavior they have seen rewarded (a process called **vicarious reinforcement**) and less likely to imitate a behavior they have seen punished (**vicarious punishment**). Finally, the characteristics of the model also influence the likelihood of a subject repeating/imitating the behavior. Research has found that individuals are more likely to pay attention to and imitate a person they think is an expert, is attractive, has high social status and is socially powerful.

Social Learning theory has serious implications for parenting and television programming. In a landmark study by **Bandura, Ross, and Ross (1963),** children were randomly assigned to either watch a film depicting an adult model behaving aggressively toward an inflated Bobo doll or to watch an aggression-free film. Following the film, the children were left alone in a room with toys (which included a Bobo doll) during which time their behaviors were recorded on a hidden camera. Interestingly, those children who had observed the aggressive model displayed significantly more aggressive behavior toward the Bobo doll than the children who had watched the aggressive-free film. Moreover, those children who had watched the aggressive model showed additional aggressive behaviors that had not been modeled by the adult in the film.

Cognitive Processes in Learning

Not everything that humans do and learn can be explained by operant and classical conditioning. Some cognitive psychologists focus on **higher-order learning,** learning that requires conscious and deliberate processing of information, and on the specific cognitive and mental factors that mediate various learning processes.

A classic study by **Edward Tolman** in 1948 illustrates two important cognitive factors involved in learning: motivational factors and latent learning. In his study, Tolman had two groups of rats run a maze for 10 days. One group of rats was allowed to wander around the maze without receiving any rewards, while the second group of rats was given a reward (food) each time they ran the maze. The key question concerned whether the two groups of rats performed differently in running the maze. They did. The group of rats that had been rewarded (**motivated**) for running the maze made fewer errors and completed the maze more quickly than the group of rats that did not receive any reward for running the maze.

Tolman went on to examine what happened if the rats who initially did not receive any reward for running the maze began to be rewarded for their behavior. Interestingly enough, when the rats were reinforced for their behavior, they showed an immediate, sharp reduction in the number of errors made while running the maze. Tolman suggested that while running the mazes, the rats had formed **cognitive maps,** internal mental representations of the maze, but were not displaying this learning in their behavior. However, when their behavior was reinforced, the learning became observable. According to Tolman, learning can take place, but might not be displayed until a later point in time. Tolman referred to learning that has occurred but is not immediately displayed or expressed as **latent learning.**

Review Questions

Questions 1 and 2 are based on the following scenario: A cook makes soup the same way every day. He always chops the carrots right before the onions. Initially, the onions make his eyes tear up, but the carrots do not. After he makes the soup several times, however, the cook notices that his eyes tear up when he is chopping carrots.

1. The cook's change in behavior is a result of:
   A. classical conditioning
   B. operant conditioning
   C. social learning
   D. systematic desensitization
   E. latent learning

2. In the preceding scenario, the unconditioned stimulus is the _____ and the conditioned stimulus is the _____.

   A. carrots; soup
   B. onions; soup
   C. carrots; onions
   D. soup; onions
   E. onions; carrots

3. If you buy your sister gas every time she takes you shopping so that she will take you more often, you are using _____ to influence her behavior.

   A. positive reinforcement
   B. negative reinforcement
   C. shaping
   D. a token economy
   E. counterconditioning

4. _____ is most closely aligned with Thorndike's Law of Effect.

   A. latent learning
   B. classical conditioning
   C. operant conditioning
   D. social learning
   E. higher-order learning

5. Taste-aversive learning is a type of learning most closely associated with:

   A. higher-order learning
   B. latent learning
   C. social learning
   D. classical conditioning
   E. operant conditioning

6. If your credit card company lowers your interest rate when you make your first 12 payments on time, the company is using _____ to influence your behavior.

   A. a token economy
   B. shaping
   C. negative punishment
   D. negative reinforcement
   E. systematic desensitization

7. Bill is using a shock collar to keep his dog from running out of the yard. Every time his dog leaves the yard, the collar shocks the dog. What operant conditioning technique is being used here?

   A. counterconditioning
   B. negative punishment
   C. negative reinforcement
   D. positive punishment
   E. systematic desensitization

8. Mark is hiking for the first time. He sees a snake coiled in front of him and slowly backs away because that is what he has seen people do on Animal Planet. What type of learning is Mark displaying?

   A. social learning
   B. latent learning
   C. classical conditioning
   D. operant conditioning
   E. shaping

Answers

1. A. Classical conditioning is a type of learning in which an individual changes their behavior as a result of making an association between two stimuli in the environment. Prior to making an association between the carrots and onions, the cook did not tear up while cutting the onions. However, after numerous pairings of the carrots with the onions, the cook now makes the same response to the carrots that he initially only made to the onions. The cook has been conditioned to respond to the carrots in this way as a result of associating the carrots with the onions.

2. E. An unconditioned stimulus is any stimulus that elicits a natural, automatic response. A conditioned stimulus is a stimulus that one has learned to make a response to based on its association with an unconditioned stimulus. In this example, onions naturally elicit teary eyes, but carrots do not. However, because the carrots are repeatedly presented prior to the onions, the carrots now produce teary eyes. Thus, the onions are an unconditioned stimulus, and the carrots are a conditioned stimulus.

3. A. Positive reinforcement is designed to increase the likelihood of a behavior occurring again; it involves following a desired behavior with a positive consequence. In this example, you are trying to increase the likelihood that your sister will take you shopping by buying her gas. Negative reinforcement is also designed to increase the likelihood of a behavior occurring again, but it involves the removal of a negative stimulus following the desired behavior. Shaping involves the use of reinforcement to encourage an altogether new behavior. A token economy also uses reinforcement, but it involves providing tokens for desired behaviors. The tokens can later be exchanged for real reinforcers. Counterconditioning is a technique that utilizes the principles of classical conditioning in an attempt to eliminate a classically conditioned response.

4. C. Operant conditioning is based on Thorndike's Law of Effect (which states that behaviors followed by positive consequences are likely to be repeated, whereas behaviors followed by negative consequences are less likely to be repeated). All the other types of learning are based on different principles. Classical conditioning is based on learning associations between two environmental stimuli. Social learning involves copying or imitating the behavior of others. Higher-order learning involves forms of learning that require deliberate and conscious processing of information.

5. D. Taste-aversive learning is a type of learning based on the principles of classical conditioning. Like classical conditioning, taste-aversive learning occurs when an individual makes an association between two stimuli. In taste-aversive learning, the stimuli that are associated are a particular food and nausea/illness. As a result of the association, the individual avoids the food.

6. D. Negative reinforcement involves the removal of a negative stimulus to increase the likelihood of a behavior occurring again. If you make your first 12 payments on time, your credit card company lowers your interest rates, thus removing something undesirable in an attempt to increase the likelihood that you will make your payments on time. Negative punishment involves the removal of a positive stimulus to decrease the likelihood of a behavior occurring again (for example, taking away television privileges when a child misbehaves). Shaping involves the use of reinforcement to bring about an altogether new behavior. A token economy involves the presentation of tokens for desired behavior that can be exchanged later for meaningful reinforcers, such as a candy bar or ice cream.

7. D. Bill is using positive punishment, which involves the presentation of a negative stimulus (shock) to decrease the likelihood of a behavior (leaving the yard) occurring again. Negative punishment involves the removal of a positive stimulus to decrease the likelihood of a behavior occurring again. Negative reinforcement involves the removal of a negative stimulus to increase the likelihood of a behavior occurring again. Systematic desensitization and counterconditioning are variants of classical conditioning used to extinguish a behavior.

8. A. Mark is engaging in a behavior that he learned by watching others on Animal Planet. Social learning involves learning by watching others. Classical conditioning is a type of learning in which one changes their behavior as a result of associating two stimuli together. Operant conditioning is a type of learning in which one changes their behavior as a result of associating a particular consequence with a behavior.

Cognitive psychology is a branch of psychology that focuses on the various types of mental processing engaged in by humans and the factors that influence our ability to process information, solve problems and make decisions. Cognitive psychologists study a variety of mental processes (including thinking, speaking, comprehending, remembering, forgetting, problem solving, decision making and reasoning).

This chapter reviews what is currently known about memory, language, thought, reasoning and problem solving. The chapter begins with an examination of the different memory systems and why we sometimes forget information. It then looks briefly at language—how it is used by humans to communicate and how infants and children learn the language of their culture. The chapter ends with a review of various types of thinking and the variety of strategies used to reason, solve problems and make decisions.

Memory

Many mistakenly think of memory as a large filing cabinet where information is simply stored away for later retrieval. In reality, **memory** is a complex mental system involving multiple stages of information processing. According to the Information-Processing model of memory, four major processes are involved in remembering information:

- **Attention:** We must direct our attention to the information.
- **Encoding:** The information must be transformed into a neural impulse and mental representation that can be processed, interpreted, and organized by the brain.
- **Storage:** The information must be processed in some form and stored away.
- **Retrieval:** Stored information must be brought to conscious awareness.

In addition to the processes involved in memory, psychologists have also identified a number of memory systems. **Sensory memory** is a memory system associated with each of our senses and is responsible for the initial intake of information from the environment. Sensory memory for our visual sense is called **iconic memory** and for our auditory sense is called **echoic memory.** Sensory memory holds a great deal of information without much processing for a very brief period of time.

If we choose to attend to and further process the information held in sensory memory, it moves into our working **(short-term) memory** system. Previously known as short-term memory, many prefer to call this system **working memory** because it is the system where we actually work on and process information. How much information can be held in short-term memory? In a set of classic experiments, **George Miller** discovered that on average seven items can be held in short-term memory at any given time. In fact, George Miller coined the phrases *the magical number seven* and *seven plus or minus two* when referring to the number of items that can be held in short-term memory. However, the capacity of short-term memory can be increased by a process known as chunking. **Chunking** involves grouping items into meaningful units. For example, if you are read a list of 14 numbers (1, 4, 7, 8, 4, 3, 6, 9, 8, 6, 2, 5, 1, 0) and asked to recall the list, this exceeds the capacity of short-term memory. However, you might have chunked some of the numbers into groups (for example, 147, 843, 698, 251, 0).

Long-term memory is a relatively permanent memory store that holds an infinite amount of information for long periods of time, sometimes indefinitely. Though much of what is put in long-term memory is held permanently, it is possible for information to fade, to be lost or to not be recalled when needed.

Memory Processes

The nature of the processing that occurs in short-term/working memory determines whether the information enters long-term memory or is lost. Thus, merely encountering information does not guarantee that it will reach long-term memory for future recall. Information is only stored in long-term memory if it is processed at a deep enough level in short-term/working memory. **Fergus Craik** and **Robert Lockhart** (1972) proposed the **Levels of Processing theory** of memory, which argues that information is more likely to be remembered when the information is processed at a deep level. **Rote or maintenance rehearsal** (repeating information over and over to oneself) is not enough to remember information over long periods of time. Instead, information needs to be elaborated on, made meaningful, related to already stored information, organized in a meaningful way or made distinctive in some way—a form of processing known as **elaborative rehearsal.**

Putting all this information together, we get a full picture of how the overall memory system functions.

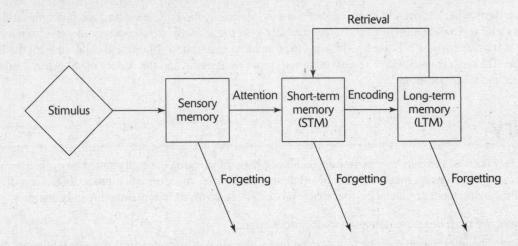

Information from the external world is taken in through sensory receptors, at which point it is held briefly in sensory memory. If we choose to attend to and further process this information, it is transferred to short-term/working memory where we begin the process of encoding and storing the information. The degree to which we process the information determines whether the information is merely held for a brief period in short-term memory and then lost, or the information is transferred to long-term memory. For the information to be transferred to long-term memory, it must be processed at a deep level (for example, organized, made meaningful and/or elaborated on). We again utilize short-term memory when we wish to retrieve or recall information previously put in long-term memory. At this point, short-term memory aids in the search for and retrieval of information, assists in piecing the information back together and allows conscious awareness of the memory. All systems and all processes are critical to remembering information. Breakdowns or problems in any component or process of the memory system can lead to difficulties remembering information.

Types of Memory

Long-term memory is not a single, large storage bin. A number of distinct memory systems exist within long-term memory. Two main divisions within long-term memory are declarative (explicit) and non-declarative (implicit). **Declarative memory** stores facts and knowledge about oneself and the world and can be further divided into semantic and episodic memory. **Semantic memory** stores general knowledge about the world such as facts, concepts and ideas. Information concerning the four lobes of the brain, the president of the United States, the 50 states and their capitals are all stored in semantic memory. **Episodic memory** stores information about personal life experiences and events such as one's first date, one's personal experiences on 9/11 when the terrorists attacked New York City or where one was when they were told something important. **Flashbulb memories** refer to highly vivid and detailed memories that endure over long periods of time. They are typically associated with dramatic and emotional events in one's life. Non-declarative (implicit) memory refers to unintentional learning that occurs outside of conscious awareness. Non-declarative memory includes procedural memory and priming. **Procedural memory** stores information about skills and how to do things such as how to ride a bike, how to drive and how to type. **Priming** occurs when prior exposure to a stimulus influences the processing of new information, even if we do not consciously remember the prior exposure. In essence, the prior exposure to the stimulus serves as a prime to the processing and interpretation of subsequent information.

The Reconstructive Nature of Memory

We used to think of memories as being stored in some exact location within the brain with each memory occupying its own space in the memory system. However, we know today that any given memory is actually stored in cells distributed throughout the cerebral cortex. When information is recalled or retrieved from long-term memory, these cells must be activated, and the information must be pieced back together in short-term memory. As a result of this piecemeal process of memory storage and retrieval, our memories are susceptible to all sorts of errors. Upon recall, parts might be missing that must be filled in by the individual, and the process of filling in missing parts might alter the memory and reduce its accuracy. Memories can also be distorted by new information, changing attitudes, views, opinions and leading questions by others.

Elizabeth Loftus has done a great deal of research on eyewitness testimony and the accuracy of memory for various events. Loftus's research highlights how easily memories can be altered by the power of suggestion and by leading questions. In her most famous study, Loftus had subjects watch a video in which two cars collide. Following the video presentation, half of the subjects were asked, "How fast were the cars going when they smashed into each other?" The remaining subjects were asked, "How fast were the cars going when they hit each other?" The key question of interest was whether altering the wording in the question would have any effect on subjects' recollection of the event, and, in fact, it did! She found that subjects in the first condition (who were asked how fast the cars were going when they *smashed* into each other) estimated the cars were going much faster than subjects in the second condition (in which the word *hit* was used instead of *smash*). Merely inserting a word that implies greater speed and damage led individuals to "remember" the cars going much faster.

Forgetting

We might not be able to recall a piece of information for several reasons. **Encoding failure** occurs when we cannot recall information because it was never put into our internal storage bin to begin with. If we fail to effectively encode new information, it is not put into our memory store and cannot be recalled later.

Sometimes we are unable to recall information in long-term memory because other information is interfering with its retrieval. Two types of interference can block the retrieval of information from long-term memory: proactive interference and retroactive interference. **Proactive interference** occurs when previously learned information hinders our memory of new information. When you move to a new house or apartment, you might have difficulty remembering your new address, telephone number or zip code because the old address, phone number or zip code keeps blocking the new. **Retroactive interference** occurs when more recently learned information interferes with the recall of information learned earlier. Sometimes, try as we might, we cannot remember our old address and phone number because a new one has overwritten or interfered with the old.

In some instances, we have difficulty recalling information because we fail to use or do not have retrieval cues to aid in the retrieval process. This type of forgetting is referred to as **cue-dependent forgetting.** Cognitive psychologists point out that when information is encoded, features of the context surrounding the information are also encoded (for example, where the information was, who provided the information and so on). These same features of context can be used later to aid in retrieval of stored information. For example, some students are able to look up at the blackboard to help recall something written on the board earlier. Some might look to the professor to help recall something the professor said. In 1983, **Tulving** proposed the **Encoding Specificity hypothesis,** which states that memory of information is improved if the cues present during learning are also present at the time of retrieval because those cues can be used to facilitate retrieval.

Language

Language refers to the complex system of sounds, words, meanings and rules used as a mode of communication among humans. Much debate exists over the extent to which humans are preprogrammed to decipher the sounds and structure of language. **Phonemes** refer to the basic sounds of language such as *p-, b* and *d-*. Combinations of phonemes make up **morphemes,** the smallest meaningful units of a language (words, prefixes, suffixes). Morphemes can be combined into phrases that are then combined to form sentences. **Syntax** refers to the grammatical rules for forming sentences and statements, and governs how words and phrases can be arranged in a sentence. Semantics refers to the meanings of words and the process of choosing appropriate words based on their meaning. Pragmatics refers to the process of adjusting language to fit the situation.

Noam Chomsky argued that humans are biologically hard-wired to learn and acquire language. He proposed the existence of a **language acquisition device (LAD),** an inborn mechanism responsible for processing language and deciphering the rules of the language one hears. In contrast, learning theorists argue that children learn language through experience (by associating words with objects, and imitating and repeating phrases they hear in the environment). According to learning theorists, the environment assists children in learning language.

Which view is correct? There is evidence to support both views. With respect to a language acquisition device, there are specific regions of the brain involved in language production (Broca's area) and language comprehension (Wernicke's area). In addition, all children (regardless of the language spoken) follow a similar developmental sequence in the development of language. However, learning theorists point out that children learn to speak the language they hear around them and learn grammar more rapidly when adults model correct syntax. Debate also exists over the extent to which language influences thought. **Benjamin Whorf** (1956) proposed the **Whorfian Hypothesis of Linguistic Relativity,** which argues that language shapes thought. According to the Whorfian hypothesis, thought is influenced and constrained by the language one speaks. Others choose to look at language as being shaped by thought. According to this view, language constantly evolves and changes to reflect the thought patterns of individuals in a given time and society.

Thinking involves the mental manipulation and processing of information. Two major components of thinking are mental images and concepts. **Mental images** refer to internal representations of objects or events in the world. **Concepts** refer to mental representations of classes of objects, events or people that share common properties. Some concepts are clearly defined by specific properties or features. Other concepts have less clearly defined boundaries. For less clearly defined concepts, individuals often think in terms of **prototypes,** the most typical or best example of the concept. For example, a robin is a more prototypical example of a bird than a chicken or ostrich. How we think about, respond to, and choose to interact with objects and people are influenced by the concepts we have formed.

How are concepts organized in memory? A popular view is that concepts are organized in **semantic networks,** a complex web of associations in which specific objects, people and events are linked together based on their relationships with one another. The following figure is an example of a simple network.

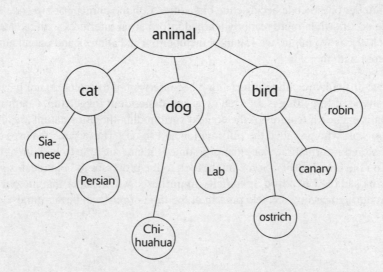

According to this view, the shorter the link between items, the stronger the association and the more likely it is that the activation or retrieval of one item will trigger the activation or retrieval of the related item.

Reasoning

Reasoning refers to a mental process in which one generates and/or evaluates ideas, arguments, beliefs and/or statements. Cognitive psychologists, mathematicians, and philosophers typically distinguish between two types of reasoning: inductive reasoning and deductive reasoning. **Inductive reasoning** involves reasoning from specific ideas or observations to more general propositions. In other words, one draws general conclusions based on specific pieces of information. When investigators draw conclusions based on several individual pieces of information, they are using inductive reasoning. **Deductive reasoning** involves reasoning that moves from general principles to more specific inferences. For example, if you know that all cats have fur and that your friend's pet, Bailey, is a cat, you can deduce that Bailey has fur even if you have never seen Bailey before.

Problem Solving

A major area of interest for cognitive psychologists concerns the manner in which people attempt to solve problems. The specific strategy or approach used to solve a problem depends on a number of factors, including the nature of the problem and the way in which the problem is represented and approached by an individual.

Probably the simplest of all problem-solving strategies is **trial and error.** When using trial and error, individuals unsystematically try a number of different solutions until the correct one is reached. Though effective at times, it is a hit-or-miss approach that often takes too long and does not work well with more complex problems. In many cases, a more systematic, planned approach proves more beneficial.

A second approach to solving problems is **means-end analysis.** When using means-end analysis, one breaks a problem down into subgoals, and then repeatedly assesses the discrepancy between the desired outcome and the current status of the problem after each step taken toward a solution. Like trial and error, some problems do not lend themselves well to means-end analysis.

Cognitive psychologists have found that humans frequently utilize cognitive shortcuts, called heuristics, when solving problems. **Heuristics** are cognitive shortcuts (or rules of thumb) that increase the likelihood of success on a problem or task, but might or might not lead to the correct solution. Two common heuristics that lead to inaccurate solutions are the availability heuristic and the representativeness heuristic. The **availability heuristic** is used when individuals judge the probability of an event occurring *based on how readily the event comes to mind*. The availability heuristic often leads one to assume that an event is more likely to occur than it actually is. For example, people often report a greater fear of dying in a plane crash than in a car crash, despite the fact that statistics clearly point to a higher risk of dying in a car crash. Why? Most likely because plane crashes receive more publicity and are thus more easily remembered than car crashes. The **representativeness heuristic** refers to the tendency of humans to estimate the likelihood of an event occurring *based on how typical it seems*. In doing so, many people ignore the actual statistical probability of an event. **Algorithms** are systematic, step-by-step rules that guarantee a solution to a problem if applied correctly. Mathematical formulas, such as how to do long division and how to add or subtract, are algorithms.

Problem solving can be hindered by the following psychological and cognitive phenomena: framing, functional fixedness, mental sets, confirmation bias and belief perseverance. **Framing** refers to the presentation and/or organization of a problem in such a way that one fails to reach the correct solution. Some problems are presented or worded in such a way that they lead one to focus on irrelevant aspects and ignore other important components of the problem. A related problem is functional fixedness. **Functional fixedness** refers to the tendency to think of an object only in terms of its typical use. For example, most people are likely to think of a book as something to read and less likely to think of a book as a weapon or kindling for a fire. As a consequence, when given the task of lighting a fire in a place where no firewood or sticks can be found, but many books are available, one might fail to think to use the books as kindling for the fire.

Both framing and functional fixedness contribute to the problems that many people experience when trying to solve the candlestick problem. In the **candlestick problem,** individuals are presented with three boxes: one containing a set of tacks, another containing a set of candles and the third containing several matches.

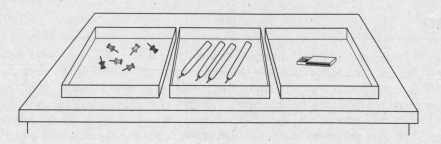

The individual is to place the candles at eye level on a nearby wall in such a way that the wax does not drip on the floor when the candles are lit. Many individuals have difficulty with this problem. Most fail to think of the boxes as useful for the task, instead viewing them as merely items holding the tools needed for the task. In actuality, the boxes holding the matches, candles and tacks are key to solving the problem. The solution to the problem is to tack the boxes to the wall and put the candles inside the boxes so that the boxes catch the wax.

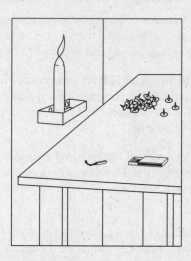

A broader phenomenon, **mental set,** occurs when individuals stick to old solution patterns that do not apply to a current problem. Many people have difficulty solving the following **jar problem** as a result of a mental set. The jar problem requires that one obtain, in jar B, the quantities of liquid indicated in the last column using three jars that can hold the quantities listed in their respective columns.

	A	B	C	Obtain:
1.	21	127	3	100
2.	14	163	25	99
3.	18	43	10	5
4.	9	42	6	21
5.	20	59	4	31
6.	28	76	3	25

The first five rows are all solved by filling jar B first, then taking the water in jar B and filling jar A once and jar C two times. Many attempt to use this same solution to solve the sixth row of the problem. However, this row requires a different, simpler solution than the previous five rows.

Confirmation bias occurs when individuals stick to their original hypothesis or belief about a problem, ignore any information that contradicts their initial hypothesis and search only for confirmation of what they already believe. In many situations, individuals only look for evidence that supports or verifies their original hypothesis, often leading them to miss important information that could help in solving a problem.

Belief perseverance refers to the phenomenon in which individuals cling to their initial beliefs even after contradictory evidence has been presented. In instances in which this contradictory information is useful for the task, the individual is likely to fail at solving the problem.

Creativity

Creativity refers to the ability to produce something novel or to derive unique and novel ideas and responses. Why are some people more creative than others? Cognitive psychologists differentiate between divergent and convergent thinking. **Divergent thinking** refers to the ability to generate unusual responses to questions and/or problems. It is in contrast to **convergent thinking,** which involves the generation of responses based on existing knowledge and/or strict logical reasoning. Most of the types of thinking we have discussed throughout this chapter involve convergent thinking in which a correct answer/solution is reached in the end. In contrast, creativity requires divergent thinking.

Review Questions

1. Bob is trying to remember the following list of words: letter, cat, truck, cow, wagon, paper. If Bob tries to remember the words simply by repeating them over and over to himself, he is utilizing:

   A. elaborative rehearsal
   B. maintenance rehearsal
   C. sensory memory
   D. procedural memory
   E. semantic memory

2. Again, Bob is trying to remember the list of words: letter, cat, truck, cow, wagon, paper. If Bob now tries to remember the words by thinking about personal experiences he has had with each of the words, he is now utilizing:

   A. elaborative rehearsal
   B. maintenance rehearsal
   C. sensory memory
   D. procedural memory
   E. semantic memory

3. Iconic and echoic memory are specific types of:

   A. short-term memory
   B. sensory memory
   C. episodic memory
   D. flashbulb memory
   E. working memory

4. After hearing a dog barking, Lori thinks of the time a dog bit her when she was 6 years old. This type of memory is illustrative of:

   A. sensory memory
   B. procedural memory
   C. semantic memory
   D. episodic memory
   E. echoic memory

5. The capital of Iowa, the 49th president of the United States of America and the names of the various bones in the body are stored in:

   A. semantic memory
   B. episodic memory
   C. iconic memory
   D. sensory memory
   E. procedural memory

6. If information is not properly attended to, it might not be remembered. This type of forgetting is referred to as:

   A. proactive interference
   B. cue-dependent forgetting
   C. motivated forgetting
   D. encoding failure
   E. retroactive interference

7. When we assume that events are more likely to occur because they are readily recalled, we have fallen prey to:

   A. the representativeness heuristic
   B. the influence of mental sets
   C. functional fixedness
   D. the availability heuristic
   E. framing

8. An individual is asked to identify as many uses for a fork as possible. The type of thinking required for this task best reflects:

   A. analytical thinking
   B. convergent thinking
   C. prototypical thinking
   D. trial-and-error thinking
   E. divergent thinking

Answers

1. **B.** Maintenance rehearsal involves repeating material over and over to oneself. Elaborative rehearsal involves expanding on material by organizing it or making the material more meaningful or distinctive in some way. The other options (sensory memory, procedural memory and semantic memory) are all memory systems and not memory processes.

2. **A.** Elaborative rehearsal involves expanding on material by organizing it, or by making it more meaningful or distinctive in some way. Maintenance rehearsal involves repeating material over and over to oneself. The other options (sensory memory, procedural memory and semantic memory) are all memory systems and not memory processes.

3. **B.** Iconic and echoic memory are specific types of sensory memory. Each sensory system has its own distinct sensory memory. Iconic memory is the sensory memory for the visual sense. Echoic memory is the sensory memory for the auditory sense.

4. **D.** Episodic memory stores information about personal life experiences such as being bit by a dog when one was 6 years old. Semantic memory stores general knowledge and facts acquired over time. Procedural memory stores information about skills and how to do things. Sensory memory is a memory system that holds information briefly in its raw form prior to processing. Echoic memory is a specific type of sensory memory that exists in the auditory sense.

5. **A.** Semantic memory stores general knowledge and facts acquired over time. Episodic memory stores information about personal life experiences. Procedural memory stores information about skills and how to do things. Sensory memory is a memory system that holds information briefly in its raw form prior to processing. Iconic memory is a specific type of sensory memory that exists in the visual sense.

6. **D.** Encoding failure occurs when one fails to attend to or properly encode information in memory. Proactive and retroactive interference involve the inability to recall a piece of information because other information is interfering with its retrieval. Cue-dependent forgetting occurs when one is unable to recall a piece of information because appropriate retrieval cues are not used to aid in the retrieval process. Motivated forgetting occurs when one represses information into the unconscious.

7. **D.** The availability heuristic leads one to judge the probability of an event occurring based on how readily the event comes to mind, rather than on its actual statistical probability. The representativeness heuristic leads one to judge the probability of an even occurring based on how typical it seems, rather than on its actual statistical probability. Framing occurs when a problem is presented or organized in such a way that one fails to reach the correct solution. Functional fixedness occurs when one fails to think of uses for an object other than its original or typical use.

8. **E.** Divergent thinking refers to the ability to generate unusual responses to questions and/or problems. Convergent thinking involves the generation of responses based on existing knowledge and/or strict logical reasoning.

Motivation and Emotion

Motivation refers to an inner state that guides and drives human behavior. **Emotion** refers to feelings that are usually accompanied by physiological arousal, cognitive interpretations and related behavioral responses. Both motivation and emotion are important components of human behavior. Not only do they prepare us for action, but they also influence our behavioral, cognitive and physiological responses to events and people in the environment. Psychologists who study motivation seek to identify the goals or motives that underlie behavior. Those who study emotion seek to understand the various emotions experienced by humans and the role that such emotions play in our daily lives and behavior.

This chapter begins by reviewing the major theories of motivation and identifying the various needs, desires and motives that drive human behavior. It first considers biologically based motives underlying behavior. It then reviews social and psychological motives that underlie behavior such as the needs for achievement, belonging and approval. The chapter then takes a look at major theories of emotion and how people understand and explain their emotional experiences. The chapter ends with a review of how stress affects us physically and psychologically.

Theories of Motivation

The first explanations of motivation were biologically based and focused on **instincts,** inborn patterns of behavior that are not learned. **Instinct theory** argues that organisms are preprogrammed to engage in behaviors that ensure survival and reproduction. In 1908, **William McDougall** suggested that 18 primary instincts drive behavior, whereas other theorists claim that more than 18 basic instincts exist. Over the years, instinct theories were replaced with theories focused on drive and drive reduction.

Drive-reduction approaches are based on the premise that organisms seek to obtain some basic biological need that is lacking. According to this view, an organism is motivated by a **drive,** a state of tension or arousal that mobilizes the organism to fulfill some need. A number of primary drives have been identified. **Primary drives** all involve basic biological needs such as hunger, thirst, sleep and sex. Primary drives are in contrast to secondary drives in which behavior is driven by a desire to obtain a nonbiological reinforcer such as money or love.

Homeostatic-Regulation theory takes Drive-Reduction theory a step further by suggesting that organisms are driven to maintain a steady and balanced internal state. According to this view, the body constantly monitors temperature and nutrient levels. When deviations from the ideal, balanced state occur, the body adjusts to maintain homeostasis. But, not all behavior is motivated by a desire to reduce a drive or to fulfill some need. What about behaviors driven by the desire to climb an 8,000-foot mountain or to jump from a flying airplane? Drive-Reduction theory alone does not explain all human behaviors.

Arousal theory argues that individuals are often motivated by a desire to either maintain or increase their level of stimulation or excitement. This theory suggests that if activity or stimulation levels are too high, we try to reduce them. If activity or stimulation levels are too low, we try to increase them. In essence, we are motivated to maintain a moderate level of arousal. Related to this theory, the **Yerkes-Dodson Law** states that we perform at our best when we are functioning at a moderate level of arousal. According to this law, both over-arousal and under-arousal inhibit performance. Over the years, research has discovered that individuals vary tremendously in their optimal level of arousal. As a result, some have chosen to identify **sensation seeking,** the general level of stimulation or arousal that one prefers, as a personality characteristic.

Incentive theory proposes that individuals are motivated by a desire to obtain external incentives such as money, affection and grades. Such external incentives are referred to as **secondary drives.** Many psychologists believe that secondary drives work in tandem with primary drives (biological drives) to motivate behavior.

The Cognitive Theory of Motivation proposes that individuals are motivated as a result of their own thoughts, desires, goals and expectations. The Cognitive Theory of Motivation differentiates between intrinsic and extrinsic motivation. **Intrinsic motivation** leads individuals to engage in behaviors for their own enjoyment or needs. **Extrinsic motivation** drives individuals to engage in behaviors for external, tangible rewards such as money or to avoid punishment.

The Psychological Theory of Motivation focuses on social and psychological needs as powerful motivators underlying behavior. **David McClelland** focused on the need for achievement, or **achievement motivation,** arguing that individuals are motivated by a desire to accomplish tasks and to excel. However, the extent to which one strives for achievement differs among individuals. Some individuals have a high need for achievement, whereas others have a low need for achievement.

Abraham Maslow saw human behavior as motivated primarily by a drive toward growth and fulfillment of needs, ranging from the most basic physiological needs to higher psychological needs such as belonging and self-esteem. Maslow proposed a **hierarchy of needs,** in which he outlined the various needs that drive human behavior, and suggested that human behavior is driven by where one is in the hierarchy.

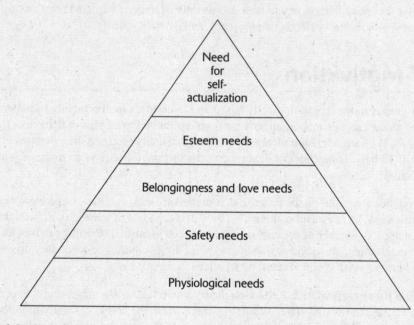

The most basic **physiological needs** appear at the bottom of the hierarchy and include primary drives such as the need for water, food and sleep. The second level identifies **safety needs,** which include the need for a safe, secure environment. Both physiological and safety needs compose what Maslow called lower-order needs. Maslow placed **love/belongingness needs** and **esteem needs** at the third and fourth levels, respectively. Together, the third and fourth levels include the need to belong, to contribute to society and to feel valued by others. At the highest level of the hierarchy is the need for **self-actualization** in which one is able to recognize their fullest potential. According to Maslow, lower-order needs must be satisfied before working to satisfy higher-order needs; only after all other needs are met is one able to work on self-actualization. Maslow believed that only a few rare individuals actually attain full self-actualization and that most individuals are focused on the lower needs in the hierarchy.

Theories of Emotion

William James and Carl Lange proposed one of the first theories of emotion. The **James-Lange theory** of emotion argues that the physiological changes in the body that accompany arousing events lead us to experience a particular emotion. According to this view, every emotion has an accompanying pattern of physiological changes called a **visceral experience** that the brain interprets as a particular emotion. Thus, we feel afraid because we tremble, and we feel sad because we cry.

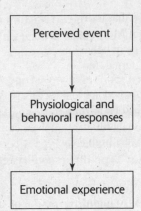

Walter Cannon and Philip Bard proposed an alternative theory of emotion. According to the **Cannon-Bard theory,** physiological arousal and the emotional experience occur simultaneously following activation of brain regions responsible for processing emotionally arousing experiences. In this view, the hypothalamus and limbic system are the major players in producing emotional experiences. When activated, these structures send signals to the body that produce a visceral response (physiological changes in the body) while simultaneously sending signals to the cerebral cortex concerning the nature of the emotional experience.

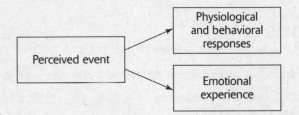

The **Schacter-Singer theory** of emotion focuses on cognitive factors as the key components in producing emotion. According to this view, as we experience certain physiological changes, we rely on environmental and contextual cues to help identify the specific emotion we are experiencing. Thus, the physiological arousal is nonspecific to the particular emotion. We look to our surroundings to determine the emotion we are experiencing.

Stress

A final area of concern for psychologists interested in motivation and emotion is stress. **Stress** refers to the emotional and physiological processes that occur as one attempts to deal with threatening or harmful circumstances. **Stressors** refer to events or situations that present harm or danger, or cause anxiety and worry in individuals. A variety of stressors exists in our everyday lives, from major catastrophes to daily hassles. It is important to distinguish between acute and chronic stressors. **Acute stressors** are fleeting, short-term stressors that come and go rather quickly. In contrast, **chronic stressors** are more persistent and enduring.

How does stress affect us physically and psychologically? All stressors trigger a sympathetic nervous system, or fight-or-flight, response in which heart rate and blood pressure increase, respiration increases and so on. When the stressor subsides, a parasympathetic response kicks in to return our bodies to a normal level of functioning. However, when stressors are chronic, the body maintains a state of heightened arousal that can tax the body and increase one's risk of illness and disease.

Hans Selye described how chronic stressors tax the body and lead to physical damage and illness. Selye proposed the **General Adaptation Syndrome (GAS) model** in which he identified three stages that the body goes through in response to chronic stressors: alarm-reaction stage, resistance stage and exhaustion stage. The **alarm-reaction stage** involves the immediate fight-or-flight response associated with the sympathetic nervous system. During this stage, the body mobilizes itself to either fight off the stressor or flee. In the **resistance stage,** the sympathetic response wanes, but the body continues to fight off the stressor at a hormonal level. During this stage, the immune system kicks into high gear in an attempt to fight off or adapt to the stressor. In the **exhaustion stage,** the body tires and weakens as a result of its continued fight, resources are depleted, and the individual becomes increasingly vulnerable to exhaustion, disease and even death.

The actual effects of stress on the body vary as a result of how we cope with stressors in our lives. Over the years, research has found that a number of social and psychological factors play an important role in mediating the effects of stress on the body. First, personality plays an important role. It is important to distinguish between Type A and B personalities. **Type A personality** refers to individuals who are intense, competitive, aggressive and high strung. Their reactions to stress and their ways of dealing with stress leave Type A personalities highly susceptible to health problems, particularly heart disease and heart attacks. **Type B personality** refers to individuals who take a more laid-back, relaxed approach to life.

Richard Lazarus and **Susan Folkman** proposed a **cognitive model of stress** in which they argue that how we respond to stressors in our lives is dependent on two cognitive processes: a primary-appraisal process and a secondary-appraisal process. According to this model, when faced with a potentially stressful event or situation, individuals first undergo a **primary-appraisal process** in which they assess the potential threat or harm posed by the situation. If the event is perceived as harmful or threatening, the individual moves into a **secondary-appraisal process** in which they assess their ability to cope with the event and the resources available to deal with the stressor. The ultimate stress response that ensues depends on the outcome of the primary and secondary appraisals made by an individual (how much harm or threat they perceive and whether they believe they have adequate resources to cope with the stressor).

Review Questions

1. The Yerkes-Dodson Law states that we perform at our best when we are:

   A. at a moderate level of arousal
   B. at a relatively high level of arousal
   C. experiencing homeostasis
   D. working for extrinsic rewards
   E. working for intrinsic rewards

2. The notion that specific patterns of physiological arousal are associated with specific emotional experiences is referred to as:

   A. the James-Lange theory
   B. the Cannon-Bard theory
   C. the Two-Factor theory
   D. the Schacter-Singer theory
   E. Arousal theory

3. If Melinda works hard to make a lot of money, she is motivated by:

   A. a basic biological drive
   B. extrinsic factors
   C. intrinsic factors
   D. homeostasis
   E. self-actualization

4. According to Arousal theory, humans are motivated to:

    A. fulfill drives and needs that are lacking

    B. maintain a balanced internal state

    C. seek extrinsic rewards and incentives

    D. achieve their optimal level of functioning

    E. maintain an optimal level of stimulation

5. Which of the following theories is most likely to argue that human behavior is primarily motivated by a natural desire to survive and reproduce?

    A. Homeostatic-Regulation theory

    B. Drive-Reduction theory

    C. Incentive theory

    D. Arousal theory

    E. Instinct theory

6. Abraham Maslow is most closely linked to the notion of:

    A. drives

    B. instincts

    C. self-actualization

    D. achievement motivation

    E. sensation seeking

7. In the GAS model, describing the body's reaction to chronic stressors, a sympathetic nervous system response is associated with the:

    A. exhaustion stage

    B. alarm-reaction stage

    C. resistance stage

    D. alarm-reaction and resistance stage

    E. alarm-reaction and exhaustion stage

8. According to the GAS model, the correct order of bodily reactions to stress is:

    A. alarm reaction, resistance, exhaustion

    B. resistance, alarm reaction, exhaustion

    C. resistance, exhaustion, alarm reaction

    D. alarm reaction, exhaustion, resistance

    E. exhaustion, resistance, alarm reaction

Answers

1. A. The Yerkes-Dodson Law states that individuals perform at their best when they are at a moderate level of arousal. According to this law, both over-arousal and under-arousal hinder performance on tasks. The Yerkes-Dodson Law is associated with Arousal theory. Homeostatic-Regulation theory argues that we are motivated to maintain a state of homeostasis. The Cognitive Theory of Motivation distinguishes between instrinsic and extrinsic rewards as motivators for behavior.

2. A. The James-Lange theory of emotion argues that the physiological changes in the body that accompany arousing events lead us to experience a particular emotion. The Cannon-Bard theory argues that physiological arousal and the emotional experience occur simultaneously following activation of brain regions responsible for processing emotionally arousing experiences. The Schacter-Singer theory argues that we rely on environmental and contextual cues to help identify the specific emotion we are experiencing. Thus, the physiological arousal is nonspecific to the particular emotion. Arousal theory primarily addresses motivational factors and not how we experience emotion.

3. B. In this example, Melinda is being motivated by extrinsic factors. The Cognitive Theory of Motivation differentiates between intrinsic and extrinsic motivation. Extrinsic motivation drives individuals to engage in behaviors for external, tangible rewards such as money. Intrinsic motivation leads individuals to engage in behaviors for their own enjoyment. Self-actualization refers to the process of attaining one's fullest potential.

4. E. Arousal theory argues that individuals are motivated by a desire to maintain a moderate level of arousal. This theory suggests that if activity or stimulation levels are too high, we try to reduce them. If activity or stimulation levels are too low, we try to increase them.

5. E. Instinct theory argues that organisms are preprogrammed to engage in behaviors that ensure survival and reproduction. Drive-Reduction theory is based on the premise that organisms seek to obtain some basic biological need that is lacking. Homeostatic-Regulation theory takes Drive-Reduction theory a step further by suggesting that organisms are driven to maintain a steady and balanced internal state. Arousal theory argues that individuals are motivated by a desire to either maintain or increase their level of stimulation or excitement. Incentive theory proposes that individuals are motivated by a desire to obtain external incentives such as money, affection and grades.

6. C. Abraham Maslow is most closely linked to the notion of self-actualization. Maslow saw human behavior as motivated primarily by a drive toward growth and fulfillment of needs, ranging from the most basic physiological needs to higher psychological needs such as belonging and self-esteem. At the highest level of the hierarchy is self-actualization in which individuals are motivated to reach their fullest potential.

7. B. A sympathetic nervous system response is associated with the first stage of the GAS model, the alarm-reaction stage. In this stage, the body responds to a stressor with a fight-or-flight/sympathetic response that prepares the body for action. The resistance stage is the second stage of the GAS model and involves a hormonal and immune system response to a stressor. The exhaustion stage is the third stage of the GAS model and occurs when the body wears down and resources are depleted.

8. A. The correct order of stages in the GAS model is alarm reaction, resistance, exhaustion. The alarm-reaction stage involves the immediate fight-or-flight response associated with the sympathetic nervous system. In the resistance stage, the sympathetic response wanes, but the body continues to fight off the stressor at a hormonal level. In the exhaustion stage, the body tires and weakens as a result of its continued fight, resources are depleted, and the individual becomes increasingly vulnerable to exhaustion, disease and even death.

Developmental Psychology

Developmental psychology is a field of psychology that aims to understand how individuals change physically, psychologically, socially and cognitively across the life span. This chapter provides an overview of the field of developmental psychology and major research findings emerging from the study of development. The chapter begins with an introduction to the life span approach to studying development and a review of the various research designs used by developmental psychologists to study behavior over time. The chapter then provides an overview of the major physical, cognitive, and psychosocial changes that occur during each stage of the life span.

Life-Span Approach

Today, most developmental psychologists hold to a **life-span developmental perspective** in which they view development as a lifelong process, beginning at the moment of conception and not ending until the moment of death. Still, many developmental psychologists choose to focus on specific age periods, thus defining themselves as child psychologists, gerontologists (who study primarily adult development and aging) and thanatologists (who study how individuals cope with the issues of death and dying in their lives). The life span is typically broken down into a number of **developmental stages,** periods of life characterized by distinct changes or transitions in physical, cognitive, social and psychological functioning. Several stages have been identified: prenatal, neonatal, infancy, childhood, adolescence and adulthood. The following chart shows each of the developmental stages and the age periods associated with each stage. It is important to note that the ages associated with each stage are arbitrary and the actual age ranges of various stages are a matter of debate even among developmental psychologists. Developmental psychologists also speak of **critical periods** (key periods for specific types of learning that shape future development) and **sensitive periods** (periods that are important but not crucial in determining future development).

Developmental Stage	Age Period
Prenatal	Conception to birth
Infancy/toddlerhood	Birth–3 years
Early childhood	3–5 years
Middle/late childhood	8–12 years
Adolescence	13–20 years
Early adulthood	20–40 years
Middle adulthood	40–65 years
Late adulthood	65 years and older

Research Methods

To study age-related changes and age-related differences, developmental psychologists typically employ one of three research designs: longitudinal designs, cross-sectional designs and cross-sequential designs. **Longitudinal designs** involve following the same group of people over time and assessing them on the variable(s) of interest on multiple occasions. The researcher then compares the scores of individuals from one time to another to see whether scores change or remain the same. Such designs allow one to examine how individuals change or remain the same over time on the variable(s) of interest.

Cross-sectional designs involve assessing individuals of multiple age groups (for example, a group of 40-year-olds, 50-year-olds and 60-year-olds) on only one occasion, and then comparing the scores of each age group. Such designs allow one to examine how individuals of various ages compare on the variable(s) of interest.

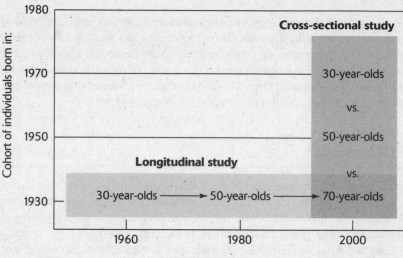

Cross-sequential designs involve a combination of the longitudinal and cross-sectional design (taking multiple age groups and assessing them on multiple occasions). Such designs are rarely employed as they are extremely time-consuming and complex. However, cross-sequential designs provide a great deal of information concerning both age changes and age differences.

Heredity-Environmental Issues

Consider the following questions: Why is it that some people turn out to be well adapted and highly functional individuals, and others turn out to be emotionally unstable, less intelligent or aggressive? Are these characteristics or behaviors the result of inborn, genetic tendencies that manifest across the life span, or are they the result of life experiences and circumstances? Developmental psychologists recognize two main factors that contribute to development: nature and nurture.

Nature refers to the genetic unfolding of an individual. This genetic unfolding, also known as maturation, leads to a pattern of physical growth and development that is fairly universal among most humans. Still, we all differ with respect to our exact genetic make-up, and these individual differences in genetic make-up also lead to variations in development. **Nurture** refers to the process in which experiences with the world and others lead to change.

For years, developmental psychologists debated over the relative importance of the two factors for behavior and development. Some argued that maturation (or heredity) plays the greater role, while others argued that experience plays the crucial role in who we become. Today, the divide between those who support nature and those who support nurture is less clear. Most modern developmental psychologists take an **interactionist view** in which they view developmental outcomes as a result of an interaction between nature and nurture. Who we are today and who we become in the future are a result of both our unique genetic make-ups and our unique experiences as individuals.

Dimensions of Development

Development involves changes and continuities in several aspects of an individual (including physical, cognitive, social, and psychological development). The following section reviews major changes across the life span in each of these areas of development.

Physical Development

Physical development begins at the moment of conception and continues across the entire life span. It involves changes in body growth, muscles, motor skills and brain development.

During the prenatal period, an individual moves through three stages of physical development. In the **germinal stage** (lasting from about 0 to 2 weeks of age), the single cell created by the union of sperm and egg begins the process of cell division and replication. The end of this stage is marked by implantation in the uterine wall, where the cells receive all the oxygen and nutrients they need to grow into a full human infant. During the **embryonic stage** (lasting from about 2 weeks to about 8 weeks of age), all major organ systems (for example, the central nervous system, respiratory system, digestive system, eyes, ears, limbs and so on) differentiate. In the **fetal stage** (lasting from about 2 months of age until birth), the fetus continues to grow, sexual differentiation occurs, and organ systems begin to function. Physical growth is rapid during this stage with the fetus tripling its size in a matter of weeks. Across the prenatal period, the fetus is highly vulnerable to a number of harmful environmental agents and substances known as **teratogens.** Teratogens can exert a number of negative effects on the developing fetus including altered physical development and/or impaired cognitive development. Some of the more well-known teratogens include alcohol, nicotine, cocaine, lead, a variety of prescription drugs and a number of viruses and illnesses.

To the passive observer, infants appear fairly limited in their physical abilities. They are not yet able to take care of themselves nor are they able to perform any complex motor behaviors or behavioral responses. However, at a deeper level, infants are able to do quite a bit physically. All **sensory systems** are intact and functioning, and from the moment of birth infants are taking in a great deal of information about the world around them. In addition, infants come into this world equipped with a number of **reflexive behaviors** that allow them to respond to and interact with the world. Finally, across the infancy years, a number of motor milestones are acquired that allow for increased interaction with the world. The following chart lists some of the major motor milestones achieved across the infancy years and the average age at which each is achieved.

Milestone	*Typical Age Achieved*
Lifts head up	2 months
Rolls over	2 1/2 months
Sits propped up	3 months
Sits without support	6 months
Stands holding on	6 1/2 months
Walks holding on	9 months
Stands alone	11 months
Walks alone	12 months
Walks up steps	17 months

Across childhood, children become able to perform more complex behavioral responses. In addition, a number of motor skills are attained, including advances in fine and gross motor skills. **Fine motor skills** are skills that require coordination of small muscles and include activities such as grasping, writing, drawing and eye-hand coordination. **Gross motor skills** are skills that require use of larger muscles in the body and involve activities such as walking, running and jumping.

In adolescence, individuals undergo dramatic physical changes. The major physical changes occurring during adolescence involve those associated with **puberty.** With the onset of puberty, a surge of hormones is released into the body bringing on a multitude of physical and psychological changes. **Sexual maturation** of the internal reproductive organs completes, and adolescents become able to produce children. **Secondary sex characteristics** emerge that lead to outwardly observable changes in physical appearance, such as broader shoulders in males and breast development in females. All these changes exert a significant impact on the social and psychological development of adolescents as they must adjust to the changes in physical appearance and to the changes in how others interact with and respond to them.

Physical development does not cease in adulthood. Across the adult years, we continue to see changes (as well as continuities) in the physical aspects of individuals. The physical changes seen in old age are typically referred to as **senescence.** The sensory systems themselves undergo changes. Though these changes are relatively minor, they do affect the quality of information that enters the system and might have an impact on other aspects of functioning, including cognitive functioning. In addition, muscles atrophy and become less elastic, making certain behavioral responses more difficult in old age.

Cognitive Development

Cognitive development involves changes in mental processing, reasoning, problem solving and other cognitive skills. Probably the most comprehensive theory of cognitive development is that of **Jean Piaget.**

Piaget's Four Stages of Development

Piaget proposed that individuals move through four stages of cognitive growth (the sensorimotor stage, preoperational stage, concrete operational stage and formal operational stage) across the childhood and adolescent years.

During the **sensorimotor stage,** infants think about the world through their senses and motor actions. Piaget described thought during the early months of life as **out of sight out of mind,** arguing that if an object is not currently being acted on or directly sensed, infants are not able to think about it. Piaget recognized that infants are able to learn during this stage. As they continue to interact with the environment, they learn how things work and that certain objects look and feel certain ways. He also noted that as infants discover new things about themselves and the world, they repeat actions and behaviors over and over. He called these repetitive behaviors **circular reactions** and argued that they allow for greater understanding of oneself and the surrounding environment. By the end of the sensorimotor period (about 2 years), infants have learned enough about the world that they can now think about objects in their absence and form internal mental representations of objects, a feat Piaget termed **object permanence.**

The major feature of the **preoperational stage** (lasting from about 2 to 7 years of age) is **symbolic thought**—the ability to internally represent the world. Symbolic thought allows children to think about objects and events in their absence; this ability is especially tied to the increased ability to use language at this age. Despite advances in the ability to internally represent objects and events, a number of limitations still exist in thought at this stage. First, children display a great deal of **egocentrism** (an inability to recognize that others might see, think or perceive an object or event differently than oneself). Second, those in the preoperational stage also display **centration** (an inability to focus on more than one aspect of a situation at one time).

In the **concrete operational stage** (lasting from about 7 to 11 years of age), children overcome many of the limitations of the preoperational stage and show mastery of several new cognitive skills (including decentration, transformational thought and conservation). **Decentration** refers to the ability to consider multiple features of objects or situations simultaneously. **Transformational thought** refers to the ability to reverse actions and events mentally to see how actions can be undone or reversed. **Conservation** refers to the awareness that many objects in the world remain the same despite changes in their physical appearance.

It is during the **formal operational stage** (associated with the adolescent years and beyond) that individuals develop the ability to think and reason about abstract notions and hypothetical situations. Adolescents also acquire the ability to engage in hypothetical deductive reasoning. **Hypothetical deductive reasoning** refers to the ability to draw conclusions based on several pieces of information. Together, these newfound abilities open a whole new world of thought to adolescents.

Adult Cognitive Development

Although Piaget's theory does not address cognitive development beyond the adolescent years, modern developmental psychologists recognize that cognitive development continues into the adult years. A number of new ways of thinking have been described as typical of adult thinking. **Postformal thought** maintains the ability to think logically and abstractly, but also incorporates emotion and life experience into thought and reasoning. Postformal thought allows for greater tolerance for ambiguity and contradiction. It is more open, flexible and adaptive than the strict logical reasoning of formal operational thought. **Relativistic thought** involves a more flexible way of thinking in which individuals recognize that any given situation can be viewed in multiple ways and that gray areas often exist in which there might not be one single right or wrong solution to a problem.

A major question with respect to cognitive development in adulthood involves the issue of whether cognitive and intellectual skills decline with age. For the most part, research suggests that many adults experience increases in **crystallized intelligence** (knowledge and information acquired through education and experience, which is tested through tasks such as vocabulary, general information and reading comprehension), but decreases in **fluid intelligence** (the application of intellectual abilities to new situations, which is tested through tasks such as completing mazes, solving puzzles and analyzing relationships). Though some declines occur in cognitive abilities in the adult years, the declines are mostly minimal and do not typically occur until the late adult years.

Social Development

Social development involves changes in social skills, relationships with others and the ability to interact with others. Though infants have not yet acquired full language skills, they are social beings and display a number of social skills. Even very young infants engage in social interactions with caregivers and show synchronicity in their interactions (for example, coordinated gazes and vocalizations). They attempt to initiate interactions with caregivers and look to others concerning how to respond to events and situations (called **social referencing**).

Early Attachment

Probably the most important social relationship in infancy is the relationship that forms with parents or primary caregivers. Developmental psychologists typically refer to this relationship as the **attachment relationship.** According to **John Bowlby,** the early attachment relationship is the most important relationship in one's life as it forms the basis for all future relationships. Bowlby argued that across the early years, infants come to recognize that certain individuals are more likely to respond to their signals than others. As they do, they begin to form an attachment to those people. Important signs that an attachment has formed include proximity seeking, separation anxiety and stranger anxiety.

Another leading researcher in the area of attachment, **Mary Ainsworth,** argued that not all infants form secure relationships with caregivers. Ainsworth devised a research paradigm known as the **strange situation** test to assess the nature of an attachment relationship that has formed between an infant and caregiver. The strange situation test consists of eight brief episodes that involve exposure to an unfamiliar person and short separations from the caregiver. The overall purpose of the procedure is to observe how the infant behaves in the presence and absence of the caregiver and how the infant responds to the presence of a stranger in an unfamiliar environment.

By observing children in the strange situation, Ainsworth identified three different types of attachment: secure, insecure-avoidant and insecure-ambivalent. Infants classified as having a **secure attachment** display behaviors throughout the strange situation that reflect comfort and security in the presence of the caregiver. Securely attached infants freely explore the environment, organize their behavior around the caregiver, reference the caregiver on multiple occasions, show moderate anxiety in the presence of a stranger, show some distress in the absence of the caregiver (separation anxiety), but are easily comforted by the caregiver upon return. Infants classified as having an **insecure-ambivalent** attachment display a great deal of anxiety throughout the strange situation. They engage in little exploration of the environment, stay close to the caregiver, become extremely distressed in the absence of the caregiver and the presence of a stranger, and are difficult to console when the caregiver returns. Infants classified as having an **insecure-avoidant** attachment generally ignore the caregiver, show little distress when separated from the caregiver and when in the presence of a stranger, and do not seek contact with the caregiver upon return.

Parenting Styles

Across the childhood years, the parent-child relationship continues to be one of the most important social relationships in children's lives. A great deal of research suggests that how parents choose to discipline their children plays an important role in their child's development. **Diane Baumrind,** a leading researcher in parent-child relationships, has identified four disciplinary styles or (**parenting styles**) that parents typically employ and the child outcomes generally associated with each: authoritative, authoritarian, permissive and neglectful.

Authoritative parents are high on control and warmth/affection. They set rules and place demands on children, but the demands are typically reasonable and age appropriate. In addition, authoritative parents are loving and affectionate toward their children and open to discussing rules and changing them if needed. **Authoritarian** parents are high on control, but low in love and affection. They set many rules and expect complete obedience at all times. Discussion of rules and opinions of children are not considered, and displays of love and affection are relatively infrequent. **Permissive parents** are low on control, but high on love and affection. Children of permissive parents are allowed a great deal of freedom, provided with little guidance or discipline, and shown a great deal of love and affection. **Neglectful parents** are low on control and love and affection. Like permissive parents, they set few rules and place few demands on children. However, they are also uninvolved with their children and show little love, affection, support and communication.

Influences in Adolescence

Parents continue to have important influences on adolescents. However, across the childhood and adolescent years, peers take on an increasingly important role in the lives of children and adolescents. In fact, friendships become particularly important in the late childhood/adolescent years, and adolescents who have no friends are at high risk for social and psychological problems. It is also during adolescence that cliques and crowds form. Cliques and crowds influence adolescent development by encouraging certain behaviors, discouraging other behaviors, limiting or promoting interactions with particular individuals, and accepting or isolating adolescents from certain groups of individuals.

Adult Relationships

How do social relationships change in adulthood? Across the adult years, the number and nature of social relationships change. In middle and late adulthood, individuals establish fewer new connections and instead focus their attention on already established relationships. **Socioemotional Selectivity theory** argues that in late adulthood, individuals prefer the company of a few close friends and/or relatives and selectively invest their energy and emotions in those relationships that are most meaningful and satisfying. Family relationships continue to be important across the adult years and expand beyond parent-child relationships to relationships with aging parents, adult children, spouses and other family members. In any case, social relationships are an important source of social support across the adult years. Research indicates that adults who lack social support and meaningful relationships experience more illnesses and shorter life spans than those with strong social-support networks.

Psychological Development

What is important for healthy psychological development? What fosters positive psychosocial development? **Erik Erikson** proposed one of the most comprehensive theories of social and personality development in which he argued that we move through a series of psychosocial crises or challenges across the life span. Each **psychosocial crisis** represents a conflict between the skills and abilities of the individual and the expectations and demands of the environment. According to Erikson, resolution of each crisis is the primary determinant of social and personality development.

The first crisis occurs in infancy and is referred to as the **trust versus mistrust** crisis (0–1 year). Erikson believed that it is important for infants to develop a sense of trust in the environment. He argued that infants need consistency, predictability and sensitive care-giving if they are to develop trust. Lack of closeness, insensitivity by caregivers and/or inconsistent handling might produce a sense of mistrust, insecurity and anxiety that is carried forward into future interactions with the environment.

The second crisis faced is the **autonomy versus shame and doubt** crisis (1–3 years). During this time, infants need to establish a sense of independence from their environment. It is important during this time that parents are understanding, encouraging and patient with their children. Constant criticism, ridicule, impatience or controlled parenting might instill a sense of shame and doubt in the child that is carried forward into future stages of development.

Initiative versus guilt is the third crisis (3–6 years) and involves a need to establish initiative (the ability to plan, direct and control one's own behavior). It is important that children also establish some restraint that keeps them from doing wrong, but not so much that it inhibits their behavior or causes extreme guilt or anxiety.

In the fourth crisis, **industry versus inferiority** (6–12 years), children are expected to learn a number of new skills and abilities. It is important during this stage that children develop a sense of industry or confidence in their skills and abilities. If they do not, they run the risk of developing a sense of inferiority, inadequacy and low self-esteem. How successes and failures are handled at this time is particularly important for the successful resolution of this crisis.

The fifth psychosocial crisis, **identity versus identity confusion** (12–20 years), involves a search for one's identity and place in the world. According to Erikson, adolescents need to undergo a moratorium period (a time of searching, exploring and trying out various roles and identities). The successful resolution of this crisis involves a sense of who one is, a discovery of one's individual values and beliefs and place in the world, and establishment of goals and ideas about one's future self. Some adolescents run the risk of identity confusion, an inability to figure out who they are, to find roles they are comfortable with and/or to commit to certain beliefs and values.

The sixth crisis, **intimacy versus isolation** (20–40 years), involves the need to establish close, intimate relationships with others. Successful resolution of this crisis requires that one be open to others and committed to intimacy, compromise and so on. Unsuccessful resolution can result in social isolation, avoidance of interpersonal relationships and failure to establish meaningful relationships with others.

The seventh crisis, **generativity versus stagnation** (40–60 years), involves the need to focus attention on future generations and to contribute something meaningful to society and/or family. Individuals who are unable to do this might become preoccupied with themselves or with material possessions. Some might stagnate with respect to psychological growth and become cynical and unhappy with life.

The eighth and final crisis, **integrity versus despair** (60 years and older), involves the need to accept one's life, find meaning and purpose in life and feel a sense of integrity or wholeness. Successful resolution of this crisis involves a life review in which individuals look back on their life and accept it with a sense of satisfaction. Individuals who are unable to do this might experience despair, regret and/or self-deprecation.

Review Questions

1. Which of the following is characteristic of longitudinal research designs?

   A. The same individuals are tested on multiple occasions.
   B. People of different ages are tested on the same skill.
   C. The average scores of different groups are compared.
   D. Cohort effects can be tested.
   E. Multiple age groups are assessed on multiple occasions.

2. Mrs. Kerr believes that nurture plays the primary role in how her young child will grow and develop. Thus, Mrs. Kerr believes that:

   A. Her child will grow and develop according to an internal biological plan.
   B. The genes inherited from her and her husband will guide her child's development.
   C. She cannot do much to shape her child's future development.
   D. The environment surrounding her child will play an important role in who her child becomes.
   E. Maturation will guide and shape her child's development.

3. The primary feature of the embryonic stage of development is:

   A. the birth process
   B. growth and storage of fat
   C. cell division and multiplication
   D. differentiation of all organ systems
   E. union of the sperm and egg

4. Baby Byron is 8 months old. At this point, he should have achieved all the following skills except the ability to:

   A. lift his head on his own
   B. sit without support
   C. walk without support
   D. roll over
   E. stand holding on to a steady object

5. Which of the following behaviors involves fine motor skills?

   A. jumping
   B. walking
   C. writing
   D. running
   E. throwing

6. Jessica has been classified as a securely attached infant. In the strange situation test, we expect to see all the following except:

   A. exploration of the environment
   B. frequent references to the caregiver
   C. anxiety when separated from the caregiver
   D. continuing to be upset when the caregiver returns
   E. moderate anxiety in the presence of a stranger

7. Authoritarian parents:

   A. are overly indulgent with their children
   B. are highly controlling of their children
   C. show lots of love and affection to their children
   D. pay little attention to their children
   E. are often abusive toward their children

8. Jimmy is a 16-year-old adolescent. According to Erikson's theory, Jimmy is currently experiencing which psychosocial crisis?

   A. integrity versus despair
   B. intimacy versus isolation
   C. industry versus inferiority
   D. autonomy versus shame and doubt
   E. identity versus identity confusion

Answers

1. A. Longitudinal designs involve testing the same individuals on multiple occasions and comparing scores at different times. When people of different ages are tested on the same skill and the average scores of different age groups are compared, one is using a cross-sectional design. When multiple age groups are assessed on multiple occasions, a cross-sequential design is being employed.

2. D. A belief in nurture reflects a belief in the importance of environmental influences on growth and development. According to a nurture view, who one becomes and how one grows and develops reflect their experiences with the world around them. All the other options reflect beliefs in nature, the importance of genes and maturational processes in guiding and shaping development.

3. D. The embryonic stage is the second stage of prenatal development and involves the formation of all organ systems in the body. The union of the sperm and egg, otherwise known as conception, marks the beginning of the first stage of prenatal development, the germinal stage. Cell division and multiplication are the primary feature of the germinal stage. Growth and storage of fat are the primary features of the third stage, the fetal stage. The birth process itself marks the end of prenatal development.

4. C. In infancy, children acquire a number of important motor milestones. By 6 months of age, an infant is typically able to lift their head on their own, roll over, sit without support and stand holding on to a steady object. Most children are unable to walk without support until about 12 months of age.

5. C. Fine motor skills involve the coordination of small muscles in the body. Therefore, writing requires fine motor skills. Throwing, walking, running and jumping all reflect gross motor skills, which require use of larger muscles in the body.

6. D. Securely attached infants are infants who have established a secure and trusting relationship with their caregiver. In the strange situation, such infants show comfort in exploring the environment, frequently refer to the caregiver, become upset when separated from the caregiver, show some anxiety in the presence of strangers and are easily comforted by the caregiver when the caregiver returns from an absence. Infants who are classified as having an insecure-ambivalent attachment show continued upset and anger, and are difficult to console when the caregiver returns from an absence.

7. B. In his comprehensive theory of psychosocial development, Erik Erikson suggested that adolescents face the crisis of identity versus identity confusion. This crisis involves a search for who one is; a discovery of values and beliefs; and an integration of one's past, present and future self. The integrity versus despair crisis is associated with late adulthood. The intimacy versus isolation crisis is associated with early adulthood. The industry versus inferiority crisis is associated with late childhood, and the autonomy versus shame and doubt crisis is associated with toddlerhood.

8. E. Authoritarian parents are highly controlling of their children and show little warmth and affection toward their children. Permissive parents are overly indulgent with their children, allowing them virtually unlimited freedom while continuing to be highly affectionate toward them. Neglectful parents pay little attention to their children.

Personality

Personality refers to a pattern of enduring qualities and characteristics that make each of us unique as human beings. In this chapter, we will review a number of different theoretical perspectives on the development of personality (including psychoanalytic, humanistic, cognitive, behavioral, and trait theories of personality). The chapter then reviews various methods used by psychologists to assess one's personality and to assess individual differences in personality and behavior.

Personality Theories and Approaches

A variety of theories have been proposed to explain personality. Some theories focus on the biological aspects of personality. Other theories focus on the role of learning and culture in personality development. Still, other theories emphasize unconscious forces, self-concept, or personal growth. In this section, the most prominent theories of personality are presented.

The Psychodynamic Approach

The psychodynamic approach to personality argues that personality is derived largely from unconscious forces. **Sigmund Freud** was the first psychologist to propose the notion that much of behavior and personality are influenced by **unconscious forces** including unconscious impulses, instincts, conflicts and drives. In addition to unconscious forces, Freud believed that **early childhood experiences** played a key role in personality development and behavior. According to Freud, we come into this world with certain instincts and impulses (especially sexual impulses) already driving our behavior. Across the childhood years, family experiences teach us how to channel those impulses, assist us in meeting various needs and impulses, and ultimately determine our desire and drive to satisfy certain impulses.

Freud's Psychosexual Stages

With respect to personality development, Freud argued that children go through five stages in which they experience tension between unconscious, biological impulses and the demands of the external environment. During each stage, the focus of impulses shifts such that children desire stimulation and gratification from different body regions, called **erogenous zones.**

In the **oral stage** (0–1 year), the focus of stimulation is the mouth. Thus, stimulation of the mouth is the major source of pleasure. This pleasure can be derived through a number of behaviors including sucking, biting and eating. Freud argued that as parents begin to wean children from the bottle/nipple and as they make demands on children with respect to eating and biting, children face a conflict between meeting the impulsive desires of this stage and giving in to societal expectations and demands.

In the **anal stage** (1–3 years), the focus of stimulation is the anal region. Satisfaction and pleasure are now derived primarily through having and retaining bowel movements. The major conflict at this stage occurs when parents attempt to control children's bowel movements through toilet training.

In the **phallic stage** (3–6 years), the focus of pleasure shifts to the genital region. At this point, Freud suggested that boys experience an Oedipus complex and that young girls experience an Electra complex. Both the Oedipus and Electra complex involve a sexual longing for the opposite-sex parent. In addition, the Oedipus complex involves castration anxiety as young boys fear their father will castrate them for their feelings toward their mother. The Electra complex involves penis envy and feelings of hatred toward one's mother as little girls blame their mother for their anatomical deficit. These conflicts and extreme feelings of anxiety are resolved when children repress their sexual feelings and, in the end, identify with the same-sex parent.

The next stage, the **latency stage** (6 years to puberty), is a time of few sexual desires. Freud believed that during this time, children continue to repress their sexual desires and instead direct their energy toward nonsexual activities such as learning social and intellectual skills.

In the final stage, the **genital stage** (puberty to adulthood), sexual impulses resurface with a focus on the genitals again. The difference between the genital stage and the phallic stage is that during the genital stage, sexual impulses and drives are aimed at peers rather than parents.

How parents handle the conflicts of each stage—whether the child leaves each stage having successfully resolved the conflict or leaves each stage feeling that their needs were either underindulged or overindulged—plays an important role in shaping personality and later behavior. Freud spoke of the possibility of individuals becoming **fixated** or stuck in a particular stage as a result of either under- or overindulgence during any stage of development. When an individual becomes fixated, they display behaviors that can be traced back to a particular stage, continuing to either seek or deny gratification in a particular area. For example, an individual who is fixated at the oral stage of development might show behaviors such as overeating, smoking or using sarcasm—all reflective of a need to continue to receive gratification through oral means. An individual fixated at the anal stage might display anal-retentive characteristics such as compulsiveness and highly controlling behavior, or anal-expulsive characteristics such as messiness, disorderliness and destructive behaviors.

Freud's Personality Structures

In addition to proposing psychosexual stages, Freud also proposed three personality structures that develop across the childhood years and account for different aspects of personality: the id, the superego and the ego. The **id** is present at birth and consists of innate instincts and impulses. It is immature, impulsive and irrational—operating according to the **pleasure principle** (seeking immediate gratification of impulses at all times).

The **superego** develops across the childhood years and is representative of our moral conscience. It is the aspect of personality that demands we abide by moral principles and societal standards. Thus, it operates according to the **morality principle** (demanding that one never violate rules and standards and that one strive for perfection at all times).

The final component of personality to develop, the **ego,** serves to mediate the conflict between the id and the superego. Both the id and the superego are irrational, with the id demanding constant gratification of impulses and the superego demanding constant perfection and moral behavior. The ego represents the executive branch of personality, making decisions about how to meet the needs of the id while at the same time not violating the demands of the superego. The ego is said to operate according to the **reality principle** (finding realistic and acceptable means by which to satisfy impulses and continue to act in accordance with rules and expectations).

At times, the ego is overwhelmed by impulses from the id and is unable to meet its demands. In such instances, the ego might utilize **defense mechanisms**—defensive responses that operate at an unconscious level to keep anxiety and guilt-provoking thoughts out of conscious awareness. A number of different defense mechanisms might be used. The most basic of all defense mechanisms is **repression** in which anxiety or guilt-provoking thoughts are repressed into the unconscious and kept completely out of conscious awareness. The following chart outlines some additional defense mechanisms and gives examples of each.

Defense Mechanism	Description	Example
Displacement	Shift unacceptable thoughts and feelings to a more acceptable object/activity.	Feelings of sexual attraction toward a friend's mother are directed toward the friend instead.
Projection	Attribute unacceptable thoughts to others.	A desire to cheat on a significant other becomes an accusation of the significant other wanting to cheat.
Reaction formation	Express unacceptable thoughts as their opposite.	Being overly nice to someone that you absolutely don't like.

Defense Mechanism	Description	Example
Regression	Mimic the behavior of an earlier stage of development.	An adolescent reverts back to a state of high dependency in the face of a difficult situation.
Rationalization	Replace a threatening or inappropriate explanation for a behavior with a more acceptable explanation.	Having a drink because of a rough day at work.
Denial	Refuse to acknowledge anxiety- or guilt-provoking thoughts.	Refusing to accept that one's child has a learning disability.

Over the years, Freud's psychodynamic approach has been replaced with Neo-Freudian views that maintain some of Freud's basic ideas, but include additional concepts and ideas. For example, Carl Jung suggests that behavior is driven as much by drives toward growth, creativity, and resolution of conflict as it is by sexual instincts. In addition, Jung proposed a collective unconscious which contains memories inherited from our ancestors that lead us to react to certain things in innate ways. Finally, Jung emphasized introversion (a tendency to look inward and reflect on one's own experiences) and extraversion (a tendency to focus outward on others and the social world) as important aspects of personality, suggesting that individual differences in personality reflect varying degrees of introversion and extraversion. Karen Horney, another Neo-Freudian, agreed with Freud that we are motivated by unconscious forces. However, she rejected Freud's notions of penis envy and inferiority complexes in women, arguing that differences between men and women are more a result of cultural influences than sexual instincts.

Humanistic Theories

Whereas Freud saw humans as driven primarily by unconscious conflicts, impulses and desires, humanistic psychologists view humans as motivated by more positive forces. According to humanistic psychologists, human behavior is motivated by a drive toward growth, fulfillment and self-actualization.

Abraham Maslow, one of the most famous humanistic psychologists, argued that personality and behavior are merely an expression of goals and needs, ranging from the most basic physiological needs (such as food, water and shelter) to higher psychological needs (such as belonging, love and self-esteem). Maslow proposed a **hierarchy of needs,** arguing that basic needs at the bottom of the hierarchy must be satisfied before higher-growth needs at the top can be addressed. Maslow coined the term **self-actualization,** referring to the ability to realize one's fullest potential. According to Maslow, human behavior and personality are driven by where one is in the hierarchy (whether they are striving to meet basic survival needs or are striving to meet higher psychological needs) and by one's ability to meet needs at the various levels. Severe deprivation of need satisfaction might contribute to feelings of hopelessness, depression, anxiety, low self-esteem and more. In contrast, overindulgence of needs can also create problems, such as when an individual desires abnormally high levels of self-esteem or establishes additional needs—like the needs for power and control.

Like Maslow, **Carl Rogers** agreed that all humans are striving toward growth and fulfillment. In line with Maslow's concept of self-actualization, Rogers spoke of the **fully functioning person**—one who is functioning at their fullest potential. He believed that three important factors influence whether one achieves this level of functioning: self-concept, how one is treated by others and one's subjective reality. **Self-concept** refers to the information and beliefs we have about our own nature, qualities and behavior. It is essentially our thoughts and beliefs about who we are. Rogers distinguished between the **real self** (how we see ourselves in the present) and the **ideal self** (who we desire to be) as important aspects of self-concept. According to Rogers, the degree of congruence between our real self and ideal self plays an important role in personality and emotional adjustment. The greater the discrepancy that exists between the real and ideal self, the more likely one is to experience maladjustment, low self-esteem, depression and/or anxiety.

Rogers also believed that the way others treat us is an important factor in personality and behavior. An important distinction made by Rogers is one between conditional and unconditional positive regard. **Conditional positive regard** refers to love and acceptance that are contingent on behaving in certain ways. According to Rogers, conditional positive regard might lead individuals to hide or suppress their real self and/or form views of themselves that are distorted or negative, thus inhibiting their ability to grow and reach their fullest potential. Rogers believed that humans need to experience **unconditional positive regard** if they are to reach their fullest potential.

Finally, Rogers believed that all individuals have their own **subjective reality** or views of themselves, others and the world around them. This subjective reality is important for personality and behavior as it influences self-concept, approaches to others and reactions to others.

Cognitive Theories

Cognitive theories of personality argue that personality and behavior are a reflection of thought processes, beliefs and expectations. Three cognitive factors emphasized as important to personality include locus of control, self-efficacy and attributional style. **Locus of control** refers to one's beliefs about the causes and outcomes of events and experiences. **Jullian Rotter** coined the term in the 1950s and argued that individuals tend to have a cognitive style that reflects either an internal or external locus of control. Individuals with an *external* locus of control tend to think that the environment and other external forces beyond their own control (for example, luck, chance, fate) are responsible for the events and outcomes in their lives. Individuals with an *internal* locus of control tend to believe that their own skills, abilities and efforts control events and outcomes in their lives.

Self-efficacy refers to one's expectations for success and beliefs about their ability to produce desired results. *High* self-efficacy implies a belief that one can succeed regardless of past failures and/or current obstacles related to the task at hand. *Low* self-efficacy implies that one does not believe they can perform well. One's degree of self-efficacy has been linked to individual differences in behavior and personality (including one's degree of confidence, self-esteem, likelihood of approaching a task, effort expended on a task and persistence on challenging tasks).

Attributional style refers to one's pattern of explaining events in one's life. Attributions can vary on three dimensions: internal-external, stable-unstable and global-specific. The *internal-external* dimension refers to whether one attributes events and outcomes to oneself or the external environment. The *stable-unstable* dimension refers to whether one's explanation of events implies a stable cause that is always present or a temporary or fluctuating cause. The *global-specific* dimension refers to whether one's explanation of events implies that the event or outcome affects all aspects of one's life or is specific to a particular area of life. Examples of attributions that reflect each dimension are provided in the following chart.

Attributional Style	Example
Internal	It's my fault.
External	The teacher isn't fair.
Stable	I am incompetent and stupid.
Unstable	I wasn't feeling well that day.
Global	I am a failure at everything.
Specific	I am not good at math.

Social cognitive theory explains personality using both behavioral (learning) and cognitive theories. According to social cognitive theory, personality emerges as a result of unique experiences, behaviors, and thoughts. **Albert Bandura** views personality as shaped by the interaction between thoughts, behavior, and the external environment. This interaction, known as **reciprocal determinism,** suggests that the environment influences our thoughts and behavior which in turn influence the environment.

Trait Theories

Trait theories argue that personality is reflected in the various traits we possess. **Traits** refer to personal qualities or characteristics that are relatively stable and consistent over time and situations. When you describe a friend as good-natured and dependable, you are describing their traits. Trait theorists argue that certain traits are present in all humans. Individual differences emerge from the fact that we all possess traits to varying degrees (for example, some people are more good-natured than others).

Trait theorists debate the exact number of traits that constitute personality. **Raymond Cattell** suggested that 16 pairs of source traits make up the core of personality. (These 16 traits are listed in the following chart.)

Catell's 16 Source Traits

Reserved—Warm
Concrete—Abstract
Reactive—Emotionally stable
Deferential—Dominant
Serious—Lively
Expedient—Rule conscious
Shy—Socially bold
Utilitarian—Sensitive
Trusting—Vigilant
Grounded—Abstracted
Forthright—Private
Self-assured—Apprehensive
Traditional—Open to change
Group-oriented—Self-oriented
Tolerates disorder—Perfectionistic
Relaxed—Tense

Hans Eysenk argued that personality can be reduced to three trait dimensions: extraversion, neuroticism and psychoticism. The dominant model today is the **Five-Factor Model,** proposed by Costa and McCrae. The Five Factor Model argues that personality is made up of five basic traits: neuroticism, extraversion, openness to experience, agreeableness and conscientiousness. The poles of each of the five dimensions are described in the following chart.

Low	Personality Trait	High
Stable	**Neuroticism**	Unstable
Withdrawn and shy	**Extraversion**	Outgoing and talkative
Closed	**Openness to experience**	Open
Uncooperative, unfriendly	**Agreeableness**	Cooperative, friendly, easygoing
Irresponsible, undependable	**Conscientiousness**	Responsible, dependable

Assessment Techniques

Psychologists utilize a number of different tools and methods to assess and analyze personality. In general, personality assessment techniques can be placed into two broad categories: objective personality tests and projective personality tests.

Objective Personality Tests

Objective personality tests are standardized questionnaires that require individuals to respond to specific questions or statements about themselves such as "I want others to like me," "I have frequent fights with others" and "I tend to share lots about myself with others." Objective personality tests are typically self-report tests that have a limited number of possible responses. Oftentimes, individuals indicate the extent to which the statement is true or false for them, or the extent to which they agree or disagree with the statement. The major problem with such tests is the issue of social desirability (individuals responding in ways that make them "look good" to others or feel good about themselves). Three popular objective personality tests are the NEO-Personality Inventory (NEO-PI), the Minnesota Multiphasic Personality Inventory (MMPI), and the Myers-Briggs Type Indicator.

The **NEO-PI** is a self-report test designed to measure the degree to which one possesses each of the big five traits.

The Myers-Briggs Type Indicator is a personality inventory designed to assess one's personality type. It contains a number of statements focused on where one directs their energy, how one processes information, how one makes decisions, and how one organizes their life. There are 16 possible personality types based on varying combinations of these four variables.

The **MMPI** is a self-report test that identifies the presence/absence of various psychological disorders. Items on the MMPI are grouped into 10 clinical scales, each of which measures a different disorder. (See the following chart for the 10 scales of the MMPI.) It also contains validity and lie scales that are designed to detect lying or distortion of answers.

Scales of the MMPI	Focus of Scales
Hypochondriasis	Concern with bodily symptoms
Depression	Pessimism, hopelessness
Hysteria	Use of symptoms to avoid or solve problems
Psychopathic deviancy	Disregard for social standards and antisocial behavior
Masculinity/femininity	Interests related to gender
Paranoia	Suspiciousness, delusions, defensiveness
Psychasthenia	Guilt, worry, obsessiveness, compulsiveness
Schizophrenia	Loss of touch with reality, bizarre thoughts
Hypomania	Impulsiveness, excitedness, overactivity
Social introversion	Confidence levels, security in social interactions, outgoingness

Projective Personality Tests

Projective personality tests involve the presentation of ambiguous stimuli that can be interpreted or perceived in a number of different ways and asking individuals to report what they see in the various stimuli. Projective personality tests are based on two assumptions: (1) that individuals might be unwilling or unable to express their true feelings if asked directly and (2) that individuals project unconscious desires, thoughts and conflicts into their perceptions of the stimuli. While such tests avoid the issue of social desirability, analysis of responses in highly subjective and difficult to interpret. The two most widely used projective tests of personality are the Rorschach test and the Thematic Apperception Test.

Developed by **Hermann Rorschach** in 1921, the **Rorschach test** involves the presentation of a series of 10 symmetrical inkblots followed by the question "What do you see in this picture?" Responses are then interpreted as indicators of unconscious feelings and conflicts.

Developed by **Henry Murray** in 1928, the **Thematic Apperception Test** involves the presentation of ambiguous pictures of people in various situations. Individuals are asked to create a story about each of the pictures that includes what the characters are feeling, doing and thinking, and how the story turns out. Again, responses are believed to reflect unconscious needs and conflicts.

Review Questions

1. Which of the following theories of personality focuses on unconscious impulses and conflicts?

   A. Maslow's humanistic theory
   B. Roger's humanistic theory
   C. Freud's psychoanalytic theory
   D. the Five-Factor Model of personality
   E. Rotter's internal-external locus-of-control theory

2. If little Joey is in the phallic stage of personality development, we can expect him to:

   A. experience few sexual desires
   B. be angry at his mother and father
   C. experience sexual desires for his mother
   D. experience sexual desires for his peers
   E. desire stimulation of the anal region

3. According to Freud, the _____ operates according to the pleasure principle, whereas the _____ operates according to the reality principle.

    A. id; superego

    B. id; ego

    C. ego; superego

    D. ego; id

    E. superego; ego

4. The _____ demands that we behave morally at all times.

    A. id

    B. ideal self

    C. superego

    D. ego

    E. real self

5. A child is angry at his sister for something she has done. But, instead of hitting his sister, he throws and kicks one of his toys. This is an example of the defense mechanism of:

    A. regression

    B. reaction formation

    C. projection

    D. rationalization

    E. displacement

6. An individual who makes an internal-stable attribution is most likely to attribute their poor performance on the latest psychology exam to:

    A. the room being noisy and disruptive

    B. the test being extremely unfair

    C. not feeling well the day of the exam

    D. not studying hard enough for the exam

    E. being stupid and incompetent

7. When one receives love and attention only when they behave in ways that others desire, they are likely to:

    A. fixate in a stage of development

    B. attain their ideal self and self-actualize

    C. feel confident in their ability to meet others' needs

    D. experience a negative effect and insecurity in relationships with others

    E. utilize defense mechanisms to protect their self-esteem

8. An individual who scores low on a measure of extraversion is likely:

    A. outgoing and talkative

    B. irresponsible and undependable

    C. open to experiencing new things

    D. shy and withdrawn

    E. uncooperative and unfriendly

Answers

1. C. Freud introduced the idea of the unconscious as a driving force of personality. Maslow believed personality was driven by a desire to meet goals and needs. Rogers believed personality was driven by the desire for growth and fulfillment. The Five-Factor Model is a trait theory of personality that focuses on stable and enduring personality qualities present at birth and driven by biological/genetic factors. Rotter's internal-external locus-of-control theory focuses on thought patterns and whether individuals believe they have control over events and outcomes in their lives.

2. C. The phallic stage is marked by a sexual desire for the opposite-sex parent and fear or dislike of the same-sex parent. Few sexual desires are experienced during the latency stage. It is during the genital stage (associated with adolescence) that sexual impulses resurface and are focused toward peers. Stimulation of the anal region is desired during the anal stage of psychosexual development.

3. B. The id operates based on the pleasure principle, seeking immediate gratification of impulses at all times. The ego operates based on the reality principle, balancing the impulses of the id and the demands of the superego in ways that are realistic and in line with societal rules and expectations. The superego operates according to the morality principle and demands strict adherence to rules and norms.

4. C. The superego demands that we behave morally at all times. It operates according to the morality principle and demands perfection and adherence to rules and standards at all times. The id operates according to the pleasure principle, seeking immediate gratification of all impulses at all times. The ego operates according to the reality principle, seeking a balance between the impulses of the id and the desire for moral behavior from the superego. The ideal self and the real self are concepts proposed by Carl Rogers. They represent our current self and the self we wish to become.

5. E. Displacement involves shifting behavior to a more appropriate target. In the example, the boy has shifted his anger and aggression away from his sister and displaced it onto one of his own toys. Regression involves reverting to behaviors reflective of an earlier stage of development. Reaction formation is marked by expression of inappropriate thoughts as their opposite. Projection involves attributing unacceptable thoughts to others. Rationalization replaces inappropriate explanations of behavior with more acceptable ones.

6. E. An internal attribution involves attributing the cause or outcome of an event to oneself or one's own skills, abilities or efforts. A stable attribution involves attributing the cause or outcome of an event to a permanent and persistent factor. Thus, because stupidity and incompetence represent individual and stable characteristics, the choice that best reflects an internal-stable attribution states that one is stupid and incompetent. Although stating that one did not study hard enough or did not feel well the day of the exam are internal attributions, they are not stable. Both imply only temporary or unstable causes. The other two choices (the room being noisy and disruptive, and the test being unfair) are both external attributions.

7. D. Carl Rogers proposed that conditional positive regard occurs when one receives love and attention only when they behave in ways that others desire. He argued that such love and attention can lead to negative effects and insecurity in relationships with others. Roger's argued that individuals can only attain their ideal self and self-actualize when they receive unconditional positive regard (love and affection regardless of their behaviors). Defense mechanisms are employed to counteract anxiety and guilt, and to keep anxiety- and guilt-provoking thoughts in the unconscious.

8. D. Extroversion is a personality trait that represents the degree to which one is outgoing, social and talkative. Individuals who score low on a measure of extroversion are shy and withdrawn. Individuals who are irresponsible and undependable score low on a measure of conscientiousness. Individuals who are open to experiencing new things score high on the trait of openness to experience. Individuals who are uncooperative and unfriendly score low on a measure of agreeableness.

Testing, Intelligence, and Individual Differences

This chapter examines the field of psychometrics, or psychological testing. The chapter begins with a review of issues in test development and construction. It then turns to a more detailed review of intelligence and intelligence testing. The chapter also addresses theories of intelligence, tests of intelligence and the factors that influence intelligence. The chapter ends with a brief review of individual differences in intellectual abilities.

Standardization and Norms

Norms refer to standard test scores that are used as a basis for comparison and interpretation of scores. **Standardization** is the process of establishing norms for a test. The process of standardization involves administering the test to a large sample of individuals (from a variety of socioeconomic and racial backgrounds) and determining the average score and variation of scores.

Reliability and Validity

Tests used to measure any ability, characteristic or psychological trait must have established reliability and validity. **Reliability** refers to the consistency of a test. A test is reliable if it consistently measures the skill or ability it purports to measure. Reliability for a test can be established in many ways. One method is to give the same group of people the same test on more than one occasion. This is called **test-retest reliability.** When the same people are tested and then retested, a reliable test yields nearly the same score each time. In some cases, researchers choose to use an alternative, but equivalent, form of the test at the time of retesting rather than the exact same test. This is called **equivalent-forms reliability.** In other cases, researchers examine the correlation between items on one half of the test and items on the other half of the test. This is called **split-half reliability.** The test is considered reliable if the two halves are highly correlated because this suggests that the two halves are measuring the same construct.

Validity refers to the capability of a test to measure what it is intended to measure. This most basic form of validity is also called **construct validity** and is determined by examining how scores on a test correlate with other measures that assess the same construct. For example, if you develop a new test designed to assess one's level of depression, you might give individuals your new test and a test already shown to measure depression. If your test is valid, individuals' scores on *your* test of depression should be similar to their scores on the other test of depression. **Predictive validity** refers to the capability of a test to predict future performance. **Content validity** refers to the capability of a test to be fully representative of the construct it is intended to measure.

Types of Tests

A variety of tests are used to assess abilities and characteristics in psychology. Tests used to assess psychological attributes, abilities and skills are referred to as **psychometric tests. Intelligence tests** are used to measure one's cognitive abilities and/or knowledge in an area. The two general types of intelligence tests are achievement tests and aptitude tests. **Achievement tests** are designed to assess one's level of knowledge in a given area. They are focused on how much one has learned rather than on one's general ability level. **Aptitude tests** are designed to predict one's general ability.

Intelligence

Intelligence can be defined as the application of cognitive skills and knowledge to learn or solve a problem. The earliest theories viewed intelligence as a general ability that one either had or did not have. **Charles Spearman** (1927) argued that intelligence is a general ability that is applied to all kinds of tasks. He called this general cognitive ability the **g factor.** Though Spearman recognized some specific abilities, which he called "s" factors, he emphasized the role of general intellectual ability in influencing performance on intellectual tasks. According to Spearman, individuals perform at a similar level on a variety of different cognitive tasks as a result of their g factor. Over the years, the notion of a g factor has been replaced by the idea that intelligence is a multidimensional construct made up of several related, yet distinct abilities. Several variations of this idea have been proposed.

Louis Thurstone (1938) argued that mental performance depends on several distinct abilities that he called **primary mental abilities.** The seven primary mental abilities identified by Thurstone are outlined in the following chart:

Louis Thurstone's Primary Mental Abilities	
Perceptual speed	Speed of information processing
Memory	Ability to remember information
Word comprehension	Ability to understand verbal statements
Word fluency	Ability to produce verbal statements
Number facility	Ability to deal with numbers and perform mathematical calculations
Inductive reasoning	Ability to deal with novel problems and unfamiliar situations
Space	Visual-spatial skills

In the 1960s, **Cattell** and **Horn** distinguished between crystallized and fluid intelligence. **Crystallized intelligence** refers to the ability to apply acquired knowledge to current problems. It is based on previous learning and includes vocabulary skills, language skills and other acquired methods for solving problems. In contrast, **fluid intelligence** refers to the ability to deal with novel problems and to use the mind in new and adaptive ways. It is a more creative type of thinking and is typically tested by asking individuals to identify relationships among objects and underlying patterns in stimuli.

Howard Gardner (1999) proposed a theory of **multiple intelligences** in which he identified eight distinct types of intelligence. The eight types of intelligence, **or frames of mind,** are described in the following chart:

Howard Gardner's Multiple Intelligences	
Linguistic	Ability to use language
Spatial	Ability to solve spatial problems
Bodily-kinesthetic	Ability to control body movements and to manipulate objects
Intrapersonal	Ability to understand oneself
Musical	Ability to perceive pitch and rhythm, and to produce music
Interpersonal	Ability to understand and relate to others
Logical/mathematical	Ability to reason
Naturalistic	Ability to see patterns in nature

Robert Sternberg (1985) proposed a **triarchic theory of intelligence** in which he identified three types of intelligence: analytical, practical and creative. **Analytical intelligence** refers to one's ability to judge, reason, evaluate, criticize and solve problems. It is most closely linked to academic performance and is the type of intelligence most often assessed through intelligence tests. **Practical intelligence** refers to one's ability to deal with everyday tasks and demands, to navigate through life, and to manage oneself and others. **Creative intelligence** refers to one's ability to deal with novel situations and to invent, discover, theorize and hypothesize.

Daniel Goleman (1995) coined the term **emotional intelligence (EQ)** to refer to one's ability to manage and regulate their emotions. According to Goleman, EQ underlies one's ability to socialize, to get along with others, and to maintain psychological health. Moreover, Goleman argued that EQ and IQ are separate and distinct abilities.

Assessing Intelligence

The first intelligence test was developed by **Alfred Binet** and **Theodore Simon** in the early 1900s to assist overcrowded schools in identifying students in need of special attention. The test contained a number of **age-graded items,** items reflective of what individuals of different ages should be able to do. Thus, there were a set of tasks and questions that all average 6-year-olds should be able to complete, and a set of tasks and questions that all average 8-year-olds should be able to complete. On the basis of one's performance on the test, they were assigned a **mental age,** reflecting the level of age-graded items the child was able to complete. A mental-age score provides information about one's performance on a test in comparison with others of the same age. Later tests yielded an intelligence quotient (IQ) score rather than a mental-age score. To calculate one's IQ, their mental-age score is divided by their chronological (actual) age, then multiplied by 100. Thus, if a person has a mental age of 10 and a chronological age of 8, their IQ is calculated as follows: $10 \div 8 \times 100 = 125$. The benefit of translating a mental-age score into an IQ score is that scores can be compared across individuals of different ages. When calculating IQ, an IQ score of 100 always indicates average intelligence, regardless of one's age. An IQ above 100 indicates above-average intelligence, and an IQ below 100 indicates below-average intelligence.

The most commonly used intelligence tests today are the Stanford-Binet Intelligence Scale and the Wechsler Scales. The **Stanford-Binet Intelligence Scale** is a modern version of the initial test developed by Simon and Binet in the early 1900s. The modern Stanford-Binet test contains sets of age-graded items that can be given to individuals of a variety of ages. The **Wechsler Scales** refer to three different scales developed by **David Wechsler:** the Wechsler Preschool and Primary Scale of Intelligence (designed for use with preschool-aged children), the Wechsler Intelligence Scale for Children (designed for use with school-aged children and young adolescents) and the Wechsler Adult Intelligence Scale (designed for use with older adolescents and adults). Both the Stanford-Binet and the Wechsler scales are administered individually and involve an experimenter giving a variety of tasks to the test taker. Group intelligence tests, paper-and-pencil tests that can be given to large groups of people at one time, are also used. Examples of group intelligence tests are the **SAT** and **ACT,** which are designed to assess one's ability to succeed in college.

Heredity/Environment and Intelligence

Heritability refers to the extent to which a given trait or ability is influenced by hereditary or genetic influences. Heritability is typically established using twin and adoption studies. **Twin studies** involve a determination of the extent to which the IQ scores of monozygotic (identical) twins are similar or different. Because monozygotic twins are genetically identical, any differences in IQ scores must be due to environmental influences. Some researchers choose to look at monozygotic twins who were raised apart. In this instance, any similarities in IQ scores must be due to genetic similarity, and any differences in IQ scores must be due to environmental influences. **Adoption studies** examine children who have been adopted and look at how similar or different they are from their biological and adoptive parents. If their IQ score more closely resembles their biological parents, this suggests a genetic influence. If their IQ score more closely resembles their adoptive parents, this suggests an environmental influence. In each case, statistical analyses yield a **heritability coefficient,** which indicates the proportion of variation among individuals that can be attributed to genetic or hereditary influences. Most studies converge on the finding that the heritability coefficient for IQ is about .50–.60, suggesting that about half the variation in IQ scores among individuals can be attributed to genetic influences. The other half can be attributed to differences in environment. In the end, studies suggest that heredity, environment and their interaction all influence one's actual level of intelligence.

Human Diversity

Skills and abilities vary a great deal among humans. In fact, research finds that most psychological traits and abilities follow a normal distribution, or bell curve, when plotted on a graph. A distribution is a chart of scores on a test that reflects the spread of scores around the average. In a normal/bell distribution, the majority of scores cluster around the average, and fewer scores fall far away from the mean.

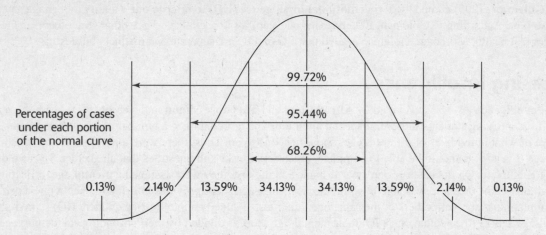

Scores on intelligence tests typically follow a normal/bell distribution. Researchers have identified several levels of intelligence, ranging from gifted to mentally retarded. Individuals who score in the upper extreme of the bell curve (the upper 2%–3% of the population) are considered **gifted.** Individuals who score below 70, and who have a severe deficiency in their ability to care for themselves and relate to others are considered mentally retarded. **Mental retardation** can range in degree from **mild** (IQ scores between 55 and 70), **moderate** (IQ scores between 40 and 55), **severe** (IQ scores between 25 and 40) and **profound** (IQ scores below 25). As can be seen from the following chart, roughly 2% of the population is mentally retarded. Of those considered mentally retarded, the majority fall in the mild-to-moderate range.

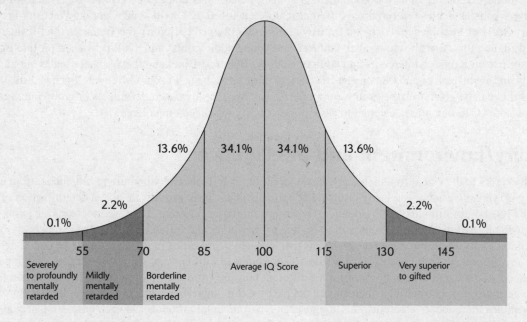

Review Questions

1. If an individual's score on a test one week is highly correlated with their score on the same test the following week, the test is said to have high:

    A. predictive validity
    B. standardization
    C. test-retest reliability
    D. equivalent-forms reliability
    E. split-half reliability

2. Brian has learned a lot of information in his eight years of schooling. The knowledge and skills Brian has learned in school best represents:

    A. crystallized intelligence
    B. fluid intelligence
    C. practical intelligence
    D. creative intelligence
    E. interpersonal intelligence

3. If Kyle has a mental age of 9 and a chronological age of 6, his IQ is:

    A. 15
    B. 66
    C. 166
    D. 150
    E. 100

4. When given to large groups of individuals, the average score on a test is called:

    A. a deviation score
    B. reliability
    C. validity
    D. the norm
    E. a base score

5. An individual classified as moderately mentally retarded has an IQ score:

    A. between 100 and 115
    B. right at 100
    C. between 55 and 70
    D. between 40 and 55
    E. between 25 and 40

6. Of the following individuals, who is most likely to agree that intelligence represents a general cognitive ability?

    A. Howard Gardner
    B. Robert Sternberg
    C. David Goleman
    D. Louis Thurstone
    E. Charles Spearman

7. According to Robert Sternberg, a person who deals well with everyday tasks and demands has high:

    A. fluid intelligence

    B. practical intelligence

    C. crystallized intelligence

    D. emotional intelligence

    E. intrapersonal intelligence

8. Which of the following conclusions can be drawn from studies examining the influence of genes and environment on intellectual skills?

    A. Intelligence is a fixed trait influenced solely by genetic factors.

    B. Intelligence is not influenced by genes at all.

    C. Environment solely influences intelligence.

    D. Both genes and environment influence one's level of intelligence.

    E. The effects of genes and environment on intelligence cannot be disentangled.

Answers

1. C. Test-retest reliability refers to the capability of a test to consistently measure the construct of interest. It is established by having the same group of subjects take the test on more than one occasion and examining the correlations among individuals' scores across testing times. High test-retest reliability is indicated by high correlations among scores at different testing times.

2. A. Crystallized intelligence refers to one's level of acquired knowledge and information, and their ability to apply acquired knowledge and information to current problems. It is most closely aligned with academics. Fluid intelligence is a type of intelligence that enables one to deal with novel problems. Practical intelligence refers to one's ability to deal with everyday problems and to navigate through life. Creative intelligence refers to one's ability to invent, discover and hypothesize. Interpersonal intelligence refers to one's ability to understand and relate to others.

3. D. The formula for calculating IQ based on one's mental age (MA) and chronological age (CA) is MA ÷ CA × 100. Thus, to calculate Kyle's IQ, perform the following calculation: 9 ÷ 6 × 100. The answer is 150. One hundred represents average intelligence. Scores above 100 represent above-average intelligence. Scores below 100 represent below-average intelligence. Because Kyle has a mental age (9) that is far above his chronological age (6), his IQ score is above 100. Thus, 15, 66 and 100 can be eliminated automatically.

4. D. The average score on a test, when given to a large group of individuals, is called the norm. Norms are used as a basis for comparison and interpretation of scores. Reliability refers to the capability of a test to consistently measure the construct of interest. Validity refers to the capability of a test to measure what it is intended to measure.

5. D. Mental retardation can range in degree from mild to severe. Those classified as moderately mentally retarded have an IQ score that falls between 40 and 55. Those with an IQ score between 25 and 40 are considered severely mentally retarded. Those with an IQ score between 55 and 70 are considered mildly mentally retarded. Those with an IQ of 100 are considered average, and those with an IQ score between 100 and 115 are considered above average with respect to intelligence.

6. E. Charles Spearman was the first to propose that intelligence represents a general cognitive ability when he proposed the notion of a g factor. Louis Thurstone, Robert Sternberg and Howard Gardner all believed that intelligence is made up of several related, but independent abilities. David Goleman proposed a distinction between academic intelligence and emotional intelligence.

7. **B.** In Sternberg's triarchic theory of intelligence, a person who deals well with everyday tasks and demands has high practical intelligence. None of the other options are types of intelligence proposed by Sternberg. Fluid and crystallized intelligence were proposed by Cattell and Horn as two distinct types of intelligence. Emotional intelligence was proposed by David Goleman. Intrapersonal intelligence was proposed by Howard Gardner to refer to one's ability to understand oneself and to manage one's emotions.

8. **D.** Most twin and adoption studies converge on the finding that both genes and environment influence one's level of intelligence. Intelligence is not influenced solely by genetic factors, nor it is influenced solely by environmental factors. Rather, intelligence seems to be influenced by the constant interaction of genetic and environmental influences.

Abnormal Psychology

This chapter will review major classifications of abnormal behavior and the way in which abnormal behavior is defined and classified. The use of the Diagnostic and Statistical Manual of Mental Disorders as a diagnostic tool in identifying and classifying abnormal behavior is discussed. The chapter ends with a review of the major disorders found in the DSM-IV and the key symptoms and features of each disorder.

Definitions of Abnormality

Abnormal behavior, or **psychopathology,** refers to patterns of behavior, thought and emotion that are abnormal for one or more of the following reasons:

- **The behavior is rare in the general population.** Some behaviors are considered abnormal because they occur rarely or infrequently in the general population. However, this criteria alone is not sufficient in determining abnormality. A number of behaviors occur infrequently in the population that are quite normal, such as extremely high intelligence and exceptional athletic ability.

- **The behavior causes personal distress.** A second indicator that a behavior might be abnormal is if the individual is distressed by the behavior, thoughts, or emotions and desires them to stop. One must be careful in using this as a criterion for abnormality because in some disorders the individual denies the problem, or the problem causes little or no emotional discomfort to the individual.

- **The behavior is maladaptive.** A third indicator is if the behavior, thought or emotion is maladaptive (meaning that it results in a loss of normal functioning or impairs normal functioning). Some psychological disorders leave individuals unable to get along with others, to hold a job, to eat properly or to function on a daily basis.

- **The behavior is unconventional.** If a behavior violates the norms or standards of society, it might be considered abnormal. However, not all behaviors that violate norms or standards are signs of psychopathology. In fact, what is seen as abnormal in one particular culture might be perfectly normal in another culture. In addition, it is not uncommon to see culture-bound disorders that are unique to specific cultures.

- **The behavior causes discomfort to others.** Sometimes the behavior of an individual causes little discomfort to the individual, but others find the behavior discomforting.

- **The behavior is irrational.** Behavior, thought or emotion might be considered abnormal if it impairs one's ability to think clearly and to make rational decisions.

- **The behavior is unpredictable.** If behavior, thought or emotion fluctuates from one extreme to another for no apparent reason, or if behavior, thought or emotion is inappropriate for the situation one is in, it might be considered abnormal.

Theories of Psychopathology

Views of psychopathology and mental illness have fluctuated over the years. In the 1600s, abnormal behavior was believed to be caused by evil spirits and witchcraft. Individuals displaying odd or abnormal behavior were believed to be witches or to be possessed by demons. In the eighteenth century, explanations for abnormal behavior shifted from a focus on supernatural processes to medical or physical conditions. During this time, mental illness was viewed as a disease of the mind. Today, abnormal behavior is believed to be the result of multiple factors (including biological, cognitive, social and psychological factors). Each of the modern perspectives in psychology offers a unique explanation for abnormal behavior.

The **psychoanalytic perspective** holds that abnormal behavior is the result of childhood conflicts that were not adequately resolved. Over- and under-indulgence of desires across infancy and childhood, conflicts with parents early in life, and the formation of personality structures that result from these early experiences all contribute to abnormal behavior.

The **humanistic perspective** focuses on one's self-concept and one's relationship with society as important influences on behavior. From this perspective, abnormal behavior can result from denial, distortion or questioning of one's true self; lack of acceptance by others; and/or judgment and criticism by others.

The **cognitive perspective** holds that faulty thoughts and beliefs are central to abnormal behavior. According to this perspective, abnormal behavior results from maladaptive and inappropriate thoughts, distorted and inaccurate perceptions, irrational beliefs, and self-defeating and automatic thoughts.

The **biological perspective** focuses on biological and/or genetic influences on behavior. According to the biological perspective, abnormal behavior results from structural/anatomical, chemical and/or functional abnormalities in the brain.

The **behavioral perspective** argues that abnormal behavior is a product of faulty learning through conditioning and/or modeling. According to this view, abnormal behaviors are learned through past experience and present environmental conditions and circumstances.

The **sociocultural perspective** emphasizes social and cultural factors as important contributors to abnormal behavior. This perspective recognizes that abnormal behavior is defined by the culture and influenced by socialization and cultural values, beliefs and practices. Thus, behavior (including abnormal behavior) is shaped by the family group, society and culture in which one lives.

The **diathesis-stress model** is a more modern explanation that incorporates elements from each of the above perspectives including biological, psychological, and sociocultural factors. According to this model, inherited characteristics, underlying biological processes, and personality traits, and learning experiences combine to create varying degrees of predisposition for a psychological disorder. Whether or not an individual actually develops a disorder or not depends on the degree of stress/negative experiences one experiences. Thus, for those who have a strong predisposition, relatively mild levels of stress can trigger a disorder. For those with a weak predisposition, much higher levels of stress are required to trigger a disorder.

Diagnosis of Psychopathology

The **Diagnostic and Statistical Manual of Mental Disorders (DSM-IV TR)** is a manual used by professionals to aid in the diagnostic process. Published by the American Psychological Association, the DSM-IV TR provides a classification system for mental disorders and describes in detail the criteria and symptoms that must be present for a particular diagnosis to be made. The DSM-IV TR classifies behavior across five dimensions, or axes. The first three axes assess an individual's clinical condition. **Axis I** assesses the presence of clinical conditions such as mood disorders, anxiety disorders, schizophrenic disorders and addictive disorders. **Axis II** assesses the presence of personality disorders and mental retardation. **Axis III** assesses for general medication conditions that might or might not be involved in the conditions assessed in Axes I and II. **Axis IV** assesses the presence of psychosocial and environmental stressors that the individual might currently be facing. **Axis V** involves an overall assessment of the person's level of functioning.

Disorders

The DSM-IV TR identifies over 300 specific psychological disorders. The most prevalent of the various disorders include mood disorders, anxiety disorders, schizophrenic disorders, somatoform disorders, dissociative disorders, and personality disorders.

Mood Disorders

Mood disorders are characterized by disturbances or extreme fluctuations in emotion or mood. The two most common mood disorders are unipolar disorder and bipolar disorder.

Unipolar disorder, also known as major depressive disorder, is characterized by persistent and intense sadness, despair, feelings of worthlessness, helplessness, low self-esteem, and high guilt and shame. For individuals who suffer from major depression, the sadness they feel is so intense that it interferes with their ability to function, to feel pleasure, and to maintain interest in life. In addition to the emotional disturbances, major depression is often accompanied by physiological changes, including sleep and eating disturbances and reports of physical illness and pain.

Bipolar disorder is characterized by alternating periods of depression and mania. An individual who suffers from bipolar disorder experiences depressive episodes similar to those of unipolar depression. However, depressive episodes are interspersed with periods of mania and extreme elation. During a manic episode, an individual might be overly excited and extremely active. They might show unrealistically high self-esteem and an inflated sense of importance (possibly even delusions of grandeur). They might make elaborate plans, be impulsive, hyperactive and sleepless for days at a time (without becoming fatigued). Speech often becomes rapid and the individual might show *rapid flight of ideas* and *pressured speech.*

What factors contribute to mood disorders? Evidence suggests that depressive disorders might be partially *inherited.* Individuals are at increased risk of developing depression if a family member suffers from depression, and this risk increases as the degree of genetic relatedness increases. There appears to be a stronger genetic link for bipolar disorder than for unipolar disorder. *Biological factors* have also been found to be associated with depressive disorders. Brain-imaging techniques reveal significant differences in brain activity during depressive and manic episodes. Additional research has found that depression is linked to chemical imbalances, particularly levels of serotonin and norepinephrine in the brain.

With respect to *environmental factors*, depressive episodes are often precipitated by certain negative experiences, particularly high stress, loss and trauma. Finally, a number of *cognitive and psychological factors* are also associated with depressive disorders. Beliefs about oneself, one's abilities and control over events are all related to depression.

Depressed individuals are more likely than nondepressed individuals to attribute failures to internal factors and abilities (It's my fault; I'm not smart enough), while at the same time attributing successes to external factors (I got lucky). Depressed individuals are also more likely than nondepressed individuals to make global attributions (I am a failure at everything) rather than specific attributions (I am not good at psychology). Additionally, depressed individuals are more likely to report feelings of helplessness and to believe that they have no control over events in their lives. Such cognitive patterns and attributional styles can fuel the cycle of depression, making it difficult to break out of a depressive state.

Anxiety Disorders

Anxiety disorders are a class of disorders characterized by tension, worry, nervousness, panic or fear that is debilitating, distressing and interferes with an individual's ability to function on a daily basis. A number of disorders fall under this classification (including generalized anxiety disorder, panic disorder, phobic disorder, obsessive-compulsive disorder and post-traumatic stress disorder).

Generalized anxiety disorder involves a chronic state of high anxiety, tension and worry (free-floating anxiety) in which the individual cannot pinpoint any particular cause of the anxiety. Individuals who suffer from generalized anxiety disorder report a sense of impending doom and a feeling that something dreadful is about to happen, but cannot identify any specific reason for the anxiety and worry.

Panic disorder involves anxiety attacks that produce a sudden and intense rush of anxiety, fear or impending doom that arises abruptly and for no apparent reason. The attacks are usually relatively brief (10–15 minutes) but leave the individual worrying excessively about future attacks and avoiding activities for fear of having an attack.

Phobic disorder involves an intense, irrational fear and avoidance of a specific object or situation that (in reality) poses little or no objective danger. In many cases of phobia, the individual recognizes the irrationality, but still experiences overwhelming anxiety and goes to extremes to avoid or escape the presence of the feared object. (Imagine being so afraid of spiders that you would jump out of a speeding car to get away from one.) Some common phobias found in the general population include fear of spiders (arachnophobia), heights (acrophobia) and closed spaces (claustrophobia).

Agoraphobia is a more severe and debilitating phobia involving an intense fear of social situations or crowded places. Individuals who suffer from agoraphobia frequently withdraw from society, isolate themselves and have great difficulty functioning in the everyday world.

Obsessive-compulsive disorder (OCD) involves persistent, unwanted thoughts (called obsessions) that cause anxiety and lead the individual to engage in repetitive acts or rituals (called compulsions) in an attempt to reduce the anxiety. Unfortunately, with OCD, the compulsive behaviors reduce the anxiety only temporarily, and the obsessions quickly return to cause another surge in anxiety. In fact, with OCD the repetitive thoughts and ritualistic actions become uncontrollable and, as with most mental disorders, interfere with an individual's ability to function in daily life. Many sufferers of OCD do not enjoy the rituals and realize that their actions are senseless, but find that the anxiety can only be relieved by giving in to the urges. Common compulsions seen in individuals who suffer OCD are endless counting, checking locks and repeatedly washing their hands.

Schizophrenic Disorders

Schizophrenic disorders are considered some of the most serious and debilitating forms of mental illness. The major feature of all schizophrenic disorders is a break from reality (or a psychotic episode). In addition to experiencing psychotic episodes, additional symptoms of schizophrenic disorders include disturbances in perception, language, thought, emotion and behavior. Following is a more detailed description of the various symptoms associated with schizophrenia.

- **Perceptual symptoms:** Individuals might experience *hallucinations,* in which they perceive things without external stimulation. (Though hallucinations can occur in any of the senses, hearing voices and sounds are the most common forms of hallucinations reported.)
- **Language disturbances:** Individuals might exhibit disorganized and incoherent speech including *word salad,* in which words become scrambled and jumbled together. For example, individuals might create artificial words called *neologisms* (such as *smever* for smart and clever); they might also speak in rhythmic, rhyming phrases called *clang associations.*
- **Thought disturbances:** In many types of schizophrenia, logic is impaired and thoughts are disorganized and bizarre. Individuals might experience *delusions* (distorted beliefs that are maintained despite evidence to the contrary). Some common types of delusions seen among individuals with schizophrenia include *delusions of persecution* in which they believe they are the target of a plot to harm or assassinate them or that they are being watched, followed or sought after. *Delusions of grandeur* cause individuals to believe they are someone very important, such as Napoleon, or that they have special powers. *Delusions of reference* cause individuals to believe that someone is giving or sending them special messages through radio programs, newspaper articles, television programs and so on.
- **Emotional disturbances:** Schizophrenia involves a variety of emotional disturbances including inappropriate affect, exaggerated affect, blunted or flat affect, and rapid fluctuations in affect.
- **Motor/behavioral disturbances:** Certain types of schizophrenia involve unusual mannerisms and movements in which the individual might show excessive, uncontrollable motor activity or tics. In some cases, individuals display catatonic behavior in which they assume a nearly immobile stance for an extended period of time.

Schizophrenic disorders are typically divided into 4–5 basic types:

- **Paranoid:** The dominant symptoms are hallucinations, delusions, and erratic or unpredictable behavior.
- **Catatonic:** The dominant symptom is motor disturbances in which the person might display complete loss of motion (catatonic stance) or experience uncontrollable and erratic movement.
- **Disorganized:** The dominant symptoms include incoherent speech, emotional disturbances, social withdrawal and bizarre behavior.
- **Undifferentiated:** This refers to instances in which an individual's behavior meets the criteria for a diagnosis of schizophrenia, but no defining symptom exists; rather, the individual shows a mixture of major symptoms of schizophrenia.
- **Residual:** A major psychotic episode or symptoms are not present, but minor signs of schizophrenia are still evident.

Many psychologists now distinguish between positive and negative symptoms of schizophrenia. Positive symptoms involve additions or exaggerations of normal thought processes and behaviors (such as bizarre delusions, hallucinations and disorganized speech). Negative symptoms involve the loss or absence of normal thought processes and behaviors (such as impaired attention, limited speech, blunted affect and social withdrawal).

What factors contribute to schizophrenia? Psychologists used to speak of schizogenic mothers with the assumption that harsh, cold parenting contributed to the development of schizophrenia. However, we now know this is not true. In fact, schizophrenia appears to result from a complex interaction of genetic, biological and environmental factors. For example, we know that one's risk of developing schizophrenia increases as genetic relatedness to an individual with schizophrenia increases. In addition, excess levels of certain neurotransmitters in the brain (particularly dopamine) are associated with schizophrenia, and ingestion of large amounts of amphetamines (which increase the amount of dopamine in the brain) produce the positive symptoms of schizophrenia in people with no history of mental illness. Even low doses of amphetamines worsen symptoms in individuals with schizophrenia.

Brain imaging techniques point to the possibility of structural differences in the brains of individuals with schizophrenia and those without schizophrenia. Some individuals with schizophrenia have been found to have abnormally large ventricles—spaces that house fluid—in the brain. Certain life events and circumstances are also related to the onset of schizophrenic episodes. For example, traumatic events and extreme stress are frequently associated with schizophrenic episodes. The diathesis-stress hypothesis argues that the development of schizophrenia involves an interaction between genetic and environmental factors; it states that certain environmental stressors are more likely to contribute to the development of schizophrenia in individuals who have a predisposition toward schizophrenia than in those who do not have a predisposition.

Somatoform Disorders

All somatoform disorders involve problems in which one experiences physical symptoms that have no physiological or biological basis. Rather, psychological problems take on a physical form for which no biological cause exists.

Hypochondriasis is a disorder in which individuals display an extreme preoccupation with their health and a constant fear of illness. Despite medical evidence to the contrary, people who suffer from hypochondriasis continue to believe they are ill and might go as far as to doctor shop (seeking multiple medical opinions) or create factitious disorders.

Conversion disorder involves an actual physical disturbance or problem, but the cause of the problem is purely psychological. With conversion disorder, an individual might suddenly lose a particular body function (for example, eyesight, use of arm) without any underlying physiological cause, and then just as suddenly regain the function.

Dissociative Disorders

All dissociative disorders are characterized by the fragmentation of experience, memory, or consciousness and involve a number of related disorders (including dissociative amnesia, dissociative fugue, depersonalization disorder and dissociative identity disorder).

Dissociative amnesia involves memory loss that is typically highly selective (for example, not being able to recall one's own name, not recognizing loved ones, not remembering one's address). Though such individuals are unable to recall certain facts about themselves, in all other respects they generally appear normal, maintaining memories for previously learned skills and abilities.

Dissociative fugue is a form of amnesia in which one forgets who they are, wanders from home and starts a completely new life. In dissociative fugue, people flee from their usual environment and assume a completely new identity without any awareness of their past life.

Depersonalization disorder involves a separation of mind and body in which individuals experience episodes of feeling detached from their body.

Dissociative identity disorder, formerly known as multiple personality disorder, occurs when two or more distinct personalities develop in one individual. Each personality has unique memories, behaviors and social relationships, and the personalities might even be a different sex, race or age than the original personality.

Personality Disorders

Personality disorders are characterized by long-standing, inflexible and maladaptive behavior patterns that cause an individual or society impairment or distress. Several disorders fall under this classification:

- **Narcissistic:** The major characteristic is an exaggerated sense of self-importance.
- **Antisocial:** This disorder involves a chronic pattern of self-centered, manipulative and destructive behavior toward others. Individuals lack a sense of responsibility and feel little personal distress, but bring considerable harm and suffering to others.
- **Paranoid:** This disorder is characterized by suspicious, mistrustful, secretive and jealous behavior.
- **Borderline:** This disorder is characterized by instability of self-image, mood, and social relationships and an unstable and poorly defined identity. Individuals typically experience extreme difficulties in relationships and engage in destructive, impulsive behaviors. They are prone to chronic feelings of depression, emptiness, and intense fear of abandonment and are a high suicide risk group.
- **Dependent:** This disorder is characterized by extreme dependence on others, submissive and clingy behavior, difficulty making decisions, and helplessness.

Review Questions

1. When an individual's behavior interferes with their ability to carry out normal activities of daily life, their behavior is said to be:

    A. irrational
    B. unpredictable
    C. dangerous
    D. maladaptive
    E. unconventional

2. Dr. Lynn believes that abnormal behavior is most likely to reflect severe deprivation of needs such as lack of acceptance, lack of love and lack of positive regard by others. Dr. Lynn's belief is consistent with the _____ perspective of psychopathology.

    A. psychoanalytic
    B. sociocultural
    C. cognitive
    D. behavioral
    E. humanistic

3. If one believes that abnormal behavior is most frequently the result of abnormal brain function and, thus, should be treated with drugs, they are adhering to the _____ perspective.

    A. behavioral
    B. biological
    C. cognitive
    D. sociocultural
    E. psychoanalytic

4. A cognitive psychologist is most likely to attribute abnormal behavior to:

   A. poor learning experiences
   B. irrational and faulty thought patterns
   C. impoverished environments
   D. unresolved conflicts and/or desires
   E. extreme criticism by others

5. Axis V of the DSM-IV provides details for assessing:

   A. the presence of serious clinical conditions
   B. the presence of underlying medical conditions
   C. the presence of personality disorders
   D. the possibility of mental retardation
   E. one's overall level of functioning

6. Jackie has developed such a fear of social situations that she cannot bear to leave her house or answer the telephone for fear of having to speak to another person. Jackie's problems are most reflective of:

   A. bipolar disorder
   B. phobic disorder
   C. obsessive-compulsive disorder
   D. paranoid schizophrenia
   E. panic disorder

7. Janice has been making frequent statements reflecting hopelessness and despair, and states that she doesn't even want to get out of bed. Her friend notes that three weeks earlier, Janice was overly happy, hyperactive, and had made elaborate and excited plans about her future. Her friend is concerned that Janice might be suffering from:

   A. bipolar disorder
   B. unipolar disorder
   C. narcissistic personality disorder
   D. obsessive-compulsive disorder
   E. undifferentiated schizophrenia

8. Dissociative identity disorder differs from dissociative fugue in that individuals with dissociative identity disorder:

   A. completely forget who they are
   B. replace their old personality with a new personality
   C. flee from their normal environment
   D. develop more than one personality
   E. cannot remember their past at all

Answers

1. D. Maladaptive behavior disrupts daily life and normal functioning. Irrational behavior implies impaired thinking and decision making. Unpredictable behavior fluctuates for no apparent reason or is inappropriate given the situation. Unconventional behavior violates societal norms.

2. E. Humanistic theories focus on an individual's needs and goals in addition to their self-concept. Psychoanalysts focus on childhood experiences and unconscious drives and conflicts. Sociocultural psychologists look to the influence of societal and cultural values, beliefs and norms in explaining abnormal behavior. Cognitive theorists believe that faulty and illogical thought patterns contribute to abnormal behavior. Behaviorists argue that poor conditioning, negative experiences and poor role models contribute to abnormal behavior.

3. B. Biological theories look to genetic and physiological influences in explaining abnormal behavior. Treatments appropriate to this perspective are drugs, surgery and other physiological treatments. Behaviorists argue that external factors such as environmental experiences and conditions contribute to abnormal behavior. Cognitive psychologists believe that irrational, illogical and faulty thought patterns contribute to abnormal behavior.

4. B. Cognitive psychologists believe that irrational and faulty thought patterns are important influences on behavior. Behaviorists emphasize poor learning experiences in explaining abnormal behavior. Psychoanalysts look to unresolved conflicts and/or desires as key factors influencing abnormal behavior. Humanistic psychologists argue that abnormal behavior results from extreme criticism by others.

5. E. Axis V of the DSM-IV assesses the overall level of functioning of an individual. Axis I tests for the presence of clinical conditions. Axis II denotes the presence of mental retardation and personality disorders. Axis III tests for underlying medical conditions. Axis IV assesses psychosocial and environmental stressors.

6. B. Phobic disorder is marked by irrational fear and avoidance of some external object or stimulus. Bipolar disorder is characterized by extreme mood fluctuations. Obsessive-compulsive disorder is marked by obsessive thoughts and compulsive behaviors. Paranoid schizophrenia is a psychotic disorder with prevailing symptoms of hallucinations and delusions of persecution. Panic disorder involves sudden rushes of intense fear and anxiety for no apparent reason.

7. A. Bipolar disorder involves extreme mood fluctuations ranging from extreme despair and hopelessness to extreme elation and hyperactivity. Narcissistic personality disorder is marked by an inflated sense of self-importance. Obsessive-compulsive disorder involves obsessive thoughts that create anxiety and compulsive behaviors employed to reduce the anxiety. Undifferentiated schizophrenia is a psychotic disorder involving breaks from reality and several additional symptoms including hallucinations, delusions and erratic behavior.

8. D. Dissociative identity disorder, formerly known as multiple personality disorder, involves the development of two or more distinct personalities in one individual. Dissociative fugue involves amnesia concerning one's identity, fleeing from one's home and assuming a completely new identity in a new environment.

Treatment of Psychological Disorders

Psychotherapy, in general, refers to a variety of methods used to treat emotional and behavioral disorders. This chapter reviews a number of different therapeutic approaches including psychodynamic, humanistic, behavioral, cognitive and biological approaches to therapy. It also addresses various modes of therapy including individual, group and family therapy. The chapter ends with a brief review of the role of community psychologists in preventing and treating mental disorders.

Treatment Approaches

Insight therapies refer to a number of specific therapies that all strive for increased self-understanding of one's thoughts, emotions, behaviors and motives. Both psychodynamic and humanistic approaches fall under the broader heading of insight therapies.

Psychodynamic Therapies

Psychodynamic therapy, also known as **psychoanalysis,** focuses on two key areas:

- Searching for the unconscious roots or motives of an individual's problem
- Uncovering early childhood experiences that might have contributed to unconscious conflicts and problems

Psychoanalysts utilize a variety of techniques to uncover unconscious motives and early childhood experiences that might drive behavior. One such technique is **free association** in which the patient is asked to share thoughts and feelings as they come to mind. The therapist listens to the patient's free flow of thoughts, paying particular attention to key patterns of thoughts and feelings and nonverbal behaviors. The therapist then assists the patient in gaining insight into the thoughts, experiences and behaviors underlying their problem. Another technique used by psychoanalysts is **dream analysis,** which involves analyzing dreams for their hidden meaning. **Sigmund Freud,** the founder of dream analysis, distinguished between the manifest and the latent content of dreams. The **manifest content** refers to the actual content of the dream (what we recollect about the dream). The **latent content** is the dream's underlying meaning (what the dream *really* means). Thus, dream analysis involves analyzing dreams for their latent content.

Humanistic Therapies

The primary goal of all humanistic therapies is to provide an open and trusting environment in which an individual can discover and cultivate their true self. The most frequently used humanistic therapy is **client-centered therapy,** developed by **Carl Rogers.** Rogers believed that all humans are striving for growth and fulfillment, and that psychological problems result when one's drive toward growth and fulfillment is blocked by others or oneself. According to Rogers, one's perception of self, one's perception of reality and the way one is treated by others are important factors influencing psychological well-being. Specifically, a negative perception of oneself and/or large discrepancies between one's perception of self and actual experiences contributes to psychological disorders. In addition, conditional positive regard, love and affection that is provided only when an individual meets the expectations of another, contributes to psychological problems and disorders. Thus, Roger's client-centered therapy focuses on providing the patient with empathy, unconditional positive regard, and an open and trustworthy environment in which the patient can reflect on who they are and develop their true self.

Another humanistic approach is **Gestalt therapy,** developed by **Fritz Perls.** Gestalt therapy emphasizes the need for clients to fully acknowledge and experience their feelings and thoughts and to become more self-aware and self-accepting. Gestalt therapy focuses more on recognizing *how* one feels than *why* one feels that way. Most importantly, Gestalt therapists emphasize that one become aware of feelings that he/she has disowned or disregarded and accept only those feelings that are their own. One popular Gestalt technique is the **empty-chair technique** in which the patient sits in front of an empty chair and imagines that the person to whom they need to express their feelings is in the chair. The patient then expresses their feelings to the person as though the person were there. Other techniques involve imaginary conversations with oneself or others to foster awareness of feelings.

Behavioral Therapies

Behavioral therapies rely on learning principles to eliminate or extinguish maladaptive behaviors and replace them with more adaptive behaviors. Most behavioral therapies begin the therapeutic process by conducting a **behavioral analysis,** a careful examination of the problem behavior and the stimuli associated with the behavior. The information gained from the behavioral analysis is used to tailor the therapeutic process to the specific behavior and associated stimuli. Behavioral therapists have a multitude of techniques available to treat psychological disorders and behavioral problems. Some techniques are based on operant conditioning; other techniques are based on classical conditioning.

Behavior modification is a general technique that attempts to eliminate inappropriate behaviors and replace them with more adaptive behaviors by controlling the consequences that follow the behavior (for example, reinforcing a desirable behavior to increase its frequency and extinguishing undesirable behavior by withholding reinforcement). **Token economies** are a variant of behavior modification in which appropriate behaviors are rewarded with tokens (for example, stars, poker chips) that can be exchanged at a later time for activities or objects that are desired by the individual. Another technique sometimes used to eliminate undesirable behaviors is **timeout.** In timeout, individuals are removed from a desired situation or activity and must spend a period of time in an area without any reinforcers.

A number of additional behavioral therapies rely on principles of classical conditioning. One such technique is **systematic desensitization,** a therapeutic technique typically used to treat phobic disorders. In systematic desensitization, patients first undergo relaxation training. They are then gradually exposed to the object or situation they fear over a series of trials while employing the relaxation technique. Another technique, **flooding,** involves exposing patients to the object or situation they fear instantly and all at once for an extended period of time until their anxiety decreases. **Aversion therapy** involves pairing an undesirable behavior with an unpleasant or painful stimulus over repeated trials until the behavior becomes associated with discomfort and the person begins to avoid the behavior.

Cognitive Therapies

Based on the cognitive perspective, cognitive therapies assume that irrational and maladaptive thought patterns and beliefs contribute to psychological disorders. Thus, the goal of all cognitive therapies is to change dysfunctional thought patterns. Two popular cognitive therapies are **Albert Ellis's** rational-emotive therapy (**RET**) and **Aaron Beck's** cognitive-behavior therapy (**CBT**).

According to Ellis, **irrational beliefs** elicited by events in one's life are the underlying causes of emotional distress. Ellis proposed the **ABCDE model** as a framework for RET. In his model, A refers to the activating event, B to beliefs elicited by the event, and C to the emotional and behavioral consequences that result from the beliefs. Ellis goes on to argue that, at step B, the beliefs that arise can be rational or irrational. If beliefs are rational, they are likely to result in moderate emotions that enable one to act constructively and to achieve their goals. If the beliefs are irrational (which often include *musts* and *shoulds*), disturbed emotions such as anger, anxiety and depression can result and impair behavior and performance. According to Ellis, irrational beliefs often include *musts* and *shoulds,* such as I must look good at all times, or I must always excel in everything that I do.

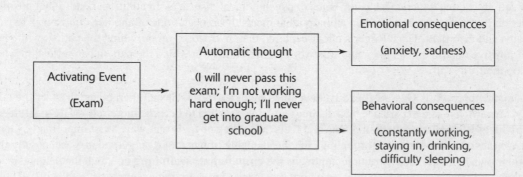

The ultimate goal of RET is to increase a client's awareness of their irrational thought patterns and beliefs, dispute or challenge those beliefs, and replace irrational beliefs with more adaptive thought patterns. The therapeutic process is represented in steps D and E in the model. D refers to the process of disputing or challenging beliefs. E refers to the process of replacing irrational and maladaptive thought patterns with more rational beliefs. In the final step, the therapist works with the client to establish a more balanced and productive way of thinking.

Like RET, CBT focuses on replacing maladaptive thought patterns with more adaptive thoughts. CBT focuses on **automatic thoughts** as the culprit in psychological disorders. According to Beck, automatic thoughts can be negative or positive. When automatic thoughts are negative or pessimistic, individuals might fall prey to anxiety, depression, and other emotional and behavioral problems. The goal of CBT is to break the cycle of negative thoughts by assisting clients in identifying negative self-talk; refuting the negative thoughts; and replacing them with more rational, accurate and positive thoughts. In CBT, clients are taught **self-monitoring** techniques in which they keep track of their automatic thoughts and the situations that produce them. They are also taught **thought-catching** techniques to recognize negative thoughts when they occur and evaluate the thoughts for their accuracy and validity. Finally, individuals are assisted in a process of **cognitive restructuring** in which they modify their thoughts to elicit more adaptive thought patterns.

Biological Therapies

Biological therapies are therapies that focus on biological and physiological factors that might underlie behavioral and psychological disorders. **Electroconvulsive therapy** (ECT) is a biological therapy in which high-voltage waves of electricity are passed through the brain. ECT is primarily used to treat severe depression that is unresponsive to drug treatments. Though ECT can be effective, its benefits must be weighed against its side effects. Potential side effects of ECT include memory loss (especially for events directly preceding the shock), speech disorders, bone fractures during convulsions, and cardiac arrest. **Psychosurgery** is another biological therapy in which parts of the brain are removed or disconnected. The **prefrontal lobotomy,** in which connections between the frontal lobe and other portions of the brain are severed, is a form of psychosurgery. Though a popular technique in the early 1900s, especially with patients who were highly aggressive, the prefrontal lobotomy is no longer performed.

Psychopharmacology involves the use of drugs to treat behavioral and psychological disorders. Drugs that exert effects on the brain and behavior are called psychotropic drugs. The three broad classes of psychotropic drugs are antidepressants, antipsychotics and antianxiety drugs. **Antidepressants** are used primarily to treat mood disorders. The three types of antidepressant drugs are monoamine oxidase inhibitors (MAOIs), selective reuptake inhibitors (SRIs) and tricyclics. All three drugs serve to reduce the symptoms of depression by increasing the amount of serotonin and norepinephrine in the brain. MAOIs exert their effects by inhibiting the function of monoamine oxidase, which serves to break down serotonin and norepinephrine following their reuptake from the synaptic cleft. SRIs exert their effects by blocking the reuptake of serotonin following its release into the synaptic cleft, leaving it active for a longer period of time. **Antipsychotics, also known as neuroleptics,** are drugs used primarily to reduce the symptoms of schizophrenia. Most antipsychotic drugs exert their effects by blocking dopamine receptors in the brain. Examples of antipsychotic drugs include Haldol and Thorazine. **Antianxiety drugs,** also known as anxiolytics, serve to reduce anxiety, reduce insomnia and/or increase positive feelings of well-being. Two general types of anxiolytics are barbiturates and benzodiazapenes.

Other Modes of Therapy

The therapeutic approaches discussed thus far all reflect individual therapy in which a therapist works with an individual client to overcome a problem. Other modes of therapy include others in the therapeutic process (for example, family or others who are experiencing similar problems). **Group therapy** is a form of therapy in which several clients meet together with one or more therapists to work on issues and problems together. Group therapy can be beneficial for some clients as it provides opportunities to receive feedback and support from others who might be experiencing similar problems. Group therapy can also help people to see that they are not alone in their problems. A variant of group therapy is self-help groups. **Self-help groups** are made up of people who share a common problem (for example, substance abuse) and involve regular meetings in which individuals both give and receive support. **Family therapy** is a form of therapy that involves working with an entire family. The goal of family therapy is to assist family members in communicating with one another and developing a better understanding of each family member's needs and desires.

Community psychologists are psychologists who work within the community and are focused on the prevention of mental illness in the population as a whole. Community psychologists provide varying levels of prevention and intervention services within the community. **Primary prevention** focuses on preventing the emergence of disorders before they have appeared. **Secondary prevention** focuses on early detection of problems and timely intervention to reduce the incidence of full-blown mental disorders. **Tertiary prevention** involves the treatment of existing disorders to lessen the impact of the disorder and/or prevent the disorder from becoming worse.

Review Questions

1. Free association and dream analysis are techniques associated with:

   A. client-centered therapy

   B. CBT

   C. Gestalt therapy

   D. psychoanalysis

   E. RET

2. Empathy and unconditional positive regard are key elements in:

   A. CBT

   B. RET

   C. client-centered therapy

   D. behavior therapy

   E. aversion therapy

3. Dr. Jones put an empty chair in front of his patient, Julie. He then instructed her to pretend that her father was in the chair and to express her feelings to her father. Dr. Jones is utilizing a technique commonly used in:

   A. systematic desensitization

   B. flooding

   C. RET

   D. free association

   E. Gestalt therapy

4. Five-year-old Jason receives a star on his behavior chart every time he cleans up his toys. As the stars add up, Jason can choose to exchange his stars for other desired objects and activities such as a trip to the video arcade, a bowl of ice cream and even a new toy. Jason's parents are utilizing a therapeutic technique known as a(n) _____ to foster appropriate behavior in Jason.

   A. token economy

   B. timeout

   C. systematic desensitization

   D. flooding

   E. aversion therapy

5. When an individual is gradually exposed to a feared stimulus while employing relaxation techniques to reduce anxiety, _____ is being used.

   A. flooding

   B. systematic desensitization

   C. behavior modification

   D. timeout

   E. psychoanalysis

6. RET and CBT are both based on the notion that _____ underlie(s) most psychological and behavioral problems.

    A. physiological problems
    B. unconscious conflicts
    C. dysfunctional thought patterns
    D. conditional positive regard
    E. negative environmental stimuli

7. MAOIs and SRIs are types of:

    A. antidepressants
    B. antipsychotics
    C. benzodiazapenes
    D. barbiturates
    E. anxiolytics

8. A community psychologist focuses her efforts on preventing the incidence of mental disorders in the general population. Her work is reflective of:

    A. group therapy
    B. primary prevention
    C. tertiary prevention
    D. secondary prevention
    E. comprehensive prevention

Answers

1. **D.** Free association and dream analysis are psychoanalytic techniques used to uncover unconscious forces and conflicts underlying psychological and behavioral problems. In free association, the therapist listens to the patient's free flow of thoughts in an attempt to gain insight into unconscious drives. In dream analysis, the therapist assists the patient in analyzing the latent content, or hidden meanings, of their dreams.

2. **C.** Empathy and unconditional positive regard are key elements of client-centered therapy. Taking a humanistic approach, client-centered therapy is aimed at providing an open and trusting environment in which patients can reflect on, discover and develop their true self.

3. **E.** Gestalt therapy is a technique that focuses on acknowledging and experiencing one's thoughts and feelings. The empty-chair technique is a specific type of Gestalt therapy used to help a person acknowledge and experience their feelings in a safe environment. Free association is a psychoanalytic technique in which an individual shares thoughts and feelings as they come to mind. Flooding and systematic desensitization are behavioral techniques used to help patients overcome fears. RET is a cognitive therapy aimed at pointing out and changing dysfunctional thought patterns.

4. **A.** Jason's parents are using a token economy in which tokens are provided for appropriate behavior and can be exchanged at a later time for real reinforcers. All the other options listed are techniques designed to eliminate maladaptive or inappropriate behaviors. Timeout involves removing an individual from a desired situation or activity as a result of inappropriate behavior. Systematic desensitization involves gradually exposing an individual to a feared stimulus while employing relaxation techniques. Flooding involves immersing an individual in a feared stimulus instantly and over a period of time until their anxiety wanes. Aversion therapy involves pairing an undesirable behavior with an unpleasant stimulus so that the individual later avoids the behavior to avoid the painful stimulus.

117

5. **B.** Systematic desensitization involves gradually exposing an individual to a feared stimulus while employing relaxation techniques. It is a behavioral technique designed to help an individual overcome irrational fears. In contrast, flooding involves immersing a patient in the feared stimulus instantly and over a period of time until their anxiety wanes. Behavior modification and timeout are techniques aimed at fostering appropriate behaviors and eliminating inappropriate behaviors by manipulating the consequences that follow behaviors.

6. **C.** RET and CBT are both cognitive therapies based on the notion that dysfunctional thought patterns contribute to psychological and behavioral problems. RET focuses on identifying and disputing irrational thought patterns. CBT focuses on identifying automatic negative thoughts and establishing more adaptive ways of thinking.

7. **A.** MAOIs and SRIs are types of antidepressant drugs. Both MAOIs and SRIs exert their effects by altering the functioning of the neurotransmitter serotonin in the brain. An abnormally low level of serotonin has been implicated as a potential contributor to depressive symptoms. MAOIs and SRIs serve to enhance levels of serotonin in the brain.

8. **B.** Primary prevention refers to efforts aimed at preventing the incidence or emergence of disorders in the general population. Secondary prevention refers to efforts aimed at individuals at risk for psychological disorders. Tertiary prevention refers to efforts aimed at reducing the impact of existing disorders on individuals.

Social Psychology

Social psychology is a field of psychology that studies how thought, behavior and emotion are influenced by social factors. A basic assumption of social psychology is that the immediate social context plays an important role in human behavior. This assumption is often referred to as **situationism.** Social psychologists point to the importance of social roles and social norms in guiding much of our behavior and argue that humans often change their behavior to coincide with the social norms for a given situation. Thus, one focus of social psychology is to understand behavior in its social context. Social psychologists also believe that humans behave differently when in the presence of others than when alone. According to social psychologists, the mere presence of others can lead to drastic changes in behavior, especially when an individual is embedded within a large group. Thus, a second focus of social psychology is to understand group processes and phenomena. Finally, social psychologists also believe that we are influenced by and in turn influence others in important ways throughout our lives. So, a final area of interest for social psychologists concerns interpersonal relationships and processes.

This chapter reviews each of these areas in turn. It begins with a review of group processes and phenomena that occur when individuals are put into groups to work on tasks and make decisions. It then considers the reasons people choose to help or not to help others. The third part of the chapter addresses the factors involved in forming opinions and making judgments of others as well as the factors influencing the formation of relationships with others. It then turns to a review of classic studies examining conformity and obedience. The chapter ends with a brief review of research on attitudes and attitudinal change.

Group Dynamics

Social psychologists are interested in group dynamics and the way individual behavior changes when one is in the presence of others. **Social facilitation** occurs when the presence of others increases or improves one's performance on a task. An opposite effect is **social inhibition,** which occurs when the presence of others leads to poorer performance on a task. Social facilitation is most likely to occur when a task is easy or familiar, whereas social inhibition is more likely when a task is difficult or unfamiliar. We see additional processes when individuals must work on a task with others. **Social loafing** refers to the tendency of group members to reduce their effort on a task when many individuals are working on the task. Social loafing is most likely to occur in instances in which individual performance is not evaluated and when rewards for group effort are divided equally among group members rather than according to individual effort.

Additional phenomena are seen when individuals are put into groups to make decisions. **Group polarization** refers to the tendency of group decisions to be more extreme than decisions made by individual members. **Groupthink** refers to the tendency of groups to strive for consensus and unanimity to such an extent that they no longer evaluate the consequences or implications of their decisions. Groupthink is most likely to occur when a group is isolated from outsiders, has a charismatic leader, is highly homogenous and is feeling pressured to make a decision.

Helping Behavior

Why do individuals help others? Do we help others out of altruistic motives (to benefit a person other than oneself) or out of egoistic and self-centered motives (to feel better about ourselves)? According to the **self-centered helping model,** when we see a person in need, it creates a degree of personal distress. We are motivated to help the person to reduce our own distress. This model also recognizes that some people help to derive a sense of satisfaction, or a *helper's high.* According to the **altruistic helping model,** we are motivated to help others out of a desire to relieve their distress. We help out of a true concern for others and a desire to benefit others. The top portion of the following figure illustrates the self-centered helping model, whereas the bottom portion of the figure illustrates the altruistic helping model.

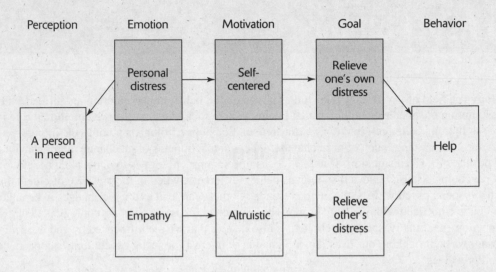

Why do individuals fail to help others in need of assistance? Back in March of 1964 in Queens, New York, a young lady named Kitty Genovese was attacked outside her apartment complex. A number of neighbors heard her screams, looked out the window and even saw her struggling with the attacker. Yet, not a single person went to her aid, and only one person called the police—not until the attacker was gone. In the end, Kitty died. Social psychologists were fascinated by the lack of assistance provided by Kitty's neighbors! What could have happened? Why did no one help? In follow-up interviews with the neighbors, it was discovered that most of them had assumed someone else had called the police. This phenomenon is known as **diffusion of responsibility,** the tendency of individuals to feel less responsible for taking action when others are present who can also help. As the number of individuals present increases, diffusion of responsibility becomes more likely.

Social Cognition

A major area of interest for social psychologists concerns how we make judgments of others and how we explain others' behavior. This area of interest is generally referred to as **social cognition.** The earliest work in this area focused on **impression formation,** how individuals from opinions of others. Social psychologists have found that when forming overall impressions of others, individuals typically base their judgments on a few key traits, called **central traits.** Central traits often influence additional judgments of others. For example, research has shown that individuals tend to assume that people who are physically attractive also possess a number of additional favorable qualities. This tendency to assume that positive qualities cluster together is known as the **halo effect.**

Research also indicates that individuals form social **schemas,** mental categories that represent various types of people and social experiences. Social schemas guide the way in which we process and evaluate information about others, and what we remember about others and the social situations we encounter. In fact, research finds that when asked about certain people or events, individuals are most likely to recall **schema-relevant information,** those behaviors and characteristics that are congruent with a particular schema. For example, if one reads a paragraph about a librarian and is asked one week later what they remember about the librarian, they are most likely to remember information that falls into their schema of a librarian. When schemas are applied automatically and/or rigidly, stereotypes can result.

Attitudes and Attitude Change

Attitudes refer to evaluations of a particular person, behavior, belief or object. Attitudes typically have an *affective* component consisting of the emotions aroused by a stimulus, and a *cognitive* component consisting of the thoughts and evaluations of a stimulus. In addition, attitudes also have a behavioral component consisting of behaviors reflective of them. The three components of attitudes are reflected in stereotypes, prejudice, and discrimination. **Stereotypes** refer to characteristics attributed to a person based on that person's association with a particular group. Related to stereotypes is the issue of **prejudice,** prejudgment of others based on stereotypes. Prejudice often underlies **discrimination,** behaviors directed at members of a group following negative evaluations.

Social psychologists have also examined the tendency of humans to make **ingroup-outgroup distinctions,** distinctions between members of groups to which one belongs (ingroup) and members of groups to which one does *not* belong (outgroup). Research has found that such distinctions can lead individuals to interpret others' behavior based on their ingroup-outgroup status (usually favoring the ingroup and denigrating the outgroup) and can also contribute to prejudice and discrimination. Ultimately, in-group/out-group distinctions contribute to **ethnocentrism** in which one views the group to which they belong more favorably than other groups.

Persuasion and Attitude Change

Persuasion refers to the process of trying to change one's attitudes or beliefs. One's ability to persuade another is dependent on a number of factors including the source of the message, the nature of the message and the characteristics of the individual one is trying to persuade. People in positions of authority and people who are experts are typically more persuasive than people who are not authorities or experts. In addition, individuals who are attractive and trustworthy are more persuasive than those who are unattractive or untrustworthy. The choice of how to present the message also influences its persuasiveness. Some messages utilize fear in an attempt to change attitudes. For example, campaigns aimed at changing people's attitudes about smoking might incorporate pictures of lungs blackened from years of smoking or images of individuals dying of lung cancer. Lastly, characteristics of the individual one is trying to persuade also influence the ease with which the message leads to attitudinal change. Typically, individuals with high self-esteem and individuals of high intelligence are less easily persuaded than those with low self-esteem or of lower intelligence.

Social psychologists have identified two types of processing engaged in by individuals evaluating persuasive messages: central-route processing and peripheral-route processing. **Central-route processing** focuses heavily on the nature of the message being presented and involves a thoughtful consideration of the arguments and issues presented. It involves conscious and deliberate processing of the arguments and issues presented. **Peripheral-route processing** focuses on factors unrelated to the actual message, such as characteristics of the person delivering the message and the length of the argument. Although both types of processing can lead to attitude change, central-route processing generally leads to a more lasting attitude change.

Leon Festinger (1957) suggested that attitude change is likely to occur when individuals experience **cognitive dissonance,** a conflict or discrepancy between two contradictory attitudes or thoughts. According to Festinger, cognitive dissonance creates a state of tension and unease. This unpleasant state motivates individuals to change their attitude or behavior to achieve cognitive consistency.

Daryl Bem (1967) proposed the **self-perception theory** in which he argues that often individuals are unsure of their attitudes. When this occurs, they look to their own behavior in certain circumstances and infer from their behavior what their attitude must be.

Attribution Processes

Attribution theory seeks to identify the way humans explain the causes of others' behavior. According to attribution theory, we interpret the cause of others' behavior based on several factors. **Fritz Heider** (1958) distinguished between situational and dispositional attributions for behavior. **Situational attributions** ascribe behavior to environmental or external causes. (For example, he yelled at that woman because she provoked him.) **Dispositional attributions** ascribe behavior to internal personality traits or characteristics. (For example, he yelled at that woman because he is a mean person.)

Psychologists have found that humans are prone to two particular biases (or errors) when evaluating behavior. The fundamental attribution error involves the tendency to attribute behavior more to dispositional factors and somewhat overlook the situational factors that might have influenced the behavior. The **fundamental attribution error** leads us to blame others for their behavior and contributes to blame-the-victim thinking in which we view victims of certain events and crimes as somehow responsible for what has happened to them. (For example, a person is homeless, and we view them as lazy rather than a victim of circumstances.) The **self-serving bias** occurs when we evaluate our own behavior and involves a tendency to attribute our successes and positive behaviors to dispositional factors, and to attribute our failures and negative behaviors to situational factors. Ultimately, the self-serving bias leads one to see themselves in a more positive light than others.

Interpersonal Perception

Social psychologists are interested in interpersonal attraction and the formation of friendships and romantic relationships among humans. Psychologists have identified several factors that influence the formation of relationships. **Physical attractiveness** is one of the most important factors influencing our initial attraction to another individual. Individuals are more likely to want to form a relationship with an attractive individual than with an unattractive individual. **Similarity** is another deciding factor in the formation of relationships. Research finds that individuals have a tendency to select as friends and partners those who are similar to themselves with respect to attractiveness, attitudes, beliefs and values. This finding is also referred to as the **matching principle.** The formation of relationships also depends on **physical proximity** or geographic location. The **mere exposure effect** refers to the tendency of an attraction to a stimulus to increase as exposure to that stimulus increases. **Self-disclosure** and intimacy are also important in forming relationships. When an individual discloses personal information, closeness tends to increase, and the relationship is more likely to be maintained (as long as that disclosure is reciprocated).

A number of theories have been proposed to explain the formation and maintenance of relationships among individuals. **Reward theory** argues that individuals judge relationships based on the costs and benefits associated with the relationship. According to reward theory, we like those who provide maximum rewards at minimum cost the best. Moreover, if the costs exceed the rewards, we might choose to discontinue the relationship. **Exchange theory** argues that we seek reciprocity and equality in relationships. According to this theory, if one feels that they are giving more than their partner, they are likely to become disappointed and frustrated with the relationship and might choose to discontinue the relationship.

Conformity and Obedience

Social psychologists are also interested in social influence (how individuals influence the behavior of others). Psychologists recognize that the degree of social influence/pressure put on an individual and the nature of the behavioral response can range from conformity at the low end of social pressure to obedience at the high end of social pressure.

Conformity refers to the alteration of one's behavior to match that of a group. **Solomon Asch** performed a series of classic studies examining the tendency of individuals to conform to group judgments. Individuals were told they were participating in a study on perceptual judgments. Participants were seated around a table with six other individuals. The group was then shown two cards, one with 3 lines of varying lengths labeled A, B and C and another with just 1 line. The task was for participants to indicate which line (A, B or C) was similar in length to the line on the other card. The task was designed in such a way that the correct answer was always obvious.

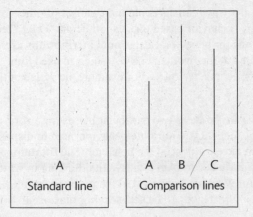

Each participant was to state their answer out loud in turn around the table. What the participants didn't know was that the other six individuals were confederates of the experimenter and were instructed to answer incorrectly on certain trials. The confederates were arranged around the table so that the real participant was always the last to answer. The key question was whether participants would conform to the group's incorrect answer or stick with their own conviction. Findings revealed that more than one-third of the participants conformed to the group's obviously incorrect answer! In follow-up studies, Asch went on to identify factors that influence conformity. Some of these factors include the size of the group (the larger the group, the more likely individuals are to conform), the cohesiveness of the group (the more cohesive the group, the more likely individuals are to conform) and the unanimity of the group (the more unanimous the group is in their answers, the more likely individuals are to conform). In fact, a person is much less likely to conform if just one other person in the group does not conform.

Obedience involves doing something because one is told to or commanded to by another individual. **Stanley Milgram** discovered that individuals sometimes obey commands to hurt an authority figure, even when they know what they are doing is wrong! In an experiment, Milgram told individuals they would be participating in a study examining the effects of punishment on learning and that they would be playing the role of the *teacher* in the study. Participants were then introduced to a man they believed was another participant who would play the role of the *learner* in the study. The learner was actually a confederate of the experimenter and had been instructed to behave in certain ways. The teacher watched as the learner was hooked up to an electric shock machine. The teacher was then placed in front of a shock generator with switches marked sequentially from 15 to 450 volts and labeled Slight Shock, Danger: Severe Shock, XXX and so on. The teacher was then instructed to give a series of questions to the learner. Whenever the learner answered incorrectly, the teacher was to deliver an electric shock. For each incorrect response given, the teacher was to increase the electric shock by 15 volts. As the experiment continued, the learner began to make multiple mistakes, and the teacher was faced with the issue of obeying the experimenter's command to shock the learner. It is important to note that although the teacher was led to believe that they were shocking the learner, at no time was the learner actually shocked.

Did the participants obey the experimenter and shock the individual? Milgram's original study consisted of 40 participants. All 40 participants administered shocks up to 300 volts, and only 5 of the 40 refused to continue beyond this point. Of the 40 participants, 26 (65%) continued beyond the Danger: Severe Shock switch to the maximum voltage of 450 volts. How could individuals do this? What leads someone to obey a request to hurt another individual? Could it be that the participants in the study were sadistic or flawed in some way? Not likely. Personality tests taken prior to the study found that personality traits and characteristics were unrelated to obedience in the Milgram study. In fact, follow-up studies found that situational factors (for example, whether the experimenter was an authority figure, whether the experimenter was physically present, whether the learner could physically see the teacher) were better predictors of obedience than any internal personality trait or characteristic.

Review Questions

1. Group polarization occurs when group members:

   A. become more extreme in their views
   B. assume that others will take action
   C. fail to evaluate the implications of their decisions
   D. hold extremely conflicting opinions
   E. view outsiders as different from themselves

2. The failure of Kitty Genovese's neighbors to help her because they believed someone else would help is an example of:

   A. groupthink
   B. deindividuation
   C. diffusion of responsibility
   D. conformity
   E. group polarization

3. When members of a large group reduce their efforts on a task, _____ is at play.

   A. social inhibition
   B. social facilitation
   C. social loafing
   D. diffusion of responsibility
   E. group polarization

4. When the presence of others improves one's performance on a task, it is called:

   A. diffusion of responsibility
   B. social facilitation
   C. group polarization
   D. social loafing
   E. social inhibition

5. Karen's friend just aced her psychology test. If Karen makes a dispositional attribution for her friend's behavior, she is likely to argue that:

   A. The test must have been very easy.
   B. The teacher must have curved the grades.
   C. Her friend must have cheated on the test.
   D. Her friend was lucky that day.
   E. Her friend is a very smart girl.

6. According to exchange theory, we seek out:

   A. partners who are similar to us
   B. partners who are different from us
   C. relationships where the benefits outweigh the costs
   D. relationships where the costs outweigh the benefits
   E. equality and reciprocity in relationships with others

7. The name to associate with famous studies on conformity is:

   A. Kitty Genovese
   B. Solomon Asch
   C. Stanley Milgram
   D. Leon Festinger
   E. Fritz Heider

8. Leon is listening to a talk on the reasons the United States should not go to war. If Leon is engaged in central-route processing, he is focusing on the:

   A. attractiveness of the speaker
   B. length of the argument
   C. specific issues presented by the speaker
   D. gender of the speaker
   E. clothing of the speaker

Answers

1. **A.** Group polarization refers to the tendency for groups to make more extreme decisions than those made by individuals. When groups fail to evaluate the implications of their decisions, groupthink is at play. When individuals are in the presence of others and assume that others will take action, diffusion of responsibility is at play.

2. **C.** When individuals assume that others will help a person in need and, thus, do not offer help themselves, diffusion of responsibility is at play. Diffusion of responsibility refers to the dilution of responsibility to offer help to a person in need when many people are present. Group polarization and groupthink are processes that occur when groups are making decisions. Deindividuation is a phenomenon in which individuals in a crowd feel more conspicuous and, thus, engage in behaviors that they might not engage in if they were alone.

3. **C.** Social loafing occurs when members of a group reduce their efforts on a task. Social facilitation occurs when the presence of others increases or improves one's performance on a task. Social inhibition occurs when the presence of others leads to poorer performance on a task. Group polarization refers to the tendency for group decisions to be more extreme than those made by each member individually. Diffusion of responsibility occurs when the presence of others leads individuals to feel less responsible to help someone in need.

4. **B.** Social facilitation occurs when the presence of others increases or improves one's performance on a task. Social loafing occurs when members of a group reduce their efforts on a task. Social inhibition occurs when the presence of others leads to poorer performance on a task. Group polarization refers to the tendency for group decisions to be more extreme than those made by each member individually. Diffusion of responsibility occurs when the presence of others leads individuals to feel less responsible to help someone in need.

5. **E.** Dispositional attribution involves ascribing behavior to internal personality factors. Thus, in making a dispositional attribution, Karen attributes her friend's good performance on the test as a result of her friend being very smart. All the other options (the test being easy, the teacher curving the grades, her friend possibly cheating or her friend having a lucky day) reflect external causes and therefore represent a situational attribution.

6. **E.** Exchange theory argues that we seek equality and reciprocity in relationships with others. According to this view, unequal contributions result in disappointment and frustration with the relationship. The matching principle argues that we seek partners similar to ourselves. Reward theory argues that we seek relationships in which the benefits outweigh the costs.

7. **B.** Solomon Asch conducted the famous studies on conformity. Stanley Milgram conducted the famous studies on obedience. Leon Festinger proposed cognitive dissonance theory. Fritz Heider distinguished between situational and dispositional attributions. Kitty Genovese is the young woman who was killed outside her apartment with a number of neighbors nearby. Her murder spawned interest in bystander intervention and led to the theories of diffusion of responsibility and the bystander effect.

8. **C.** Central-route processing involves careful consideration of the specific arguments and issues being discussed about a topic. In contrast, peripheral-route processing focuses on factors unrelated to the actual arguments and issues raised by a presenter (such as the length of the argument and characteristics of the speaker). All the other options represent peripheral-route processing.

PART II

PRACTICE EXAMS

Answer Sheet for Practice Test 1

1 (A) (B) (C) (D) (E)		26 (A) (B) (C) (D) (E)	
2 (A) (B) (C) (D) (E)		27 (A) (B) (C) (D) (E)	
3 (A) (B) (C) (D) (E)		28 (A) (B) (C) (D) (E)	
4 (A) (B) (C) (D) (E)		29 (A) (B) (C) (D) (E)	
5 (A) (B) (C) (D) (E)		30 (A) (B) (C) (D) (E)	
6 (A) (B) (C) (D) (E)		31 (A) (B) (C) (D) (E)	
7 (A) (B) (C) (D) (E)		32 (A) (B) (C) (D) (E)	
8 (A) (B) (C) (D) (E)		33 (A) (B) (C) (D) (E)	
9 (A) (B) (C) (D) (E)		34 (A) (B) (C) (D) (E)	
10 (A) (B) (C) (D) (E)		35 (A) (B) (C) (D) (E)	
11 (A) (B) (C) (D) (E)		36 (A) (B) (C) (D) (E)	
12 (A) (B) (C) (D) (E)		37 (A) (B) (C) (D) (E)	
13 (A) (B) (C) (D) (E)		38 (A) (B) (C) (D) (E)	
14 (A) (B) (C) (D) (E)		39 (A) (B) (C) (D) (E)	
15 (A) (B) (C) (D) (E)		40 (A) (B) (C) (D) (E)	
16 (A) (B) (C) (D) (E)		41 (A) (B) (C) (D) (E)	
17 (A) (B) (C) (D) (E)		42 (A) (B) (C) (D) (E)	
18 (A) (B) (C) (D) (E)		43 (A) (B) (C) (D) (E)	
19 (A) (B) (C) (D) (E)		44 (A) (B) (C) (D) (E)	
20 (A) (B) (C) (D) (E)		45 (A) (B) (C) (D) (E)	
21 (A) (B) (C) (D) (E)		46 (A) (B) (C) (D) (E)	
22 (A) (B) (C) (D) (E)		47 (A) (B) (C) (D) (E)	
23 (A) (B) (C) (D) (E)		48 (A) (B) (C) (D) (E)	
24 (A) (B) (C) (D) (E)		49 (A) (B) (C) (D) (E)	
25 (A) (B) (C) (D) (E)		50 (A) (B) (C) (D) (E)	

51 Ⓐ Ⓑ Ⓒ Ⓓ Ⓔ		76 Ⓐ Ⓑ Ⓒ Ⓓ Ⓔ
52 Ⓐ Ⓑ Ⓒ Ⓓ Ⓔ		77 Ⓐ Ⓑ Ⓒ Ⓓ Ⓔ
53 Ⓐ Ⓑ Ⓒ Ⓓ Ⓔ		78 Ⓐ Ⓑ Ⓒ Ⓓ Ⓔ
54 Ⓐ Ⓑ Ⓒ Ⓓ Ⓔ		79 Ⓐ Ⓑ Ⓒ Ⓓ Ⓔ
55 Ⓐ Ⓑ Ⓒ Ⓓ Ⓔ		80 Ⓐ Ⓑ Ⓒ Ⓓ Ⓔ
56 Ⓐ Ⓑ Ⓒ Ⓓ Ⓔ		81 Ⓐ Ⓑ Ⓒ Ⓓ Ⓔ
57 Ⓐ Ⓑ Ⓒ Ⓓ Ⓔ		82 Ⓐ Ⓑ Ⓒ Ⓓ Ⓔ
58 Ⓐ Ⓑ Ⓒ Ⓓ Ⓔ		83 Ⓐ Ⓑ Ⓒ Ⓓ Ⓔ
59 Ⓐ Ⓑ Ⓒ Ⓓ Ⓔ		84 Ⓐ Ⓑ Ⓒ Ⓓ Ⓔ
60 Ⓐ Ⓑ Ⓒ Ⓓ Ⓔ		85 Ⓐ Ⓑ Ⓒ Ⓓ Ⓔ
61 Ⓐ Ⓑ Ⓒ Ⓓ Ⓔ		86 Ⓐ Ⓑ Ⓒ Ⓓ Ⓔ
62 Ⓐ Ⓑ Ⓒ Ⓓ Ⓔ		87 Ⓐ Ⓑ Ⓒ Ⓓ Ⓔ
63 Ⓐ Ⓑ Ⓒ Ⓓ Ⓔ		88 Ⓐ Ⓑ Ⓒ Ⓓ Ⓔ
64 Ⓐ Ⓑ Ⓒ Ⓓ Ⓔ		89 Ⓐ Ⓑ Ⓒ Ⓓ Ⓔ
65 Ⓐ Ⓑ Ⓒ Ⓓ Ⓔ		90 Ⓐ Ⓑ Ⓒ Ⓓ Ⓔ
66 Ⓐ Ⓑ Ⓒ Ⓓ Ⓔ		91 Ⓐ Ⓑ Ⓒ Ⓓ Ⓔ
67 Ⓐ Ⓑ Ⓒ Ⓓ Ⓔ		92 Ⓐ Ⓑ Ⓒ Ⓓ Ⓔ
68 Ⓐ Ⓑ Ⓒ Ⓓ Ⓔ		93 Ⓐ Ⓑ Ⓒ Ⓓ Ⓔ
69 Ⓐ Ⓑ Ⓒ Ⓓ Ⓔ		94 Ⓐ Ⓑ Ⓒ Ⓓ Ⓔ
70 Ⓐ Ⓑ Ⓒ Ⓓ Ⓔ		95 Ⓐ Ⓑ Ⓒ Ⓓ Ⓔ
71 Ⓐ Ⓑ Ⓒ Ⓓ Ⓔ		96 Ⓐ Ⓑ Ⓒ Ⓓ Ⓔ
72 Ⓐ Ⓑ Ⓒ Ⓓ Ⓔ		97 Ⓐ Ⓑ Ⓒ Ⓓ Ⓔ
73 Ⓐ Ⓑ Ⓒ Ⓓ Ⓔ		98 Ⓐ Ⓑ Ⓒ Ⓓ Ⓔ
74 Ⓐ Ⓑ Ⓒ Ⓓ Ⓔ		99 Ⓐ Ⓑ Ⓒ Ⓓ Ⓔ
75 Ⓐ Ⓑ Ⓒ Ⓓ Ⓔ		100 Ⓐ Ⓑ Ⓒ Ⓓ Ⓔ

CUT HERE

Practice Test 1

Section 1: Multiple-Choice Questions

Time: 70 Minutes

Questions: 100

1. The spinal cord is part of the _____ nervous system.

   A. central
   B. peripheral
   C. somatic
   D. autonomic
   E. sympathetic

2. Which perspective in psychology rejects the concept of "mind" and views mental events as the contents of a "black box" that cannot be studied scientifically?

   A. cognitive
   B. behaviorist
   C. evolutionary
   D. psychodynamic
   E. both A and D

3. A practitioner of cognitive psychology is most likely to:

   A. explore the effect that changes in one's physical environment are likely to have on behavior
   B. explore theories of language and information processing
   C. dissect the brain of a human or animal who suffered a behavior disorder
   D. experiment with drug treatments for mental illness
   E. regard genetics as a primary influence in mental health

4. A major limitation of psychoanalytic (psychodynamic) theory is:

   A. its lack of a theory of personality
   B. its focus on current behaviors and influences, with limited focus on past experiences
   C. its relatively new status in psychology
   D. its approach to biologically based mental illnesses, such as schizophrenia
   E. its disregard for case studies

5. Which school of psychology asserts the importance of free will and questions the applicability of scientific methods to human psychology?

   A. Humanistic
   B. Gestalt
   C. Cognitive
   D. Structuralism
   E. Psychoanalytic

6. What type of study should you use to observe the mating habits of gorillas?

   A. outcome
   B. experiment
   C. survey
   D. naturalistic observation
   E. case studies

7. Which of the following does a survey *not* reflect?

   A. a participant's opinions
   B. a participant's beliefs
   C. a participant's attitudes
   D. a participant's preferences
   E. a participant's abilities

GO ON TO THE NEXT PAGE

8. In psychology, reliability:

   A. refers to how consistently individuals score on a test

   B. measures whether a test measures what the examiner wants it to measure

   C. reflects how effective a test is in predicting an individual's behavior in other particular situations

   D. B and C

   E. A only

9. In upholding ethics of psychological research, an experimenter does *not* need to:

   A. practice informed consent

   B. allow subjects to leave the experiment

   C. tell subjects in advance what the experiment is measuring

   D. protect confidentiality

   E. protect subjects from harm

10. Inferential statistics include:

    A. t-tests, chi-squares and z-scores

    B. chi-squares, t-tests and analysis of variance

    C. z-scores, chi-squares and analysis of variance

    D. z-scores, measures of variability and analysis of variance

    E. chi-squares, standard scores and z-scores

11. Which of the following is true of a normal distribution?

    A. It has one mode.

    B. It has two modes.

    C. It has a skewed curve.

    D. It has two medians.

    E. The mode and the mean vary by more than 2%.

12. The different ways in which a speaker can influence an individual's attitude toward a particular product would most likely be studied by:

    A. developmental psychologists

    B. counseling psychologists

    C. educational psychologists

    D. social psychologists

    E. clinical psychologists

13. Industrial and organizational psychologists apply psychological principles to areas such as:

    A. consumerism and working conditions

    B. production efficiency

    C. substance abuse in the workplace

    D. A and B

    E. C only

14. Which of the following brain areas is most directly involved in memory?

    A. hippocampus

    B. hypothalamus

    C. medulla

    D. reticular formation

    E. tectum

15. The forebrain includes the following structures:

    A. cerebral cortex, corpus callosum, hypothalamus

    B. cerebral cortex, tegmentum, tectum

    C. cerebral cortex, pons, medulla

    D. cerebral cortex, cerebellum, pons

    E. cerebral cortex, tectum, hypothalamus

16. The hypothalamus is *not* related to:

    A. mating

    B. the endocrine system

    C. fight and flight impulses

    D. the motor system

    E. foraging

17. The most invasive technique that psychologists use to study the brain is:

    A. ablation

    B. direct stimulation

    C. EEGs

    D. brain scans

    E. reticular activation

18. Which of the following statements is *true*?

    A. All neurons have myelin sheaths.

    B. Neuron cell bodies have receptor sites.

    C. Used neurotransmitter is absorbed by cytophages.

    D. There is frequent physical contact between neurons.

    E. The soma is separate from the cell nucleus.

19. The coordination and control of functions such as reproduction, metabolism and energy balance is performed by:

   A. anabolics
   B. temporal coding
   C. RAS
   D. hormones
   E. pons

20. Messenger RNA is responsible for:

   A. ensuring that the correct amino acid is attached to a protein being constructed at the ribosome
   B. carrying DNA instructions from the cell nucleus to ribosomes
   C. mapping out the sites where proteins are constructed
   D. determining single versus multiple alleles
   E. A and C

21. What is the "rubber band" in the Rubber Band theory of heritability?

   A. environment
   B. gender
   C. genetics
   D. behavior
   E. socialization

22. The part of the eye that focuses images is the:

   A. retina
   B. lens
   C. sclera
   D. iris
   E. pupil

23. Which of the following is a binocular depth perception cue?

   A. temporal coding
   B. spatial coding
   C. sensory transduction
   D. retinal disparity
   E. homeostasis

24. Which of the following statements about pain is *false*?

   A. Pain can inspire learning.
   B. Pain receptors in the body are highly specialized.
   C. Felt pain has a large psychological component.
   D. Pain can sometimes be controlled with acupuncture or hypnosis.
   E. Pain can provoke aggression.

25. The back of the tongue is most sensitive to:

   A. salt
   B. sour
   C. sweet
   D. pungent
   E. bitter

26. Which of the following theories of frequency transduction holds that different areas of the basilar membrane respond to different frequencies?

   A. transduction theory
   B. frequency theory
   C. Ohm's theory
   D. Mho's theory
   E. place theory

27. To keep information in short-term memory, people practice a technique called:

   A. rehearsal
   B. encoding
   C. sensory registration
   D. retrieval
   E. interference

28. Which of the following is *not* a type of long-term memory?

   A. episodic
   B. semantic
   C. sensory
   D. declarative
   E. procedural

GO ON TO THE NEXT PAGE

29. The incubation stage of problem solving is characterized by:

   A. the person withdrawing from the problem, only to return with an unexpected solution
   B. the person withdrawing from the problem, only to return having forgotten the nature of the problem
   C. the person engaging in problem assessment
   D. the person actively searching for all possible solutions
   E. the person evaluating all possible solutions and selecting the best one

30. Which of the following statements about creativity is *false*?

   A. Creativity and intelligence tests correlate reliably.
   B. Creativity cannot be tested reliably.
   C. Creativity is the ability to produce novel solutions or objects.
   D. There might not be much construct validity to psychologists' measure of creativity.
   E. As a group, exceptionally creative people are more emotionally stable than others.

31. *Pop* and *quiz* are linguistic examples of:

   A. phonemes
   B. morphemes
   C. syntax
   D. prosody
   E. synonyms

32. Which of the following disorders is characterized by cessation of breathing for brief periods of time during sleep?

   A. insomnia
   B. sleep apnea
   C. pseudoinsomnia
   D. narcolepsy
   E. somnambulism

33. While studying children, Freud found that most dreams had to do with:

   A. sex
   B. animals
   C. abuse
   D. wish fulfillment
   E. adults

34. The hypnotic state can be diagnosed through which of the following characteristics?

   A. selective attention and distorted perception
   B. rapt attention and clear perception
   C. exaggerated emotionality
   D. high activity and alertness
   E. B and D

35. Which of the following is not a category of psychoactive drug?

   A. depressants
   B. narcotics
   C. stimulants
   D. hallucinogenics
   E. nicotine

36. Cold sweats, vomiting, convulsions and hallucinations are symptoms of:

   A. sleep deprivation
   B. light deprivation
   C. drug withdrawal
   D. nightmares
   E. emotional abuse

37. Much of our knowledge of learning has been discovered by:

   A. Psychoanalytic research
   B. Behavioral research
   C. Cognitive research
   D. Humanistic research
   E. Gestalt research

38. Select the series of abbreviations that follow the correct order to complete this sentence:

   If a ___, which produces a ___, is paired with a ___, then a ___ will in turn produce a new instance of the ___ termed the ____.

   A. US, UR, CS, CS, UR, CR
   B. CS, CR, US, US, CR, CS
   C. US, CR, CS, CS, CR, UR
   D. UR, US, UR, UR, CS, US
   E. US, CR, US, US, CR, US

39. The number of responses needed before reinforcement is given is intermittent and irregular in a:

   A. fixed-ratio schedule
   B. fixed-interval schedule
   C. variable-interval schedule
   D. variable-ratio schedule
   E. variable-response schedule

40. The gradual removal of an interrupting variable is known as:

   A. fading
   B. backward chaining
   C. total task presentation
   D. shaping
   E. forward chaining

41. Distinctiveness, the likeability of the model and the complexity of the behavior to be modeled are all factors affecting which process of modeling?

   A. awareness process
   B. attention process
   C. retention process
   D. reproduction process
   E. motivational process

42. Which of the following factors does *not* affect a reinforcer's effectiveness?

   A. contingency
   B. immediacy
   C. size
   D. satiation
   E. likeability

43. Which of the following is *not* related to the psychometric approach to intelligence?

   A. t-factor
   B. g-factor
   C. s-factor
   D. factor analysis
   E. two-factor theory

44. On the Performance Scale of the Wechsler Adult Intelligence Scale (WAIS), which of the following subsets is tested?

   A. General Comprehension
   B. Arithmetic Reasoning
   C. Digit-Symbol Substitution
   D. Vocabulary
   E. Digit Span

45. On the Bayley Scales of Infant Development, the mental scale tests functions such as:

   A. perception and coordination
   B. learning and problem solving
   C. memory and walking
   D. sitting and stair climbing
   E. none of the above

46. If a person has an IQ ranging from 52 to 67, they are classified as having:

   A. borderline mental retardation
   B. mild mental retardation
   C. moderate mental retardation
   D. severe mental retardation
   E. profound mental retardation

47. Which chromosome pair is abnormal in a person with Down syndrome?

   A. 10
   B. 12
   C. 20
   D. 21
   E. 22

48. Which of the following drives did Machiavelli *not* believe served as the basis for political leadership?

   A. egotism
   B. fear
   C. love
   D. sex
   E. pain

GO ON TO THE NEXT PAGE

49. An unchanging sequence of behaviors that is observed in all members of a species and released by specific stimuli without learning is:

A. operant conditioning
B. a drive
C. a motive
D. an instinct
E. a stimulus

50. Which of the following categories of need goes in the center of Maslow's hierarchy of motivation?

A. physiological needs
B. self-actualization
C. esteem and self-esteem
D. love and belonging
E. safety and security

51. Which theory upholds that emotion is the result of an individual's interpretation of their aroused physical state?

A. Emergency theory
B. Opponent Process theory
C. Cognitive Dissonance theory
D. Cognitive theory
E. Physiological theory

52. The approach-avoidance situation of Equilibrium theory was developed by:

A. Schachter-Singer
B. Miller
C. Festinger
D. Freud
E. Cannon-Bard

53. Erikson, Freud, and Piaget developed models of development that focused on _____, _____, and _____ stages, respectively.

A. cognitive, psychosexual, psychosocial
B. psychosocial, psychosexual, cognitive
C. psychosexual, psychosocial, cognitive
D. cognitive, psychosocial, and psychosexual
E. psychosocial, cognitive, psychosexual

54. According to Shirley (1933), by the age of 14 months, most children who follow a standard motor sequence of development should be able to:

A. walk alone
B. begin to run
C. stand alone
D. skip alone
E. hop on one foot

55. Which of the following skills improves between the ages of 25 and 64?

A. math
B. spatial
C. small motor
D. gross motor
E. verbal

56. In general, girls tend to suffer from fewer _____ defects than boys.

A. social
B. physical
C. sexual
D. speech
E. intellectual

57. Which of the following is *not* an example of traits that have been studied by psychologists?

A. extroversion/introversion
B. submission/dominance
C. honesty/dishonesty
D. intelligence
E. friendliness/unfriendliness

58. Stanley Milgram's study of _____ was conducted with white, middle-class American men.

A. punishment
B. obedience
C. anger
D. learning
E. racial discrimination

59. The overproduction of ordinary bile was thought to cause what kind of personality type, according to Hippocrates and Galen?

   A. choleric

   B. sanguine

   C. melancholic

   D. phlegmatic

   E. salacious

60. According to Freud, the _____ consists of rules that the person has internalized, while the _____ represents goals and aspirations that the person's parents or other authority figures admire.

   A. superego, id

   B. conscience, ego ideal

   C. id, ego ideal

   D. conscience, ego

   E. id, conscience

61. Which of the following is *not* an example of a defense mechanism?

   A. regression

   B. reaction formation

   C. denial

   D. repression

   E. intellectualization

62. According to Jung's theory of personality structure, the animus is:

   A. a man's internalized male image

   B. a man's internalized female image

   C. a woman's internalized female image

   D. a woman's internalized male image

   E. an adult's internalized child image

63. Raymond Cattell divides traits into which two categories?

   A. common traits and rare traits

   B. common traits and special traits

   C. surface traits and source traits

   D. single traits and cluster traits

   E. disposition traits and behavior traits

64. The California Psychological Inventory (CPI) is an example of what kind of personality test?

   A. projective

   B. objective

   C. subjective

   D. strategic

   E. deviant

65. In the Harlow experiment (1958), which object was given to baby monkeys as a mother surrogate?

   A. stuffed bear

   B. washcloth

   C. fuzzy cloth

   D. doll

   E. stuffed monkey

66. A tendency to overestimate the influence of natural traits while minimizing the impact of the environment, identified by Ross (1977), is known as the:

   A. Fundamental Attribution Error

   B. Fundamental Blame Dilemma

   C. Fundamental Human Error

   D. Fundamental Influence Conflict

   E. Fundamental Locus of Control

67. A person's belief about how they should act and what goals they should strive for is labeled:

   A. an attitude

   B. a more

   C. a value

   D. a trait

   E. a behavior

68. The thought that a person hides behind a mask of conscious intentions, known as the *persona*, was developed by:

   A. Jung

   B. Bandura

   C. Skinner

   D. Freud

   E. Erikson

GO ON TO THE NEXT PAGE

69. Hans Eyseneck's theory of personality lies in the belief that individual differences in the introversion/extroversion split are caused by differences in arousal of the:

   A. phallus
   B. libido
   C. pons
   D. cerebral cortex
   E. body temperature

70. Carl Rogers's belief that the structure of the personality is based on two constructs—the organism and the self—is a key component in which theory?

   A. Structuralist
   B. Gestalt
   C. Cognitive
   D. Behaviorist
   E. Humanistic

71. The interpretation of the Rorschach test is supposed to reveal how subjects solve problems, their intellectual levels and their:

   A. mores
   B. attitudes
   C. values
   D. emotional stability
   E. creativity

72. Which of the following is *not* a cause of prejudice?

   A. economic competition
   B. political competition
   C. history of abuse
   D. personality needs
   E. displacement of aggression

73. When an individual adopts the beliefs of a group as their own, it is known as:

   A. conformity
   B. compliance
   C. identification
   D. over-identification
   E. internalization

74. In any given position in a group, which roles are likely to be demonstrated?

   A. self-orientation and self-awareness
   B. task orientation and maintenance
   C. control orientation and task orientation
   D. control orientation and maintenance
   E. none of the above

75. When individual performance is enhanced in the presence of others, it is known as:

   A. groupthink
   B. social influence
   C. social facilitation
   D. group facilitation
   E. social performance enhancement

76. In Latane and Darley's experiment on bystander intervention, under which condition did subjects respond to the need for help most frequently?

   A. when alone
   B. when in the presence of a passive confederate
   C. when in the presence of a stranger
   D. when in the presence of a friend
   E. when in the presence of a family member

77. Which steroid hormones have been conclusively linked to an increase in aggressive behavior?

   A. testosterone
   B. hexosterone
   C. estrogen
   D. endocrine
   E. progesterone

78. Which of the following statements is in line with cognitive-social views of aggression?

   A. The amygdala and hypothalamus play important roles in aggression.
   B. Aggression is inborn and gets activated under conditions that affect reproductive success.
   C. Aggression is instinctive, and activated by frustration and/or anger.
   D. People learn to behave aggressively through social rewards and punishments and observational learning.
   E. Aggression is partially controlled by hormones, especially testosterone.

79. Whether an aggressive behavior is harmful or not is judged by the _____ of the behavior.

- A. duration
- B. outcome
- C. intent
- D. frequency
- E. side-effects

80. The role of a _____ is to plan, design and produce structures and machines useful to people.

- A. industrial psychologist
- B. organizational psychologist
- C. human factors engineer
- D. mechanical engineer
- E. cognitive behavioral engineer

81. Which view proposes that mental disorders come from mental malfunctions and was the origin of Freud's early work?

- A. Psychoanalytic theory
- B. Psychotic theory
- C. Psychogenic theory
- D. Dementia theory
- E. Psychotropic theory

82. Which of the following is *not* a model of abnormal behavior?

- A. statistical
- B. medical
- C. psychoanalytic
- D. cognitive behavioral
- E. social learning

83. Panic disorder, phobic disorder and stress disorder are types of:

- A. anxiety disorders
- B. affective disorders
- C. somatoform disorders
- D. personality disorders
- E. psychosexual disorders

84. If a person has symptoms including rapid heart rate, sweating, dizziness and irregular breathing, they might suffer from:

- A. major depressive disorder
- B. schizophrenia
- C. panic disorder
- D. stress disorder
- E. hallucinations

85. An example of the first nosological dimension of affective disorders is:

- A. mania
- B. episodic depression
- C. chronic energy loss
- D. atypical mood swings
- E. undetermined illness

86. After committing an antisocial act, a sociopath is likely to:

- A. express shame and remorse
- B. experience shame and remorse, without expressing it
- C. experience severe emotional arousal
- D. actively seek forgiveness
- E. lack emotional response

87. When a person who suffers from schizophrenia speaks incoherently or makes up words, it is an example of:

- A. a thought disorder
- B. disorganized speech
- C. creative flow
- D. flattened effect
- E. asocial personality

88. Which of the following is *not* one of the four main types of schizophrenia, as listed in the DSM IV?

- A. violent
- B. catatonic
- C. paranoid
- D. disorganized
- E. undifferentiated

GO ON TO THE NEXT PAGE

89. An individual who cannot recall their identity prior to the onset of disease and begins a new life is likely suffering from:

    A. undifferentiated personality disorder
    B. schizophrenia
    C. amnesia
    D. dissociative fugue
    E. dissociative identity disorder

90. On Axis V of the DSM IV, a patient's prognosis is closely related to:

    A. their level of function before disease onset
    B. stress levels
    C. how well their immediate family is functioning
    D. genetic predetermination
    E. none of the above

91. In psychodynamic approaches to treatment of psychological disorders, the most effective way for an analyst to respond to transference is to:

    A. help the patient suppress feelings
    B. maintain compassionate neutrality
    C. engage in countertransference
    D. use free association
    E. refer the patient to a different analyst

92. Before they can begin practice, all therapists trained as psychoanalysts must:

    A. undergo their own psychoanalytic treatment
    B. get a mentor
    C. teach an undergraduate psychology course
    D. publish an article in a scholarly journal
    E. cross-train with a therapist from another psychological approach

93. If a patient wants to eliminate their gambling habit, a therapist might give the patient electric shocks while showing him video footage of gambling. As a result, the patient's gambling elicits fear instead of excitement. In this situation, the fear is the:

    A. undesired response
    B. desired response
    C. new response
    D. stimulus
    E. condition

94. Which of the following is *not* a class of antipsychotic drug?

    A. barbiturates
    B. phenothiazines
    C. butyrophenones
    D. thioxanthines
    E. All the above are antipsychotic drugs.

95. Family therapy developed from which theory originated by von Bertalanffy?

    A. Cognitive Group theory
    B. Interpersonal Group theory
    C. General Systems theory
    D. Progressive Segregation theory
    E. Encounter theory

96. In the following series of numbers, which is the mean, median and mode (in that order)?

    1, 2, 3, 3, 4, 4, 4, 4, 4, 5, 6

    A. 3.636, 4, 4
    B. 4, 4, 4
    C. 4, 4, 3.636
    D. 4, 3.636, 4
    E. 3.363, 4, 4

97. Which of the following is an effect of parasympathetic nervous system activity?

    A. perspiration
    B. slowed digestion
    C. reduced heart rate
    D. elevated blood sugar
    E. constricted pupils

98. When a patient who takes a fake drug experiences relief from symptoms, it is referred to as the _____ effect.

    A. blind
    B. hallucinatory
    C. delusional
    D. malingering
    E. placebo

99. The function of the vestibular organs is to provide:

    A.   balance and equilibrium

    B.   neurotransmitters

    C.   cell repair

    D.   auditory conduction to the brain

    E.   red blood cell production

100. The normal, average IQ score is:

    A.   140

    B.   125

    C.   115

    D.   100

    E.   85

IF YOU FINISH BEFORE TIME IS CALLED, CHECK YOUR WORK ON THIS SECTION ONLY. DO NOT WORK ON ANY OTHER SECTION IN THE TEST.

Section 2: Free-Response Questions

Time: 50 Minutes

Questions: 2

Directions: You have 50 minutes to answer both of the following questions. It is not enough to answer a question by just presenting facts. You must present a strong argument based on your critical analysis of the questions posed, using appropriate psychological terminology.

Free-Response Question #1

Suppose a client wants to have her 10-year-old child given a Wechsler Intelligence Scale for Children, third edition, (WISC III) IQ test. How would you explain how and what the test measures, as well as its strengths and weaknesses?

_____
_____
_____
_____
_____
_____
_____
_____
_____
_____
_____
_____
_____
_____
_____
_____
_____
_____
_____
_____
_____
_____
_____
_____
_____

GO ON TO THE NEXT PAGE

Free-Response Question #2

Compare and contrast Freud's stages of psychosexual development with Erickson's stages of psychosocial development.

_____
_____
_____
_____
_____
_____
_____
_____
_____
_____
_____
_____
_____
_____
_____
_____
_____
_____
_____
_____
_____
_____
_____
_____
_____
_____
_____
_____
_____
_____
_____
_____
_____

GO ON TO THE NEXT PAGE

Answer Key for Practice Test 1

1.	A	26.	E	51.	D	76.	A
2.	B	27.	A	52.	B	77.	B
3.	B	28.	C	53.	B	78.	D
4.	D	29.	A	54.	C	79.	B
5.	A	30.	A	55.	E	80.	C
6.	D	31.	B	56.	D	81.	C
7.	E	32.	B	57.	E	82.	D
8.	E	33.	D	58.	B	83.	A
9.	C	34.	A	59.	A	84.	C
10.	B	35.	E	60.	B	85.	A
11.	A	36.	C	61.	A	86.	E
12.	D	37.	B	62.	D	87.	A
13.	D	38.	A	63.	C	88.	A
14.	A	39.	D	64.	B	89.	D
15.	A	40.	A	65.	C	90.	A
16.	D	41.	B	66.	A	91.	B
17.	A	42.	E	67.	C	92.	A
18.	B	43.	A	68.	A	93.	C
19.	D	44.	C	69.	D	94.	A
20.	B	45.	B	70.	E	95.	C
21.	C	46.	B	71.	D	96.	A
22.	B	47.	D	72.	C	97.	C
23.	D	48.	E	73.	E	98.	E
24.	B	49.	D	74.	B	99.	A
25.	E	50.	D	75.	C	100.	D

Complete Answers and Explanations for Practice Test 1

1. **A.** The nervous system is divided into two main parts: the central nervous system and the peripheral nervous system. The spinal cord and brain are the two components of the central nervous system. The peripheral nervous system is further split into the somatic and autonomic divisions. The somatic division relays sensory information to the central nervous system and sends motor commands to muscles. The autonomic division controls basic life functions, such as heart rate, breathing, and fear responses. The autonomic nervous system is further divided into the sympathetic and parasympathetic branches. The sympathetic division activates the body in response to a threat, while the parasympathetic calms the body down.

2. **B.** To behaviorists, psychology is the science of behavior. The behaviorist perspective focuses on learning and examines the way environmental events control behavior (stimulus-response releationships). In general, cognitive psychologists view the mind as a computer. The cognitive perspective focuses on the way humans process, store, and retrieve information. Evolutionary psychologists study how behavior evolved because it was adaptive, and allowed survival and reproduction. Sigmund Freud founded the psychodynamic perspective, and based his theory of mind on his patients whose symptoms were not based on physiological problems. He believed that many of our behaviors reflect unconscious motives that conflict with one another, leading to compromises among competing motives.

3. **B.** Explore theories of language and information processing. Cognitive psychology is primarily concerned with processes of thinking, memory, attention, imagery, creativity, problem solving and language use. Choices **A, C, D** and **E** reflect the wide range of study that falls within biological psychology, including the interaction between the body and the brain.

4. **D.** Its approach to biologically based mental illnesses, such as schizophrenia. Psychoanalysis is one of the oldest types of psychotherapy, and was developed by Sigmund Freud based on case studies of his patients. Psychoanalytic treatment focuses on past conscious and unconscious experiences and memories to address current issues and problems. Today, other forms of treatment for mental illness have proved more effective biologically based illnesses, such as schizophrenia (e.g., pharmacotherapy).

5. **A.** Humanistic. Humanistic psychologists believed that behaviorism focused too much on science over experience and that psychoanalysis concentrated too much on human frailty. Humanistic psychologists emphasize the importance of free will and reject the idea that environmental and genetic factors determine all behavior.

6. **D.** Naturalistic observation. This type of study involves the systemic observation of an event or phenomenon in the environment as it naturally occurs. This type of social behavior might be exhibited differently in a laboratory setting than it is in the wild.

7. **E.** A participant's abilities. As a method of psychological investigation, surveys ask individuals to rate a series of items that provide insight into their opinions, beliefs, attitudes and preferences.

8. **E.** A only. Reliability measures the extent to which differences between individuals' scores show true differences, not errors in test construction. Choices **B** and **C** reflect the question of validity.

9. **C.** Tell subjects in advance what the experiment is measuring. This might influence the outcome of the experiment, and is not part of considering the ethical implications of research. Choices **A, B, D** and **E** are required by the United States government for every experiment receiving federal funding.

10. **B.** Chi-squares, t-tests and analysis of variance. Inferential statistics use formulas to determine whether the results obtained with a sample are likely to reflect characteristics of the population as a whole. These statistical procedures include tests of statistical significance, which determine the probability that a positive finding (e.g., a difference between a control and experimental group) was a matter of chance.

11. **A.** It has one mode. A normal distribution is defined by a bell-shaped curve, a single mode, and the equality of the mean, median and mode.

12. **D.** Social psychology is a field of psychology that studies the way thought processes, interpersonal feelings, and behavior are shaped by the presence of others.

13. D. A and B. Industrial/organizational (I/O) psychologists generally work for public and private businesses or the government and apply psychological principles to personnel policies, consumerism, working conditions, production efficiency and decision making in an attempt to solve organizational problems. Some questions that an I/O psychologist might ask are a) What leadership style results in the greatest productivity in workers? or b) What types of rewards or benefits do workers value the most?

14. A. The hippocampus is part of the limbic system and is necessary for the formation of new memories. The classic example of this is the patient identified as H.M., who had his hippocampus removed to control epileptic seizures. H.M. could not form new memories after the surgery. If he met the same person every day for a year (if he had not known the person previous to the surgery), each day would be like the first meeting to H.M. The hypothalamus is involved in a wide range of behaviors, but one of its most important functions is to maintain homeostasis—that is, keep body temperature, glucose levels, and metabolism within a fairly narrow range. The medulla is the lowest brainstem structure and controls vital processes, such as heart rate, breathing, and circulation. The reticular formation is a diffuse network of neurons that together regulate arousal levels. The tectum is part of the midbrain and is involved in visual and auditory processing.

15. A. Cerebral cortex, corpus callosum, hypothalamus. The midbrain comprises the tegmentum and the tectum. The hindbrain comprises the pons, medulla and cerebellum.

16. D. The motor system. The hypothalamus is the small structure at the base of the brain that controls parts of the autonomic nervous system, the endocrine system and certain reactions including those described in choices **A, C** and **E.**

17. A. Ablation. In ablation, researchers remove part of an organism's brain, and then test that organism for behavior changes. While ablation is extremely invasive, it has helped scientists localize brain regions important in memory, learning, speech and other functions.

18. B. Neuron cell bodies have receptor sites. Receptor sites receive the chemical messages from other cells' terminal buttons, which travel across the synapse to communicate with other neurons.

19. D. Hormones. Hormones influence neural function and behavior and are controlled by the central nervous system. Hormones coordinate and control sexual behaviors as well.

20. B. Carrying DNA instructions from the cell nucleus to ribosomes. RNA occurs in both the nucleus and cytoplasm of cells, and is concerned with manufacturing new proteins according to DNA instructions. This is the process by which all proteins are made, including proteins in neuronal membranes, such as neurotransmitter receptors, ion channels, and sodium-potassium pumps.

21. C. Genetics. Inherited traits (or nature) are seen as the rubber band in Stern's (1956) writings. The environment (nurture) determines how much the rubber band can stretch. This is the age old nature vs. nurture discussion. Every behavior is determined by genetics, and almost every behavior is influenced to some extent by the environment.

22. B. Lens. Directly below the cornea sits the lens, a transparent tissue that focuses images on the retina, the light-sensitive layer of receptor cells at the back of the eye.

23. D. Retinal disparity (a binocular depth cue) is the slight difference between the retinal images of the right and left eyes; this disparity is most pronounced when objects are very close, and diminishes as objects move away. Another depth perception cue is convergence, or the way the eyes move toward each other as an object moves closer to the eyes.

24. B. Pain receptors in the body are highly specialized. Pain receptors are actually unspecialized, free nerve endings that respond to cellular damage. A prominent theory holds that when cells are damaged, they release chemicals (such as substance P) that stimulate free nerve endings.

25. E. Bitter. While you can taste any taste anywhere on your tongue, the back of the tongue is most sensitive to bitter. The tip is most sensitive to sweet, the sides are most sensitive to sour, and the front is most sensitive to salt. About one third of taste buds are sensitive to all four tastes. Taste receptors (located in taste buds) stimulate neurons that carry information to the hindbrain. From here the information can take one of two paths. One path leads to the primary gustatory cortex located between the temporal and parietal lobes and allows the identification of tastes. The other pathway leads to the limbic system and allows for immediate behavioral responses, such as spitting out a bitter substance.

26. E. There are two major theories that explain how different frequencies are transduced (changed from physical energy to neural impulses) by the auditory system. The place theory, which explains transduction at high frequencies, holds that different areas of the basilar membrane respond to different frequencies. The frequency theory, which explains transduction at low frequencies, holds that the rate of vibration of the basilar membrane converts frequency into pitch.

27. A. Rehearsal. Rehearsal means paying active attention to information by consistently repeating it without interruption.

28. C. Sensory. The sensory register is a very short-lived recording of sensory information, where memory begins.

29. A. The person withdrawing from the problem, only to return with an unexpected solution. One explanation for this is that while the person is engaged in some other activity, their unconscious mind continues to work on the problem. Problem solving is the process of transforming an initial state into a more satisfying goal state using operators. There are several strategies one can use to accomplish this goal. Some of these strategies are algorithms (systematic procedures that are certain to produce a solution), hypothesis testing (trying solutions based on educated guesses), and mental simulations (imagining the steps involved in the solution before actually doing them).

30. A. Creativity and intelligence tests correlate reliably. Creativity is the ability to produce valued outcomes in a novel way. Creativity in and of itself is a difficult ability to test and measure, and it does not correlate with intelligence tests. One way to assess creativity in the laboratory is to measure divergent thinking, or the ability to generate multiple possibilities in a given situation.

31. B. Morphemes. Phonemes combine to form morphemes, the smallest units of meaning in a language. These can be whole words, suffixes or prefixes. English has more than 100,000 morphemes.

32. B. Sleep apnea. This breathing disorder is commonly associated with snoring. During sleep apnea, the level of carbon dioxide in the blood rises until the person wakes up and begins to breathe. When the level of oxygen in the blood returns to normal, the person falls asleep again and the cycle repeats itself.

33. D. Wish fulfillment. A child who wants a new puppy might dream that they get one. Adults' dreams are less clear in their motives. However, Freud proposed that all dreams are reflections of unconscious associative thoughts, feelings, and wishes.

34. A. Selective attention and distorted perception. The additional major characteristics of the hypnotic state include passivity, altered awareness, lack of emotion, altered memory, altered identity and regression. A hypnotic state is one of several states of consciousness. States of consciousness are different ways of orienting to internal and external events.

35. E. Nicotine. Nicotine is one example of a stimulant drug (or "upper"). This category also includes caffeine, amphetamines and cocaine.

36. C. Drug withdrawal. Addictive drugs cause a physiological dependence, and withdrawal from these drugs has physiological as well as psychological side effects.

37. B. Behavioral research. Learning can be defined as a change in behavior caused by experience. Behaviorists believe that observable external behavior is the only valid topic for study.

38. A. US, UR, CS, CS, UR, CR. If an unconditioned stimulus that produces an unconditioned response is paired with a conditioned response, then a conditioned response will in turn produce a new instance of the unconditioned response (termed the conditioned response).

39. D. Variable-ratio schedule. This type of schedule produces the highest rate of performance, whereby response continues at a rate approaching the maximum physical capacity of an organism.

40. A. Fading. When a response doesn't exist in an organism's behavioral repertoire, it can be created through operant conditioning. Operant conditioning is learning that occurs when an organism associates a response with a particular effect. Fading is a way for the psychologist to remove the prompts or stimulus that helped the subject learn the response.

41. B. Attention process. This is the first process in modeling. Other factors affecting this process include the learner's history of reinforcement for paying attention to similar models and the psychological state of the observer.

42. E. Likeability. Because behavioral conditioning is objective and scientific in its approach, the subjective likeability of the reinforcer is not relevant. The other answer choices are some of the many variables that can affect a reinforcer's effectiveness (i.e., its ability to evoke an operant response).

43. A. The psychometric approach to intelligence uses factor analysis to identify groups of items in a test that correlate highly with one another. Using this approach, Spearman formed his two-factor theory in which he identified correlations that he felt were due to two types of factors. The g-factor (general intelligence) was based on his observation that children with the highest academic ranking scored well on a variety of subject areas, such as arithmetic, general knowledge, and vocabulary. The second factor, or s-factor, referred to specific abilities unique to certain tests or shared only by a subset of tests. Thus, individuals vary in overall intelligence, but some individuals are proficient at certain kinds of reasoning, but poor at others.

44. C. Digit-Symbol Substitution. The other subsets of the Performance Scale include Picture Completion, Block Design, Picture Arrangement and Object Assembly. The WISC was designed by David Wechsler in an attempt to avoid the problems of other intelligence tests of the time (e.g., the Army Beta), which were linguistically and culturally biased toward native-born English speakers.

45. B. Learning and problem solving. Other functions measured on this scale include perception and memory. The other functions are measured on the Motor scale.

46. B. Mild mental retardation. Children in this category are eligible for special classes for the educable mentally retarded. Adults in this category can likely hold unskilled jobs, while needing assistance with social and financial issues.

47. D. 21. The overwhelming majority of Down syndrome children have 47 chromosomes instead of 46, with a third chromosome on pair 21. Down syndrome is also known as Trisomy 21.

48. E. Pain. Machiavelli also believed that the motive of hunger served as a basis for political leadership. Other theories of motivation would focus on other motives. Drive-reduction theory asserts that deprivation of basic needs creates an unpleasant state of tension, and the organism tries to produce behaviors that reduce the tension. Cognitive theories focus on motivation in terms of goals. Goal-setting theory holds that conscious goals regulate human behavior. Expectancy-value theories maintain that humans perform behaviors that they believe will produce valued outcomes, and they also believe the goals are attainable.

49. D. An instinct. Behaviors produced by instinct are unaffected by practice over time. Each instinct is a relatively fixed pattern of behavior that an organism emits without learning. Instinct theory purports that human behavior is driven by instinct; however, most psychologists believe that other factors, such as learning, drive human behavior.

50. D. Love and belonging. The bottom of the pyramid reflects physiological needs, such as food and water. These are followed by safety and security, love and belonging, and esteem and self-esteem. Self-actualization is at the top.

51. D. Cognitive theory. The primary belief is that the physical states accompanying many emotions are similar, and these differences often cannot be sensed when states differ. They only seem different because we interpret them differently and experience the emotion we feel is most fitting to the current state.

52. B. Miller. According to Neal Miller, when a person is confronted with a situation that is both appealing and unappealing, they experience conflict. The person's response varies depending on the strength of the motives in play and the physical distance from the goal.

53. B. Erikson's theory of development included psychosocial stages, or stages in the development of the person as a social being. Erikson intended to supplement Freud's psychosexual stages of development, which viewed the libido as the driving force underlying development. Piaget's theory of cognitive development holds that children move through a sequence of stages in which they use a distinct underlying logic to guide their thinking during each stage.

54. C. Stand alone. A child can stand with help by 8 months of age and can walk with help by 11 months. They should be able to stand alone by 14 months of age, and by 15 months, many children can walk unaided.

55. E. Verbal. While skills and abilities such as motor control and concentration decline with age, verbal skills improve, and tasks that require the application of learned material are maintained well into the 60s.

56. D. Speech. In general, girls tend to speak earlier, speak more fluently and suffer from fewer speech defects than boys. Conversely, males tend to score higher on tests of mathematical ability and spatial processing. Another notable gender difference is that in virtually all species, males are more aggressive than females.

57. E. Friendliness/unfriendliness. Traits are classified as enduring and stable characteristics that provoke a person to act in a consistent manner. Friendliness is a behavior rather than a trait.

58. B. Obedience. Milgram discovered that the average, middle-class, white, American male would deliver electric shocks to other people in an experimental setting under the direction of an authority figure. Even when their "subjects" were communicating that they felt terrible pain, 65% of the participants delivered shocks of maximum voltage. Milgram also found that several factors influence obedience. Obedience is reduced if the victim (the person who receives the shock) is in close proximity to the subject. Obedience is *enhanced* if the *experimenter* (the authority figure) is close to the subject. Finally, the presence of dissenters who refuse to proceed with shock reduces obedience.

59. A. Choleric. The ancient Greeks classified people according to the dominance of one of four basic humors, or bodily fluids. Cholerics were angry personalities, ascribed to having too much ordinary bile.

60. B. Conscience, ego ideal. The superego represents the taboos and ethics of society, and develops between 18 months and 6 years of age. The conscience and the ego ideal are the two divisions of the superego, often in conflict with one another. The id is the pool of sexual and aggressive energy. The ego is the structure that must balance the id, the external world, and the superego.

61. A. Regression. Defense mechanisms (including **B–E**, as well as displacement and projection) occur when the ego needs to compensate for an unfulfilled need.

62. D. A woman's internalized male image. Like the male anima, this image, or archetype, determines one's relationship to the opposite gender and is based on a combination of real, personal experiences as well as the collective gender experience throughout history (collective unconscious). Jung proposed that certain archetypes, such as the image of a mother or a wise elder, arise in all cultures and reflect innate tendencies derived from the collective unconscious.

63. C. Surface traits and source traits. Trait theories of personality rely on words people commonly use to describe themselves and others to define an individual's personality. Surface traits can be described as groups of related behaviors, while source traits are what underlie these behaviors. Surface traits can be observed, while source traits can only be extracted through statistical analysis. Some traits on Cattell's list are warm, cheerful, intelligent, suspicious, and sensitive.

64. B. Objective. The CPI and the Minnesota Multiphasic Personality Inventory (MMPI) are the two primary objective psychological personality tests. Their objectivity is defined by the fact that the test is standardized, and responses are limited and controlled. Projective tests assess personality by confronting subjects with an ambiguous stimulus and asking them to define it in some way. The idea is that subjects will project their own personalities into their responses. The Rorschach inkblot test is an example of a projective test in which subjects view a set of inkblots and tell the tester what each inkblot resembles.

65. C. Fuzzy cloth. The baby rhesus monkeys in this experiment preferred spending time with a fuzzy cloth that gave no milk, while feeding from a wire surrogate. This experiment suggested that security, not nourishment, is the basis of attachment in monkeys.

66. A. Fundamental Attribution Error. The FAE is seen as the tendency to *blame the person for everything* rather than carefully examining the intersection between nature and nurture.

67. C. A value. Values are what steer actions over the long term, while attitudes cause behaviors toward a particular person or situation.

68. A. Jung. He theorized that the persona is the front a person presents to other people and is only one of many themes that derive from the collective unconscious.

69. D. Cerebral cortex. More specifically, differences exist in the ascending reticular activating system (ARAS), which produces arousal in the cerebral cortex. According to Eysenck, introverts tend to be more highly aroused in normal situations and behave in a more subdued manner to prevent excess arousal.

70. **E.** Humanistic. Humanistic psychology emphasizes the whole human, rather than relying on components. Carl Rogers believed that the organism is where the all experience and sensation occurs, and the self represents the organism's attitudes and feelings about itself.

71. **D.** Emotional stability. Nevertheless, many question the validity of the test, as well as its diagnostic merits.

72. **C.** History of abuse. While aggression that cannot otherwise be expressed can be a cause of prejudice, abuse in and of itself does not have a causal link to prejudice. An additional cause is conformity to preexisting prejudices. Prejudice requires a distinction between ingroups (people who belong to a group) and outgroups (people who do not belong to a group). It appears that contact between groups can actually increase prejudice unless it is accompanied by shared goals, personal acquaintance with outgroup members, equal status, and enough shared culture to dissolve stereotypes.

73. **E.** Internalization. Based on an overwhelming desire to be right, internalization is a social response with intrinsic rewards. When internalized, beliefs are unlikely to be changed.

74. **B.** Task orientation and maintenance. Task-oriented group members are concerned with accomplishing the goals of the group. Maintenance-focused group members are concerned with group morale. Self-oriented group members are primarily concerned with their self-interest. Research on group processes suggests that the most effective group leaders are extroverted, conscientious, and agreeable.

75. **C.** Social facilitation. This phenomenon also accounts for poorly performing groups negatively impacting individual performance.

76. **A.** When alone. In this situation, subjects responded to the perceived need for help 91% of the time. Diffusion of responsibility suggests that in the presence of other people, each person's sense of responsibility diminishes. There are also other variables that affect bystander intervention. The more attractive and the more similar the victim is to the bystander, the more likely the bystander is to intervene. Bystanders who are anonymous are less likely to help.

77. **B.** Androgens. While a clear link has been shown, it has not been determined whether high levels of aggression result in the production of testosterone or whether high levels of testosterone produce aggression. One thing that is fairly consistent across all species, however, is that males are more aggressive than females.

78. **D.** This statement is in line with cognitive-social theories. Answer choices A, B, C, and E are in line with biological, evolutionary, psychodynamic, and biological perspectives, respectively.

79. **B.** Outcome. Simply put, harmful aggressive behavior has injurious outcomes, while nonharmful behavior does not.

80. **C.** Human factors engineer. A person with this job combines knowledge about human behavior with mechanical, electrical, chemical or other types of engineering to create functional devices. An example of a question that this type of psychologist might ask is "How should instruments be placed on the control panel of a plane to avoid potentially dangerous pilot errors?"

81. **C.** Psychogenic theory. This theory developed in the eighteenth, nineteenth and twentieth centuries as an alternative hypothesis to demonic possession as the cause for mental illness and to theories that ascribed mental illness to something wrong with the body.

82. **D.** Cognitive behavioral. The statistical model deals with how often certain characteristics occur in the general population. The medical model regards mental illness as either a physical or mental disease. The psychoanalytic model takes the idea of mental illness as a mental disease to the next level. The social learning model assumes that abnormal behavior is learned.

83. **A.** Anxiety disorders. The other two types of anxiety disorders are obsessive-compulsive disorder and generalized anxiety disorder.

84. **C.** Panic disorder. These symptoms characterize a panic attack, which take place when there is no actual threat to life or limb. The patient might confuse a panic attack with a heart attack.

85. **A.** Mania. The first nosological dimension has to do with the predominant mood displayed by the patient. The second nosological dimension refers to the onset of the disorder.

86. **E.** Lack emotional response. Someone with antisocial personality syndrome (or sociopathy) has no regard for other people or their feelings. Because people with this syndrome experience no guilt or shame, they are unlikely to change their antisocial ways.

87. **A.** A thought disorder. This is a disorder of cognition characterized by disconnected (or made-up) speech, loose associations and speaking in rhyme.

88. **A.** Violent. While some people who suffer from schizophrenia might become violent in response to hallucinations or paranoia, violence is not a main type—or primary symptom—of this disease.

89. **D.** Dissociative fugue. While similar to dissociative amnesia, this state is evidenced by a person suddenly traveling away from their surroundings and beginning a new life, which can often be quite different from the previous one. The fugue is usually produced by overwhelming psychological stress.

90. **A.** Their level of function before disease onset. Axis V describes the patient's highest level of functioning during the previous year.

91. **B.** Maintain compassionate neutrality. Transference is the process by which people transfer thoughts, feelings, conflicts, etc., from past relationships (usually childhood) onto new relationships (i.e., with the therapist). Freud believed that transference was important for developing emotional insight. As the patient transfers to the analyst, the analyst must be receptive to these emotions so that they can be brought into the open and discussed. The analyst must also refrain from engaging in countertransference. The goal of working with transference is to deal with the old feelings in light of new information.

92. **A.** Undergo their own psychoanalytic treatment. Because psychoanalysts need to be receptive to their patients' transference of childhood emotions, while refraining from countertransferring their own issues onto their patients, they need to have worked through their own issues stemming from childhood before treating others.

93. **C.** New response. In this example of aversive conditioning, which works by attaching negative feelings to stimuli that are undesirable, the gambling is the stimulus, the fear is the new response, and the excitement is the undesired response.

94. **A.** Barbiturates. These are a type of sedative, which (along with alcohol) was historically used to control anxiety. However, meprobamates such as Miltown have since been shown to be more effective.

95. **C.** General Systems theory. In von Bertalanffy's theory, humans are autonomous organisms regulated by family systems. For a family system to undergo positive change, each individual in that system must contribute to the improvement. Communications within the system are highly stressed. The family systems model views an individual's symptoms as symptoms of family dysfunction.

96. **A.** 3.636, 4, 4. The mean is the average, the median is the number that falls in the middle of the series, and the mode is the number that occurs most frequently in the series.

97. **C.** Reduced heart rate. When the sympathetic nervous system produces arousal, the parasympathetic nervous system works to reduce these symptoms.

98. **E.** Placebo. The placebo effect is the phenomenon that a patient's symptoms can be alleviated by an otherwise ineffective treatment, apparently because the individual *expects* or *believes* that it will work. The fake drug is also known as a placebo.

99. **A.** Balance and equilibrium. They play a major role in the subjective sensation of motion and of spatial orientation. Vestibular input to areas of the nervous system involved in motor control helps adjust muscle activity and body position to allow for upright posture. Furthermore, vestibular input to regions of the nervous system controlling eye movements helps stabilize the eyes in space during head movements.

100. **D.** 100. IQ tests use a standardized scale with 100 as the median score. On most tests, a score between 90 and 110, or the median plus or minus 10, indicates average intelligence. A score above 130 indicates exceptional intelligence, while a score below 70 might indicate mental retardation.

Free-Response Question #1—Explanation

Overall approach

- Keep in mind the wording of the question, which asks you to explain the information to a client, not report facts and figures in an essay. Make sure your answer reflects this approach.

- Integrate the parts of your answer into well-constructed arguments rather than simply listing information.

- Be consistent and systematic in your approach. While you need not cover every type of test, or every strength and weakness, make sure that key points are covered.

- Use examples to show that you understand and can apply the concepts, rather than that you've memorized them.

Key points to include

- There are two main types of cognitive tests: those that measure general ability and those that measure acquired ability or learning.

- An IQ test is the first type, and an achievement test is the second type.

- An example of an IQ test is the WISC III. An example of an achievement test is the Scholastic Aptitude Test (SAT).

- The two types of tests are often given together so that the scores can be compared to see whether a child is living up to their potential.

- A high IQ score with a relatively low achievement score indicates that the child is not learning at the rate they are able to, which *might* indicate a learning disability.

- An IQ is generally found by dividing a person's mental age (what they accomplish on an IQ test compared with their peers) by their chronological age, and multiplying the result by 100 (MA/CA × 100).

- IQ scores don't factor in creativity, athletic ability, personality and so on—all of which can affect the results. Because of these extraneous factors, IQ scores are often presented as a range.

- On the WISC III, in addition to the IQ score (also called the Full Scale IQ), Verbal IQ and Performance IQ scores are included.

- Quality IQ tests use a highly standardized set of procedures for testing a person. Standardized IQ scores have the following features:

  - The average is always 100. If you score above 100, you have a higher-than-average IQ. If you score below 100, you have a lower-than-average IQ.

  - IQ scores are normally distributed, meaning that if all the IQ scores for any given age group are plotted on a graph, the graph has a bell shape.

  - Percentiles are sometimes given alongside the IQ or standard score, which represent a person's score in relation to their peers.

  - Sometimes scores (particularly achievement scores) are presented in terms of grade levels. Grade levels represent the theoretical level of achievement that a person should have at any particular grade.

- The WISC III is the most widely used test in the United States for measuring IQ and can be used for testing children aged 6 to 16 1/2.

- The WISC III is administered individually, usually by a clinical psychologist or school psychologist, and takes about 1.5 hours. The test consists of 13 subtests, 11 of which are given in a standard test. Two of the other subtests can be given if 1 of the original 11 is somehow spoiled. The 13th test is designed to detect attention deficit disorder.

- The WISC III has good research data behind it, has a good correlation with academic success and is well understood by almost every school in the country.

- The WISC III underestimates high IQs because it has an artificial ceiling of 160. It is time-consuming to administer and relies too heavily on timed tasks to measure ability. (The relevance of timed tasks in measuring IQ is being questioned by more current research.)

- A frequent problem that parents have after their children receive some type of standardized testing is interpreting the results. Sometimes test reports give verbal descriptions without giving the numbers and statistics behind the report. Explaining testing results should be part of any thorough assessment.

Free-Response Question #2—Explanation

Overall approach

- In answering a compare and contrast question, make sure to demonstrate your understanding of *compare* (examine for similarities) and *contrast* (show to be different)—and be sure to do both.

- Integrate the parts of your answer into well-constructed arguments rather than simply listing characteristics.

- Be consistent and systematic in your approach. While you need not compare and contrast every aspect of each theory, make sure the key differences and similarities are covered.

- Use examples to show that you understand and can apply the concepts, rather than that you've memorized them.

Key points for comparison and contrast

Similarities

- Both are theories of personality development.

- Both emphasize the importance of the unconscious in the development of personality.

- Both represent stage theories where individuals progress through stages in a predictable order.

- Both theories begin at birth and have five stages that describe personality development through adolescence. However, Erikson's model continues through adulthood with three more stages (young adulthood, midlife, and old age) for a total of eight stages.

- A direct comparison can be made between the five stages of each theory in terms of the ages at which they occur.

Differences

- Freud emphasized the role of sexual drive, or libido, in personality.

- Erickson emphasized the influence of parents and society in the development of personality.

- Freud's theory focused on the individual unconscious.

- Erickson's theory focused on the collective unconscious.

- Freud believed that personality development ends at adolescence with the resolution of the Oedipal conflict.

- Erickson's stages extend through the life span.

- Freud believed that the ego serves only to satisfy the id.

- Erickson believed that ego is more important than id and that the culture serves the ego as the ego serves the culture.

- Freud believed that dreams are the keys to unlocking the unconscious and are means to an end.

- Erickson believed that dream themes focus on the strengths of the ego and that they are constructive ends in and of themselves.

- Freud believed that the purpose of therapy is to uncover traumatic and repressed events.

- Erickson believed that therapy is for the purpose of strengthening one's ego so that everyday problems can be handled well.

- Freud had his patients reclining and not facing the analyst.

- Erickson sat face to face with his patients to create a more equitable environment.

- Freud had a pessimistic view of religion, believing that "it is merely a collective neurosis based on infantile fears and desires."

- Erickson believed that religion is a necessary part of the human experience to make lives meaningful and understandable.

Answer Sheet for Practice Test 2

1 Ⓐ Ⓑ Ⓒ Ⓓ Ⓔ		26 Ⓐ Ⓑ Ⓒ Ⓓ Ⓔ
2 Ⓐ Ⓑ Ⓒ Ⓓ Ⓔ		27 Ⓐ Ⓑ Ⓒ Ⓓ Ⓔ
3 Ⓐ Ⓑ Ⓒ Ⓓ Ⓔ		28 Ⓐ Ⓑ Ⓒ Ⓓ Ⓔ
4 Ⓐ Ⓑ Ⓒ Ⓓ Ⓔ		29 Ⓐ Ⓑ Ⓒ Ⓓ Ⓔ
5 Ⓐ Ⓑ Ⓒ Ⓓ Ⓔ		30 Ⓐ Ⓑ Ⓒ Ⓓ Ⓔ
6 Ⓐ Ⓑ Ⓒ Ⓓ Ⓔ		31 Ⓐ Ⓑ Ⓒ Ⓓ Ⓔ
7 Ⓐ Ⓑ Ⓒ Ⓓ Ⓔ		32 Ⓐ Ⓑ Ⓒ Ⓓ Ⓔ
8 Ⓐ Ⓑ Ⓒ Ⓓ Ⓔ		33 Ⓐ Ⓑ Ⓒ Ⓓ Ⓔ
9 Ⓐ Ⓑ Ⓒ Ⓓ Ⓔ		34 Ⓐ Ⓑ Ⓒ Ⓓ Ⓔ
10 Ⓐ Ⓑ Ⓒ Ⓓ Ⓔ		35 Ⓐ Ⓑ Ⓒ Ⓓ Ⓔ
11 Ⓐ Ⓑ Ⓒ Ⓓ Ⓔ		36 Ⓐ Ⓑ Ⓒ Ⓓ Ⓔ
12 Ⓐ Ⓑ Ⓒ Ⓓ Ⓔ		37 Ⓐ Ⓑ Ⓒ Ⓓ Ⓔ
13 Ⓐ Ⓑ Ⓒ Ⓓ Ⓔ		38 Ⓐ Ⓑ Ⓒ Ⓓ Ⓔ
14 Ⓐ Ⓑ Ⓒ Ⓓ Ⓔ		39 Ⓐ Ⓑ Ⓒ Ⓓ Ⓔ
15 Ⓐ Ⓑ Ⓒ Ⓓ Ⓔ		40 Ⓐ Ⓑ Ⓒ Ⓓ Ⓔ
16 Ⓐ Ⓑ Ⓒ Ⓓ Ⓔ		41 Ⓐ Ⓑ Ⓒ Ⓓ Ⓔ
17 Ⓐ Ⓑ Ⓒ Ⓓ Ⓔ		42 Ⓐ Ⓑ Ⓒ Ⓓ Ⓔ
18 Ⓐ Ⓑ Ⓒ Ⓓ Ⓔ		43 Ⓐ Ⓑ Ⓒ Ⓓ Ⓔ
19 Ⓐ Ⓑ Ⓒ Ⓓ Ⓔ		44 Ⓐ Ⓑ Ⓒ Ⓓ Ⓔ
20 Ⓐ Ⓑ Ⓒ Ⓓ Ⓔ		45 Ⓐ Ⓑ Ⓒ Ⓓ Ⓔ
21 Ⓐ Ⓑ Ⓒ Ⓓ Ⓔ		46 Ⓐ Ⓑ Ⓒ Ⓓ Ⓔ
22 Ⓐ Ⓑ Ⓒ Ⓓ Ⓔ		47 Ⓐ Ⓑ Ⓒ Ⓓ Ⓔ
23 Ⓐ Ⓑ Ⓒ Ⓓ Ⓔ		48 Ⓐ Ⓑ Ⓒ Ⓓ Ⓔ
24 Ⓐ Ⓑ Ⓒ Ⓓ Ⓔ		49 Ⓐ Ⓑ Ⓒ Ⓓ Ⓔ
25 Ⓐ Ⓑ Ⓒ Ⓓ Ⓔ		50 Ⓐ Ⓑ Ⓒ Ⓓ Ⓔ

51	Ⓐ Ⓑ Ⓒ Ⓓ Ⓔ
52	Ⓐ Ⓑ Ⓒ Ⓓ Ⓔ
53	Ⓐ Ⓑ Ⓒ Ⓓ Ⓔ
54	Ⓐ Ⓑ Ⓒ Ⓓ Ⓔ
55	Ⓐ Ⓑ Ⓒ Ⓓ Ⓔ
56	Ⓐ Ⓑ Ⓒ Ⓓ Ⓔ
57	Ⓐ Ⓑ Ⓒ Ⓓ Ⓔ
58	Ⓐ Ⓑ Ⓒ Ⓓ Ⓔ
59	Ⓐ Ⓑ Ⓒ Ⓓ Ⓔ
60	Ⓐ Ⓑ Ⓒ Ⓓ Ⓔ
61	Ⓐ Ⓑ Ⓒ Ⓓ Ⓔ
62	Ⓐ Ⓑ Ⓒ Ⓓ Ⓔ
63	Ⓐ Ⓑ Ⓒ Ⓓ Ⓔ
64	Ⓐ Ⓑ Ⓒ Ⓓ Ⓔ
65	Ⓐ Ⓑ Ⓒ Ⓓ Ⓔ
66	Ⓐ Ⓑ Ⓒ Ⓓ Ⓔ
67	Ⓐ Ⓑ Ⓒ Ⓓ Ⓔ
68	Ⓐ Ⓑ Ⓒ Ⓓ Ⓔ
69	Ⓐ Ⓑ Ⓒ Ⓓ Ⓔ
70	Ⓐ Ⓑ Ⓒ Ⓓ Ⓔ
71	Ⓐ Ⓑ Ⓒ Ⓓ Ⓔ
72	Ⓐ Ⓑ Ⓒ Ⓓ Ⓔ
73	Ⓐ Ⓑ Ⓒ Ⓓ Ⓔ
74	Ⓐ Ⓑ Ⓒ Ⓓ Ⓔ
75	Ⓐ Ⓑ Ⓒ Ⓓ Ⓔ

76	Ⓐ Ⓑ Ⓒ Ⓓ Ⓔ
77	Ⓐ Ⓑ Ⓒ Ⓓ Ⓔ
78	Ⓐ Ⓑ Ⓒ Ⓓ Ⓔ
79	Ⓐ Ⓑ Ⓒ Ⓓ Ⓔ
80	Ⓐ Ⓑ Ⓒ Ⓓ Ⓔ
81	Ⓐ Ⓑ Ⓒ Ⓓ Ⓔ
82	Ⓐ Ⓑ Ⓒ Ⓓ Ⓔ
83	Ⓐ Ⓑ Ⓒ Ⓓ Ⓔ
84	Ⓐ Ⓑ Ⓒ Ⓓ Ⓔ
85	Ⓐ Ⓑ Ⓒ Ⓓ Ⓔ
86	Ⓐ Ⓑ Ⓒ Ⓓ Ⓔ
87	Ⓐ Ⓑ Ⓒ Ⓓ Ⓔ
88	Ⓐ Ⓑ Ⓒ Ⓓ Ⓔ
89	Ⓐ Ⓑ Ⓒ Ⓓ Ⓔ
90	Ⓐ Ⓑ Ⓒ Ⓓ Ⓔ
91	Ⓐ Ⓑ Ⓒ Ⓓ Ⓔ
92	Ⓐ Ⓑ Ⓒ Ⓓ Ⓔ
93	Ⓐ Ⓑ Ⓒ Ⓓ Ⓔ
94	Ⓐ Ⓑ Ⓒ Ⓓ Ⓔ
95	Ⓐ Ⓑ Ⓒ Ⓓ Ⓔ
96	Ⓐ Ⓑ Ⓒ Ⓓ Ⓔ
97	Ⓐ Ⓑ Ⓒ Ⓓ Ⓔ
98	Ⓐ Ⓑ Ⓒ Ⓓ Ⓔ
99	Ⓐ Ⓑ Ⓒ Ⓓ Ⓔ
100	Ⓐ Ⓑ Ⓒ Ⓓ Ⓔ

CUT HERE

Practice Test 2

Section 1: Multiple-Choice Questions

Time: 70 Minutes
Questions: 100

1. A researcher conducted a survey and concluded that the more often an individual watches soap operas, the more likely it is that the individual is unemployed. This type of study is:

   A. experimental
   B. nonexperimental
   C. correlational
   D. both A and C
   E. both B and C

2. Which measure of central tendency is *least* representative of the following set of student test scores: 7, 96, 97, 98, 99, 99, 100?

   A. mean
   B. median
   C. mode
   D. variance
   E. standard deviation

3. Variables such as length, weight and reaction time are measured on a/an _____ scale.

   A. nominal
   B. ordinal
   C. interval
   D. ratio
   E. both C and D

4. A researcher wants to determine whether packaging information affects the way individuals rate the flavor of orange juice. The same orange juice is put in three packages: (1) an orange container that says "100% of daily vitamin C," (2) a yellow container that says "a healthy way to start your day" and (3) a red container that says "for a fit and fun lifestyle." In this experiment the confounding variable is:

   A. flavor ratings
   B. packaging information
   C. color of container
   D. personal taste
   E. reading ability

5. When conducting scientific research, it is always unethical to:

   A. use deception
   B. use mentally ill participants
   C. use participants younger than 12 years of age
   D. expose humans to discomfort during an experiment
   E. none of the above

6. A researcher is interested in investigating how different types and amounts of reinforcement affect the amount of time college students spend exercising on a stationary bicycle. This researcher most likely takes which type of approach to psychology?

   A. biological
   B. cognitive
   C. psychodynamic
   D. behaviorist
   E. evolutionary

GO ON TO THE NEXT PAGE

7. You conduct an experiment using a factorial design and find that the effect of your first independent variable depends on the level of your second independent variable. You have just discovered a/an:

   A. main effect
   B. interaction
   C. carry-over effect
   D. confound
   E. extraneous variable

8. A well-known correlation exists between the consumption of ice cream and deaths due to drowning. Thus, as ice cream consumption increases, drowning deaths also increase. The relationship between these two variables is:

   A. positive and linear
   B. negative and linear
   C. positive and nonlinear
   D. negative and nonlinear
   E. causal

9. What statistical test *is not* used to determine whether three groups are significantly different from each other?

   A. analysis of variance
   B. factorial analysis of variance
   C. independent t-test
   D. dependent t-test
   E. both C and D

10. Which of the following psychologists is considered behaviorist(s)?

    A. Ivan Pavlov
    B. John B. Watson
    C. B.F. Skinner
    D. E.L. Thorndike
    E. all the above

11. Experimental methods of data collection are *least* likely to be used by an individual with a background in which of the following perspectives in psychology?

    A. biological
    B. cognitive
    C. social
    D. psychodynamic
    E. evolutionary

12. Of the following brain areas, which is most directly involved in coordinating smooth movements?

    A. hippocampus
    B. cerebellum
    C. hypothalamus
    D. medulla
    E. amygdala

13. When an action potential is fired, neurotransmitters are released from which part of the neuron?

    A. soma
    B. dendrites
    C. axon
    D. axon hillock
    E. terminal buttons

14. What is the resting membrane potential of a neuron?

    A. +70 mV
    B. +55 mV
    C. –20 mV
    D. –70 mV
    E. –120 mV

15. Tom accidentally ran into an angry grizzly bear on his hike. His heart races, his breathing accelerates, and he takes off running in the other direction. Which division of Tom's nervous system is activated?

    A. ganglionic
    B. somatic
    C. sympathetic
    D. parasympathetic
    E. automatic

16. Which cerebral cortical lobes are the loci of auditory cortex?

    A. frontal
    B. occipital
    C. cerebellar
    D. parietal
    E. temporal

17. Jim suffered a stroke that damaged a discrete part of his cerebral cortex. Since the stroke, Jim has experienced severe problems comprehending speech, although he has no problems speaking. Which part of Jim's cerebral cortex was most likely damaged?

    A. Broca's area
    B. Wernicke's area
    C. Lashley's area
    D. Carlson's area
    E. Westman's area

18. Of the following relatives, who has the greatest degree of genetic relatedness?

    A. monozygotic twin
    B. dizygotic twin
    C. sibling
    D. mother
    E. father

19. Which of the following research techniques is most likely to be used on a human participant?

    A. intracellular recording
    B. lesioning
    C. functional magnetic resonance imaging
    D. track tracing
    E. ablation

20. Which of the following chemicals functions as both a neurotransmitter in the central nervous system and a hormone in the periphery?

    A. glutamate
    B. adrenaline
    C. GABA
    D. dopamine
    E. serotonin

21. Which of the following brain areas is most directly linked to the endocrine system?

    A. frontal lobes
    B. cerebellum
    C. hypothalamus
    D. temporal lobes
    E. amygdala

22. The point at which a physical energy is just strong enough to be noticed is referred to as the:

    A. absolute threshold
    B. difference threshold
    C. just-noticeable threshold
    D. minimum threshold
    E. maximum threshold

23. Which of the following statements about color vision is *not true*?

    A. Thomas Young and Hermann von Helmholtz developed the Trichromatic theory of color vision.
    B. The Opponent-Process theory of color vision explains the phenomenon of afterimages.
    C. Rods are more sensitive to light, and cones are more sensitive to color.
    D. Color photoreceptors are concentrated in the fovea.
    E. The Opponent-Process theory appears to be at work at the retinal level, whereas the Trichromatic theory is more applicable to the lateral geniculate nucleus.

24. The optic nerve is made up of _____.

    A. photoreceptors
    B. bipolar cells
    C. complex cells
    D. ganglion cells
    E. simple cells

25. Retinal disparity, interposition, relative size, linear perspective, texture gradient and motion parallax are all cues that help us perceive _____.

    A. motion
    B. depth
    C. form
    D. length
    E. contrast

GO ON TO THE NEXT PAGE

26. When we look at an ink sketch, we inherently know that we should focus on the black picture as opposed to the white paper around it. In Gestalt psychology this phenomenon is referred to as:

A. proximity

B. similarity

C. figure-ground perception

D. good continuation

E. closure

27. The visual pathway that runs from the primary visual cortex in the occipital lobes through the lower portion of the temporal lobes (inferior temporal cortex) is known as the:

A. who pathway

B. what pathway

C. when pathway

D. where pathway

E. why pathway

28. Which of the following statements is *least* true of sensory adaptation?

A. Sensory adaptation is the tendency of sensory systems to respond more to continuous, unchanging stimuli.

B. Sensory adaptation is adaptive from an evolutionary perspective.

C. Severe pain is an exception to the rule of sensory adaptation.

D. Afterimages are the result of sensory adaptation.

E. Sensory adaptation is a phenomenon shared by all sensory systems.

29. Which of the following psychoactive drugs is a stimulant?

A. lysergic acid diethylamide (LSD)

B. marijuana

C. amphetamine

D. alcohol

E. PCP ("angel dust")

30. During which stage of sleep do both men and women show signs of sexual arousal?

A. Stage 1

B. Stage 2

C. Stage 3

D. Stage 4

E. REM stage

31. A psychologist from which of the following perspectives is most likely to believe that dreams have no underlying meaning?

A. cognitive

B. Freudian

C. psychodynamic

D. biological

E. both B and C

32. Which of the following activities could induce an altered state of consciousness?

A. ingestion of drugs

B. meditation

C. hypnosis

D. sleep

E. all the above

33. Susan has enjoyed eating clams all her life. Recently she ate a spoiled clam and became violently ill. Since then, the sight or smell of a clam makes her nauseous. Her nausea at the sight or smell of a clam is referred to as a/an:

A. conditioned stimulus

B. unconditioned stimulus

C. conditioned response

D. unconditioned response

E. neutral response

34. Which of the following is an example of a fixed-ratio schedule of reinforcement?

A. receiving a gumdrop for every homework problem that is completed

B. receiving a dollar each hour if at least one homework problem is completed since the last hour

C. winning a trophy after the third season of playing baseball

D. winning at chess every other game, on average

E. receiving a food pellet, on average, every five minutes if a bar is pressed

35. A young child was stung by a bee, which scared and hurt him very much. For a year following the incident, the child screamed and cried at the very sight of a bee. Eventually, however, after seeing bees hundreds of times, without the consequence of a sting, the child lost his fear of bees. In classical conditioning terms, the process by which the child *lost his fear* of bees is known as:

A. conditioning
B. backwards conditioning
C. extinction
D. stimulus discrimination
E. deceleration

36. Which of the following is an example of a fixed-interval schedule of reinforcement?

A. receiving a gumdrop for every homework problem that is completed
B. receiving a dollar each hour if at least one homework problem is completed since the last hour
C. winning a trophy after the third season of playing baseball
D. winning at chess every other game, on average
E. receiving a food pellet, on average, every five minutes if a bar is pressed

37. Martin Seligman's animal model of depression is known as:

A. negative learning
B. acquired despair
C. animal depressive syndrome
D. learned helplessness
E. latent learning

38. John feels that it doesn't matter how hard you work; being successful at anything is simply a matter of getting the right lucky breaks. According to Cognitive-Social theory, John has:

A. an internal locus of control
B. an external locus of control
C. generalized expectancies
D. both A and C
E. both B and C

39. A rat is placed in a box that delivers a constant mild electric shock through the floor. The rat quickly learns that if it presses a nearby bar, the shock will be turned off. This is an example of:

A. positive reinforcement
B. negative reinforcement
C. positive punishment
D. negative punishment
E. reverse punishment

40. Which type of conditioned stimulus–unconditioned stimulus (CS-UCS) pairing is *least* effective at conditioning?

A. simultaneous conditioning
B. delayed conditioning
C. trace conditioning
D. backward conditioning
E. both B and C

41. An organism will quickly associate a taste with the feeling of nausea, but will not easily associate an audiovisual cue with nausea. This example illustrates the phenomenon of:

A. paradoxical conditioning
B. conditioned tolerance
C. prepared learning
D. latent conditioning
E. extinction

42. Which of the following symptoms of schizophrenia is classified as a negative symptom in the DSM-IV?

A. flat effect
B. disordered thought
C. hallucinations
D. bizarre behavior
E. delusions

43. Which of the following statements is *least* true of paranoid schizophrenia?

A. It is dominated by positive symptoms.
B. Onset usually occurs during the late 20s.
C. It responds better to antipsychotic medication than catatonic schizophrenia.
D. Heritability is around 50%.
E. Imbalance in norepinephrine levels appears to contribute to the disorder.

GO ON TO THE NEXT PAGE

44. For the past two years, Lisa has had bouts of depression that have been interspersed with periods of relatively normal moods, each lasting several weeks. Her depression is not debilitating; rather, she feels tired, sleeps more than normal, and has very low self-esteem. Lisa is *most* likely to be diagnosed with:

- **A.** major depressive disorder
- **B.** dysthymic disorder
- **C.** mania
- **D.** bipolar disorder
- **E.** anhedonia

45. The most widely prescribed drugs for the treatment of bipolar disorder are:

- **A.** tricyclics
- **B.** monoamine oxidase inhibitors (MAOIs)
- **C.** selective serotonin reuptake inhibitors (SSRIs)
- **D.** lithium salts
- **E.** antipsychotics

46. An individual with borderline personality disorder is best described as:

- **A.** distrustful and suspicious
- **B.** excessively emotional and attention seeking
- **C.** impulsive and unstable in interpersonal relationships, self-concept and emotion
- **D.** submissive and clinging
- **E.** disregarding of the rights of others

47. A cognitive therapist is *most* likely to use which of the following modes of treatment?

- **A.** altering of problematic thought patterns
- **B.** psychoanalysis
- **C.** unconditional positive regard
- **D.** drug treatment
- **E.** operant techniques

48. Someone who exhibits hypochondriasis (excessive fear of disease without a valid basis for concern) is most likely suffering from which of the following types of disorders?

- **A.** dissociative
- **B.** mood
- **C.** adjustment
- **D.** somatoform
- **E.** personality

49. Which of the following anxiety disorders is *most* likely to be treated with an antidepressant drug, such as an SSRI?

- **A.** post-traumatic stress
- **B.** agoraphobia
- **C.** social anxiety
- **D.** generalized anxiety
- **E.** obsessive-compulsive

50. Which of the following is *not* a diagnostic category of the DSM-IV?

- **A.** substance-related disorders
- **B.** hyperactivity disorders
- **C.** eating disorders
- **D.** adjustment disorders
- **E.** sexual and gender identity disorders

51. Which of the following psychological disorders is most likely to be treated with the technique of systematic desensitization?

- **A.** paranoid schizophrenia
- **B.** mania
- **C.** arachnophobia
- **D.** drug addiction
- **E.** attention deficit/hyperactivity disorder

52. Which of the following types of drugs is associated with a disorder called tardive dyskinesia?

- **A.** antipsychotics
- **B.** SSRIs
- **C.** benzodiazepines
- **D.** psychostimulants
- **E.** hallucinogenics

53. A depressed patient, Mary, tells her therapist that she is not pretty enough to go on a date, even though she has won several beauty contests. According to Aaron Beck, this patient is experiencing the cognitive error of:

- **A.** magnification
- **B.** minimization
- **C.** personalization
- **D.** overgeneralization
- **E.** arbitrary inference

54. Which of the following terms is *not* associated with psychodynamic therapy?

   A. insight

   B. free association

   C. interpretation

   D. negative triad

   E. transference

55. What is the main difference between a psychiatrist and a psychologist?

   A. Psychiatrists generally use psychodynamic therapy, while psychologists use a variety of approaches to therapy.

   B. A psychiatrist has a doctorate in medicine and a psychologist has a doctorate in philosophy.

   C. Psychiatrists can prescribe medications for psychological disorders, but psychologists cannot prescribe medications.

   D. Both A and C.

   E. Both B and C.

56. In social psychology, conformity means a change in attitude or behavior to fit the views of a group majority. Which of the following circumstances increases the likelihood that an individual will conform?

   A. The individual has high self-esteem.

   B. The individual is concerned with their own status.

   C. The individual was previously committed to another position.

   D. The majority does not have a unanimous position.

   E. The situation is private.

57. Results of the famous Milgram experiments on obedience showed that:

   A. Subjects will not obey an authority figure if they feel that doing so will harm another person.

   B. Subjects are more likely to obey when an authority figure is close in proximity.

   C. The results of the study were not surprising to most psychologists at the time.

   D. Both A and B.

   E. Both A and C.

58. In the famous Zimbardo Prison Study, Philip Zimbardo was interested in how _____ influence social behavior.

   A. biases

   B. prison foods

   C. roles

   D. heuristics

   E. individual differences

59. While Kelly was at the grocery store, a checkout clerk was somewhat rude to her. The clerk is normally a very polite and respectful person; however, she just broke up with her boyfriend and was feeling very upset. When Kelly arrived home, she told her husband that she encountered one of the meanest people she had ever met. This is an illustration of:

   A. fundamental attribution error

   B. hindsight bias

   C. halo effect

   D. self-fulfilling prophecy

   E. false consensus bias

60. A car commercial appears on TV, and the speaker says, "Why should you buy a Corvette? Simple; because women love a man in a hot sports car." The speaker is attempting to use the _____ route of persuasion.

   A. fundamental

   B. central

   C. external

   D. peripheral

   E. hormonal

61. Which of the following circumstances increases the likelihood that a bystander will intervene in a crisis to help another individual?

   A. The bystander senses a diffusion of responsibility.

   B. The bystander is a man.

   C. The bystander is a woman.

   D. The bystander is part of a group.

   E. The bystander is alone.

GO ON TO THE NEXT PAGE

62. A psychologist with a cognitive-social background is *most* likely to make which of the following statements about aggression?

   A. If a child observes their parents fighting regularly, they will be more aggressive as an adult.

   B. Aggression occurs in all species; thus, it evolved because of its value in maintaining survival and reproductive success.

   C. Aggression is a basic human drive, and aggressive behavior is pleasurable.

   D. When we mature, we learn to regulate direct physical aggression; however, our aggression comes out in indirect ways, such as passive aggressive behavior.

   E. Aggressive behavior must be reinforced in some way, or it does not continue.

63. According to the Serial Processing model of memory, stages of memory occur in which of the following orders?

   A. sensory registers, rehearsal, short-term memory, long-term memory, retrieval

   B. short-term memory, sensory registers, rehearsal, long-term memory, retrieval

   C. sensory registers, short-term memory, rehearsal, long-term memory, retrieval

   D. short-term memory, sensory registers, long-term memory, rehearsal, retrieval

   E. retrieval, sensory registers, short-term memory, rehearsal, long-term memory

64. Which type of rehearsal is most useful for storing information in long-term memory?

   A. complex
   B. elaborative
   C. structured
   D. maintenance
   E. preservation

65. Approximately how many pieces of information can be held in short-term memory at one time?

   A. 7
   B. 10
   C. 15
   D. 20
   E. 25

66. Consider this list of words: *house, dog, tree, apple, hair, water, paper, ball, child, sky, ship, flag, shoe*. According to the serial position effect, which of these words would you recall best after a short delay if they were read to you in the preceding order?

   A. House, dog.
   B. Flag, shoe.
   C. Water, paper, ball.
   D. Both A and B.
   E. Each word has the same chance of being remembered.

67. Tom's teacher asked him what he ate for breakfast earlier in the morning. To answer that question, Tom uses his _____ memory.

   A. episodic
   B. declarative
   C. semantic
   D. both A and B
   E. both B and C

68. Every time you tie your shoes, you are using _____ memory.

   A. declarative
   B. episodic
   C. semantic
   D. explicit
   E. procedural

69. Which of the following examples illustrates the encoding specificity principle?

   A. To remember items that needed to be picked up from the store, Angela imagined each item in a specific location in her bedroom while trying to make each vision as vivid as possible.

   B. Angela always performed very well on her introductory psychology tests; however, the final exam was given in a different room than usual, and she performed very poorly.

   C. Angela and Lisa are both good students, but for their last biology exam Angela studied the material over several sessions during the preceding week, while Lisa crammed the night before the test. Angela received an A+, and Lisa earned a C+.

   D. Both A and B.
   E. Both B and C.

70. Bill is on a date with Ashley. Based on their conversations, Bill is not sure whether Ashley has a brain. However, Bill knows that all living human beings have a brain. Bill also knows that Ashley is a living human being. Armed with this knowledge, Bill deduces that Ashley has a brain. The type of reasoning that Bill used to reach his conclusion regarding Ashley's possession of a brain is known as:

A. inductive
B. deconstructive
C. deductive
D. theological
E. constructive

71. Kevin has been dating Erin for about two months. Erin has recently begun to cancel dates often. Kevin remembers that when his last girlfriend started canceling dates often, she broke up with him shortly thereafter. Therefore, Kevin assumes that Erin will break up with him soon and decides to break up with Erin so that he will beat her to the punch. The type of reasoning that Kevin used is called:

A. analogical
B. faulty
C. inductive
D. deductive
E. pragmatic

72. In regard to language, which of the following terms refers to the rules that govern the *meanings* of words and phrases?

A. phonemes
B. morphemes
C. syntax
D. pragmatics
E. semantics

73. The four phases of Masters and Johnson's sexual response cycle are:

A. excitement, plateau, orgasm, termination
B. initiation, excitement, orgasm, resolution
C. excitement, plateau, orgasm, resolution
D. foreplay, excitement, plateau, orgasm
E. foreplay, excitement, plateau, termination

74. The James-Lange theory of emotion asserts that:

A. Emotion is too complex to understand from a biological perspective.
B. The subjective experience of emotion results from the brain's interpretation of autonomic responses.
C. Emotional states are really figments of our imagination.
D. Emotional reactions are highly dependent on individual personality characteristics.
E. The amygdala is the brain center of emotion.

75. Which two psychologists challenged the James-Lange theory of emotion?

A. Singer and Winglet
B. Watson and Skinner
C. Jung and Lange
D. Cannon and Bard
E. Watson and Rainer

76. This theory of emotion takes into consideration cognitive appraisal.

A. Schachter-Singer
B. Kluver-Busy
C. Arnold-Anderson
D. Cohen-Poplawsky
E. Kontos-Beck

77. According to Selye's general adaptation syndrome, exhaustion is the end result of chronic _____.

A. physical exertion
B. stress
C. failure
D. rejection
E. physical pain

78. John is very concerned that he will fail publicly. To deal with this, John never attempts anything difficult in public, avoiding any chance of public failure. Apparently, John has _____.

A. a need for achievement
B. performance-approach goals
C. performance-avoidance goals
D. both A and B
E. both A and C

GO ON TO THE NEXT PAGE

79. Under normal circumstances, our body temperature is maintained at approximately 98.6° Fahrenheit. If our temperature drops too low, we shiver; and if it gets too high, we sweat. This example illustrates the process of _____.

    A. thermo induction
    B. drive reduction
    C. homeostasis
    D. allostasis
    E. thermostasis

80. Which of the following is *not* a level in Maslow's hierarchy of needs?

    A. self-actualization
    B. safety
    C. physiological
    D. sexual gratification
    E. esteem

81. An individual with an IQ score of 72 is considered:

    A. gifted
    B. superior
    C. average
    D. borderline mentally retarded
    E. profoundly mentally retarded

82. Which of the following tests is a group test?

    A. Scholastic Assessment Tests (SAT)
    B. Wechsler Adult Intelligence Scale, third edition (WAIS III)
    C. Wechsler Intelligence Scale for Children, third edition (WISC III)
    D. Stanford-Binet Scale
    E. both C and D

83. Which of the following statements regarding intelligence is *least* accurate?

    A. To a large extent, intelligence can be attributed to genetic factors.
    B. Environmental factors have little or no influence on intelligence.
    C. Howard Gardner proposed the theory of multiple intelligences.
    D. Fluid intelligence is used when approaching a novel problem.
    E. Crystallized intelligence varies considerably between different cultures.

84. Which of the following statements regarding mental retardation is *least* accurate?

    A. Severe forms of mental retardation are mostly due to genetic or other physical causes.
    B. Most cases of mental retardation are *not* diagnosed at birth.
    C. Most cases of mild retardation seem to be environmentally influenced.
    D. Most cases of mental retardation are mild to moderate.
    E. Down syndrome is caused by the absence of a chromosome.

85. Approximately what proportion of the general population is considered either profoundly mentally retarded or gifted according to their IQ score?

    A. 10%
    B. 5%
    C. 2%
    D. 0.2%
    E. 0.002%

86. Which of the following is the definition of *sublimation*?

    A. the indirect expression of anger toward others
    B. justifying one's actions in a seemingly logical way to avoid guilt or shame
    C. converting sexual or aggressive impulses into socially acceptable activities
    D. an unconscious mechanism that keeps threatening thoughts or memories from conscious awareness
    E. refusal to acknowledge external realities

87. Which of the following personality types is most closely linked with heart disease?

    A. type A
    B. type B
    C. neurotic
    D. optimistic
    E. pessimistic

88. A psychologist with a background in humanistic theories is *most* likely to make which of the following statements concerning personality?

   A. Personality consists of several underlying traits on which individuals vary.

   B. Every individual has a true self.

   C. Personality is very dependent on the type of schema an individual uses to encode and retrieve social information.

   D. Personality develops through several psychosexual stages.

   E. An individual's conscious, preconscious and unconscious mental processes determine behavior.

89. One of the major criticisms of trait theories of personality is that:

   A. Genetic influences are not acknowledged.

   B. They do not lend themselves to empirical measurement.

   C. Trait psychologists cannot identify one agreed upon dimension of personality.

   D. They explain behavior, but do not describe behavior.

   E. Changes in behavior across different situations are not considered.

90. Which of the following personality assessments is a projective test?

   A. Thematic Apperception Test (TAT)

   B. Rorschach test

   C. life history method

   D. both A and B

   E. both B and C

91. Mark sees a strikingly beautiful woman across a bar and feels the overwhelming urge to run over and kiss her. However, he knows that this behavior would cause problems, perhaps embarrassment or even physical injury if a bouncer or angry boyfriend got involved. Therefore, he decides against it. According to Freud, the rational part of Mark's psyche that stopped him from giving in to his impulse is the:

   A. id

   B. ego

   C. superego

   D. ultraego

   E. logic monitor

92. Which of the following applies to longitudinal studies?

   A. comparison of people of different ages at a single time

   B. immunity to cohort effects

   C. following the same individuals over time

   D. both A and B

   E. both B and C

93. The period of gestation between nine weeks post-conception and birth is known as the _____ period.

   A. fetal

   B. germinal

   C. embryonic

   D. gestation

   E. nascent

94. A child who has just developed object permanence is most likely in Piaget's _____ stage of cognitive development.

   A. presensorimotor

   B. preoperational

   C. formal operational

   D. concrete operational

   E. sensorimotor

95. According to Piaget, a child who has just learned that water maintains the same volume when poured from a small container to a large container must be in which of the following stages?

   A. sensorimotor

   B. preoperational

   C. concrete operational

   D. formal operational

   E. postsensorimotor

96. Healthy senior citizens show the *least* decline in which of the following aspects of cognition?

   A. processing speed

   B. working memory capacity

   C. explicit memory retrieval

   D. crystallized intelligence

   E. fluid intelligence

GO ON TO THE NEXT PAGE

97. Which of the following parenting styles appears to produce the most well-adjusted children?

    A.   Authoritative.

    B.   Authoritarian.

    C.   Permissive.

    D.   Both A and C.

    E.   All parenting styles are equally successful.

98. According to Kohlberg's theory, during which of the following stages does a child come to understand that their gender remains constant over time?

    A.   gender identity

    B.   gender stability

    C.   gender constancy

    D.   gender solidity

    E.   gender distinctiveness

99. In Kohlberg's theory of moral development, a child who follows moral rules either to avoid punishment or to obtain reward is at which of the following levels of moral development?

    A.   preconventional morality

    B.   conventional morality

    C.   midconventional morality

    D.   postconventional morality

    E.   late conventional morality

100. According to Erikson's theory of lifespan development, a middle-aged person is *most* concerned with:

    A.   integrity

    B.   intimacy

    C.   identity

    D.   autonomy

    E.   generativity

IF YOU FINISH BEFORE TIME IS CALLED, CHECK YOUR WORK ON THIS SECTION ONLY. DO NOT WORK ON ANY OTHER SECTION IN THE TEST.

Section 2: Free-Response Questions

Time: 50 Minutes

Questions: 2

Directions: You have 50 minutes to answer both of the following questions. It is not enough to answer a question by just presenting facts. You must present a strong argument based on your critical analysis of the questions posed, using appropriate psychological terminology.

Free-Response Question #1

An experimenter wants to test the effect of a new appetite suppressant drug on hunger in rats. The experimenter also wants to test three different doses of the drug (low, medium and high). How many levels of the independent variable are in this experiment? Explain why each level is necessary. Further, provide two possible dependent variables that could be used to measure hunger in rats, being sure to provide specific operational definitions of each variable. Give a possible outcome of the experiment, and provide an interpretation of the results.

Free-Response Question #2

Part 1. Consider these two psychological disorders: paranoid schizophrenia and major depressive disorder. For both disorders:

- Describe the disorder and list the major symptoms associated with it.
- List the category of drug most commonly used to treat the disorder.
- Describe the mechanism of action of the drug (that is, the neurotransmitter system it targets and how it affects the system).

Part 2. Explain what a phobia is, and explain how an individual with arachnophobia (fear of spiders) would be treated with the techniques of systematic desensitization and the exposure technique of flooding. Also, discuss the theory behind the two treatments.

GO ON TO THE NEXT PAGE

GO ON TO THE NEXT PAGE

Answer Key for Practice Test 2

1. E	26. C	51. C	76. A
2. A	27. B	52. A	77. B
3. D	28. A	53. E	78. E
4. C	29. C	54. D	79. C
5. E	30. E	55. E	80. D
6. D	31. D	56. B	81. D
7. B	32. E	57. B	82. A
8. A	33. C	58. C	83. B
9. E	34. A	59. A	84. E
10. E	35. C	60. D	85. D
11. D	36. B	61. E	86. C
12. B	37. D	62. A	87. A
13. E	38. E	63. C	88. B
14. D	39. B	64. B	89. E
15. C	40. D	65. A	90. D
16. E	41. C	66. D	91. B
17. B	42. A	67. D	92. C
18. A	43. E	68. E	93. A
19. C	44. B	69. B	94. E
20. B	45. D	70. C	95. C
21. C	46. C	71. A	96. D
22. A	47. A	72. E	97. A
23. E	48. D	73. C	98. B
24. D	49. E	74. B	99. A
25. B	50. B	75. D	100. E

Complete Answers and Explanations for Practice Test 2

1. E. The most important question to ask when deciding whether a study is experimental or nonexperimental is *was a variable manipulated?* If a variable was manipulated and measures were taken to control confounding (extraneous) variables, it is most certainly an experimental study. The important difference between experimental and nonexperimental studies is that experimental studies allow researchers to make cause-and-effect statements about their results. A correlational study, such as the one in this question, can provide information regarding the way in which two variables change in relationship to each other (which has predictive value), but it cannot tell whether a cause-and-effect relationship exists between the variables.

2. A. The mean is the most skewed measure of central tendency in this example. The mean (sum of scores/number of scores), median (score in middle of the distribution) and mode (most frequently occurring score) for this set are 85, 98 and 99, respectively. The extreme score of 7 lowered the mean, which is much lower than the score received by most students in the sample. For this set of scores, the median and mode provide a more accurate representation of the entire sample. Variance and standard deviation are measures of variability, not central tendency, and were just listed as distractions.

3. D. Nominal variables have no quantitative (numerical) properties. Rather, they are qualitative variables such as male, female, Republican, Democrat and so on. Ordinal variables, as the name implies, are rank ordered from first to last. However, the interval between each order in the ranking is not necessarily equal. For example, if a group of runners were rank ordered based on finishing times, you would not know how far behind the second-place finisher was from the first place finisher, or the third-place finisher from the second, and so on. With interval variables the intervals between numbers on the scale are always equal, but there is no absolute zero. For example, temperature and IQ scores are measured along an interval scale. The zero point is only relative; thus, zero does not indicate the absence of temperature or intelligence. Ratio variables *do* have an absolute zero indicating the absence of the variable. Ratio variables include length, width, height, number of correct responses, number of lever presses, firing rate of a neuron and so on. Typically, students have the most trouble deciding whether a variable is interval or ratio. Two important questions to answer are *does a score of zero indicate the complete absence of the variable in question* and *if two measures are taken of this variable, is it possible to conclude that one measure is twice the value of the other (a ratio)?* If the answers are yes, the measurement scale is ratio.

4. C. A confounding variable is any variable other than the independent variable (IV) that might have an effect on the dependent variable (DV). In this study the researcher is interested in the effect of packaging information (IV) on flavor ratings (DV). Thus, the only variable that should change between groups in this experiment is packaging information. However, the color of the containers also changes systematically between groups and is therefore a confounding variable. Subject-relevant variables such as personal taste and reading ability are dealt with by randomly assigning individuals to experimental groups.

5. E. Deception is most often used during social psychology experiments. The use of deception is sometimes necessary and is ethical as long as certain conditions are met, such as the use of reasonable procedures and a debriefing at the conclusion of the experiment. Participants may also be subjected to reasonable discomfort during experiments provided that they give informed consent prior to the commencement of the experiment. Special populations such as the mentally ill and the very young are also used in experimental research to study certain phenomena, but exceptional care must be taken to ensure the safety of these participants.

6. D. Behaviorists focus on learning and experimentally study the way environmental variables control responses (behaviors). In this example, the reinforcements are the environmental variables, and exercising is the behavior. Generally, a behaviorist studies various aspects of classical conditioning and/or operant conditioning. The broad area of biological psychology includes neurobiology, neuroscience, behavioral neuroscience or any other subdiscipline that focuses on the physiological bases of behavior. Cognitive psychologists study phenomena such as thought, memory and language, often using information processing models. The psychodynamic perspective has its roots in the writings of Sigmund Freud, who believed that individuals' actions are driven by several unconscious motives that might conflict with each other. Finally, evolutionary psychologists study how adaptation through natural selection has come to shape animal and human behavior.

7. **B.** A factorial experimental design incorporates more than one independent variable (IV) in the same experiment. By using a factorial design, a researcher can study how one IV can influence the effect of another IV on the dependent variable (DV). If the effect of one IV *depends* on the level of another IV, you have an interaction. It is also possible to observe a *main effect* in a factorial design. A main effect occurs when one IV has a significant effect on the DV regardless of the level of the other IV(s). A carryover effect can occur in repeated measures experimental designs (i.e., designs that use the same subjects in every level of the IV). It means that being exposed to one level of the IV can affect an individual's performance in another, subsequent level of the IV. To deal with this problem, *counterbalancing* is used (e.g., half of the participants are exposed to the control condition first, while the other half is exposed to the experimental condition first). A confound occurs when an extraneous variable (an unwanted variable that is not the IV) causes a change in the dependent variable and it is not possible to interpret the results.

8. **A.** A positive relationship is one in which increases in the values of one variable are associated with increases in the values of the other variable. Likewise, decreases in one variable are accompanied by decreases in the other variable. Linear refers to the fact that the relationship is simple and can be drawn on a graph with a straight line (see example A). A negative relationship is one in which increases in the values of one variable are associated with decreases in the values of the other variable, or vice versa (see example B). A positive or negative correlation is necessarily linear. Therefore, C and D would never be correct. Causal relationships can only be determined by conducting an experiment, which was not done in this example.

9. **E.** A T-test is used to compare the means of two groups and determine whether they are significantly different. An independent t-test is used when the groups are independent from each other, and a dependent t-test is used when the groups are related in some way (e.g., the same subjects are used in each group). An analysis of variance tests for differences between three or more groups. A factorial analysis of variance is used to analyze data from an experiment with three or more groups *and* two or more independent variables.

10. **E.** All four famous psychologists are considered behaviorists. Thorndike proposed the Law of Effect, which stated that the more a behavior is rewarded, the more the behavior will be performed. Although Pavlov won a Nobel Prize for his research on digestion, he serendipitously discovered a phenomenon now called classical conditioning (or Pavlovian conditioning) while studying the salivation responses of dogs. Expanding on the work of Pavlov, Watson began the school of behaviorism and conducted the now famous (or infamous) experiments with Little Albert. Skinner extended the work of Thorndike by formally studying stimulus-response relationships and developing the rules of operant conditioning.

11. **D.** The scientific method is the foundation of any scientific discipline, including psychology. Most psychologists use experimental methods as their main vehicle for discovery. However, this is *least* true of Sigmund Freud, who founded the psychodynamic perspective in psychology. His theory of behavior was based on patient case studies (in-depth analysis of individuals). Thus, a major criticism of Freud's work is that it was never experimentally tested. Also, it might not be applicable to normal individuals because it is based on case studies of abnormal patients.

12. **B.** It is important to remember that no brain region is dedicated to just one behavior. In fact, most brain areas are involved in the control or modulation of numerous behaviors. However, in a question such as this one, you must choose the *best* answer based on the functions that each brain region is historically most associated with. The hippocampus is part of the limbic system and is necessary to form new memories, particularly explicit memories. The cerebellum is a large structure at the back of the brain originally found to be involved in coordinating smooth movements and in maintaining balance and posture. The hypothalamus is a tiny structure that activates pituitary hormones and also provides homeostatic control over glucose levels and metabolism. The medulla resides in the lowest portion of the brainstem and controls vital physiological processes, such as respiration, heartbeat and circulation. The amygdala is really a collection of forebrain nuclei that are best known for their involvement in emotional processes, such as the formation of emotionally significant memories.

13. **E.** The soma is the cell body of the neuron and contains the nucleus. Extending from the soma are branch-like processes called dendrites. The dendrites receive most of the information from other neurons. When the net excitatory post-synaptic potentials (EPSPs) are sufficient to move the membrane potential to the spike threshold, an action potential is initiated at the axon hillock (the first segment of the axon that is attached to the soma). The action potential travels down the axon until it reaches the end, where it causes the release of neurotransmitter from the terminal buttons.

14. D. The resting membrane potential of a neuron is the difference between the electrical charge inside and outside the neuron when it is not firing an action potential. The resting potential can vary quite a bit between different types of neurons, but in general, the resting membrane potential is somewhere around –70 millivolts (mV; one-thousandth of a volt). If you were to receive this question on a test and –70 mV was not an answer choice, you would just pick the choice that was closest to –70 mV. It is also important to know that an excitatory post-synaptic potential (EPSP) moves the resting membrane potential in a positive direction; that is, it depolarizes the neuron (for example, –50 mV). Conversely, an inhibitory post-synaptic potential (IPSP) moves the resting potential in a negative direction; that is, it hyperpolarizes the neuron (for example, –90 mV).

15. C. The nervous system is separated into two major divisions: the central nervous system (CNS) and the peripheral nervous system (PNS). The CNS consists of the brain and spinal cord and nothing else. The PNS is everything outside of the CNS. It carries information to and from the CNS. The PNS is further broken down into the somatic and autonomic subdivisions. The somatic division of the PNS transmits sensory information to the CNS and relays motor commands to skeletal muscle. The autonomic division of the PNS regulates internal organs such as the heart, lungs, intestines and so on. The autonomic nervous system is further segregated into the sympathetic and parasympathetic divisions. When an organism is threatened, the sympathetic nervous system readies the body for fight or flight by sending oxygen and other resources where they are needed. When no threat is present, the parasympathetic nervous system controls everyday bodily functions and stores the body's energy reserves. *Ganglionic* and *automatic* are not divisions of the nervous system.

16. E. The cerebral cortex is the folded, layered covering of the brain. The left and right hemispheres of the brain are divided into four symmetrical areas or lobes. The occipital lobes are located in the rear portion of the cortex and are largely made up of the primary visual cortex, which is the first cortical area to receive visual information. The parietal lobes are located in front of the occipital lobes and are the locus of somatosensory cortex, which receives tactile information from every part of the body. Other parts of the parietal lobes are involved in spatial orientation and the perception of movement. The frontal lobes are involved in a wide variety of higher functions, including attention, planning, problem solving and personality. The frontal lobes are also the locus of motor cortex, which is centrally involved in the control of movement. The temporal lobes reside in the lower side portions of the cortex and contain auditory cortex. The temporal lobes are also involved in pattern and object recognition. The cerebellar cortex covers the cerebellum and is not a cerebral cortical area.

17. B. Wernicke's area is located in the left temporal lobe, and damage to this area can result in Wernicke's aphasia. Wernicke's aphasia is characterized by difficulty understanding the meaning of spoken words. Patients with Wernicke's aphasia might speak clearly and fluently, but the syntax (word order) makes little sense. Broca's area is located in the left frontal lobe and is specialized to control the mouth and tongue during speech production. Injury to this area often results in Broca's aphasia, in which a patient has problems producing words and fluent speech, but might have no difficulty comprehending simple sentences. Although damage to either area can affect both speech production and comprehension, historically Wernicke's and Broca's areas have been associated with speech comprehension and production, respectively. The remaining choices are not actual cortical areas.

18. A. Because half of an individual's genes come from each parent, a child shares 50% genetic relatedness with each parent. Accordingly, siblings also share 50% genetic relatedness. Dizygotic (fraternal) twins are formed from two different sperm and egg unions. Therefore, they share the same genetic relatedness as siblings. Monozygotic (identical) twins develop from the union of one sperm and one egg. Thus, they possess the same genetic makeup and share 100% genetic relatedness.

19. C. Functional magnetic resonance imaging is a research tool that uses magnetic fields to measure metabolic activity in the brain. This is a noninvasive procedure; that is, it involves no surgery. Other commonly used noninvasive imaging techniques used in human research are electroencephalogram (EEG), computerized axial tomography (CAT) and positron emission tomography (PET). These techniques are used in human research to understand how various manipulations change neuronal activity in specific areas of the brain. The remaining answer choices are all invasive procedures. Intracellular recording involves the implantation of a recording electrode into the brain. Lesioning or ablation involves killing or removing a discrete area of the brain. Track tracing is an anatomical technique that requires a die or tracer of some kind to be injected into the brain. Invasive techniques such as these are only used in animal research for obvious reasons. These invasive procedures allow a much more detailed investigation of brain functioning.

179

20. B. Adrenaline (also called epinephrine) is secreted by the adrenal glands as a hormone during emergencies, but it is also used by certain neurons in the brain as a neurotransmitter. The remaining chemicals are important neurotransmitters and do not serve as hormones. Glutamate and GABA are, respectively, the major excitatory and inhibitory transmitters in the brain. Glutamate and GABA are both amino acid transmitters. Abnormal glutamate and GABA transmission can contribute to epileptic seizures and certain anxiety disorders, respectively. Dopamine neurons serve a variety of functions in the brain, and loss of these neurons causes Parkinson's disease. Serotonin also has wide-ranging effects, and abnormal serotonin transmission can contribute to depression. Dopamine and serotonin (as well as epinephrine and norepinephrine) are in a family of transmitters called monoamines.

21. C. The hypothalamus is an important link between the brain and the endocrine (hormone) system. The hypothalamus has a direct link to the pituitary gland and regulates a wide range of behaviors, largely by stimulating the release of pituitary hormones.

22. A. When a stimulus becomes just strong enough to be perceived (that is, perceived 50% of the time), it has reached the absolute threshold. Difference threshold refers to the amount of stimulation that is necessary to produce a just-noticeable difference (jnd). The difference threshold needed to detect a jnd varies depending on the baseline stimulus intensity. For example, if you were holding a bucket containing 20 pebbles, you would be able to detect a difference in weight if 50 pebbles were added. However, if 50 pebbles were added to a bucket containing 2000 pebbles, you would not be able to detect the change.

23. E. The two types of photoreceptors in the retina are *rods* and *cones*. Rods are very sensitive to light, but not sensitive at all to color. Cones respond to color, but require more light than rods. Cones are concentrated in the center of the retina, called the fovea, whereas rods are denser in the periphery of the retina. There are three types of cones, each maximally sensitive to blue, green or red wavelengths of light. This is the basis of the Young-Helmholtz, or Trichromatic, theory of color vision. The Opponent-Process theory of color vision, proposed by Ewald Hering, holds that our visual system possesses three antagonistic color systems—blue/yellow, red/green and black/white. Research has supported this theory by revealing that certain cells higher in the visual pathway (that is, the lateral geniculate nucleus of thalamus) are excited by color wavelengths of one member of the antagonistic pair and inhibited by the other. The Opponent-Process theory nicely explains *afterimages*, images that persist after a stimulus is removed. For example, if you stare at a red dot for a long time and then look at a white wall, you will perceive a green dot. This phenomenon is the result of *sensory adaptation*. In all sensory modalities, the system adapts to constant stimulation by responding less. When staring at a red dot, the cells that normally inhibit green adapt and respond less, thereby contributing to a green afterimage.

24. D. Photoreceptors absorb energy in the form of light, and then stimulate neighboring bipolar cells. Bipolar cells combine information from many photoreceptors and send it on to ganglion cells. Ganglion cells integrate information from several bipolar cells. Ganglion cells send this information down their long axons, which form the optic nerve. This information passes through the lateral geniculate nucleus of the thalamus and on to the primary visual cortex (V1). Simple cells in V1 respond most strongly to lines of a particular orientation located in a specific location in the visual field. Complex cells in V1 respond most strongly to lines of a particular orientation within a larger receptive field and, sometimes, moving in a specific direction. The discovery of simple and complex cells helped David Hubel and Thorsten Wiesel win a Nobel Prize. Damage to any one part of this pathway can cause loss of vision.

25. B. Perception is the process of organizing sensory stimuli into meaningful information. This requires organization, interpretation, and attention. One of the most important aspects of perceptual organization is depth perception. The ability to perceive depth is dependent on a variety of binocular and monocular cues. All the cues in this question are depth-perception cues. Retinal disparity is a binocular cue made possible because our eyes are located in different positions. As an object moves closer to us, our eyes converge, creating a greater disparity between the images on each retina. Interposition occurs when one object overlaps with another. We always know that the partially occluded object is farther away. When we know the relative sizes of objects, we can tell which is farther away based on the size discrepancy. If an elephant appears smaller than a human, we know it must be far away. Linear perspective is a cue in which lines seem to converge in the distance, as when looking down railroad tracks. Texture gradient is a cue based on how we see texture at different distances—we see every nook and cranny of a cookie when held close, but from across the room we see much less detail. Finally, motion parallax is a depth cue in which more distant objects seem to move more slowly compared to closer objects even when moving at the same speed. This is best illustrated by looking out a car window—things along the road wiz by, but a distant mountaintop seems to barely move at all.

26. **C.** All the answer choices are Gestalt principles. Gestalt theory proposes that the brain automatically organizes sensory input into meaningful wholes. When we look at a scene, we effortlessly distinguish between the object we are viewing and the background surrounding it. This is the principle of figure-ground perception. Proximity is the tendency to group objects together if they are near each other. The principle of similarity holds that the brain groups objects together that are similar. Good continuation means that the brain organizes discontinuous stimuli into coherent patterns based on our expectations. Lastly, the principle of closure states that we tend to perceive incomplete figures as complete.

27. **B.** Information flows from the primary visual cortex (V1) along two main pathways known as the *what* and *where* pathways. These streams perform complex computations in parallel that allow us to recognize *what* objects are, and *where* they are located. The what pathway runs from V1 through the inferior (lower) temporal cortex. This stream processes information about things like color and texture, and ultimately determines what object we are viewing. The where pathway extends from V1 to the superior (upper) regions of temporal cortex as well as parietal cortex. This pathway processes information about where an object is located in space and guides movement toward the object. Patients with damage to the what pathway might have difficulty naming objects, colors or familiar faces, but have no problem following the movement of an object. Conversely, patients with damage along the where pathway might have no difficulty naming objects, but might have problems reaching in the proper direction to grasp an object.

28. **A.** Sensory adaptation is the tendency of sensory systems to respond *less* to continuous, unchanging stimuli, and it is a phenomenon shared by all sensory systems. This type of system makes sense from an evolutionary perspective; thus, it is not very adaptive to keep attending to stimuli that provide no new information about your environment. However, in rare cases, such as severe pain, it is maladaptive to ignore repeated stimuli, and adaptation does not occur. Please refer to the answer to question 23 for an explanation of afterimages.

29. **C.** Amphetamine, cocaine, nicotine and caffeine are all psychomotor stimulants. These drugs increase alertness, energy and autonomic responses such as heart rate and blood pressure. LSD and PCP are examples of hallucinogens, drugs that create sensations and perceptions in the absence of outside stimulation. Alcohol is a depressant, which means that it has a sedative effect on the central nervous system. Marijuana induces a high that can be very different depending on the person experiencing it; however, most users report pleasurable feelings.

30. **E.** Rapid eye movement (REM) sleep, as the name implies, is the stage of sleep when the eyes begin to dart around. Brain waves during REM sleep are very different from all other sleep stages and actually look more like brain waves during waking. This is also the time when the vast majority of dreaming occurs. Additionally, autonomic activity increases, and both men and women show signs of sexual arousal.

31. **D.** Freudian and psychodynamic are synonyms. A psychologist with a Freudian perspective is *most* likely to believe that dreams have a deeper, hidden meaning. Freud believed that below the story line of a dream (manifest content) there was an underlying meaning (latent content) that usually involved a forbidden or suppressed desire. A cognitive psychologist is likely to suggest that dreams reflect current concerns or events in one's life, but might have no underlying meaning. A biological psychologist is most likely to argue that dreams have no deeper meaning, but rather, they are the result of (or the interpretation of) random neuronal discharges during REM sleep.

32. **E.** In an altered state of consciousness, an individual's normal, waking pattern of thought and perception is modified for a period of time. The most common example of an altered state of consciousness is sleep. In fact, it is a state of consciousness that most people enter at least once a day. However, several other activities can induce an altered state of consciousness, including the ingestion of drugs, meditation, hypnosis, or even certain cultural or religious experiences. Keep in mind, however, that the capability of certain activities (for example, hypnosis) to induce altered states of consciousness is controversial.

33. **C.** Before Susan ate the spoiled clam, the sight of a clam did not elicit nausea. Therefore, in classical conditioning terms, the clam was a neutral stimulus. The bacteria in the spoiled clam are referred to as unconditioned stimuli (UCS) because illness after exposure to these types of pathogens is an innate reflex that requires no learning. The nausea and vomiting *in response to the bacteria* are referred to as unconditioned responses (UCRs). However, after the previously neutral stimulus (a clam) was paired with the bacteria (UCS), the sight or smell of a clam alone came to elicit nausea. The nausea *in response to the sight of a clam* is called a conditioned response (CR), or a response attributable to learning. Thus, in Susan's case, clams are now a powerful conditioned stimulus (CS).

34. A. With a fixed-ratio (FR) schedule of reinforcement, a reinforcer is received after a fixed proportion of responses are emitted. The example in answer **A** is an FR-1 schedule of reinforcement; that is, the homework problem to gumdrop ratio is 1:1. Answer **D** is an example of a variable ratio (VR) schedule of reinforcement. A chess game is won, *on average*, every other time it is played (VR-2); however, this is only an average—five games might be won in a row, followed by five games lost in a row.

35. C. Extinction is the opposite of acquisition (the learning of a response). Extinction is the process by which a conditioned response (CR; fear at the sight of a bee) is weakened by several presentations of the conditioned stimulus (CS; a bee) without the unconditioned stimulus (UCS; a sting). After enough presentations of the bee without the sting, the CR of fear to the sight of a bee is extinguished.

36. B. With a fixed-interval (FI) schedule of reinforcement, a reinforcer is delivered after a fixed interval of time has passed as long as the correct response has been made at least once after the interval has passed. The example in answer **B** is an FI-1 hr schedule, in that a dollar is received as long as one problem is completed after each hour. A variable-interval (VI) schedule, as illustrated in answer **E**, is also tied to an interval of time, but the time is averaged. A food pellet will be available after an interval of time passes, but each interval will be different, averaging 5 minutes (VI-5 min).

37. D. In a nutshell, Seligman's experiments involved dogs that were harnessed in one side of a shuttlebox and exposed to mild shock for a day. The next day the dogs were unharnessed and allowed to jump to the other side of the shuttlebox to escape shock. Compared to control animals that were not previously exposed to inescapable shock, dogs in the experimental group did not attempt to escape the shock. Additionally, these dogs failed to learn even when they occasionally escaped. Seligman argued that humans might develop a similar type of depression if they feel that they have no control over negative events in their lives. Other theories of depression focus on genetic factors, neural transmission (particularly the transmitters serotonin and norepinephrine), environmental factors, cognition, and culture.

38. E. People with an internal locus of control feel that they have power and control over their own destiny. Individuals with an external locus of control, like John, believe that their destiny is determined by outside forces and they can do little to change their fate. John also has generalized expectancies, in that he believes in an external locus of control in virtually every aspect of his life.

39. B. First, let's define some operant conditioning terms. If an environmental consequence makes a behavior more likely to occur, it is called a *reinforcement*. Conversely, if an environmental consequence makes a behavior less likely to occur, it is called a *punishment*. If the environmental consequence is the presentation of a stimulus (a reward), it is positive. If the environmental consequence is the removal of an aversive stimulus, it is negative. When a rat presses a lever to stop a shock, it is removing an aversive stimulus, which in turn increases the likelihood that the behavior will occur again. This is called *negative reinforcement*.

40. D. Classical conditioning does not necessarily occur every time two stimuli are paired together in time. The specific way in which the stimuli are paired predicts the level of conditioning that will occur. Forward conditioning occurs when the conditioned stimulus (CS) precedes the unconditioned stimulus (UCS). The two types of forward conditioning are *delayed* and *trace*. Delayed conditioning occurs when the CS is presented first and lasts until the UCS is presented. Trace conditioning is similar, except for an interval between the termination of the CS and the presentation of the UCS. Delayed and trace conditioning are most effective. As the name implies, simultaneous conditioning occurs when the CS and UCS are presented at the same time (this type is slightly less effective). With backward conditioning, the CS is presented after the UCS. This type of conditioning is very ineffective because the CS does not predict the UCS. From the perspective of an evolutionary psychologist, it is not adaptive, and perhaps maladaptive, to learn something about a neutral stimulus if it predicts nothing that is biologically relevant.

41. C. Many early behaviorists believed that any stimulus could be associated with any response, based on the laws of classical conditioning. However, years of research has shown that certain responses can be conditioned to some stimuli more easily than to others. Prepared learning relates to the idea that organisms are biologically prepared to learn some associations more readily than others. The evolutionary explanation is that organisms can more easily make an association if that association is important for survival (and ultimately reproductive success). Evolutionarily speaking, the ability to make fast associations between the taste of a poisonous plant and nausea is very important to survival.

42. A. Negative symptoms of schizophrenia reflect the absence of a behavior that is normally present. Negative symptoms include flat effect (absence of appropriate emotion) and any other deficit in thought, speech or movement. Positive symptoms signal the presence of abnormal behavior, such as disordered thought, delusions and hallucinations. Positive symptoms are more responsive to traditional antipsychotic medications compared to negative symptoms, which suggests that distinct neural circuitry might underlie the two types of symptoms.

43. E. Answers A through D are all true in regard to paranoid schizophrenia, a type of schizophrenia dominated by delusions and auditory hallucinations. Another type of schizophrenia is catatonic, which is characterized by motor immobility (frozen state) and rigid posture. Disorganized schizophrenia is characterized disorganized speech, bizarre behavior, and inappropriate affect. Undifferentiated schizophrenia is a diagnosis given to patients with mixed symptoms that do not meet criteria for any other subtype. Dysfunctions in neurotransmitter systems have been implicated in the etiology of all types of schizophrenia. However, the neurotransmitters thought to be involved are dopamine and glutamate, not norepinephrine. The dopamine hypothesis of schizophrenia is largely based on the knowledge that antipsychotic medications work by blocking dopamine receptors. The glutamate hypothesis of schizophrenia is due in large part to the discovery that drugs that interact with glutamate transmission (for example, PCP) can mimic both the positive and negative symptoms of schizophrenia.

44. B. Dysthymic disorder is a much milder form of depression. It might include many of the symptoms of major depressive disorder, but the symptoms are not debilitating. Major depressive disorder is very debilitating and is characterized by disturbances in appetite and sleep, intense sadness, and anhedonia (loss of interest in pleasurable activities). Individuals with bipolar disorder experience peaks and valleys of mania and depression. Manic episodes are characterized by elevated mood, racing thoughts and inflated self-image. All of these disorders fall under the DSM-IV diagnostic category of mood disorders.

45. D. Lithium is by far the most popular treatment for bipolar disorder, although little is known about the nature of lithium's therapeutic action. Tricyclics, MAOIs and SSRIs are all used to treat depression, and all act to increase synaptic levels of one or more monoamine neurotransmitters. Antipsychotics block dopamine receptors and are used to treat paranoid schizophrenia.

46. C. All the answer choices describe various personality disorders, of which there are many. It is a good idea to become familiar with the descriptions of each type of personality disorder. Answer choices **A, B, D,** and **E** describe paranoid, histrionic, dependent and antisocial personality disorders, respectively.

47. A. Cognitive therapists attempt to alter problematic thought patterns that are believed to underlie psychological disorders. Psychoanalysis is the stereotypical Freudian therapy, in which an individual lies on a couch and talks about whatever comes to mind. Client-centered therapists use empathy and unconditional positive regard to help the client engage in self-directed growth. The main approach of a psychiatrist (who has a medical degree) is pharmacological (drug) treatment. A behavioral therapist attempts to change unwanted behavior by using reinforcement and punishment.

48. D. Somatoform disorders involve physical symptoms with no organic basis. Dissociative disorders are characterized by alterations in consciousness, memory and identity. A prime example is dissociative identity disorder, commonly known as multiple personality disorder. Mood disorders are disturbances of normal mood, such as depression and bipolar disorder. Adjustment disorders are characterized by mild emotional and behavioral symptoms that are caused by a specific stressor. Personality disorders are characterized by consistent patterns of maladaptive behavior (for example, antisocial personality disorder, schizotypal personality disorder).

49. E. The most common drug treatment for obsessive-compulsive disorder is, interestingly, antidepressant medication, usually an SSRI. Panic disorder is also sometimes treated with SSRIs. However, most anxiety disorders are treated with benzodiazepines. Benzodiazepines facilitate the action of GABA, the major inhibitory neurotransmitter in the nervous system. Pharmacotherapy (drug treatment) for psychological disorders is a very popular form of biological treatment today. Other, less common forms of biological treatment are electroconvulsive shock therapy and psychosurgery.

50. B. A hyperactivity disorder, such as attention deficit/hyperactivity disorder (ADHD) falls under the diagnostic category of disorders usually first diagnosed in infancy, childhood or adolescence.

183

51. **C.** Systematic desensitization is a very popular treatment for all types of phobias. The idea behind this treatment is that through classical conditioning, a neutral stimulus has become an anxiety-producing stimulus, and exposure to the stimulus in a relaxed state is necessary to extinguish the learned fear response. With systematic desensitization, the patient learns relaxation techniques, and then gradually confronts the fearful stimulus through progressively more accurate approximations of the phobic stimulus. Thus, a patient with arachnophobia would begin by simply imagining spiders while in a relaxed state, but gradually build (over many sessions) to the point where a live spider is placed in their hand. This type of treatment falls under the general category of cognitive-behavioral therapies.

52. **A.** Tardive dyskinesia is a movement disorder that occurs in approximately 35% of schizophrenics who have been treated with long-term antipsychotic medications. The disorder is characterized by involuntary twitching of the tongue, face and neck. The exact cause of the disorder is not known; however, one theory holds that blockade of dopamine receptors by antipsychotic medications causes the receptors to become supersensitive (a compensatory response). The overactive dopamine receptors located on neurons in motor circuits then cause unpredictable, unwanted movements. The efficacy of antipsychotic drugs in treating schizophrenia led to the "dopamine hypothesis" of schizophrenia. However, other theories of schizophrenia focus on glutamate, genetics, neural atrophy, environment, and culture.

53. **E.** The cognitive therapist Aaron Beck recognized several cognitive errors characteristic of depressed individuals. Arbitrary inferences are conclusions drawn in the absence of supporting evidence. In this example, a conclusion (unattractiveness) was drawn in the presence of *contradictory* information (winning beauty contests). Magnification and minimization are biases in assessing the relative importance of events. In other words, making mountains out of molehills or vice versa. With personalization, individuals relate external events to themselves even though no connection exists. For example, Mary might believe that Bill is dating Sue because he feels that Mary is unattractive. Overgeneralization occurs when an isolated incident is used to draw general conclusions. For example, one bad date might cause Mary to feel that dates never work out.

54. **D.** If you don't know the answer on a question like this, you can play the game *which of these things is not like the others*. Even if you have little or no knowledge of psychodynamic (Freudian) theory, you can glance over the answers and see that "negative triad" stands alone. Psychodynamic therapists attempt to change maladaptive patterns of behavior through insight into one's own psychological processes. The patient engages in free association (saying whatever comes to mind), and then together with the therapist, interprets the results. Transference refers to the process by which individuals transfer feelings, conflicts and so on from past relationships onto new relationships. Transference is part of the patient-therapist relationship and can be a tool to gain insight during therapy. The negative triad was an idea postulated by Aaron Beck, a cognitive therapist. He felt that negative views about self, the world and the future could induce depression. The Beck Depression Inventory is a diagnostic tool that measures the severity of symptoms in the negative triad.

55. **E.** Many people do not know the difference between a psychiatrist and a psychologist. A psychiatrist has a degree in medicine (M.D.), while a psychologist has a degree in philosophy (Ph.D.). Thus, only a psychiatrist can prescribe medication to a patient. Often times, the main role of a psychiatrist in a patient's treatment program is to decide what medication is most appropriate.

56. **B.** An individual is most likely to change their behavior to fit group norms if they have low self-esteem, are concerned with their status and were not previously committed to an opposing position. Conformity is also more likely if the majority is unanimous in their position, and the situation is public. Sometimes an individual changes their attitude publicly but not privately; this is referred to as *compliance*.

57. **B.** The famous experiments of Stanley Milgram surprised many social scientists by showing that the majority of individuals will inflict severe pain on another human when instructed to do so by an authority figure. In his studies, the experimenter told subjects the purpose of the study was to investigate the effect of punishment on learning. When a person in another room (actually a confederate) answered questions incorrectly, the subjects were instructed by the experimenter to deliver increasingly severe shocks to the victim. Each time the subjects asked whether they should continue, the experimenter told them that it was necessary for the experiment. Although the shocks were not real, the victims protested, screamed and eventually became unresponsive. Despite these reactions, approximately two-thirds of subjects administered the strongest shock (450 volts) to their victims. These experiments showed that most people obey, seemingly without conscience, if they believe that orders are coming from a legitimate authority figure. In related experiments, Milgram found that obedience declines when the authority figure is not close by, when the victim is nearby, and when dissenters (individuals who refuse to obey) are present.

58. C. Many social psychologists are interested in social influence, or the effects of the presence of others on the way individuals think, feel, and behave. A *role* is a position in a group that has norms of appropriate behavior for its members. Zimbardo was interested in the effects of roles on social behavior. In Zimbardo's famous study, a group of college students was randomly divided into two groups: prisoners and guards. To make the study as realistic as possible, students were "arrested" in their rooms, handcuffed, brought to the police station for processing, blindfolded, transported to "jail," stripped, deloused, and later given uniforms and put in cells with two other prisoners. The students assigned to the role of guards were given little instruction except that physical punishment was not allowed. In a short time, the student guards became immersed in their roles. Prisoners were treated aggressively, dehumanized, called by numbers instead of names and subjected to roll calls that lasted hours. Many prisoners showed signs of severe depression, anxiety or other illness. The study was intended to last two weeks, but because of the severe psychosomatic stress expressed by the inmates, the study was prematurely ended at six days. This study clearly illustrated that the behavior of individuals in a group is largely dictated by the role that they are assigned. This is an example of a form of social influence called group processes. Other forms of social influence include obedience (compliance with authority) and conformity (compliance with peers).

59. A. *Fundamental attribution error* is the propensity to believe that the behavior of others is due to internal disposition rather than an external situation. In this example, Kelly assumed that the clerk was inherently a rude person, when in fact, the clerk is normally very nice. Conversely, we tend to attribute our own reproachable behavior to external circumstances. *Hindsight bias* is the mistake of looking back on a situation and believing that you knew something all along. The *halo effect* occurs when one good quality in a person leads you to believe that the person possesses only good qualities. A *self-fulfilling prophecy* occurs when you devise a false expectation of a situation, and subsequently change your behavior in a way that causes the false expectation to come true. *False consensus bias* simply means that you believe that most individuals think and behave as you do.

60. D. An attitude is an association between an act or object and an evaluation. Persuasion refers to the deliberate effort to change an attitude. A speaker can persuade their audience through two routes: the central route or the peripheral route. If using the central route, the speaker appeals to the recipient's rational, thoughtful side by asking them to think carefully and weigh the options. This is a good strategy for a minivan commercial. For example, *if you have a large family and need a roomy and reliable vehicle, and so on,* is a message targeted at the central route. When using the peripheral route, the speaker targets the audience's less rational processes, intending to invoke gut reactions. Answer choices **A, C** and **E** are just distractions.

61. E. Researchers investigating bystander intervention have found that people often do not assist individuals in a crisis in the presence of other people. This is due to diffusion of responsibility, or a diminished sense of personal responsibility when in a group. Research in this area has shown that when people are alone, they are much more likely to help someone in an emergency (compared to a situation in which at least two other bystanders are present). Answers **B** and **C** are distracters; gender differences have not been shown to affect bystander intervention.

62. A. With this question, just knowing something about the different perspectives in psychology helps you choose the correct answer, even if you know nothing about aggression. Someone with a social psychology background is likely to focus on the influence of other people, as in choice **A**. If the words *survival* or *reproductive success* are present, you can bet it is an evolutionary perspective, as in choice **B**. Answers **C** and **D** are most aligned with a psychodynamic perspective, and the word *reinforcement* is a dead giveaway that choice **D** is from a behaviorist perspective.

63. C. According to the Serial Processing model of memory, memory formation occurs in successive steps. First, sensory registers hold information about stimuli for a second or less. Sensory registers can be iconic (visual) or echoic (auditory). From there, information is passed on to short-term memory, which has a limited capacity and can store information for no longer than approximately 30 seconds without rehearsal. Rehearsal is the repeating of information over and over again. If information is thought of for a long enough period or in a deep way, it will be transferred to long-term memory. From there it can be repeatedly recovered through the process of retrieval.

64. B. The degree to which information is processed in a meaningful way, known as the depth of processing, determines how well it is stored in long-term memory. *Maintenance rehearsal* refers to the superficial type of rehearsal in which words are just repeated over and over without really thinking about their meaning. This type of rehearsal is used to maintain information in short-term memory. *Elaborative rehearsal* is a deeper type of rehearsal in which information is stored in long-term memory by means of semantic encoding (meaningful thought). The other answer choices are not genuine types of rehearsal.

Practice Test 2

65. A. People can remember only about seven pieces of information at a time. It is often said that short-term memory has a capacity of seven, plus or minus two. That means that you can remember only about seven random digits; however, if seven digits are put together in a meaningful way, such as your own phone number, that counts as only one piece of information. This phenomenon is known as *chunking*.

66. D. The serial position effect describes the phenomenon whereby items at the beginning and end of a list are remembered more than items in the middle of the list when recalled after a short delay. One explanation for the primacy effect (better recall of items at the beginning) is that items at the beginning of a list can be rehearsed longer and are more likely to be stored in long-term memory. Items at the end might be recalled more easily (recency effect) because they are not displaced by new words (less interference).

67. D. Declarative memory refers to memory for facts and events and must be consciously recollected. Psychologists distinguish between two types of declarative memory: semantic and episodic. Semantic memory is memory of general world knowledge, such as the fact that Antarctica is very cold and the knowledge that lions live in Africa. Episodic memory is memory of specific events in one's life. For example, remembering having cereal for breakfast or breaking your ankle when you were 10 years old taps into episodic memory.

68. E. *Procedural memory* refers to memory for skills. These skills are usually motor skills, such as catching a baseball, using a clutch on a car, swimming or speaking. However, procedural memory also includes things such as reading, which requires learned motor skills (moving your eyes in the proper way), but also special nonmotor skills for decoding combinations of letters. With procedural memory, you do not need to consciously retrieve every step of a skill; you just perform them effortlessly. Thus, this type of memory is also called *implicit memory*. *Explicit memory* is memory that requires conscious recollection, such as episodic memory.

69. B. The encoding specificity principle holds that memory is improved if the encoding of information and the subsequent retrieval of that information are both performed in the same context. For example, according to this principle, you remember more of a lecture in the room where you heard it compared to your own house. The principle also predicts that if you heard the lecture while inebriated, you would later retrieve the information contained in the lecture more easily if you were again inebriated. It is believed that similar contexts during encoding and retrieval provide retrieval cues, or stimuli that can facilitate memory. Answer choice **A** illustrates a mnemonic device (memory aid) called the *method of loci,* which uses visual imagery to facilitate memory. Answer choice **C** illustrates the *spacing effect,* which means that information is remembered better when rehearsed over longer intervals compared to shorter intervals.

70. C. *Deductive reasoning* is the process of reasoning that allows you to draw conclusions from a set of assumptions. Your conclusion is true provided that your assumptions are true. Conversely, a conclusion based on *inductive reasoning* is not necessarily true because its underlying assumptions are not certain. The following is an example of inductive reasoning: I have a backache. Yesterday I did a lot of heavy lifting. I have done nothing else that could affect my back in that way. Thus, I must have injured my back while lifting yesterday. (The remaining answer choices are just distracters.)

71. A. With analogical reasoning, a novel situation is compared to a familiar one. The utility of this type of reasoning depends on several factors, such as the similarity of the situations, the ease with which individual elements of the situations can be mapped onto each other and the specific goal of the decision-maker. The remaining answer choices are just distracters.

72. E. The smallest units of sound are known as *phonemes*. The smallest unit of meaning, formed by combining phonemes, is called a *morpheme*. Morphemes are combined to form phrases and sentences. The rules that govern the placement (order) of words and phrases are called *syntax*. *Semantics* are the rules that govern the meanings of words and phrases. *Pragmatics* refers to the way in which language is used and understood in everyday life. For example, if your friend is talking during a movie and you say, "Put a lid on it," you really mean "Be quiet." This illustrates how language is processed hierarchically.

73. C. Sexual motivation and behavior are highly variable across cultures and individuals. However, in 1966, William Masters and Virginia Johnson described four phases of the sexual response cycle that occur reliably in all men and women. The first phase, excitement, is when blood engorges the genitals causing erection of the penis and lubrication of the vagina. The second phase, or plateau, is the point of maximal excitement. Autonomic responses, such as heart rate, respiration and blood pressure reach their peak during this phase. Thirdly, orgasm is when ejaculation occurs in males and vaginal contractions occur in females. The final phase, resolution, is when the body's physiology returns to normal.

74. B. William James and Carl Lange simultaneously proposed similar views on emotion, and their ideas are now known as the James-Lange theory of emotion. The theory holds that our subjective experience of emotion is the result of our central nervous system's interpretation of our peripheral nervous system's response to stimuli. For example, if you encounter a frightening stimulus, such as a lion running toward you, your heart starts pounding, you start to run, and your respiration increases. According to the James-Lange theory, your brain then interprets these bodily reactions as fear.

75. D. Cannon and Bard proposed a theory of emotional processing know known as the Cannon-Bard theory of emotion. They argued that autonomic responses are usually slower than emotional responses, which can be immediate. This contradicts the James-Lange theory of emotion. Therefore, Cannon and Bard proposed that a stimulus produces simultaneous peripheral and subjective experiences.

76. A. The Schachter-Singer theory of emotion takes a cognitive perspective. It holds that emotion results from an individual's cognitive appraisal of physiological arousal. In other words, when a person experiences nonspecific physiological arousal, they try to figure out the proper emotion by using situational cues. Simply put, if a man is feeling physiological arousal and he is standing in front of a naked woman, he is *not* likely to determine that his emotion is anger.

77. B. Based on his experimental evidence, Hans Selye proposed the general adaptation syndrome of chronic stress. The syndrome has three stages: alarm, resistance and exhaustion. When an organism first encounters stress, the autonomic nervous system responds by releasing stress hormones, such as adrenalin and cortisol. However, the alarm stage cannot last forever. Eventually the parasympathetic system returns the body to normal. If the stress continues, however, the body enters the resistance stage. In this stage, the body seems to be normal, but in fact, glucose and certain hormones are still elevated above normal levels. During this stage, the body is more susceptible to infections, such as colds, flus, bacteria and so on. If the stress continues long enough, the body eventually enters the final stage, exhaustion. By this stage the body is worn down and is highly susceptible to a variety of diseases. The general adaptation syndrome suggests that when individuals are under constant stress, they might be putting their health at serious risk.

78. E. The need for achievement is the motivation to do well—this means both succeeding *and* avoiding failure. Performance goals are components of achievement motivation. Performance-approach goals center on attaining a standard. A person who is performance-approach oriented wants to show that they can perform at the highest level possible. An individual who is performance-avoidance oriented shies away from difficult tasks to avoid failure. The need for achievement is a psychosocial need. The two general categories of psychosocial needs are relatedness (attachment, intimacy, and affiliation) and agency (self-oriented goals, such as achievement, autonomy, mastery, and power).

79. C. Homeostasis refers to the process by which the body maintains a relatively constant state, allowing normal cell functioning. Receptors in certain brain regions (for example, the hypothalamus) monitor variables such as temperature and glucose levels and provide feedback about the variables in relation to their individual optimal levels (set points). The body then responds with behaviors that move the variables toward the set point. In this way, the body's homeostatic processes are often compared to the functioning of a thermostat. Homeostatic mechanisms are involved in many functions, including hunger/satiety, metabolism, thermoregulation, etc.

80. D. Abraham Maslow proposed a hierarchy of needs and suggested that you must fulfill these needs in a particular order, from bottom to top. At the very bottom is physiological need, such as food and water. When you have these needs fulfilled, you can try to fulfill safety needs, such as housing and money. Next in the hierarchy is the need for love and belongingness, or affiliation with others. This is followed by the need for esteem (self-respect and respect from peers). Finally, at the top of the hierarchy is the need for self-actualization. This is the need for self-growth and service to others. Maslow contended that few people reach this final level.

81. D. The mean IQ score is 100. The standard deviation for IQ is 15. Thus, anyone scoring between 85 and 115 (plus or minus 1 standard deviation from the mean) is considered to be of average intelligence. Individuals scoring between 115 and 130 are considered superior, and individuals above 130 (above 2 standard deviations from the mean) are considered gifted. People scoring between 70 and 85 are considered borderline mentally retarded, and people below 70 (below 2 standard deviations from the mean) are considered mentally retarded.

82. A. A group test is a paper-and-pencil (or computer) test that can be given to a roomful of people at one time. It does not require one-on-one administration by trained staff. The Scholastic Assessment Tests (SAT) is a group test designed to predict college performance. The remaining answer choices are all intelligence tests that are administered one on one. The Wechsler Adult Intelligence Scale, third edition (WAIS III) and the Wechsler Intelligence Scale for Children, third edition (WISC III) are modern IQ tests designed for adults and children 16 and under, respectively. The Stanford-Binet Scale was an IQ test used around the turn of the twentieth century that determined IQ by the following formula: IQ = (mental age/chronological age) × 100. This test was not very suitable for adults for obvious reasons.

83. B. An important thing to remember when answering questions concerning the influence of heredity and environment is that very few variables of interest to psychologists are controlled by only one of these factors. This is no less true of intelligence. However, genetics appears to play a larger role than environment. Thus, identical twins score as similarly on IQ tests as the same person taking the test on two different occasions. Environment, however, also plays a role. Dizygotic twins have different IQ correlations compared to siblings even though their degrees of relatedness are exactly the same. (The difference, then, is presumably due to being raised at different times.) Howard Gardner proposed the existence of multiple intelligences, most of which are not measured by standard IQ tests. These intelligences are musical, kinesthetic, spatial, verbal, logical, intrapersonal and interpersonal. *Fluid intelligence* is the type of intelligence used when trying to solve a novel problem (processing information, drawing inferences and so on). *Crystallized intelligence* refers to an individual's store of general world knowledge, vocabulary and so on. This latter type of intelligence is culturally biased.

84. E. Down syndrome is a form of mental retardation caused by the presence of an *extra* chromosome. The remaining answer choices are accurate.

85. D. As with most variables, the distribution of intelligence scores falls under a bell curve. Individuals with scores below or above three standard deviations from the mean are considered profoundly mentally retarded or gifted, respectively. Over 99.7% of individuals fall within three standard deviations from the mean on any measure.

86. C. The following is an example of sublimation: A teenage boy is very angry because his father grounded him. Instead of confronting his father, the boy channels his anger into football practice later that day. Answer choices **A, B, D** and **E** are the definitions of passive aggression, rationalization, repression and denial, respectively.

87. A. Individuals with type A personalities display patterns of behavior that include ambition, competitiveness, impatience and hostility. People with type B personalities are generally more relaxed and less easily angered. Type A individuals are much more likely to develop heart disease compared to their type B counterparts. Individuals who score higher on measures of neuroticism tend to have worse reactions to daily stressors and generally feel more distressed compared to people scoring low on neuroticism. Finally, people who score high on measures of pessimism seem to have lower immune functioning compared to people who score high on measures of optimism.

88. B. Humanistic theory holds that every individual has a core aspect of being called a *true self*. The true self is often distorted by the *false self,* or the self that tries to conform to social demands. A person's view of what they should be is called the *ideal self.* Answer choices **A, C, D** and **E** are in line with trait, cognitive-social, psychodynamic and psychodynamic theories, respectively.

89. E. Trait theories posit that personality consists of several underlying emotional, cognitive and behavioral predispositions (traits) on which individuals vary. Trait theories lend themselves to empirical measurement and heritability studies, and trait psychologists have agreed on some core dimensions of personality. However, a long-time criticism of trait theories is that they do not account for changes in behavior across situations, or person-by-situation interactions. Further, they describe, rather than explain, personality.

90. D. Projective tests are assessments in which an ambiguous stimulus is presented, and the subject must project some kind of meaning onto it. With the Rorschach test, the subject views many different cards with inkblots and tells the tester what each one resembles. The TAT requires subjects to make up stories about ambiguous drawings. Proponents of projective tests say that people make up things that express individual characteristics of their personalities. Life history methods are nonprojective tests used by psychodynamic psychologists. They are basically in-depth case studies.

91. B. According to Freud's structural model, three mental forces are in conflict: the id, ego and superego. The *id* is the force that drives untamed sexual and aggressive energy. It is impulsive and irrational. The *superego* is synonymous with conscience. The superego informs one about what is morally right and wrong. The *ego* is the rational, logical force that is responsible for levelheaded cognition and decision making. The ego also balances the opposing forces of the id and superego.

92. C. The different methods for studying development each have their own advantages and disadvantages. *Cross-sectional studies* compare groups of people of different ages at a single time to assess group differences. The advantage of this design is that the study can be carried out relatively quickly. The drawback is the possibility of cohort effects. A cohort is a group of people born around the same time. Because of cultural changes, such as education, economy, nutrition and so on, over time, cross-sectional studies are susceptible to cohort effects—differences between age groups due to differences in culture. *Longitudinal studies* track the same individuals over time. Thus, they can be used to directly assess age changes, rather than age differences. However, longitudinal studies are still vulnerable to cohort effects because they cannot rule out the possibility that a different cohort would develop differently. These studies also take much longer to complete compared to cross-sectional designs. *Sequential studies* try to minimize cohort effects by combining cross-sectional and longitudinal studies. They accomplish this by studying multiple cohorts longitudinally. The obvious drawback is that this type of study takes an extremely long time to complete.

93. A. The period of gestation (from conception to birth) is divided into three stages. The first, or germinal, period is the first 2 weeks after conception. During this time, a fertilized egg becomes implanted in the uterus. The embryonic period is the second stage, and is the time from the beginning of the 3rd week to the 8th week of gestation. This is a critical period for the development of the central nervous system and organs. By the end of this stage, the heart has begun to beat. The third, or fetal, period begins after the embryonic period and lasts until birth. Rapid muscular development occurs during this time, and by approximately 28 weeks, the fetus can sustain life on its own.

94. E. A fundamental principle of Jean Piaget's developmental theory was that children move through four successive stages of cognitive development. The first stage is the *sensorimotor stage* (from approximately birth to two years of age). This is the time in development when children explore their world by mouthing, grabbing, watching and handling objects. A major achievement of the sensorimotor stage is the development of object permanence. *Object permanence* is the recognition that objects exist in time and space independent of our observations of them. For example, if you hold a toy in front of a child who has not developed object permanence, and then put it under a pillow, the child will not search for it. The child cannot see it; therefore, it does not exist.

95. C. In Piaget's theory, the sensorimotor stage (see answer 94) is followed by the *preoperational stage* (approximately age 2 through 7). The preoperational stage is when symbolic thought develops (the ability to use arbitrary symbols to represent concepts). The third stage is the *concrete operational stage* (approximately age 7 through 12), during which most children develop conservation. *Conservation* refers to the idea that the basic properties of an object remain stable even though superficial properties change. The example in this question is a classic demonstration of conservation. The final cognitive stage in Piaget's theory is the *formal operational stage* (age 12 and older). This is the stage when true abstract thinking begins to develop.

96. D. Certain aspects of cognition decline in later life. Some areas that show deficits are processing speed, working memory capacity, explicit memory retrieval, fluid intelligence (see the answer to question 83) and problem-solving strategies. Areas that do not seem to decline are encoding processes and crystallized intelligence (*see* the answer to question 83).

97. **A.** Diana Baumrind described three styles of parenting: authoritarian, permissive and authoritative. Authoritarian parents demand obedience and respect for authority. They do not listen to the child's point of view and often use physical punishment. Permissive parents impose little or no rules on their children. They accept unruly behavior and rarely give out punishments. Authoritative parents set acceptable standards for their children and firmly enforce them. However, they show respect for their children's opinions and use reasonable punishments. Research has shown that the most well-adjusted children tend to have been raised by authoritative parents.

98. **B.** In Kohlberg's cognitive-developmental theory of gender, children move through three stages in understanding gender. The first stage, *gender identity* (under age two), is the time when children first categorize themselves as either male or female. The second stage, *gender stability* (under age seven), is when children come to understand that their gender does not change over time. In the third stage, *gender constancy*, children learn that changes in appearance or activities do not change a person's gender. Later, children organize information about their culture's definitions of masculinity and femininity in gender schemas (mental representations that relate psychological characteristics to one sex or the other).

99. **A.** Kohlberg proposed three levels of moral development. The first, *preconventional morality,* is when children follow rules to avoid punishment and gain reward. The second level, *conventional morality,* is when individuals follow standards learned from others and try to maintain law and order. During the third level, *postconventional morality,* morality centers on self-defined and carefully considered principles.

100. **E.** Erik Erikson developed the best-known theory of lifespan development. It encompasses eight stages, from infancy to old age. A summary of the stages follows: Infancy—basic trust versus mistrust: development of trust for others or a view of the world as unfriendly. Toddlerhood—autonomy versus shame and doubt: development of independence. Preschool and early school years—initiative versus guilt: development of responsibility. Late childhood—industry versus inferiority: development of competence and skills. Adolescence—identity versus identity confusion: development of stable values and ideals. Young adulthood—intimacy versus isolation: establishment of long-lasting, committed friendships and romantic relationships. Midlife—generativity versus stagnation: concern for the next generation and society. Old age—integrity versus despair: satisfaction for a life lived well or regret for the loss of loved ones who have died.

Free-Response Question #1—Explanation

Overall approach

The good thing about this question is that you do not have to guess what information to include in your answer. The question asks for several specific pieces of information. Make sure you address every topic by checking off each one as you go along.

This question tests your knowledge of experimental design, but it also tests your ability to think independently (for example, "provide two possible dependent variables"), an ability that cannot be tested with multiple-choice questions. This question also tests your critical thinking skills by asking you to come up with possible outcomes and provide interpretations of those outcomes. Because knowledge of experimental methods is very important, it is likely that an essay question will deal with the topic. You should have a thorough understanding of the methods, vocabulary and logic of scientific research.

Key points to include

- The independent variable is drug dose, and there are four levels—zero (control condition), low, medium and high.

- It is important to have the zero dose level because this is the control condition, which is used to ensure that the mere administration of the drug (for example, by injection) does not have an effect on the dependent variable(s).

- It is also important to test different doses of the drug because, depending on the dose, the drug might have very different therapeutic effects.

- One possible dependent variable to measure hunger in rats is amount of food consumed. This could be measured by allowing each rat access to a specified quantity of food (for example, 20 grams of rat chow) for 6 hours following administration of the drug. At the end of 6 hours, the remaining food is weighed.

- Another possible variable to measure hunger in rats is willingness to work for food. One way to measure this is to train the rats to press a lever for food pellets. After training, administer the drug and allow rats to press the lever for food pellets for 6 hours. Record how many pellets each rat receives.

- A possible outcome of the experiment is that rats in the high-dose group consumed significantly less food than rats in any other group, and no significant difference was measured in the amount of food consumed between the remaining three groups.

- If this is the result, it appears that the drug is effective for its intended purpose, but only when administered at the highest dose.

Free-Response Question #2—Explanation

Overall approach

Psychological disorders are popular essay topics. Part 1 simply tests your knowledge of psychological disorders and pharmacological treatments (the most popular type of treatment today). Notice that each disorder is a specific subtype within a broader category. For example, the symptoms of paranoid schizophrenia are starkly different from the symptoms of catatonic schizophrenia. Be sure that your answers reflect this specificity.

Part 2 asks you to define phobia and explain how specific types of behavioral treatments are used to treat a specific type of phobia. Be sure to explain exactly how each treatment is carried out, as well as how each treatment is applied to arachnophobia. The final section of the question tests your knowledge of the theoretical concepts underlying the treatments. Most treatments are derived from fundamental principles reflecting a specific perspective in psychology. The treatments in this question come from a behavioral standpoint; thus, your answer should include an explanation of the basic behavioral principles behind the techniques.

Key points to include

Part 1

Paranoid schizophrenia

- Schizophrenia is a disorder of thought, perception and language. Paranoid schizophrenia is characterized by positive symptoms (as opposed to the negative symptoms of catatonic schizophrenia). These symptoms include delusions (false beliefs held despite contradictory evidence), hallucinations (sensory perceptions, usually auditory, in the absence of an external stimulus) and loose associations (tendency of conscious thoughts to be uncontrolled and illogical).
- Antipsychotic drugs (sometimes called neuroleptics) are used to treat paranoid schizophrenia. These drugs have little efficacy in the treatment of negative symptoms.
- These drugs work by blocking dopamine receptors; however, newer antipsychotic drugs also block certain kinds of serotonin receptors.

Major depressive disorder

- This is the most severe form of depression, characterized by depressed mood and anhedonia (loss of interest in pleasurable activities). Symptoms also include disturbances in appetite, energy level, sleep patterns and concentration. Major depressive episodes usually last several months. Some depressed individuals might be preoccupied with thoughts of suicide.
- Selective serotonin reuptake inhibitors are the most common pharmacological treatment for depression.
- As the name implies, these drugs inhibit the reuptake of serotonin into presynaptic neurons, which results in elevated levels of synaptic serotonin.
- In some cases, tricyclics or monoamine oxidase inhibitors (MAOIs) are prescribed.

Part 2

- Phobias are a subtype of anxiety disorder. A phobia is an irrational fear of a specific object or situation.
- Systematic desensitization is a behavioral technique in which the patient is induced to confront a fearful stimulus gradually while in a state that inhibits anxiety. The patient learns relaxation techniques, and then gradually confronts the fearful stimulus through progressively more accurate approximations of the phobic stimulus. These approximations are the result of a hierarchy of feared imagined stimuli constructed by the patient, beginning with scenes that provoke mild anxiety to scenes that induce intense fear.

- Systematic desensitization is based on principles of classical conditioning. The assumption is that through classical conditioning, a neutral stimulus has become an anxiety-producing stimulus, and exposure to the stimulus in a relaxed state is necessary to extinguish the learned fear response.

- A patient with arachnophobia might begin by simply imagining a spider that is miles away while in a relaxed state. They would gradually move through their hierarchy (over many sessions) to the point where a live spider is placed in their hand.

- The exposure technique of flooding is similar to systematic desensitization in that it is based on principles of classical conditioning. However, unlike systematic desensitization, flooding presents the fearful stimulus to the patient all at once.

- The theory is that inescapable exposure to the conditioned stimulus without subsequent negative outcomes will eventually extinguish the learned fear response.

- If flooding were used to treat a patient with arachnophobia, she might hold out her hands to be covered in live (harmless) spiders.

Answer Sheet for Practice Test 3

1	Ⓐ	Ⓑ	Ⓒ	Ⓓ	Ⓔ		26	Ⓐ	Ⓑ	Ⓒ	Ⓓ	Ⓔ
2	Ⓐ	Ⓑ	Ⓒ	Ⓓ	Ⓔ		27	Ⓐ	Ⓑ	Ⓒ	Ⓓ	Ⓔ
3	Ⓐ	Ⓑ	Ⓒ	Ⓓ	Ⓔ		28	Ⓐ	Ⓑ	Ⓒ	Ⓓ	Ⓔ
4	Ⓐ	Ⓑ	Ⓒ	Ⓓ	Ⓔ		29	Ⓐ	Ⓑ	Ⓒ	Ⓓ	Ⓔ
5	Ⓐ	Ⓑ	Ⓒ	Ⓓ	Ⓔ		30	Ⓐ	Ⓑ	Ⓒ	Ⓓ	Ⓔ
6	Ⓐ	Ⓑ	Ⓒ	Ⓓ	Ⓔ		31	Ⓐ	Ⓑ	Ⓒ	Ⓓ	Ⓔ
7	Ⓐ	Ⓑ	Ⓒ	Ⓓ	Ⓔ		32	Ⓐ	Ⓑ	Ⓒ	Ⓓ	Ⓔ
8	Ⓐ	Ⓑ	Ⓒ	Ⓓ	Ⓔ		33	Ⓐ	Ⓑ	Ⓒ	Ⓓ	Ⓔ
9	Ⓐ	Ⓑ	Ⓒ	Ⓓ	Ⓔ		34	Ⓐ	Ⓑ	Ⓒ	Ⓓ	Ⓔ
10	Ⓐ	Ⓑ	Ⓒ	Ⓓ	Ⓔ		35	Ⓐ	Ⓑ	Ⓒ	Ⓓ	Ⓔ
11	Ⓐ	Ⓑ	Ⓒ	Ⓓ	Ⓔ		36	Ⓐ	Ⓑ	Ⓒ	Ⓓ	Ⓔ
12	Ⓐ	Ⓑ	Ⓒ	Ⓓ	Ⓔ		37	Ⓐ	Ⓑ	Ⓒ	Ⓓ	Ⓔ
13	Ⓐ	Ⓑ	Ⓒ	Ⓓ	Ⓔ		38	Ⓐ	Ⓑ	Ⓒ	Ⓓ	Ⓔ
14	Ⓐ	Ⓑ	Ⓒ	Ⓓ	Ⓔ		39	Ⓐ	Ⓑ	Ⓒ	Ⓓ	Ⓔ
15	Ⓐ	Ⓑ	Ⓒ	Ⓓ	Ⓔ		40	Ⓐ	Ⓑ	Ⓒ	Ⓓ	Ⓔ
16	Ⓐ	Ⓑ	Ⓒ	Ⓓ	Ⓔ		41	Ⓐ	Ⓑ	Ⓒ	Ⓓ	Ⓔ
17	Ⓐ	Ⓑ	Ⓒ	Ⓓ	Ⓔ		42	Ⓐ	Ⓑ	Ⓒ	Ⓓ	Ⓔ
18	Ⓐ	Ⓑ	Ⓒ	Ⓓ	Ⓔ		43	Ⓐ	Ⓑ	Ⓒ	Ⓓ	Ⓔ
19	Ⓐ	Ⓑ	Ⓒ	Ⓓ	Ⓔ		44	Ⓐ	Ⓑ	Ⓒ	Ⓓ	Ⓔ
20	Ⓐ	Ⓑ	Ⓒ	Ⓓ	Ⓔ		45	Ⓐ	Ⓑ	Ⓒ	Ⓓ	Ⓔ
21	Ⓐ	Ⓑ	Ⓒ	Ⓓ	Ⓔ		46	Ⓐ	Ⓑ	Ⓒ	Ⓓ	Ⓔ
22	Ⓐ	Ⓑ	Ⓒ	Ⓓ	Ⓔ		47	Ⓐ	Ⓑ	Ⓒ	Ⓓ	Ⓔ
23	Ⓐ	Ⓑ	Ⓒ	Ⓓ	Ⓔ		48	Ⓐ	Ⓑ	Ⓒ	Ⓓ	Ⓔ
24	Ⓐ	Ⓑ	Ⓒ	Ⓓ	Ⓔ		49	Ⓐ	Ⓑ	Ⓒ	Ⓓ	Ⓔ
25	Ⓐ	Ⓑ	Ⓒ	Ⓓ	Ⓔ		50	Ⓐ	Ⓑ	Ⓒ	Ⓓ	Ⓔ

51 Ⓐ Ⓑ Ⓒ Ⓓ Ⓔ	76 Ⓐ Ⓑ Ⓒ Ⓓ Ⓔ
52 Ⓐ Ⓑ Ⓒ Ⓓ Ⓔ	77 Ⓐ Ⓑ Ⓒ Ⓓ Ⓔ
53 Ⓐ Ⓑ Ⓒ Ⓓ Ⓔ	78 Ⓐ Ⓑ Ⓒ Ⓓ Ⓔ
54 Ⓐ Ⓑ Ⓒ Ⓓ Ⓔ	79 Ⓐ Ⓑ Ⓒ Ⓓ Ⓔ
55 Ⓐ Ⓑ Ⓒ Ⓓ Ⓔ	80 Ⓐ Ⓑ Ⓒ Ⓓ Ⓔ
56 Ⓐ Ⓑ Ⓒ Ⓓ Ⓔ	81 Ⓐ Ⓑ Ⓒ Ⓓ Ⓔ
57 Ⓐ Ⓑ Ⓒ Ⓓ Ⓔ	82 Ⓐ Ⓑ Ⓒ Ⓓ Ⓔ
58 Ⓐ Ⓑ Ⓒ Ⓓ Ⓔ	83 Ⓐ Ⓑ Ⓒ Ⓓ Ⓔ
59 Ⓐ Ⓑ Ⓒ Ⓓ Ⓔ	84 Ⓐ Ⓑ Ⓒ Ⓓ Ⓔ
60 Ⓐ Ⓑ Ⓒ Ⓓ Ⓔ	85 Ⓐ Ⓑ Ⓒ Ⓓ Ⓔ
61 Ⓐ Ⓑ Ⓒ Ⓓ Ⓔ	86 Ⓐ Ⓑ Ⓒ Ⓓ Ⓔ
62 Ⓐ Ⓑ Ⓒ Ⓓ Ⓔ	87 Ⓐ Ⓑ Ⓒ Ⓓ Ⓔ
63 Ⓐ Ⓑ Ⓒ Ⓓ Ⓔ	88 Ⓐ Ⓑ Ⓒ Ⓓ Ⓔ
64 Ⓐ Ⓑ Ⓒ Ⓓ Ⓔ	89 Ⓐ Ⓑ Ⓒ Ⓓ Ⓔ
65 Ⓐ Ⓑ Ⓒ Ⓓ Ⓔ	90 Ⓐ Ⓑ Ⓒ Ⓓ Ⓔ
66 Ⓐ Ⓑ Ⓒ Ⓓ Ⓔ	91 Ⓐ Ⓑ Ⓒ Ⓓ Ⓔ
67 Ⓐ Ⓑ Ⓒ Ⓓ Ⓔ	92 Ⓐ Ⓑ Ⓒ Ⓓ Ⓔ
68 Ⓐ Ⓑ Ⓒ Ⓓ Ⓔ	93 Ⓐ Ⓑ Ⓒ Ⓓ Ⓔ
69 Ⓐ Ⓑ Ⓒ Ⓓ Ⓔ	94 Ⓐ Ⓑ Ⓒ Ⓓ Ⓔ
70 Ⓐ Ⓑ Ⓒ Ⓓ Ⓔ	95 Ⓐ Ⓑ Ⓒ Ⓓ Ⓔ
71 Ⓐ Ⓑ Ⓒ Ⓓ Ⓔ	96 Ⓐ Ⓑ Ⓒ Ⓓ Ⓔ
72 Ⓐ Ⓑ Ⓒ Ⓓ Ⓔ	97 Ⓐ Ⓑ Ⓒ Ⓓ Ⓔ
73 Ⓐ Ⓑ Ⓒ Ⓓ Ⓔ	98 Ⓐ Ⓑ Ⓒ Ⓓ Ⓔ
74 Ⓐ Ⓑ Ⓒ Ⓓ Ⓔ	99 Ⓐ Ⓑ Ⓒ Ⓓ Ⓔ
75 Ⓐ Ⓑ Ⓒ Ⓓ Ⓔ	100 Ⓐ Ⓑ Ⓒ Ⓓ Ⓔ

Practice Test 3

Section 1: Multiple-Choice Questions

Time: 70 Minutes

Questions: 100

1. A psychologist bases their choice of treatment on the needs of each patient. They use the following approach:

   A. eclectic
   B. psychoanalytic
   C. behavioral
   D. individualistic
   E. humanistic

2. Gestalt psychology is concerned with:

   A. individual choice
   B. family history
   C. repression
   D. environmental stressors
   E. all the above

3. Dennis undergoes Rational Emotive Therapy (RET) with his psychologist. His psychologist is most likely to suggest that:

   A. His depression is caused by an unresolved paternal conflict.
   B. He should take medication.
   C. He should engage in flooding.
   D. He should improve his self-esteem.
   E. He should shift his thinking to a more positive framework.

4. Brenda visits her boyfriend's family. At dinner, she begins to feel uncomfortable when the food is served. She has never eaten this type of cuisine. She eats the food despite reservations. A behavioralist would conclude that:

   A. She is concerned that the family will look down on her if she does not eat the meal.
   B. She hesitates to partake in the meal because it is inconsistent with her background.
   C. She feels unconscious resentment toward her boyfriend for forcing her to please his family.
   D. She is recalling the rejection of her last boyfriend's family that was related to expressing her differences.
   E. She knows that the people in her family are destined to appease their partners.

5. Joe has not joined the football team this year because he did not perform well on the team last year. A humanist psychologist might say that:

   A. Joe did not join because he has been very embarrassed about past failures.
   B. Joe decided that he wants to devote his energy to more rewarding pursuits this year.
   C. Joe has always gained respect from his peers when he chooses activities in which he excels.
   D. Joe understands from watching his older brother that he will not be able to maintain friendships with popular peers if he does not do well in a sport.
   E. Joe has an unconscious desire to please his parents, who punished him when he did not do well in the past.

GO ON TO THE NEXT PAGE

197

6. Andy is conducting research to measure the success of new physical educational requirements for the board of education. This is an example of:

   A. basic research
   B. applied research
   C. random selection
   D. operationalized research
   E. random assignment

7. Nancy, a grade school teacher, is interested in studying the ways in which grade school children interact with their learning-disabled peers in the classroom. She spends several months sitting in the back of the classroom watching the children's behavior. She is conducting:

   A. a field experiment
   B. naturalistic observation
   C. an informal survey
   D. a case study
   E. correlational study

8. How can experimenter bias be avoided?

   A. with double-blind procedures
   B. with demand characteristics
   C. with subject bias
   D. with response bias
   E. with social desirability

9. An Institutional Review Board (IRB) would most likely reject a proposal that:

   A. involves animals
   B. does not guarantee anonymity
   C. does not guarantee confidentiality
   D. permits participants to know study results
   E. involves questions already explored in the past

10. The following is/are associated with the limbic system:

    A. pons
    B. breathing
    C. body temperature
    D. heart rate
    E. fine muscle control

11. The impulse to run for cover when lightening strikes is *not* related to the:

    A. endocrine system
    B. sympathetic nervous system
    C. somatic nervous system
    D. parasympathetic nervous system
    E. fight or flight response

12. Which neurotransmitters are associated with schizophrenia?

    A. decreased dopamine and serotonin
    B. excessive dopamine
    C. endorphins
    D. those associated with depression
    E. Haldol and Stelazine

13. Gate Control theory explains that:

    A. Pain messages are arranged in priority order.
    B. Perceptions of pain are individual.
    C. Pain from temperature is more strongly felt than pain resulting from a cut on the skin.
    D. Certain people can control pain better than others.
    E. Manufactured painkillers are more effective than endorphins.

14. Eric is 5 years old. The night before his first day of kindergarten, he dreams that he can't find his mother after school. He then attempts to walk home and loses his way. According to Freud, the latent content of this dream is:

    A. nervousness that his mother is missing from home
    B. excitement that this is the first day of school
    C. confusion over the path home
    D. fear that he will lose his mother if he becomes more independent
    E. anxiety that he will not find his classroom

15. According to Maslow, what is the order of priority for a young student?

    A. a parent's appraisal of a good grade in school
    B. a cold drink after a long soccer game
    C. a hug from a grandmother that lives far away
    D. being chosen by peers for the daily basketball game
    E. completing an excellent painting

16. Mark has invited his younger brother to the movies. That day, he receives an invitation to a party from a girl he wants to date. He wants to go the party but has looked forward to his plans with his brother. Mark is experiencing:

    A. multiple approach-avoidance conflict
    B. approach-avoidance conflict
    C. achievement motivation
    D. intrinsic motivation
    E. approach-approach conflict

17. CT scans and MRIs share the following quality:

    A. measurement of brain structure
    B. use of X-rays
    C. use of magnetic field
    D. radio wave involvement
    E. tracing of brain waves

18. Developmental psychologists are researching the impact of parental death on one hundred 15-year-olds. Interviews have been conducted annually after the first interview. Which method are the researchers using?

    A. longitudinal
    B. cross-sectional
    C. cohort sequential
    D. cohort effect
    E. case study

19. According to Piaget, the following quality is associated with preoperational children:

    A. hypothetical thinking
    B. egocentrism
    C. basic logic
    D. conservation concepts
    E. transitivity

20. Mary Ainsworth's research involved the *strange situation*. The main theme of this research was:

    A. attachment
    B. temperament
    C. parenting style
    D. culture
    E. self-awareness

21. Amy, who is 16 years old, decides to invite her brother to a basketball game she is attending with her father. She does not want to share her parent, but fears she will be punished if she does not extend the invitation. She also anticipates being rewarded with more TV time later that night. Kohlberg would maintain that she is at the following level of moral development:

    A. preconventional
    B. industry
    C. postconventional
    D. autonomy
    E. conventional

22. Andy had an argument with his mother before his team's baseball game. He felt intense anger toward her. During the game he played aggressively and helped the team win. This is an example of:

    A. projection
    B. sublimation
    C. rationalization
    D. repression
    E. reaction formation

23. Jon is a psychiatric intern at a local hospital. He has always had a trusting relationship with a regular patient. One day his supervisor asked whether they could observe his session. Jon was unfocused and less sensitive than usual with the patient. His performance might have been impacted by the phenomenon of:

    A. the Hawthorn effect
    B. the Rorschach test
    C. the Thematic Apperception Test (TAT)
    D. anxiety
    E. neuroticism

24. A patient at an outpatient mental health clinic states that the government believes he is a Civil War spy and is pursuing him. He is presenting:

    A. a hallucination
    B. a delusion
    C. catatonia
    D. echolalia
    E. pica

GO ON TO THE NEXT PAGE

25. The following are symptoms that can be used to diagnose a major depressive order:

   A. diminished interest in activities, significant weight loss and flight of ideas
   B. lack of concentration, fatigue and grandiosity
   C. indecisiveness, loss of energy and insomnia
   D. suicidal ideation, pressured speech and hypersomnia
   E. impaired functioning, melancholia and inflated self-esteem

26. The following is *not* an anxiety disorder.

   A. agoraphobia
   B. panic disorder
   C. dysthymic disorder
   D. obsessive-compulsive disorder
   E. PTSD

27. The day 10-year-old Jacob's sister was born, he began to feel pain in his left leg. The next day, he told his parents that he had no feeling in this leg. Fearing paralysis, his parents rushed him to the emergency department. They were told that nothing was wrong with Jacob. He was experiencing:

   A. hypochondriasis
   B. a somatization disorder
   C. a conversion disorder
   D. mutism
   E. a histrionic personality disorder

28. Disassociation of consciousness is a theory of hypnosis stating that:

   A. Two or more streams of consciousness exist, separate from one another.
   B. Hypnosis is a role fulfillment that differs from a normal state of mind.
   C. Hypnosis is a social reaction separate from individual choice.
   D. A hypnotized individual identifies with the unconscious only.
   E. Physiological reactions in hypnosis are cut off from the alteration of consciousness.

29. A neutral stimulus in classical conditioning refers to:

   A. a change in environment that causes a response
   B. an automatic, involuntary response to a stimulus
   C. a stimulus that does not immediately predict a response
   D. discrimination
   E. spontaneous recovery

30. Carrie scans the TV listings one evening. She decides that when she finishes her chores, she will watch a certain program. She is exhibiting:

   A. the Primack principle
   B. a primary reinforcer
   C. aversive conditioning
   D. avoidance behavior
   E. escape behavior

31. As Dan walks home from school, he thinks about the choice he must make between attending his band practice or his mother's birthday celebration. Suddenly, he realizes that he can ask his mother to change the party to a time that allows him to attend the rehearsal. This experience is called:

   A. conditioning
   B. latent learning
   C. insight
   D. the blocking effect
   E. instinctive drift

32. Sanjay is 4 years old. He has just learned to use bread to eat his family's Indian meals by watching his family members. This is called:

   A. modeling
   B. abstract learning
   C. insight
   D. the contiguity model
   E. shaping

33. The following is/are involved in sex drive:

   A. hypothalamus
   B. pons
   C. thalamus
   D. medulla oblongata
   E. amygdala

34. The first stage of Selye's general adaptation syndrome is:

    A. resistance
    B. the exhaustion stage
    C. a defense mechanism
    D. the alarm reaction
    E. stress

35. The information processing model of memory is composed of:

    A. visual encoding, iconic memory, acoustic encoding
    B. rehearsal, chunking, mnemonic devices
    C. sensory memory, short-term memory, long-term memory
    D. shallow processing, deep processing, self-referent encoding
    E. echoic memory, selective attention, automatic processing

36. When blood sugar levels are low:

    A. The pancreas secretes insulin.
    B. Insulin release is inhibited.
    C. The pancreas secretes glucagon.
    D. Hunger is stimulated.
    E. Both B and C.

37. All the following are types of psychological testing except:

    A. performance tests
    B. observational tests
    C. self-report tests
    D. speed tests
    E. factor analysis

38. The following can surpass conditioning:

    A. instinctive drift
    B. generalization
    C. higher-order conditioning
    D. acquisition
    E. backward conditioning

39. The following is an example of instrumental aggression:

    A. An overworked teacher yells at a student who has not completed an assignment.
    B. A popular boy drops his food tray on another student who embarrassed him at soccer practice.
    C. A cheerleader laughs at the new student who has won the position of captain, a role that she desired.
    D. A student runs past his friends to get the best seat for a visiting theater company's performance.
    E. A girl in math class tells the teacher that her ex-boyfriend's girlfriend has cheated on an exam.

40. The James-Lange theory proposes that:

    A. Feelings can be changed by changing behavior.
    B. When a car races toward an individual, they physically feel fear and are simultaneously aware of it.
    C. Emotional reactions depend on individual interpretation.
    D. An emotion might be confronted by an opposing emotion, which might lessen the experience of the first emotion.
    E. Emotions do not depend on interpretation of the situation.

41. Dan and Sally are unable to find a solution to the problem of recruiting customers for their new store. Dan wants to take the night off, but Sally wants to continue to discuss various ideas. They are exhibiting:

    A. incubation and brainstorming
    B. divergent and convergent thinking
    C. incubation and creativity
    D. trial and error
    E. framing and bias

42. Katie is 15 months old. She says "bear" to her mother. Her mother hands her the toy. This is an example of:

    A. babbling
    B. semantics
    C. a holophrase
    D. telegraphic speech
    E. grammar

GO ON TO THE NEXT PAGE

43. A significant factor in the efficacy of the 12-step model of treatment is:

   A. peer support
   B. seasoned therapists
   C. psychological insight
   D. increased knowledge
   E. leadership

44. To ensure the reliability of a test, a psychometrician is likely to use the following method:

   A. test-retest
   B. standardization
   C. face validity
   D. content validity
   E. aptitude test

45. Jane does not like her new coworker because he does not speak to her or interact with her in any way. However, after seeing him around the office for a month, she now has positive feelings toward him. This is an example of:

   A. mere exposure effect
   B. cognitive dissonance
   C. generational conflict
   D. Freudian theory
   E. ethnocentrism

46. Professor Smith is preparing a psychological test. His students will be the participants. He plans on publishing the results in a journal article. Ethical standards require that he:

   A. provide a self-report test
   B. give a culturally relevant test
   C. inform students of the purpose of the study
   D. assure that tests are scored uniformly
   E. give an individual as opposed to a group test

47. An individual who is overdramatic, attention seeking and egocentric might have:

   A. an antisocial personality disorder
   B. obsessive-compulsive qualities
   C. manic tendencies
   D. a histrionic personality disorder
   E. narcissism

48. A top basketball player cannot make a foul line shot when he is alone, but then excels during the game. He is exhibiting:

   A. deindividuation
   B. groupthink
   C. social facilitation
   D. group polarization
   E. minority influence

49. The following term does *not* apply to behavioral therapy:

   A. systemic desensitization
   B. flooding
   C. aversive conditioning
   D. catharsis
   E. modeling

50. The following are all aspects of standardization and norms for effective psychological testing *except*:

   A. the creation of norms from the sample that initially took the test
   B. assurance that testing is administered on a uniform basis
   C. use of a standard for future test takers
   D. confirmation that testing is scored on a uniform basis
   E. development of procedures for ensuring validity of the test

51. Goslings are biologically prepared to follow whatever they see within the first few hours of hatching. If they are exposed to a human instead of their mother during this period, they will follow the human for the rest of their lives. This example illustrates the concept of:

   A. maturation
   B. gestation
   C. rooting reflexes
   D. orienting reflexes
   E. critical periods

52. Gender schema is defined as:

    A. a child's understanding that their sex won't change if they act like the opposite sex
    B. broad generalizations that express society's beliefs about being male and female
    C. a mental concept of a culture's definition of appropriate behavior of the sexes
    D. the existence of desirable male and female characteristics in one person
    E. expectations that describe how males and females should behave

53. A component of Freud's psychoanalytic approach is:

    A. mechanisms
    B. function
    C. observed behavior
    D. free will
    E. adaptation

54. Correlational research:

    A. establishes cause and effect
    B. can use the survey method
    C. involves numerical data
    D. does not use naturalistic observation
    E. is the use of case studies

55. Cognitive psychology is associated with:

    A. Maslow
    B. organic causes of behavior
    C. Rogers
    D. the processing of information
    E. James

56. Absolute threshold measures:

    A. the strongest level of a stimulus that can be determined half of the time
    B. messages below conscious awareness
    C. sensory sensitivity
    D. the difference between two stimuli half of the time
    E. the change of stimuli to neural impulses

57. Symptoms of drug dependence include:

    A. an intense desire for the drug
    B. tolerance to the drug
    C. an alteration in brain chemistry
    D. sympathetic nervous system stimulation
    E. a reduction in central nervous system activity

58. Convergent thinkers:

    A. focus on one solution to a problem
    B. underestimate the probability of incorrect judgment
    C. use framing
    D. tend to produce many solutions
    E. apply past successful solutions to current problems

59. Imprinting is rooted in:

    A. drive reduction
    B. conditioning
    C. homeostasis
    D. unconscious desire
    E. instinct

60. Kate and Alex are 5 years old and attend kindergarten together. Three assistant teachers work in their class of 15 students, who are learning the alphabet. Each adult works with one student. With the assistance of an adult, Kate can state the alphabet until the letter *S*. Alex can recite the entire alphabet without the assistance of an adult. When an assistant teacher approaches, she teaches Kate to write the entire alphabet. She shows Alex how to pronounce words he recognizes. This is an example of working with:

    A. crystallized intelligence
    B. the formal operational stage
    C. fluid intelligence
    D. the zone of proximal development (ZPD)
    E. habituation

GO ON TO THE NEXT PAGE

61. The Triarchic theory of intelligence maintains that:

    A. Three distinct primary mental abilities exist.
    B. Emotional intelligence is composed of expression, empathy and regulation.
    C. Logical, linguistic and interpersonal intelligences exist.
    D. The Wechsler intelligence tests have three age-specific IQ tests.
    E. Analytic, practical and creative intelligences exist.

62. Borderline personality disorder appears on which axis according to the diagnostic categories of the DSM-IV?

    A. Axis I.
    B. Axis II.
    C. It is not listed.
    D. Axis IV.
    E. Axis X.

63. The concepts of the ideal self, the real self, active listening and unconditional positive regard can be attributed to:

    A. Carl Rogers
    B. Karen Horney
    C. Sigmund Freud
    D. B.F. Skinner
    E. Albert Ellis

64. Community psychologists are not likely to see _____ as a primary concern.

    A. deinstitutionalization
    B. teenage suicide
    C. housing reform
    D. psychotropic medication
    E. HIV/AIDS prevention

65. At Thanksgiving dinner, the Smith children know from past years that they cannot eat their food before everyone has been served. This is an example of:

    A. roles
    B. social facilitation
    C. norms
    D. groupthink
    E. group polarization

66. Dan is a graduate student in psychology who has a sociocultural approach to the patients that he treats. When a new patient tells him that he finds the university art department too modern compared to his school in India, Dan might conclude that the patient has:

    A. an unconscious desire to return home
    B. a rigid personality structure
    C. indicated an investment in personal growth
    D. difficulty integrating the differences between American and Indian artistic values
    E. not yet attained the strengths needed to survive in a new environment

67. An empowering perspective of people's ability to solve their own problems and achieve their potential is:

    A. behavioral
    B. eclectic
    C. humanistic
    D. clinical
    E. family systems oriented

68. Latent learning can be described as learning that:

    A. is quickly forgotten
    B. causes no observable change in behavior
    C. occurs during adolescence
    D. depends on the presentation of rewards
    E. develops through watching others

69. The drug antabuse accomplishes which purpose?

    A. treatment of depression
    B. a decrease in dopamine in the brain
    C. blocking of the reuptake of serotonin
    D. controlling psychotic behavior
    E. aversive conditioning

70. Kathy discovered that she gravitated toward certain types of individuals in her freshman college class. She might have concluded that she was least comfortable with friends who:

    A. were popular and attractive
    B. held opposite political views
    C. belonged to her religious group
    D. lived in the same dorm
    E. could help her with exams

71. Validity in research is:

    A. how well an instrument measures or predicts what it is meant to
    B. how well results can be repeated
    C. specifically necessary when using the survey method
    D. an average of several scores in research data
    E. the most frequent score in research data

72. Andy saw his colleague, Carrie, yell at a student after class. He concluded that she has an impulsive personality. He found out later that the student had physically attacked another student during class. Andy might have exhibited:

    A. a self-fulfilling prophecy
    B. stereotyping
    C. self-serving bias
    D. an inclination toward situational factors
    E. fundamental attribution error

73. While entering a party, Bill notices the aroma of food and new people around him. He begins an intense conversation with a friend. His ability to ignore the food and new people is due to:

    A. visual illusion
    B. depth perception
    C. visual capture
    D. selective attention
    E. bottom-up processing

74. The following is most likely to be present in a male:

    A. color blindness
    B. Down syndrome
    C. Alzheimer's disease
    D. Tay-Sachs disease
    E. Turner's syndrome

75. A lawyer is working with a family involved in a custody battle. The parents expressed concern that their young son was negatively affected by the legal case. The lawyer referred them to counseling. He most likely referred the family to:

    A. a forensic psychologist
    B. a psychometrician
    C. an educational psychologist
    D. an ethicist
    E. an engineering psychologist

76. The following are types of somatosensation:

    A. touch and warmth
    B. cold and pain
    C. audition and vision
    D. A and B
    E. A, B and C

77. The concept of the schizophrenic mother is a theory that often blames the parent for a child's illness. Psychiatrists might suggest:

    A. a dominant gene
    B. a mutation
    C. displacement
    D. dispositional attributions
    E. a double-bind theory

78. Pamela was raised in Barbados. When her friend dies, she attends the funeral with two American friends from college. During the service, Pamela openly displays her grief by crying loudly. Her friends sit quietly. The difference between their reactions might be explained by:

    A. divergent thinking
    B. display rules
    C. conventional level
    D. denial
    E. confirmation bias

79. The following is a true statement about hearing and the human ear:

    A. Timbre and pitch are the same.
    B. Loudness is determined by pitch.
    C. A shorter wavelength has a higher frequency and higher pitch.
    D. Sound localization is the sense of hearing.
    E. The same note and pitch sound different on a cello and a violin because of the frequency.

GO ON TO THE NEXT PAGE

80. Which of the following statements is *least* true in regard to intelligence?

    A. Certain types of intelligence tests might be culturally biased.
    B. Individual differences in IQ are highly heritable.
    C. Creativity is correlated with IQ.
    D. A child with an IQ score of 140 is considered gifted.
    E. Abilities such as musical talent and interpersonal skills are not considered intelligence.

81. Carl Rogers's idea of self-acceptance and individual responsibility can be defined as:

    A. Maslow's self-actualization
    B. full functioning
    C. functional fixedness
    D. functionalism
    E. extrinsic motivation

82. The mandala is attributed to:

    A. Jung
    B. Freud
    C. Rogers
    D. Gillian
    E. Horney

83. The personal fable is associated with which stage of development?

    A. infancy
    B. latency
    C. young adulthood
    D. adolescence
    E. older age

84. Melissa is a geneticist studying the impact of adoption on the development of 6-month-old infants. She is studying identical twins who have been separated at birth. One has been adopted, and one has been raised by their biological parents. Melissa is interested in:

    A. nature versus nurture
    B. continuity versus discontinuity
    C. stability versus change
    D. longitudinal research
    E. descriptive research

85. Danny is afraid to drive a car. Each time he gets behind a wheel, he says to himself, "I know I will have an accident." He then becomes too afraid to drive. Which approach does this scenario support?

    A. rational emotive therapy (RET)
    B. aversion therapy
    C. free association
    D. counter conditioning
    E. biofeedback

86. Freud's concept of transference refers to:

    A. a patient's feelings toward their therapist that relate to early figures in the patient's life
    B. a therapist's identification with the patient (as the patient's father)
    C. resistance in the therapy process
    D. defense mechanisms that arise to sabotage treatment
    E. exchanges between patient and therapist that allow each to experience the feelings of the other

87. The memory loss from a trauma that results in a change of personal identity is called:

    A. dissociative amnesia
    B. dissociative identity disorder
    C. multiple personality disorder
    D. disassociative fugue
    E. an avoidant personality disorder

88. According to Piaget, at what age is it developmentally appropriate to show preliminary signs of object permanence?

    A. birth to 2 months old
    B. age 13
    C. age 3
    D. latency
    E. age 9 months to 1 year

89. The following is *not* a defense mechanism Freud acknowledged:

    A. projection
    B. reaction formation
    C. rationalization
    D. isolation
    E. socialization

90. A man visits his doctor regarding his sleep problem. He states that he does not sleep soundly. He reports that when he asked his wife whether she had noticed observable disruptions, she stated that it looked like he was sleeping soundly. What might the doctor explore?

   A. narcolepsy
   B. insomnia
   C. sleep apnea
   D. night terrors
   E. somnambulism

91. Bonnie receives a call from family members to buy groceries on her way home. She doesn't have a pen and paper, so she does her best to remember the requests. She tries to associate the item requested by each family member with their room in the house. This is called:

   A. a retrieval cue
   B. priming
   C. recall
   D. method of loci
   E. peg word mnemonic

92. Which of the following statements concerning consciousness and altered states of consciousness reflects a psychodynamic view?

   A. Dreams reflect the brain's interpretations of random neural transmission during REM sleep.
   B. Our unconscious processes primarily involve information-processing mechanisms that operate outside of awareness.
   C. The story line of a dream (manifest content) reflects the its latent content (underlying meaning).
   D. Consciousness is distributed across many neural pathways and circuits.
   E. Consciousness is an "on-line" workspace for focusing attention on skills relevant for solving current problems.

93. The system that allows for the movement of individual parts of the body is:

   A. kinesthesis
   B. sound localization
   C. psychophysics
   D. transduction
   E. perception

94. Opponent-Process theory pertains to:

   A. the excitation of neurons
   B. the inhibition of neurons
   C. wavelengths of light
   D. A and C
   E. A, B and C

95. Dark adaptation is a result of:

   A. going from predominantly cone vision to rod vision
   B. the formation of the optic nerve
   C. blind spots
   D. the bending of rays of light
   E. the role of the pupil

96. Males that possess XXY sex chromosomes have:

   A. a normal development
   B. a similarity to females with only one sex chromosome
   C. Klinefelter's syndrome
   D. Down syndrome
   E. Turner's syndrome

97. Which of the following glands are involved in seasonal affective disorder (SAD)?

   A. the pineal gland
   B. the hypothalamus
   C. the thyroid gland
   D. the adrenal glands
   E. the pituitary gland

GO ON TO THE NEXT PAGE

98. Quasi-experimental research:

    A. suggests a cause-and-effect relationship

    B. offers descriptive statistics that can be broadly applied

    C. lacks random assignment

    D. can often be subject to response bias

    E. both A and C

99. Explanations of behavior as adaptation belong to which psychological approach?

    A. humanistic

    B. behavioral

    C. evolutionary

    D. biological

    E. sociocultural

100. MAO inhibitors treat depression by:

    A. blocking neural receptors for dopamine

    B. causing short-term amnesia

    C. relaxing muscles and creating tranquility

    D. increasing serotonin and norepinephrine in the synaptic cleft

    E. reducing anxiety and creating feelings of well-being

IF YOU FINISH BEFORE TIME IS CALLED, CHECK YOUR WORK ON THIS SECTION ONLY. DO NOT WORK ON ANY OTHER SECTION IN THE TEST.

Section 2: Free-Response Questions

Time: 50 Minutes

Questions: 2

Directions: You have 50 minutes to answer both of the following questions. It is not enough to answer a question by just presenting facts. You must present a strong argument based on your critical analysis of the questions posed, using appropriate psychological terminology.

Free-Response Question #1

Freud maintained that defense mechanisms provide an individual with a way to manage threatening feelings, thoughts and behavior. Discuss how the following defenses contribute to that objective.

Define Freud's concept of defense mechanisms. Discuss the following defense mechanisms in the context of this theory.

- Repression
- Denial
- Projection
- Regression
- Somatization
- Displacement
- Rationalization
- Reaction formation
- Intellectualization

Free-Response Question #2

The theories of Jean Piaget are at the foundation of psychology in the area of cognitive development. Explain the major themes of his work. Include the developmental stages he outlines and their significant themes.

GO ON TO THE NEXT PAGE

Answer Key for Practice Test 3

1. A	26. C	51. E	76. D
2. E	27. C	52. C	77. E
3. E	28. A	53. A	78. B
4. D	29. C	54. B	79. C
5. B	30. A	55. D	80. E
6. B	31. C	56. C	81. B
7. B	32. A	57. B	82. A
8. A	33. A	58. A	83. D
9. C	34. D	59. E	84. A
10. C	35. C	60. D	85. A
11. C	36. E	61. E	86. A
12. B	37. E	62. B	87. D
13. A	38. A	63. A	88. E
14. D	39. D	64. D	89. E
15. B	40. A	65. C	90. C
16. E	41. A	66. D	91. D
17. A	42. C	67. C	92. C
18. A	43. A	68. B	93. A
19. B	44. A	69. E	94. E
20. A	45. A	70. B	95. A
21. A	46. C	71. A	96. C
22. B	47. D	72. E	97. A
23. A	48. C	73. D	98. E
24. B	49. D	74. A	99. C
25. C	50. E	75. A	100. D

Complete Answers and Explanations for Practice Test 3

1. **A.** Psychologists who abide by an eclectic approach view various theories as valid and applicable to many situations. Psychoanalytic, behavioral and humanistic psychologists employ specific modes of treatment. Psychoanalysis places emphasis on the unconscious mind. A humanistic psychologist observes individuals in terms of the choices they make. A behavioral perspective is concerned with behavioral reactions to stimuli. A psychiatrist takes a biological approach. Psychiatrists hold medical degrees, and their main role is to prescribe the correct psychotropic medication for patients. Individuality is not a term used to identify a major psychological perspective.

2. **E.** Gestalt psychologists look at an individual in the larger context. The whole experience of the patient is considered. This may include individual choice, family history, repression or environmental stressors.

3. **E.** Albert Ellis's Rational Emotive Therapy (RET) proposed that psychological conflict was a result of self-defeating thinking. In this confrontational approach, a therapist encourages a patient to discuss the actions, beliefs and consequences of their thought processes. In this example, a change in thought process is a basis for RET. Unconscious parental conflict is a psychoanalytic approach aimed at resolution of conflict through insight. Medication management is a more psychiatric, or biological, approach. Flooding is a behavioral tool that supports the notion that destructive behavior is a learned response that needs to be replaced by adaptive behavior. A humanistic approach would conclude that poor self-concept is responsible for the problem and that the gap between the real and ideal self needs to be reconciled.

4. **D.** Behavioralists maintain that behavior is based on conditioning. Brenda has learned through a past experience that negative consequences come from asserting a different perspective. While her concern about being looked down on relates to the fear of consequences, it is not linked to a learned reaction. The other concepts respectively refer to sociocultural, psychoanalytic and biopsychological perspectives. A sociocultural approach focuses on cultural differences in explaining behavior. The psychoanalytic perspective of Freud emphasizes unconscious motivation. A biopsychological approach emphasizes how chemical and biological systems create behavior.

5. **B.** Humanists maintain that individuals base choices on their needs. Joe has decided that he will pursue another activity that can be more fulfilling than football. Choices **A**, **C** and **D** refer to conditioned responses based on past rewards and punishments, which is deterministic behavior. The last choice is a psychoanalytic interpretation.

6. **B.** Applied research is used to solve a problem that has practical applications. Basic research is conducted to answer questions of interest rather than application; however, many findings from basic research are eventually applied to real-world problems. Random selection is a term used in sampling, or how subjects are selected for a study. Operationalize is a term used to explain how variables are measured. Random assignment refers to the way subjects are chosen to be in control or experimental groups. When assignment is random, individuals have the same chance of being placed in either group. This is the best way to ensure that any subject relevant variables (attributes that may vary between subjects) are distributed across groups.

7. **B.** Nancy's method solely involves observation. She does not intervene to impact the students. For the method to be a field experiment, she needs to manipulate an independent variable or control the study. She did not ask questions that are components of a survey. She did not isolate a section of the group to do a case study. Correlational studies measure the relationship between variables and are not a type of experimental research.

8. **A.** Double-blind procedure ensures that the experimenters cannot influence subjects toward their hypothesis. Subjects are also blind to the nature of the study. Demand characteristics are factors that participants might realize about the purpose of the study, which influence their responses. Response bias is present if, independent of the effect of any experimental manipulation, subjects are more likely to respond in one way than in another. Social desirability is a tendency to distort self-reports favorably.

9. **C.** While anonymity might not be a component of the study, confidentiality is usually required. Animal research is appropriate if it meets certain requirements. Subjects have the right to request study results. Questions studied in the past might be approached in another manner in a new research proposal.

10. **C.** The hypothalamus, which is a component of the limbic system, controls certain metabolic functions, such as body temperature. The other functions occur in the hindbrain, where the pons is located. The pons is a part of the brainstem that is responsible for arousal and that sends information between the medulla, cerebellum and cerebral cortex. Breathing and heart rate are controlled by the medulla. The cerebellum is responsible for fine muscle movement.

11. **C.** The peripheral nervous system consists of the somatic and automatic nervous systems. The somatic nervous system is responsible for voluntary muscle movement, not the involuntary response one experiences when lightening strikes. This reaction is automatically triggered by the autonomic nervous system. The autonomic nervous system is composed of the sympathetic and parasympathetic systems. The adrenal glands, which are part of the endocrine system, produce the adrenaline that alerts the body to engage in fight or flight.

12. **B.** An excess of dopamine, associated with movement and alertness, is associated with schizophrenia. A decrease in dopamine is linked to Parkinson's disease. Serotonin is responsible for mood, its decrease is linked to depression. Endorphins involve pain management, a key factor in addiction. Haldol and Stelazine are antipsychotic medications.

13. **A.** This theory maintains that messages of lower priority are shut out, as if by a gate, so only pain of higher intensity is experienced. Specifically, the theory distinguishes two kinds of neural fibers that can transmit pain— "L-fibers" and "S-fibers." Large diameter L-fibers transmit information very quickly and carry information about many forms of tactile stimulation and sharp pain to the spinal cord. Small S-fibers synapse with the same neurons in the spinal cord, but carry information about dull pain and burning more slowly. After sharp pain signals from L-fibers reach the spinal cord, they quickly inhibit the firing of the neurons with which they synapse, closing the gate to slower moving S-fiber information. Perceptions of pain vary. Pain caused by temperature is not neccesarily more intensely felt than a puncture of the skin. Because pain is individual, perceptions of control vary as well. The impact of pain management through the natural production of endorphins versus medication is dependent on the situation and individual.

14. **D.** Freud's latent content describes the unconscious meaning behind a dream. These interpretations usually include symbolism, such as that created in a dream. In the dream state, the repression employed to drive unconscious desires underground can be released. While the other answers might apply to Eric, they describe information from the dream, or manifest content.

15. **B.** According to Maslow's hierarchy of needs, physiological needs (such as hunger, thirst and sex) are the most imperative. In descending order of priority, the needs include safety, belongingness and love, esteem, and self-actualization. Choices **A** and **D** refer to esteem, **C** to belongingness and love, and **E** to self-actualization. The hierarchy of needs was Maslow's view of motivation. Evolutionary psychologists believe that basic motives evolved from basic needs for survival and reproduction. The psychodynamic perspective focuses on two basic drive states— sex and aggression. The sexual drive pushes us to seek love and intimacy, while the aggressive drive pushes us to control other people and our environment. Behaviorists focus on drive-reduction theories of motivation. These theories hold that deprivation of basic needs creates an unpleasant state of tension, and an organism emits behaviors to reduce this tension (e.g., a cat hunts a mouse to reduce the unpleasant feeling of hunger). Finally, cognitive theories of emotion revolve around goals, or valued outcomes established through social learning.

16. **E.** Approach-approach conflict refers to conflict over two attractive options. Choice **C** refers specifically to accomplishing goals. Choice **D** refers to internal rewards. Multiple approach-avoidance conflict occurs when one is choosing between several options, each of which presents attractive and unattractive factors. Approach-avoidance conflict occurs when one option has desirable and undesirable characteristics. Psychologists also study other types of conflict. Freud proposed psychodynamic conflict, or tension between opposing motives. For example, Tom tries to avoid domineering women because of unpleasant memories of his domineering mother, yet he somehow always finds himself dating dominant women because he is sexually excited by their power over him.

17. **A.** Both CT scans and MRIs show the structure of the brain or other parts of the body. MRIs use a magnetic field and radio waves to create images. CT scans employ X-rays to create a computerized image. An EEG measures brain waves through electrodes on the scalp that provide information on the electrical activity of the brain. The development of two new techniques now allows researchers to study the brain in action. Functional MRIs and positron emission tomography (PET) allow the detection of changes in brain activity in discrete regions of the brain during any task that can be performed while the head is held still.

18. **A.** In this example, longitudinal research examines the long-term impact of parental death. Cross-sectional research examines different age groups at the same time. Cohort sequential research is a combination of cross-sectional and longitudinal research to avoid the cohort effect. The cohort effect is the influence of the time period in which individuals were raised. A case study is the investigation of thought processes or behaviors of a person or group.

19. **B.** The preoperational stage is Piaget's second stage of cognitive development. It occurs in children between the ages of 2 and 7. During this phase, the child is egocentric in that they are unable to view reality from the perspective of another person. Hypothetical thinking is achieved after age 12, the formal operational stage, when a person can think abstractly. Basic logic is formed during the concrete operational stage, 7 through 12 years of age. Conservation concepts, the idea that changes in the form of an object don't change its physical properties, also develop in this stage. Object permanence (knowing that objects exist even when they are not seen) develops during the sensorimotor stage (0-2 years of age) and is firmly established by the time a child reaches the preoperational stage.

20. **A.** Ainsworth's research explored types of attachment by analyzing how babies react to the absence of their mother. If after an absence an infant was receptive to the mother, a secure attachment was identified. If following an absence an infant rejected the mother, the attachment was said to be insecure.

21. **A.** At the preconventional level of moral development, an individual obeys authority to avoid punishment and gain rewards. The conventional level involves conformity and fulfillment of obligations. The postconventional stage is motivated by social justice and societal benefit. *Industry* and *autonomy* are terms used by Erickson, not Kohlberg, in his eight stages of development.

22. **B.** This defense mechanism occurs when unacceptable sexual or aggressive feelings are channeled into socially acceptable behavior. The defense of projection occurs when unacceptable feelings or thoughts are attributed to others. Rationalization is another defense in which logical reasons are given for unacceptable behavior. Repression is the defense that occurs when an individual forgets unpleasant experiences as protection from threatening thoughts or feelings. Reaction formation is the mechanism where one acts in the opposite manner from what one feels.

23. **A.** The Hawthorne effect is a term used in the behavioral assessments of psychologists. It maintains that when people are directly observed, they alter their behavior to meet the observer's expectations. In this case, Jon was trying so hard to appear competent to his supervisor, but his nervousness interfered with his normal capacity to do well with his patient. In a Rorschach test, an individual is asked to identify inkblots and interpret what they represent. In a TAT, the subject is shown a series of pictures and is asked to create a narrative to accompany them. While Jon might have been anxious, the example does not indicate his mood. Eysenck's theory of neuroticism measures a person's level of instability based on mood and anxiety, as opposed to a calm and reliable stability.

24. **B.** The patient is presenting a belief that is inconsistent with reality, called a delusion. It is not a hallucination, which involves an erroneous sensory perception that may be visual or aural. Catatonic schizophrenia presents disorders of movement from immobile to overly active positions. Echolalia is a disturbed symptom, in which an individual repeats words or phrases of another. Pica is the eating of nonfood objects.

25. **C.** Indecisiveness, loss of energy and insomnia are symptoms of major depressive disorder. While the other choices contain correct symptoms, they also contain symptoms of manic episodes. The manic symptoms listed are flight of ideas, grandiosity, hypersomnia and inflated self-esteem.

26. **C.** Dysthymic disorder is a mood disorder characterized by depressed mood most of the time for at least two years. It is distinguished from a major depressive disorder and excludes a history of a manic or hypomanic episode. The other disorders mentioned are anxiety disorders. Agoraphobia is anxiety about being in places or situations where escape might not be possible. Panic disordered individuals experience recurrent panic attacks and worry about future episodes. Obsessive-compulsive disorder is characterized by recurrent thoughts that cause stress and anxiety, leading to symptoms such as repetitive behaviors or acts performed rigidly. Post-traumatic stress disorder (PTSD) is a reaction to a traumatic event, characterized by fear and helplessness. It might involve intrusive dreams, flashbacks and significant distress.

27. **C.** A conversion disorder is characterized by a loss of bodily function without real damage to the area. Paralysis, blindness and mutism are the most common conversion disorder symptoms. In this case, Jacob's anxiety at the birth of his sister manifested itself in the symptom of leg paralysis. Hypochodriasis is defined as a preoccupation with the notion that in the present or future one could experience serious illness. A somatization disorder involves a history of physical problems where symptoms are not readily explained by medical knowledge or have a greater-than-normal impact on functioning. A histrionic personality disorder presents as attention-seeking and overdramatic behavior.

28. **A.** Disassociation of consciousness is defined as a division between two or more streams of consciousness. One part reacts to suggestion. The other part observes this behavior. In hypnosis, an interaction occurs between the hypnotist (who is suggesting thoughts, feelings and behaviors) and the subject. One psychological theory is that hypnotized individuals enter a certain hypnotized role. In hypnosis, a complete separation from conscious awareness or individual choice does not seem to occur. Although most psychologists are doubtful that hypnosis is a real phenomenon, there is some convincing evidence that hypnosis can evoke an altered state of consciousness. For example, some hypnotized patients display unique patterns of brain activity, and there are reports of hypnotized patients undergoing extremely painful medical procedures without the use of anesthesia.

29. **C.** A neutral stimulus does not initially elicit a response. In classical conditioning, learning occurs when two or more stimuli are presented. An unconditioned stimulus is paired with a neutral stimulus until it stimulates a response. The subject can then give a response they already know to a new stimulus.

30. **A.** The Primack principle is part of Skinner's positive reinforcement or reward training. It proposes that a probable behavior can reinforce a less-probable one. A primary reinforcer is an important instinctual reward, like food and water. Aversive conditioning is a behavioral treatment model in which patients are exposed to an unpleasant association with the behavior they are seeking to change. Avoidance behavior removes the possibility of a current or future event from taking place. Escape behavior occurs when one stops an event.

31. **C.** Insight is the spontaneous solution to a problem that occurs to an individual suddenly. This should not be confused with the type of insight used in psychodynamic therapies. Therapeutic insight refers to the understanding of one's own psychological processes. This differs from conditioning, which involves a learned response. Latent learning is learning that is not currently evident as a behavioral change. The blocking effect occurs when a second stimulus cannot be conditioned because another present stimulus was conditioned already. Instinctive drift is when animals exhibit instinctual behavior that inhibits learning.

32. **A.** Modeling is observational learning, which entails learning by watching another individual. In abstract learning, the interaction between stimuli is more important than the physical manifestations of the stimuli. Insight is the sudden solution to a problem. The Contiguity model is a Pavlovian connection between the timing of a conditioned response before an unconditioned response; it proposes that this is the foundation of classical conditioning. Shaping is positive reinforcement of behavior to continually move closer to a goal.

33. **A.** Hunger, thirst and sex drives are controlled by the hypothalamus in the brain. The pons is part of the brainstem that is important for arousal and sending messages between the medulla, cerebellum and cerebral cortex. The thalamus is a part of the forebrain that communicates information regarding vision, hearing, taste and touch in the cerebral cortex. The medulla oblongata is the part of the brainstem responsible for heart rhythm, blood flow, breath rate, vomiting and digestion. The amygdala is a part of the limbic system and plays a part in memories of emotional events and fear responses.

34. **D.** The alarm reaction is triggered by stressors. The sympathetic nervous system is stimulated. This stage is followed by resistance, which includes raised temperature, heart rate and blood pressure. The exhaustion stage follows, where the immune system is weakened and the body is vulnerable to illness.

35. **C.** According to the information processing model of memory, memory consists of three stores: sensory memory, short-term memory (STM), and long-term memory (LTM). This model states that stimuli enters sensory memory (or the sensory registers) and can then either be lost or held in STM through rehearsal. If the information is rehearsed adequately, it is transferred to LTM where it can later be retrieved. The other choices are components of levels of processing theory, **D**, or the Atkinson-Shiffrin model (**A, B** and **E**), which indicates three models of memory.

36. E. Low blood sugar stimulates the pancreas to secrete the hormone glucagon. Insulin release is inhibited. The pancreas secretes insulin when blood sugar levels are high. High levels of insulin stimulate hunger. This illustrates the body's natural tendency to maintain a relatively constant state, referred to as homeostasis. This allows cells to live and function normally.

37. E. Factor analysis is a statistical method to identify closely related clusters of factors by identifying correlations. Performance tests trace the test taker's response to specific questions or tasks. Observational tests assess a test taker's behavior in a specific context. In self-report tests, the taker describes their response, beliefs or views in a survey or questionnaire. Speed tests measure how quickly an individual can answer simple questions in a period of time. All of these tests can be used for experimental or non-experimental research. Experimental research involves the manipulation of a variable by the experimenter. If no variables were manipulated by the experimenter, it is non-experimental research.

38. A. Instinctive drift is a response that goes back to the instinctive behavior of an animal. This stems from evolutionary history. In some cases, even a well-learned behavior may be interrupted by a species-specific, instinctive behavior. In classical conditioning, generalization means conditioned responses that resemble conditioned stimuli. In operant conditioning, generalization refers to the response when a similar stimulus to the discriminative stimulus is present. Higher-order conditioning in classical conditioning occurs when a conditioned stimulus is put with a neutral stimulus to produce a conditioned response to the neutral stimulus. Acquisition is the learning of new behavior at the initial stage of conditioning. Backward conditioning is when the unconditioned stimulus is presented before the conditioned stimulus in classical conditioning.

39. D. This is an example of instrumental aggression because its purpose is to obtain a reward. Whenever you see the word "instrumental" in psychology, it is referring to operant conditioning, or the relationship between a behavior and rewards or punishments. The other choices are examples of hostile aggression and are motivated by things other than tangible rewards. They illustrate aggression that is aimed at an individual who is perceived as harmful to the instigator.

40. A. The James-Lange theory proposes that awareness of physiological arousal produces the emotional experience. The theory suggests that feelings can be changed by a change in behavior.

41. A. Dan wants to put the problem aside for the time being to approach it in a new way. This is called incubation. Sally wants to freely generate solutions to the problem, or brainstorm. Divergent and convergent thinking refer to thinking that produces many alternatives and thinking directed toward one goal, respectively. Trial and error is an attempt to solve a problem and dispose of solutions that are ineffective. Framing refers to the way an issue is presented. Bias is a preconceived notion that might interfere with creative solutions.

42. C. Holophrases are used by babies at around the age of 1. A single word is used to indicate meaning. Babbling occurs at around 4 months of age and entails the making of sounds similar to speech. Semantics are rules to determine the meaning of words and sentences. Telegraphic speech occurs at about age 2, and consists of two-word sentences. Grammar is defined as rules that facilitate communication. Grammar includes syntax, or the rules that govern the placement of words and phrases in a sentence. Chomsky proposed that there is an innate universal grammar (a shared set of linguistic principles) that underlies all languages. He based this on his observation that there are many similarities of grammar across languages and cultures.

43. A. The foundation of self-help groups is the peer connection based on shared experience and mutual support. The other answers refer to more traditional models of treatment, such as working with a professional. While insight, knowledge and leadership might emerge during meetings, the philosophy of the movement is peer support. Well-known examples of self-help groups are Alcoholics Anonymous, Weight Watchers, and Gamblers Anonymous.

44. A. In the test-retest method, the same test is given to the same group on two separate occasions, and the scores are compared. If the test is reliable, there should be a high correlation between the scores. Standardization is the process of establishing test norms from a sample. Face and content validity are methods for ensuring validity, which is not reliability. An aptitude test is a kind of test, not a method.

45. A. The mere exposure effect is a phenomenon in which people feel more positively toward stimuli as their exposure to the stimuli increases. No indication is given that the other choices apply here. Cognitive dissonance refers to a dichotomy between a person's beliefs and their behavior. Generational conflict occurs when value clashes emerge due to various ages in one family. No evidence exists that an unconscious Freudian process is occurring. Ethnocentrism, the belief that certain identifying traits (such as one's culture or family) are better than others, is not relevant here.

46. C. Informed consent is a standard ethical concept in testing. Self-reporting, individual and group testing are methods of testing. Uniform scoring relates to reliability and validity, not ethics. Culturally relevant testing might be an ethical form of testing but is not likely to be required in the manner of informed consent.

47. D. An individual with a histrionic personality disorder behaves dramatically and often overreacts. A person with an antisocial personality disorder manipulates and exploits others, sometimes using criminal or violent means. Obsessive-compulsive qualities refer to preoccupations with issues such as schedules and repetitive behavior. Manic tendencies refer to manic symptoms such as those that might emerge in an individual with bipolar disorder. Symptoms include grandiosity and hypersomnia. Narcissism is a quality of a person with narcissistic personality disorder. This individual might be manipulative and egotistical.

48. C. Social facilitation is the ability to perform well-learned tasks better in front of others. Deindividuation is engagement in unusual behavior based on the anonymity of a group. Groupthink is the tendency for members of a group to minimize dissent. Group polarization occurs when an individual is in a group of similar-minded individuals, resulting in more extreme positions. Minority influence refers to the ability of a dissenter to shape the opinions of others.

49. D. *Catharsis* is a term associated with psychoanalysis. This therapy focuses on unconscious conflict and aims to increase insight. Systemic desensitization is a treatment for phobias in which a person is trained to relax in the face of the feared stimuli. Flooding is another treatment for phobias that exposes the individual to the feared experience until anxiety is overcome. Aversive conditioning is a behavioral approach in which the person is trained to associate their problem behavior with unpleasant conditions. Modeling is the observing and imitating of behavior.

50. E. Validity is a distinct concept from standardization and norms. Choices **A–D** are aspects of standardization and creation of norms. Validity is the extent to which a test measures or predicts accurately. Psychologists distinguish between several types of validity. Construct validity refers to the adequacy of the operational definitions of variables. In other words, to what extent does the operational definition of a variable measure what you are really trying to measure. For example, if you are trying to measure "love," what is an observable, measurable variable that can truly reflect love? Face validity is a related type of validity that basically asks the question "does this experiment appear to measure what it claims to measure?" External validity refers to the extent to which the results of an experiment can generalize to the real world. Internal validity refers to the level of control in an experiment. If all confounding variables are controlled for, an experiment has internal validity. Content validity is the extent to which items of a test or procedure are a representative measure of that which is to be measured. It is similar to construct validity, but for more complex variables, such as intelligence, that may be multifaceted. For example, are items relating to arithmetic ability and vocabulary ability appropriate content for an intelligence test, or should other things be included, such as spatial ability?

51. E. Critical periods are developmental periods of special sensitivity to certain kinds of learning that affect the capacity for future development and learning. Maturation refers to biologically based steps in development that occur in a specific sequence, with each step setting the stage for the next step. Gestation is the period of development between conception and birth. The rooting reflex is displayed by infants when touched on the cheek— they instinctively turn their heads and open their mouths. The orienting reflex refers to the tendency of humans to pay more attention to novel stimuli compared to redundant stimuli.

52. C. A gender schema is a mental representation that associates psychological characteristics with one sex or the other. In most every culture, children begin to show an awareness of their culture's gender schema by the age of 5, and within a few years they begin to adopt the same gender schema as their society. The other choices refer to other concepts of gender development. **A** describes gender consistency, **B** gender role stereotypes, **D** androgyny and **E** gender roles.

53. **A.** The concept of defense mechanisms is a significant factor in psychoanalytic theory. Freud maintained that individuals present multiple unconscious behaviors to manage anxiety and tension. With the goal of protecting the ego from threatening emotions, defenses emerge when the instinctual drives of the id conflict with the environmental pressures of the superego. Examples of these multiple defenses are repression, denial, projection and reaction formation. The other answers refer to different psychological approaches. Choice **B** is a component of Functionalism, a theory proposed by William James. It refers to the purpose that behavior serves. This is a practical approach that emphasizes environmental adaptation. Observed behavior, **C,** is a theme of behavioral psychologists, who analyze the role of behavior in the environment. They emphasize the importance of learning in behavior. Free will, **D,** is a humanistic approach embraced by such psychologists as Maslow and Rogers. They believed that individuals have the power for growth and the resolution of difficulties. Adaptation, **E,** is a significant component of the evolutionary approach. It is based on the theory of natural selection as a determinant of behavior.

54. **B.** Correlational research can use the survey method, in addition to other methods like tests and naturalistic observation, as in choice **D.** Correlational research does not use controlled environments that are needed to establish cause and effect, **A.** It does enable the researcher to assess the relationship between variables to conclude how one predicts the other. It is not defined as the use of the case study method, **E,** which is another research method that engages a group or individual through procedures like interviews. Correlational research does not focus on numerical data, **C.**

55. **D.** The cognitive approach to psychology emphasizes how individuals process information, use language and think. Maslow's (**A**) hierarchy of needs outlines the basic to less-significant needs of a person. He is aligned with the humanists, who emphasize individual growth. Organic causes of behavior (**B**) are the concern of biological psychologists, who maintain that mental and physical characteristics are determined by genetic make-up. Carl Rogers was also a humanist psychologist. William James (**E**) is associated with the school of functionalism, which focuses on how individuals use perceptual strengths for environmental adaptation.

56. **C.** Sensory sensitivity is measured by the absolute threshold, or the weakest level of a stimulus that can be determined at least half the time. Choice **B** describes subliminal stimulation, a protective step that allows individuals to have a slight sense of a change in stimuli. Choice **D** describes the difference threshold. This also measures a stimulus that is detected half the time, the minimum difference between two stimuli. An example of this is a sound that one is hardly aware of. Choice **E** refers generally to the concept of sensation, where environmental energy is translated as neural signals.

57. **B.** An individual who needs to use a drug despite the negative effects is dependent. They might also require more of the drug to reach the same effect, developing a tolerance. Choice **C** describes addiction, or physiological dependence. Brain chemistry is altered, resulting in serious withdrawal symptoms when the drug is stopped. Choice **A** describes the craving that develops when an addict withdraws from the substance. A reduction in CNS activity is the effect of depressants, which relax the system. Depressants include sedatives and alcohol.

58. **A.** Convergent thinkers solve problems by looking toward one correct solution. In contrast, divergent thinkers take a more creative approach by producing many answers to the same problem, as in choice **D.** Underestimating the probability of incorrect judgment is called overconfidence bias (**B**). Framing (**C**) is the way a question is posed; this can significantly impact a person's perception of a problem. The application of successful former solutions can sometimes prove ineffective. This fixation is called a mental set (**E**).

59. **E.** Imprinting is an instinctual process whereby certain animals form attachments early in life. It is associated with Konrad Lorenz, who became a parental figure to geese because he was the first moving object they saw after birth. Lorenz proposed that imprinting provides an evolutionary advantage because young animals are more likely to be fed, protected, and taught when they are close to their parents. John Bowlby argued that attachment behavior in human infants evolved for the same reasons. Drive reduction refers to states of tension that cause individuals to behave in a manner that reduces the tension and achieves the former homeostasis, or internal balance. Unconscious desire is a part of psychoanalytic theory.

60. D. The teachers are working with the children's ZPD, the range between what a child can solve on their own with difficulty and the level at which they can work with the help of adults or more advanced children. If an adult works at the top of the child's capability, the child can achieve the goal and then perform on their own with practice. When a child is able to complete this goal independently, it becomes the lower limit of the new ZPD. Crystallized intelligence refers to learned knowledge, while fluid intelligence refers to skills requiring rapid learning. Habituation refers to reaction to stimulus. It is the decreased responsiveness with repeated exposure to the same stimulus. The formal operational stage is Piaget's fourth stage of cognitive development, starting at age 12, when a child begins to think abstractly.

61. E. The Triarchic theory of intelligence is Robert Sternberg's concept that three distinct and testable intelligences exist. Analytic intelligence deals with facts. Practical intelligence is applicable to situations in reality. Creative intelligence refers to the development of multiple solutions. Choice **A** refers to the multiple intelligences theory of Howard Gardner, who maintains that individuals are unique in the way they process information. Choice **B** refers to emotional intelligence, Peter Salovey's and John Mayer's approach. It describes an individual's ability to express empathy and other emotions. Choice **C** describes a few of Gardner's intelligences. The Wechsler intelligence tests do indeed have three age-specific IQ tests, but they are not the same as the Triarchic theory of intelligence.

62. B. This question refers to the classifications of the Diagnostic and Statistical Manual (DSM-IV) that list and describe the criteria for psychological and psychiatric diagnoses. Clinicians can use the axes to correctly diagnose an individual. This can result in proper treatment and is necessary for insurance reimbursement. The correct answer, Axis II, is used to indicate whether a personality disorder (such as borderline personality disorder or histrionic personality disorder) exists. Axis I indicates a major disorder such as depression, anxiety or schizophrenia. Both I and II can be on the axes at the same time. The other axes are Axis III (general medical conditions), Axis IV (environmental problems such as poverty) and Axis V (Global Assessment of Functioning [GAF]). GAF is a numerical rating system on a mental health spectrum of psychological, social and occupational functioning.

63. A. Rogers was a humanist who emphasized that problems resulted from conflicts between the ideal self, or person one thinks they have to be for acceptance, and the real self, or positive person the individual was before society deemed them lacking. He believed the best treatment was to approach the patient with unconditional positive regard, empathy and encouragement, and to uncover strengths to achieve personal growth. Karen Horney contributed to functional theory, focusing on understanding anxiety and striving as signs of a mature individual. Freud laid the foundation of contemporary psychology with psychoanalytic theory. Skinner emphasized operant conditioning, in which a learner repeats or ceases behavior based on consequences. Ellis developed a cognitive theory, stating that when thoughts, beliefs or self-talk are irrational, people develop dysfunctional behavior and emotions.

64. D. While the use of psychotropic medication might have social and political ramifications, community psychologists are more concerned with pressing social issues than mental health treatment. Deinstitutionalization is when institutions discharged many mentally ill patients who need the structure of a residential setting. This results in an increase in urban homeless populations. While teenage suicide is a psychological problem, it can be viewed as a social issue related to community education and prevention. This is also the case with HIV/AIDS prevention. Housing reform is a social issue that interests community psychologists.

65. C. This is an example of norms because of the implicit rule that underlies the behavior of this group composed of family members. Roles refer to social status and expectations in groups. Social facilitation occurs when well-learned tasks improve when performed for others. Groupthink is when individual beliefs are repressed in the service of preventing conflict in a group and is not indicated in the example. Likewise, group polarization, the growth of a more extreme position because of the shared beliefs of members, is not evident here.

66. D. A sociocultural approach emphasizes that cultural differences are significant to behavior, beliefs and feelings. Social and environmental factors are important in this approach. In this example, a sociocultural psychologist would view the patient as conflicted about the cultural discrepancies they are confronting. Choice **A** describes a psychoanalytic interpretation, which states that the unconscious is motivating the patient to seek early figures and comfort in their conflict. Choice **B** also refers to a psychodynamic approach, maintaining that unconscious conflict can explain personality. Personal growth analysis, choice **C,** is more in the realm of humanistic psychology. Behavioralists explain behavior as influenced by environment more than culture.

67. C. Humanistic psychology can be seen as empowering in that it emphasizes that people can solve their own problems. Behavioral techniques are based on the idea that learning influences behavior. An eclectic approach to psychology is a combination of approaches that can be applied to the needs of specific individuals. Family systems theory is used in holistic approaches to family therapy. *Clinical* is a term that can be applied to any direct practice work with clients.

68. B. The term latent learning was coined by behaviorist Edward Tolman in 1948 after the discovery that his rats could learn how to navigate a maze even without being rewarded. He simply let rats wander around in a maze for several days. To his surprise, when these rats were later presented with a reward at the end of the maze, they could navigate the maze as quickly as rats that had a history of being rewarded for navigating the maze. Although his unreinforced rats were learning something about the maze while they were exposed to it, the learning was not manifest as a behavioral change until they were presented with a reinforcement for navigating the maze. Tolman believed that the rats formed a cognitive map, or mental representations, of the maze even though they did not receive reinforcement.

69. E. Antabuse is used to treat alcoholism by an aversive technique. Individuals become ill with severe nausea if the drug is mixed with alcohol. This is a classical conditioning technique. If the sight, smell, and taste of alcohol are paired with nausea, eventually just the presence of alcohol alone should evoke unpleasant feelings. The other answers relate to psychotropic drug treatment. Neuroleptics block receptors for the neurotransmitter dopamine. These drugs are used to treat schizophrenic symptoms like hallucinations and delusions, controlling psychotic behavior. SSRIs are one of three classes of medications used to treat depression by blocking the reuptake of serotonin.

70. B. Kathy would most likely have a harder time adjusting to people with different backgrounds or beliefs. Potential conflict between friends might feel more threatening and less comforting than familiar circumstances. Another aspect of interpersonal attraction is interpersonal rewards. Behaviorists talk about social exchange theories, which hold that interpersonal attraction is the degree to which interaction with another person is rewarding.

71. A. An instrument has validity if it measures what it sets out to measure. Questions need to be geared toward obtaining the relevant information needed to draw conclusions from the data. Reliability is a measure of how results stand up when an experiment is repeated. The more reliable a test is, the more consistent the results are. Validity is important in any study, but is not particular to the survey method. The average of several scores in research data is called the central tendency. Central tendency measures include the mode, median and mean. The most frequently occurring score in the data is called the mode.

72. E. Fundamental attribution error is defined as overestimating personality factors and underestimating situational factors when assessing behavior. In this example, Andy is drawing conclusions about Carrie's disposition without information about the situation. A self-fulfilling prophecy is when preconceived expectations of others cause those expectations to come true. Stereotyping refers to generalizing the characteristics of one particular group. Self-serving bias is when an individual takes credit for achievements and blames failures on situational factors to maintain a positive self-image.

73. D. Selective attention allows the brain to choose between various external stimuli. Bill has focused on a limited aspect of the stimuli of the party. Visual illusion refers to the difference between the perception of a visual stimulus and its physical reality. Depth perception is the phenomenon that the eye can see objects in three dimensions even though images the eye receives are two-dimensional. Visual capture occurs when vision dominates in a conflict between various senses. Bottom-up processing takes place when sensory receptors send external information regarding stimuli to the brain to be processed.

74. A. Color blindness, a condition where certain colors cannot be distinguished, is hereditary and most common in males. Turner's syndrome afflicts females who only possess one X chromosome and therefore do not develop secondary sex characteristics at puberty. The other answers are not significantly linked to sex. Down syndrome, a form of mental retardation, occurs when an individual has three copies of chromosome 21. Alzheimer's disease is a progressive brain disorder that might include a deterioration of a person's memory, learning and communication. Tay-Sachs disease is a recessive trait that causes nervous system damage and death in early childhood.

75. A. A forensic psychologist focuses on psychology and legal issues. This professional is knowledgeable about the impact of a legal battle on the emotional life of a child. A psychometrician is responsible for obtaining and analyzing data. An educational psychologist focuses on learning and teaching issues as they impact academic success or difficulty. An ethicist is not a relevant term here because it does not refer to a psychological approach. An engineering psychologist studies the interaction of people and machines.

76. D. Somatosensation refers to tactile sensations on the skin. These sensations include touch/pressure, warmth, cold and pain. Audition (hearing) also refers to sensation, but occurs when hair cells attached to the basilar membrane respond to vibrations of the fluid-filled cochlea of the inner ear. Vision involves light of different wavelengths traveling through the cornea, aqueous humor, pupil, lens and vitreous humor, eventually forming an image on the retina, which contains the photoreceptors that respond to light.

77. E. Double-bind theory states that serious mental illness has roots in inconsistent parental messages. Dominant genes and mutations are aspects of genetic make-up. When genes for a trait are different, the dominant gene is the one that is expressed. A mutation is a change in genetic structure. Displacement is a Freudian defense mechanism. It occurs when an unacceptable feeling or thought regarding a more-threatening object is transferred to a less-threatening object. Dispositional attributions are when an individual is held responsible for their behavior.

78. B. Display rules are culturally based and are established to detail appropriate emotional reactions to certain scenarios. In this example, it might be the case that in Pamela's culture, overt expressions of mourning are encouraged more so than in the United States. Divergent thinking is defined as thought processes that produce many ideas and spurn creativity. Conventional level is part of Kohlberg's model of moral development. This second level is when individuals have the awareness that societal rules are put in place to maintain order and for the betterment of members. Denial is one of Freud's defense mechanisms to defend the self against threatening emotions; an individual unconsciously denies aspects of reality. Confirmation bias occurs when an individual gathers information that supports their preconceived notions, leaving out a search for knowledge that might challenge their perspective.

79. C. A shorter wavelength has a higher frequency and higher pitch. This explains how pitch is determined. Timbre differs from pitch in that it refers to the quality of a sound. Timbre is what determines the different qualities of various instruments and sounds in the environment. Audition, not sound localization, is responsible for the sense of hearing. Sound localization is defined as the process by which one determines where a sound is coming from. The loudness of a sound is determined by the height of a sound wave, not the pitch.

80. E. Answers A through D are generally true. Answer E is not true because of Howard Gardner's theory of multiple intelligences. Gardner identified seven intelligences: musical (virtuosity), bodily/kinesthetic (athleticism), spatial (use of mental maps), linguistic (language skills), logical/mathematical, intrapersonal (self-understanding), and interpersonal (social skills).

81. B. While this concept is similar to Maslow's self-actualization theory, with full functioning, Rogers was referring to the concept of self-acceptance. He defined it as broad self-acceptance of the current and future self. This includes personal responsibility for behavior. Maslow's theory focused on realization of emotional and intellectual potential. Functional fixedness entails a rigid definition of the use of an object that rules out new uses, thereby inhibiting problem solving. Functionalism is a psychological approach concerned with the purpose of behavior and with environmental adaptation. Extrinsic motivation is the will to behave in a certain manner to gain a reward or avoid punishment.

82. A. Jung was considered a neo-Freudian because he accepted the idea of unconscious processes, but rejected the central role of sexuality. Jung was interested in expanding Freud's concept of the unconscious to what he called the collective unconscious. This consists of a universal shared past that is mythological and symbolic. He believed the mandala was a magical circle that symbolized the self-archetype in the subconscious. This Sanskrit word came to symbolize the wholeness and completeness of the self. Jung also argued that all men possess an unconscious feminine archetype, or anima, and all women possess a masculine side, or animus. A goal of Jungian treatment is individuation, the development of a sense of identity.

83. D. The personal fable is a strong element of the developmental period of adolescence. Adolescents often exaggerate notions of uniqueness and immortality. This stage involves a great push for independence and separation from parental figures to achieve individuation, one of the tasks of this stage. Adolescents also begin to realize that their personality changes when they are around different people and in different situations. This fits with Walter Mischel's argument that an individual's personality largely reflects situational variables rather than enduring aspects of personality.

84. A. Nature versus nurture deals with the extent to which environment and heredity play a part in individual development and behavior. In this example, Melissa is studying the differences between children with the same genetic make-up raised in separate environments, and in an adoptive versus a biological family. Continuity versus discontinuity is a different debate in developmental psychology. It is concerned with whether development is continuous, whether gradual change occurs throughout a life span or whether growth is composed of specific stages. Another controversy is that of stability versus change. It is concerned with whether personality is the same from infancy to death. The other answers refer to types of research. Longitudinal studies observe the same group over time. Descriptive research does not manipulate variables or identify causal relationships, but describes events.

85. A. RET is Ellis's cognitive treatment that emphasizes the power of irrational thinking on behavioral change. Aversion therapy is a treatment that associates unpleasant conditions with behavior problems that an individual is trying to change. Free association is the psychoanalytic technique of a patient speaking freely without the self-censorship of unacceptable thoughts and feelings. Counterconditioning is the substituting of one emotion with its opposite. Biofeedback is a method for learning to control physiological responses of the body.

86. A. Transference is a major component of psychoanalytic theory. It proposes that a patient transfers feelings toward early figures in their life to the therapist. Freudian thought maintains that transference must be analyzed as part of the therapy process. Choice **B** refers to countertransference, the transfer of early feelings of a therapist to the patient. Resistance and defense mechanisms are elements that arise in this process. Exchanges between patient and therapist can be due to many factors, including transference.

87. D. Dissociative fugue is one of several dissociative disorders that involve a sudden loss of memory or identity. This is caused by extreme stress that results in a separation from past memories. Dissociative fugue afflicts a person by wiping out personal memory. A person leaves their home and creates a new identity. Knowledge and abilities remain with the individual. Dissociative amnesia is the loss of memory following a trauma. Multiple personality disorder is a former term for what is now known as dissociative identity disorder (DID). In this diagnosis, an individual has two or more separate personalities. It has been linked to a history of physical or sexual abuse. An avoidant personality disorder is not a dissociative disorder. It is a personality disorder in which an individual is overly sensitive to rejection and withdraws socially.

88. E. Piaget's four major stages of cognitive development include the sensorimotor stage, from birth to 2 years. At 9 months to 1 year of age, an infant should show preliminary signs of object permanence. This is the understanding that objects have an existence independent of the child seeing or interacting with them. Children in this stage can differentiate themselves from the world and can retain a mental image of an object when it is not present.

89. E. Socialization is not one of the many defense mechanisms of Freud. Defense mechanisms develop as a way to function when the ego is unable to control anxiety. All individuals, despite level of functioning, have a repertoire of defenses.

90. C. Sleep apnea is when an individual stops breathing repeatedly during sleep. While it is possible that the sufferer or sleep partner notices when the individual wakes up or is restless, the cause needs to be diagnosed and is not readily apparent. The other answers are noticeable occurrences. This includes narcolepsy, when an individual falls into a deep sleep suddenly, at any time during the day or night. Insomnia is difficulty falling asleep, waking up too early or experiencing unrefreshing sleep. Night terrors occur when a person, most likely a child, wakes up in a state of fear, perhaps screaming. Somnambulism, or sleep walking, usually occurs in childhood.

91. D. Method of loci serves as a technique to remember details. It associates a place with certain words or concepts. Bonnie is connecting certain members' requests with their rooms. A retrieval cue is a reminder that is associated with details that are stored in memory. These include words, moods or emotions. Priming is what is activated when retrieval cues are instigated; it stimulates memory. Recall is the retrieval of learned material. A peg word mnemonic is used to remember lists, like Bonnie's. It involves memorizing images that link one word to another.

92. **C.** Answers A, B, C, D, and E reflect, respectively, biological, cognitive, psychodynamic, biological, and cognitive perspectives. As with any topic in psychology, different schools of psychology have different views on consciousness. In general, the psychodynamic view focuses on unconscious, often conflicting mental processes. A biological psychologist always focuses on the neural processes underlying a phenomenon. A cognitive psychologist focuses on the way people process, store, and retrieve information.

93. **A.** Kinesthesia is a proprioceptive sense that provides information about the movement and position of parts of the body *in relation to* one another. Sensory receptors in nerve endings in muscles, tendons and joints provide the kinesthesis system with this information. The other proprioceptive sense, vestibular sense, provides information about the position of the body in space. It senses gravity and movement, and works together with kinesthesia to register body position and movement. Sound location allows a person to locate a sound through brain processing. Psychophysics is the study of the interplay between physical energy and psychology. Transduction occurs when the energy of stimuli is changed to the energy of neural impulses. Perception is the process of understanding sensations to enable an individual to identify meaningful objects and events.

94. **E.** The Opponent-Process theory of color vision was developed by Ewald Hering. The theory proposes three antagonistic color systems: blue-yellow, red-green, and black-white. The blue-yellow and red-green systems underlie hue, and the black-white system is responsible for perceptions of brightness.

95. **A.** When conditions go from light to dark suddenly, sensitivity to light increases gradually. This is called dark adaptation. It occurs because the eyes shift from a dominance of cone vision to rod vision. The optic nerve is part of the structure of the eye. It is formed by the ganglion cell axons. Its purpose is to carry neural impulses from the eye to the thalamus in the brain. Blind spots are parts of the retina without receptor cells and, therefore, without vision. This is the area where the optic nerve leaves the eye. When light hits the eye, it is bent by the cornea, passes through the humor and pupil, and is then bent by the lens. It then goes through the vitreous humor to the rods and cones in the back of the eye. The pupil is an opening in the iris that gets smaller in brighter light and increases in darker light.

96. **C.** Klinefelter's syndrome is identified in males with XXY sex chromosomes. Symptoms are noticed at puberty, when the male secondary sex characteristics do not develop. Breast tissue development and passivity might also be present. This is not a normative individual development, which is composed of XX (female) or XY (male) chromosomes. Females with only one sex chromosome have Turner's syndrome. With only one X chromosome, females do not develop secondary sex characteristics at puberty. Symptoms include a webbed neck, lack of ovaries and some cognitive defects. Down syndrome occurs when an individual has three copies of chromosome 21. This results in mental retardation and specific physical characteristics. This presentation might include a round head, flat nose, small ears and a protruding tongue. Individuals might have weak muscle tone or coordination.

97. **A.** The pineal gland, located in the brain, is an endocrine gland that produces melatonin, which regulates circadian rhythms. SAD includes symptoms of depression that are experienced during winter months and subside in the spring and summer. This mood disorder is associated with seasonal variations of light. The hypothalamus, thyroid gland, adrenal glands and pituitary gland are all part of the endocrine system (like the pineal gland). This system is composed of ductless glands that secrete hormones for body regulation. The hypothalamus stimulates or inhibits hormones secreted by the pituitary. The thyroid gland produces thyroxin, which is involved with metabolism. The adrenal glands produce cortisol, a stress hormone, and epinephrine and norepinephrine, responsible for the fight-or-flight impulse. The pituitary gland produces stimulating hormones that encourage secretion in other glands.

98. **E.** Quasi-experimental research shares qualities with controlled experiments, but does not include random assignment to groups. Quasi-experimental designs are conducted in applied research settings (outside of the laboratory) in which the control features of true experimental designs cannot be achieved. Data from this kind of research yield cause-and-effect results; however, the results are not as strong as those from a true laboratory experiment. It is made up of surveys and tests that are subject to incorrect results due to factors including response bias. Descriptive statistics describe interval or ratio data.

99. C. Evolutionary psychologists explain behavior as being derived from adaptations to the environment, based on the theory of natural selection. Humanistic approaches emphasize free will and personal growth. Behavioral psychologists focus on learning as the determinant of behavior. The biological view emphasizes organic motivations for behavior. Sociocultural theorists state that culture and environment impact the formation of behavior.

100. D. Antidepressant medication encourages positive moods by increasing the neurotransmitter(s) serotonin and/or norepinephrine at synapses. There are three kinds of antidepressants. MAOIs (monoamine oxidase inhibitors) weaken chemicals that break down these neurotransmitters. Tricyclics inhibit reuptake of these neurotransmitters. SSRIs (selective serotonin reuptake inhibitors) limit only serotonin. Choice **A** refers to neuroleptic medications, used to treat disorders like schizophrenia, which minimize dopamine production. Choice **B** explains one possible side effect of electroconvulsive shock treatment (ECT), where a small electric shock is administered to a patient to decrease severe depression. Choices **C** and **E** refer to anxiolytics, or tranquilizers, which include benzodiazepines that increase the neurotransmitter, GABA. This reduces anxiety and tension.

Free-Response Question #1—Explanation

Point 1 (Definition of Defense Mechanisms)

- Defense mechanisms develop when the ego is unable to control anxiety, creating a means to function.
- All individuals, despite level of functioning, have a repertoire of defenses.
- Defenses can be grouped according to level of maturity.
- Narcissistic defenses are the most primitive, seen in children and psychotic adults.
- Immature defenses are seen in adolescents and some nonpsychotic adults.
- Neurotic defenses are seen in obsessive-compulsive and hysterical individuals as well as adults under stress.

Point 2 (Repression)

- Defined as pushing away an idea or feeling from consciousness.
- *Primary repression* is the pushing down of thoughts or feelings before they enter the unconscious mind.
- *Secondary repression* is the withholding of a previously conscious thought or feeling from conscious awareness.

Point 3 (Denial)

- Defined as avoiding an awareness of a painful reality by negating its existence.
- This defense can be seen in normal and pathological behavior.

Point 4 (Projection)

- Locating unacceptable urges outside oneself.
- Placing undesirable wishes and thoughts on another.

Point 5 (Regression)

- Moving backward developmentally to an earlier behavior.
- This enables conflict at the current developmental stage to be avoided.
- Degrees of regression are often a normal process that is required in certain instances like sleep and sex.

Point 6 (Somatization)

- Psychological conflict is converted into physical symptoms
- A psychological issue is often presented as a physical complaint.

Point 7 (Displacement)

- Moving unacceptable thoughts or feelings regarding a more threatening object or idea to a less threatening one.
- The less-threatening object or idea resembles the original.
- The idea or object can then have expression without the unbearable conflict.

Point 8 (Rationalization)

- A socially acceptable justification for inappropriate behavior.
- This process is used to rationalize beliefs, feelings or actions that the individual deems unacceptable.

Point 9 (Reaction Formation)

- Behaving in the manner opposite what an individual is feeling.
- An unacceptable impulse can be changed to its opposite.

Point 10 (Intellectualization)

- Avoidance of emotion or experience by intellectualizing.
- Emphasis is placed on objects as opposed to people to avoid intimacy.
- Emphasis is placed on external reality to avoid self-expression of feelings.

Free-Response Question #2—Explanation

Point 1

Piaget focused on the development of cognitive abilities in children. He studied the ways children think and gain knowledge.

Point 2

There are four major stages of development:

- Sensorimotor
- Preoperational thought
- Concrete operations
- Formal operations

Point 3

Sensorimotor Stage

- Birth to 2 years.
- Use of innate reflexes.
- Display of symbolic thought with objects and events.
- Achievement of object permanence at end of stage. (Object permanence is the ability to grasp that objects, such as people, exist independently of the child seeing them or being involved with them.)
- Development of symbolization—The visual image of an object symbolizes the real object, as with a toy.

Point 4

Stage of Preoperational Thought

- Age two through seven.
- Intuitive thinking and reasoning.
- More extensive use of language and symbols.
- Difficulty dealing with moral dilemmas, but understanding of good and bad.
- Egocentric—Considers self the center of the universe; cannot see other perspectives.
- Magical thinking–phenomenalistic causality—Believing that simultaneous events cause one another. (For example, mommy died because I was bad.)
- Animistic thinking—Events and objects are given psychological characteristics, like feelings.
- Semiotic function—Use of symbols as the equal of real objects. (For example, drawing a dog signifies my real dog.)

Point 5

Stage of Concrete Operations

- Thought goes from egocentric (of the previous period) to operational thought—Things can be seen from others' perspective.
- Concrete perception of the world.
- Syllogistic reasoning—Conclusion is logically drawn from two notions.
- Grouping of things according to the same characteristics.
- Can reason and follow rules.
- Beginning of moral sensibility, values.

- Conservation—Objects might change, but they have characteristics that allow them to remain the same.
- Reversibility—Relationships between things; one thing into another.
- Concepts of quantity.

Point 6

Stage of Formal Operations

- Age 11 through end of adolescence.
- Can think abstractly.
- Deductive reasoning.
- Concept of probabilities (adolescence).
- Complex use of language.
- Hypotheses can be made and tested.
- Deductive reasoning—general to specific.
- Inductive reasoning—specific to general.

Answer Sheet for Practice Test 4

1 (A) (B) (C) (D) (E)	26 (A) (B) (C) (D) (E)
2 (A) (B) (C) (D) (E)	27 (A) (B) (C) (D) (E)
3 (A) (B) (C) (D) (E)	28 (A) (B) (C) (D) (E)
4 (A) (B) (C) (D) (E)	29 (A) (B) (C) (D) (E)
5 (A) (B) (C) (D) (E)	30 (A) (B) (C) (D) (E)
6 (A) (B) (C) (D) (E)	31 (A) (B) (C) (D) (E)
7 (A) (B) (C) (D) (E)	32 (A) (B) (C) (D) (E)
8 (A) (B) (C) (D) (E)	33 (A) (B) (C) (D) (E)
9 (A) (B) (C) (D) (E)	34 (A) (B) (C) (D) (E)
10 (A) (B) (C) (D) (E)	35 (A) (B) (C) (D) (E)
11 (A) (B) (C) (D) (E)	36 (A) (B) (C) (D) (E)
12 (A) (B) (C) (D) (E)	37 (A) (B) (C) (D) (E)
13 (A) (B) (C) (D) (E)	38 (A) (B) (C) (D) (E)
14 (A) (B) (C) (D) (E)	39 (A) (B) (C) (D) (E)
15 (A) (B) (C) (D) (E)	40 (A) (B) (C) (D) (E)
16 (A) (B) (C) (D) (E)	41 (A) (B) (C) (D) (E)
17 (A) (B) (C) (D) (E)	42 (A) (B) (C) (D) (E)
18 (A) (B) (C) (D) (E)	43 (A) (B) (C) (D) (E)
19 (A) (B) (C) (D) (E)	44 (A) (B) (C) (D) (E)
20 (A) (B) (C) (D) (E)	45 (A) (B) (C) (D) (E)
21 (A) (B) (C) (D) (E)	46 (A) (B) (C) (D) (E)
22 (A) (B) (C) (D) (E)	47 (A) (B) (C) (D) (E)
23 (A) (B) (C) (D) (E)	48 (A) (B) (C) (D) (E)
24 (A) (B) (C) (D) (E)	49 (A) (B) (C) (D) (E)
25 (A) (B) (C) (D) (E)	50 (A) (B) (C) (D) (E)

51 Ⓐ Ⓑ Ⓒ Ⓓ Ⓔ	76 Ⓐ Ⓑ Ⓒ Ⓓ Ⓔ
52 Ⓐ Ⓑ Ⓒ Ⓓ Ⓔ	77 Ⓐ Ⓑ Ⓒ Ⓓ Ⓔ
53 Ⓐ Ⓑ Ⓒ Ⓓ Ⓔ	78 Ⓐ Ⓑ Ⓒ Ⓓ Ⓔ
54 Ⓐ Ⓑ Ⓒ Ⓓ Ⓔ	79 Ⓐ Ⓑ Ⓒ Ⓓ Ⓔ
55 Ⓐ Ⓑ Ⓒ Ⓓ Ⓔ	80 Ⓐ Ⓑ Ⓒ Ⓓ Ⓔ
56 Ⓐ Ⓑ Ⓒ Ⓓ Ⓔ	81 Ⓐ Ⓑ Ⓒ Ⓓ Ⓔ
57 Ⓐ Ⓑ Ⓒ Ⓓ Ⓔ	82 Ⓐ Ⓑ Ⓒ Ⓓ Ⓔ
58 Ⓐ Ⓑ Ⓒ Ⓓ Ⓔ	83 Ⓐ Ⓑ Ⓒ Ⓓ Ⓔ
59 Ⓐ Ⓑ Ⓒ Ⓓ Ⓔ	84 Ⓐ Ⓑ Ⓒ Ⓓ Ⓔ
60 Ⓐ Ⓑ Ⓒ Ⓓ Ⓔ	85 Ⓐ Ⓑ Ⓒ Ⓓ Ⓔ
61 Ⓐ Ⓑ Ⓒ Ⓓ Ⓔ	86 Ⓐ Ⓑ Ⓒ Ⓓ Ⓔ
62 Ⓐ Ⓑ Ⓒ Ⓓ Ⓔ	87 Ⓐ Ⓑ Ⓒ Ⓓ Ⓔ
63 Ⓐ Ⓑ Ⓒ Ⓓ Ⓔ	88 Ⓐ Ⓑ Ⓒ Ⓓ Ⓔ
64 Ⓐ Ⓑ Ⓒ Ⓓ Ⓔ	89 Ⓐ Ⓑ Ⓒ Ⓓ Ⓔ
65 Ⓐ Ⓑ Ⓒ Ⓓ Ⓔ	90 Ⓐ Ⓑ Ⓒ Ⓓ Ⓔ
66 Ⓐ Ⓑ Ⓒ Ⓓ Ⓔ	91 Ⓐ Ⓑ Ⓒ Ⓓ Ⓔ
67 Ⓐ Ⓑ Ⓒ Ⓓ Ⓔ	92 Ⓐ Ⓑ Ⓒ Ⓓ Ⓔ
68 Ⓐ Ⓑ Ⓒ Ⓓ Ⓔ	93 Ⓐ Ⓑ Ⓒ Ⓓ Ⓔ
69 Ⓐ Ⓑ Ⓒ Ⓓ Ⓔ	94 Ⓐ Ⓑ Ⓒ Ⓓ Ⓔ
70 Ⓐ Ⓑ Ⓒ Ⓓ Ⓔ	95 Ⓐ Ⓑ Ⓒ Ⓓ Ⓔ
71 Ⓐ Ⓑ Ⓒ Ⓓ Ⓔ	96 Ⓐ Ⓑ Ⓒ Ⓓ Ⓔ
72 Ⓐ Ⓑ Ⓒ Ⓓ Ⓔ	97 Ⓐ Ⓑ Ⓒ Ⓓ Ⓔ
73 Ⓐ Ⓑ Ⓒ Ⓓ Ⓔ	98 Ⓐ Ⓑ Ⓒ Ⓓ Ⓔ
74 Ⓐ Ⓑ Ⓒ Ⓓ Ⓔ	99 Ⓐ Ⓑ Ⓒ Ⓓ Ⓔ
75 Ⓐ Ⓑ Ⓒ Ⓓ Ⓔ	100 Ⓐ Ⓑ Ⓒ Ⓓ Ⓔ

CUT HERE

Practice Test 4

Section 1: Multiple-Choice Questions

Time: 70 Minutes
Questions: 100

1. What was Wilhelm Wundt's contribution to psychology?

   A. He opened the first psychology laboratory in Germany.
   B. He proposed that behavior can be shaped by the environment.
   C. He trained John Watson and B.F. Skinner in the methods of psychology.
   D. He discovered the techniques of free association and dream analysis.
   E. He established the first psychology lab in the United States.

2. _____ believe that psychologists should not study mental processes, but should study only observable behaviors.

   A. Functionalists
   B. Psychoanalysts
   C. Humanists
   D. Behaviorists
   E. Structuralists

3. A(n) _____ study provides a researcher with the greatest amount of control when conducting research.

   A. correlational
   B. experimental
   C. quasi-experimental
   D. observational
   E. descriptive

4. Judy recently suffered a stroke that affected parts of her left hemisphere. Given this information, Judy is most likely to show which of the following problems?

   A. loss of sensation in the left side of her body
   B. difficulty understanding spoken language
   C. difficulty recognizing faces
   D. complete paralysis (loss of motor movement)
   E. changes in mood and personality

5. To measure electrical activity in the brain, one should conduct a(n):

   A. MRI
   B. PET scan
   C. CT scan
   D. lobotomy
   E. EEG

6. According to Erik Erikson:

   A. Personality is fixed by the adolescent years.
   B. Personality is determined solely by environmental experiences.
   C. Personality is a result of biological and genetic influences.
   D. Personality evolves across an entire life span.
   E. Early childhood experiences determine adult personality.

GO ON TO THE NEXT PAGE

7. All the following accurately depict ethical principles of the American Psychological Association *except:*

  A. Participants must be informed of what their participation entails.

  B. Participants must be rewarded for their participation.

  C. Participants may withdraw from the study at any time.

  D. Participants must be told of any deceptions immediately following participation.

  E. Participants responses must be kept confidential.

8. Which process explains why you no longer notice the sound of an air conditioner running after sitting in a room for 5 minutes?

  A. Weber's law

  B. top-down processing

  C. classical conditioning

  D. sensory adaptation

  E. response bias

9. Most psychoactive drugs exert their effects on behavior, thought and emotion by:

  A. inhibiting neuronal functioning in the frontal lobes of the brain

  B. changing the functioning of the peripheral nervous system

  C. temporarily increasing the number of neurons in the brain

  D. altering the activity of neurotransmitters in the brain

  E. temporarily decreasing the number of neurons in the brain

10. The sound of a microwave alarm stimulates the _____ region of your cerebral cortex. The sight of a microwave stimulates the _____ region.

  A. parietal; temporal

  B. temporal; occipital

  C. frontal; temporal

  D. limbic; frontal

  E. parietal; occipital

11. According to the General Adaptation Syndrome (GAS), when startled by a cat that runs in front of your car, you initially experience a:

  A. heightened sympathetic nervous system response

  B. temporary state of shock and confusion

  C. primary appraisal process

  D. brief period of unconsciousness

  E. slight decrease in immune system functioning

12. A researcher plans to test the following hypothesis: Exposure to older adults who depict either negative or positive aging influences one's level of anxiety about aging. In this study, what is the dependent variable?

  A. the individuals being tested

  B. anxiety about aging

  C. the amount of exposure to older adults

  D. the older adults depicting positive aging

  E. the older adults depicting negative aging

13. Fundamental attribution error is most likely to contribute to:

  A. diffusion of responsibility

  B. deindividuation

  C. moral relativism

  D. high self-efficacy

  E. blame-the-victim thinking

14. Basic life functions such as breathing, swallowing and heartbeat are primarily regulated by the:

  A. cerebellum

  B. brainstem

  C. cerebral cortex

  D. frontal lobes

  E. limbic system

15. A behavioral psychologist who is interested in studying the effects of punishment on children's behavior is most likely to:

   A. Ask children to report their thoughts and feelings concerning punishment.

   B. Ask parents to report how their children typically respond to punishment.

   C. Observe the reactions of children to instances of punishment.

   D. Give children personality tests that assess their perceptions of punishment.

   E. Measure brain activity using a PET scan while a child is being punished.

16. Which of the following is a key symptom/feature of somatoform disorders?

   A. extreme anxiety

   B. manic behavior

   C. physical complaints

   D. psychotic episodes

   E. hallucinations and delusions

17. Gestalt psychologists argue that the brain:

   A. organizes sensory input according to certain principles

   B. breaks sensory input into individual elements based on certain principles

   C. ignores certain sensory input to focus on other input

   D. engages in sequential processing of information

   E. must rely solely on incoming sensory information to understand it

18. A basketball player who is able to ignore the sound of the crowd and the band playing in the background while focusing on his coach's words during a timeout is utilizing:

   A. selective attention

   B. sustained attention

   C. divided attention

   D. dichotic listening skills

   E. sensory adaptation

19. A developmental psychologist wishes to assess changes in memory skills across the adult years. They decide to take a group of 40-year-olds and follow them over the next 30 years, assessing memory skills at 5-year intervals. This psychologist is using:

   A. a cross-sectional research design

   B. a case study approach

   C. naturalistic observation

   D. a cross-sequential research design

   E. a longitudinal research design

20. An individual who supports the nurture side of the nature-versus-nurture debate would argue that:

   A. One's biological make-up is a primary determinant of mental illness.

   B. Genetic predispositions are the primary causes of abnormal behavior.

   C. Life experiences play an important role in the development of mental illness.

   D. Abnormal levels of neurotransmitters in the brain are the key cause of mental illness.

   E. Structural changes in the frontal lobes are the most likely explanation for serious mental illness.

21. When given a list of words to remember, individuals typically remember items at the beginning and end of the list better than items in the middle of the list. This is referred to as the:

   A. rote rehearsal effect

   B. chunking effect

   C. serial position effect

   D. retroactive interference effect

   E. proactive interference effect

GO ON TO THE NEXT PAGE

22. Which of the following statements is most consistent with Spearman's notion of a general intelligence (g factor)?

   A. An individual who scores high on one math test will also score high on other math tests.

   B. An individual will show similar levels of functioning on a variety of different types of tests.

   C. Those who score low on IQ tests in infancy will continue to score low on IQ tests in childhood and adolescence.

   D. Individuals will show declines in intelligence during the late adult years.

   E. An individual who scores high on one type of intelligence test will score low on another type of intelligence test.

23. Taking car privileges away from an adolescent who comes home past curfew is an example of:

   A. vicarious punishment
   B. negative punishment
   C. negative reinforcement
   D. positive reinforcement
   E. positive punishment

24. A cognitive psychologist would argue that abnormal behavior results when:

   A. An abnormal level of neurotransmitters exists in certain regions of the brain.

   B. Structural damage has occurred in the frontal lobe regions of the brain.

   C. An individual represses tension and conflict into the unconscious.

   D. An individual is unable to meet their psychological and social needs.

   E. An individual experiences irrational and/or negative thoughts.

25. In developing the Social Readjustment Rating Scale (SRRS), Holmes and Rahe were the first to point out that:

   A. Stress can result from both positive and negative changes in one's life.

   B. Prolonged stress decreases the functioning of the immune system.

   C. Social support is extremely important following a disaster.

   D. One's personality type plays an important role in how one copes with stress.

   E. Problem-focused coping is more effective at dealing with stress than emotion-focused coping.

26. In comparison to a Type A personality, an individual with a Type B personality is:

   A. more likely to suffer a heart attack
   B. less likely to experience stress
   C. more likely to internalize stress
   D. more emotional and volatile
   E. more relaxed and laid back

27. In a correlational design:

   A. One seeks to determine cause-and-effect relationships.

   B. Variables are not directly manipulated.

   C. One must rely on self-report techniques.

   D. One restricts the sample to only a single individual.

   E. One must use a double-blind design.

28. If one is concerned about expectancy effects in a study they are conducting, they should:

   A. Strive to make the experimental and control groups as similar as possible.

   B. Use random assignment when putting participants into the experimental and control groups.

   C. Refrain from informing the participants whether they are in the experimental or control group.

   D. Be sure to draw a sample that represents the population one seeks to describe.

   E. Obtain informed consent prior to beginning data collection.

29. An individual who looks to messages portrayed by the media as a prime influence on human thought and behavior is taking a:

   A. sociocultural perspective
   B. psychoanalytic perspective
   C. cognitive perspective
   D. eclectic perspective
   E. humanistic perspective

30. Rational Emotive Therapy (RET) focuses on:

   A. analyzing early childhood experiences
   B. improving self-concept and increasing self-esteem
   C. identifying the external factors that influence behavior
   D. slowly bringing an individual back to a nonpsychotic state
   E. identifying and changing negative and self-defeating thought patterns

31. Self-actualization is a process by which we:

   A. express genetic predispositions and tendencies
   B. become the person others wish us to be
   C. express traits and characteristics inherited from our parents
   D. strive to reach our fullest potential
   E. overcome emotional and psychological problems such as depression

32. The concept of *tabula rasa* is most consistent with:

   A. a biological perspective on behavior
   B. a belief in genetic influences on behavior
   C. a focus on unconscious forces in driving behavior
   D. the nature side of the nature-nurture debate
   E. an emphasis on experience in shaping behavior

33. Psychology falls under the category of science because it:

   A. seeks to describe, explain and predict behavior
   B. systematically collects and analyzes data about behavior
   C. studies behavior, thought and emotion
   D. uses theory as a guide to studying behavior
   E. relies on multiple perspectives to explain behavior

34. In a signal detection experiment, when an individual reports detection of a stimulus when no stimulus is presented, it is known as a:

   A. hit
   B. miss
   C. correct rejection
   D. false negative
   E. false positive

35. Which of the following correlation coefficients represents the strongest relationship?

   A. $r = +.53$
   B. $r = -.73$
   C. $r = +.62$
   D. $r = +.01$
   E. $r = -24$

36. If you were to stare at a picture of a green flower for several seconds, and then shift your gaze to a blank white sheet of paper, you would see:

   A. an afterimage of a green flower
   B. nothing but the blank white sheet of paper
   C. spots of black for a few seconds
   D. an afterimage of a red flower
   E. an afterimage of a yellow flower

37. An individual who experiences random periods of intense terror, apprehension and anxiety is likely suffering from:

   A. generalized anxiety disorder
   B. obsessive-compulsive disorder
   C. bipolar disorder
   D. panic disorder
   E. conversion disorder

38. On the Social Readjustment Rating Scale (SRRS), individuals with a high number of life-change units (LCUs) have been found to:

   A. cope better with stress than those with a low number of LCUs
   B. become more aroused during a stressful event than those with a low number of LCUs
   C. respond quicker to stressors than those with a low number of LCUs
   D. suffer more illnesses than those with a low number of LCUs
   E. have more social support than those with a low number of LCUs

GO ON TO THE NEXT PAGE

39. When looking at the following stimulus, individuals are likely to report seeing a row of circles above a row of squares rather than 4 columns, each with a circle above a square. This report is in line with the:

A. Gestalt principle of proximity
B. Gestalt principle of similarity
C. Gestalt figure-ground principle
D. Gestalt principle of closure
E. Gestalt principle of continuity

40. The claim that receptor cells in the eye function as antagonists is the basic premise of:

A. Weber's law
B. Trichromatic theory
C. Opponent-Process theory
D. Young-Helmholtz theory
E. Gestalt psychology

41. Multiple sclerosis is a condition in which the myelin sheath on neurons breaks down. What kind of effect is this disorder likely to have on neuronal functioning?

A. a longer refractory period following stimulation of neurons
B. difficulty detecting information from surrounding neurons
C. premature release of neurotransmitters into the synaptic gap
D. an inability to break down neurotransmitter molecules once they are released into the synaptic gap
E. slower transmission of impulses throughout the nervous system

42. Individuals suffering from depression and other mood disorders frequently show abnormal levels of _____ in the brain.

A. serotonin
B. acetylcholine
C. dopamine
D. endorphins
E. GABA

43. When an individual fails to help another in need because they are sure someone else will help, they are experiencing:

A. low self-efficacy
B. diffusion of responsibility
C. learned helplessness
D. moral relativism
E. the Asch effect

44. An individual with an impaired somatic nervous system is most likely to experience:

A. a chronic state of high anxiety
B. problems with automatic body functions such as heartbeat
C. a heightened fight-or-flight reaction to stressful stimuli
D. difficulties with muscle movement and control
E. problems with emotional control and regulation

45. The Yerkes-Dodson law of motivation and performance states that we perform at our best when we are:

A. experiencing cognitive dissonance
B. experiencing homeostasis
C. working for extrinsic factors
D. working to avoid punishment
E. experiencing a moderate level of arousal

46. An individual who experiences problems with alertness, attention and sleep might have a problem with their:

A. thalamus
B. hypothalamus
C. reticular activating system (RAS)
D. cerebellum
E. hippocampus

47. The sympathetic nervous system is most likely to become active when an individual is:

A. sleeping
B. calm
C. startled
D. playing the piano
E. watching television

48. The famous case of Phineas Gage illustrates the:

    A. link between the body and the mind

    B. fact that stress is related to health

    C. role of the frontal lobes in mood and personality

    D. role of thought processes in depression

    E. role of the hippocampus in memory

49. Split-brain patients refer to individuals who have had:

    A. a hemisphere of their brain removed

    B. their corpus callosum severed

    C. their cerebellum severed

    D. their hippocampus removed

    E. their frontal lobes altered

50. If an individual were to have their hippocampus removed, they would no longer:

    A. be able to form new memories

    B. recognize family members or loved ones

    C. display aggressive behaviors

    D. be able to produce meaningful speech

    E. be able to coordinate muscle movements

51. A parent first reinforces their toddler for saying "da." Later, the parent stops reinforcing "da" and reinforces only "dada." Then the parent moves to only reinforcing "daddy." In this example, the parent is using:

    A. shaping

    B. behavioral modification

    C. counterconditioning

    D. a token economy

    E. systematic desensitization

52. When information is not attended to or processed, it is likely to be forgotten. This is a form of forgetting known as:

    A. motivated forgetting

    B. repression

    C. encoding failure

    D. interference

    E. decay

53. The addictive nature of some psychoactive drugs is most likely a result of effects on reward circuits in the:

    A. peripheral nervous system

    B. limbic system

    C. reticular activating system (RAS)

    D. cerebellum

    E. somatic nervous system

54. If Ashley has high self-efficacy, she:

    A. has confidence in her ability to succeed on tasks

    B. experiences a great deal of anxiety in social situations

    C. attributes her success on tasks to external factors

    D. will give up easily when facing a difficult task

    E. has achieved her most optimal level of functioning

55. The group to which researchers wish to generalize their findings in a research study is called the:

    A. sample

    B. population

    C. experimental group

    D. control group

    E. study group

56. All the following occur during REM sleep *except:*

    A. The eyes move about rapidly.

    B. Dreaming is very frequent.

    C. The brain is highly active.

    D. Heart rate increases.

    E. Muscle movement increases.

57. Systematic desensitization is a behavioral technique most commonly used in the treatment of:

    A. depression

    B. schizophrenia

    C. phobic disorder

    D. somatoform disorder

    E. antisocial personality disorder

GO ON TO THE NEXT PAGE

58. Jesse became very ill after eating at a new restaurant. Now, every time he thinks about or sees the restaurant he feels ill, and he absolutely refuses to eat at the restaurant again. Jesse's change in behavior is the result of:

   A. aversive conditioning

   B. vicarious punishment

   C. social learning

   D. operant conditioning

   E. systematic desensitization

59. Narcotics such as heroin and codeine fall under the class of drugs known as:

   A. stimulants

   B. barbiturates

   C. depressants

   D. opiates

   E. amphetamines

60. Every fifth time that Patty does the dishes after dinner, her parents give her $2. Patty is being reinforced based on a:

   A. fixed-ratio schedule

   B. variable-ratio schedule

   C. continuous-reinforcement schedule

   D. variable-interval schedule

   E. fixed-interval schedule

61. An individual who suffers from sleep apnea is most likely to:

   A. find it very difficult to fall asleep at night

   B. experience frequent night terrors throughout the night

   C. awaken several times throughout the night

   D. fall asleep in the middle of a waking activity

   E. frequently talk or walk in their sleep

62. Stimulants are drugs that:

   A. enhance central nervous system activity

   B. decelerate breathing and heart rate

   C. increase appetite and hunger

   D. induce sadness and depression

   E. induce drowsiness and fatigue

63. If a researcher finds a correlation of +.85 between years of education and speed of typing, they could conclude that:

   A. Individuals with more years of education are also fast typists.

   B. Individuals with more years of education are also slow typists.

   C. Attending college leads to better typing skills.

   D. Attending college leads to faster processing of information.

   E. Attending college is unrelated to typing speed.

64. According to psychoanalytic theory, a person with a weak superego:

   A. experiences a great deal of anxiety

   B. experiences extreme depression and sadness

   C. is unable to repress information

   D. constantly doubts their skills and abilities

   E. feels little guilt or remorse after doing wrong

65. According to Sigmund Freud, the
_____ and _____
are in constant conflict with one another.

   A. ego; superego

   B. id; superego

   C. id; ego

   D. conscience; superego

   E. ego; conscience

66. In treating depression, a psychoanalyst is likely to focus on:

   A. negative and self-defeating thoughts

   B. abnormalities in neurotransmitter levels

   C. identifying unconscious and repressed conflicts

   D. assisting the individual in identifying needs and goals

   E. changing the socialization practices of a culture

67. Every time Jill has a quiz in her psychology class (which makes her anxious and nervous), her professor is accompanied by a graduate assistant. The graduate assistant only comes to class on quiz days. Today, Jill saw the graduate assistant as she was walking to another class and instantly became anxious and nervous. In this example, the graduate assistant has become a:

    A. conditioned response
    B. conditioned stimulus
    C. neutral stimulus
    D. unconditioned stimulus
    E. unconditioned response

68. Ivan Pavlov is credited with the discovery of:

    A. operant conditioning
    B. classical conditioning
    C. conditioned taste aversions
    D. social learning
    E. vicarious learning

69. Kara developed a dislike for hot dogs after becoming extremely ill after eating one. Kara might also develop a dislike for similar foods such as Bratwursts through a process known as:

    A. stimulus discrimination
    B. stimulus generalization
    C. forward conditioning
    D. counterconditioning
    E. trace conditioning

70. B.F. Skinner's famous Skinner box was used to train animals using the principles of:

    A. classical conditioning
    B. operant conditioning
    C. systematic desensitization
    D. observational learning
    E. backward conditioning

71. If Dr. Black deducts two points from students' grades for each day of class missed, he is utilizing _____ to decrease student absenteeism.

    A. positive punishment
    B. partial punishment
    C. negative reinforcement
    D. positive reinforcement
    E. negative punishment

72. Every time Lisa cleans her room, she gets a star on her chore chart on the refrigerator. As Lisa acquires stars, she can exchange them for other things she wants, such as cookies and bowls of ice cream. Given this example, Lisa's parents are using:

    A. the principles of shaping
    B. partial reinforcement
    C. classical conditioning
    D. a token economy
    E. vicarious reinforcement

73. According to Martin Seligman, when efforts consistently fail to bring about any sort of reward and/or consistently bring about punishment, _____ might result.

    A. a psychotic episode
    B. extreme anxiety
    C. learned helplessness
    D. latent learning
    E. instrumental conditioning

74. The statement "Mommy bottle" made by a young toddler is considered to reflect:

    A. babbling
    B. cooing
    C. telegraphic speech
    D. holophrastic speech
    E. overextension

75. When we recall personal experiences such as who we spoke to at a party over the weekend or what we did on our last birthday, we are recalling:

    A. procedural memories
    B. semantic memories
    C. flashbulb memories
    D. episodic memories
    E. implicit memories

76. At times, individuals learn a new behavior but do not express it until later. This phenomenon is known as:

    A. acquisition
    B. instrumental learning
    C. operant learning
    D. shaping
    E. latent learning

GO ON TO THE NEXT PAGE

77. Al is trying to recall his old address for an application he is filling out, but all he can remember is his new address. Al's difficulty in recalling his old address is likely the result of:

A. the serial position effect
B. the primacy effect
C. retroactive interference
D. proactive interference
E. the recency effect

78. If a psychologist shows an individual an object and asks the individual to come up with as many possible uses for that object as they can, the psychologist is likely testing:

A. convergent thinking
B. divergent thinking
C. deductive reasoning
D. inductive reasoning
E. fluid intelligence

79. According to Abraham Maslow, human behavior is motivated by a desire to:

A. maintain homeostasis within the body
B. maintain cognitive consistency
C. obtain pleasure and gratification
D. reach one's optimal level of functioning
E. seek out challenging tasks

80. The Wechsler Adult Intelligence Scale (WAIS) assesses:

A. creativity and giftedness
B. musical and kinesthetic intelligence
C. verbal and nonverbal intelligence
D. emotional and social intelligence
E. experiential and contextual intelligence

81. It is not uncommon for individuals to experience instances in which they are sure they know someone's name, but are unable to recall it at the present moment. This phenomenon, sometimes referred to as the tip-of-the-tongue phenomenon, most likely reflects a problem with:

A. the capacity of sensory memory
B. encoding information in memory
C. storing information in memory
D. retrieval of information from memory
E. attentional processes

82. According to Piaget, an infant who searches for a toy that has been removed from view is showing signs of:

A. decentration
B. logical reasoning
C. conservation
D. transformational thought
E. object permanence

83. A researcher reads the following list of numbers to an individual: 3 2 1 7 6 9 5 8 7 4 2 1 5 3. The researcher then asks the individual to repeat the list of numbers in order aloud. According to George Miller's work on short-term memory capacity, the individual is likely to remember:

A. all the items
B. about seven items
C. anywhere from two to four items
D. the last eight or nine numbers
E. the middle five or six numbers

84. A test question that asks students to list the four lobes of the brain assesses:

A. sensory memory
B. implicit memory
C. recall memory
D. recognition memory
E. short-term memory

85. Which of the following statements *best* reflects Kohlberg's postconventional level of moral reasoning?

A. If I obey my parents, I will be rewarded.
B. If I follow the rules, others will like me.
C. I must act in ways consistent with the laws at all times.
D. If I misbehave, I will be punished.
E. I must do what is in the best interest of everyone involved.

86. If Jake is experiencing the Oedipal conflict, he is likely to be:

A. focused on obtaining oral gratification
B. fixated at the oral stage of development
C. experiencing a strong desire for his mother
D. repressing sexual desires in his unconscious
E. directing his libidinal energy toward peers

87. Which of the following illustrates the defense mechanism of projection?

    A. justifying one's actions with a socially acceptable excuse
    B. attributing one's forbidden or negative thoughts to others
    C. expressing extreme affection toward someone you hate
    D. discharging anger into a game of racquetball
    E. returning to a more childlike state following a negative experience

88. According to Freud, the ego:

    A. operates at a completely unconscious level
    B. is analogous to a moral conscience
    C. strives to obtain immediate gratification
    D. operates according to the reality principle
    E. instills guilt and anxiety in individuals for misbehavior

89. People with high self-esteem tend to attribute failure to _____ factors and success to _____ factors.

    A. internal; external
    B. primary; secondary
    C. external; internal
    D. intrinsic; extrinsic
    E. secondary; primary

90. Traits refer to aspects of personality that:

    A. remain fairly stable across time and situations
    B. fluctuate across time and situations
    C. are determined to a large extent by external factors
    D. evolve from early childhood experiences
    E. do not appear until the adult years

91. An individual who is characterized as highly extroverted is likely to:

    A. enjoy solitary activities such as reading a book
    B. be open to new experiences and ways of thinking
    C. enjoy social interactions and events
    D. show instability in mood and personality
    E. be easygoing and pleasant to be around

92. Tyler believes that people should always be punished for breaking the rules set by authority figures. According to Kohlberg, Tyler is operating at the _____ stage of moral reasoning.

    A. moral relativism
    B. postconventional
    C. preconventional
    D. conventional
    E. moral absolutism

93. Projective tests are designed to:

    A. determine the presence or absence of mental disorders
    B. classify individuals as high or low on personality traits
    C. assess one's degree of extroversion and openness to others
    D. assess one's potential for learning
    E. gain insight into unconscious thoughts and desires

94. According to Erik Erikson, the late adult years are characterized by a:

    A. search for one's identity
    B. need for control over one's life
    C. distancing of oneself from friends and acquaintances
    D. desire to help younger generations
    E. review of one's life experiences and achievements

GO ON TO THE NEXT PAGE

95. Dr. Dunn wants to determine whether individuals have achieved formal operational thought. Which of the following procedures *best* achieves Dr. Dunn's goals?

   A.   presenting two similar-shaped glasses with equal amounts of water to an individual, pouring one of the glasses into a taller, thinner glass, and then asking whether the two glasses of water contain the same amount

   B.   presenting a house that can be viewed from multiple perspectives and asking an individual to report what a person standing on the side opposite the individual sees

   C.   presenting a pendulum to individuals and asking them to determine what influences the speed at which the pendulum swings

   D.   hiding an object behind a screen and observing whether and where the individual searches for the hidden object

   E.   asking an individual to sort a group of plastic bears by size and color (for example, asking them to put all large blue bears in one pile and all small red bears in another pile)

96. If an intelligence test has high reliability:

   A.   It is readily available and easy to use with any group of individuals.

   B.   All individuals score close to the mean when they take the test.

   C.   The test correlates with other tests of IQ and cognitive functioning.

   D.   The test differentiates between moderately intelligent persons and geniuses.

   E.   An individual's score on a retest will be similar to their original score on the test.

97. According to Howard Gardner's theory of multiple intelligences:

   A.   Standardized achievement tests are the best tests of intelligence available.

   B.   Intelligence tests should emphasize verbal skills over nonverbal skills.

   C.   Individuals are generally either smart or less smart.

   D.   An individual who has good language and social skills should also have good reasoning and math skills.

   E.   Current intelligence tests do not capture the variety of intelligence types evident in humans.

98. An individual awakens one morning in a hotel room with no recollection of who they are or how they got where they are. This individual is likely experiencing:

   A.   dissociative identity disorder

   B.   dissociative fugue

   C.   delusions of grandeur

   D.   a manic episode

   E.   conversion disorder

99. Which disorders fall under the same classification in the DSM-IV?

   A.   phobic disorder and schizophrenia

   B.   schizophrenia and dissociative identity disorder

   C.   conversion disorder and hypochondriasis

   D.   bipolar disorder and post-traumatic stress disorder

   E.   dissociative fugue and unipolar disorder

100. The key to client-centered therapy is:

   A.   delving into early childhood experiences

   B.   analyzing dreams for their latent content

   C.   creating an open environment that fosters self-reflection

   D.   changing maladaptive thought patterns

   E.   extinguishing maladaptive behavioral responses

IF YOU FINISH BEFORE TIME IS CALLED, CHECK YOUR WORK ON THIS SECTION ONLY. DO NOT WORK ON ANY OTHER SECTION IN THE TEST.

Section 2: Free-Response Questions

Time: 50 Minutes

Questions: 2

Directions: You have 50 minutes to answer both of the following questions. It is not enough to answer a question by just presenting facts. You must present a strong argument based on your critical analysis of the questions posed, using appropriate psychological terminology.

Free-Response Question #1

A researcher at a pharmaceutical company wants to test a new drug designed to improve immediate memory performance in older adults. Explain to the pharmaceutical researcher how they can conduct an experimental study to test the following hypothesis: *Older adults who take the new test drug 1 hour prior to a memory test recall more words on a word recall task than those who take a placebo drug 1 hour prior to the memory test*. In your response, identify the independent variable, dependent variable, experimental group, control group and how the researcher should address issues of sample selection, experimental control and expectancy effects when conducting their study.

GO ON TO THE NEXT PAGE

Free-Response Question #2

You are flashing images on a screen and asking individuals to report the objects in the images. Describe the processes of sensation and perception involved in this task. How do bottom-up and top-down processing contribute to one's analysis and interpretation of the images?

GO ON TO THE NEXT PAGE

Answer Key for Practice Test 4

1.	A	**26.**	E	**51.**	A	**76.**	E
2.	D	**27.**	B	**52.**	C	**77.**	C
3.	B	**28.**	C	**53.**	B	**78.**	B
4.	B	**29.**	A	**54.**	A	**79.**	D
5.	E	**30.**	E	**55.**	B	**80.**	C
6.	D	**31.**	D	**56.**	E	**81.**	D
7.	B	**32.**	E	**57.**	C	**82.**	E
8.	D	**33.**	B	**58.**	A	**83.**	B
9.	D	**34.**	E	**59.**	D	**84.**	C
10.	B	**35.**	B	**60.**	A	**85.**	E
11.	A	**36.**	D	**61.**	C	**86.**	C
12.	B	**37.**	D	**62.**	A	**87.**	B
13.	E	**38.**	D	**63.**	A	**88.**	D
14.	B	**39.**	B	**64.**	E	**89.**	C
15.	C	**40.**	C	**65.**	B	**90.**	A
16.	C	**41.**	E	**66.**	C	**91.**	C
17.	A	**42.**	A	**67.**	B	**92.**	D
18.	A	**43.**	B	**68.**	B	**93.**	E
19.	E	**44.**	D	**69.**	B	**94.**	E
20.	C	**45.**	E	**70.**	B	**95.**	C
21.	C	**46.**	C	**71.**	E	**96.**	E
22.	B	**47.**	C	**72.**	D	**97.**	E
23.	B	**48.**	C	**73.**	C	**98.**	B
24.	E	**49.**	B	**74.**	C	**99.**	C
25.	A	**50.**	A	**75.**	D	**100.**	C

Complete Answers and Explanations for Practice Test 4

1. **A.** Wilhelm Wundt founded the first psychology laboratory in Germany at the University of Leipzig in 1879. Wundt's research at the time was focused on identifying the structures or elements of conscious experience. To accomplish this goal, Wundt relied on the method of introspection in which individuals report aloud their conscious experience of stimuli. Wundt's approach was in direct opposition to behaviorist approaches, which argued that only direct observations should be studied. Free association and dream analysis are techniques discovered by Sigmund Freud to get at unconscious processes.

2. **D.** Behaviorists believe that psychologists should not study the mind or mental processes at all. Instead, behaviorists emphasize psychology as the study of behavior and argue that we should only study that which can be directly observed. All the other options emphasize the study of various factors that emerge from within the individual and cannot be directly observed (for example, the mind, conscious experience, unconscious forces, needs, desires, perceptions of the world).

3. **B.** Experimental studies provide the greatest amount of control when conducting research. Experimental studies allow for greater control through random assignment of participants to either an experimental group or a control group, manipulation of an independent variable and control over confounding variables. In all the other options, control is compromised in various ways.

4. **B.** The left hemisphere is known to be involved in a variety of activities, including language production and language comprehension. The left hemisphere receives sensory information from the right side of the body and controls motor movements on the right side of the body. Thus, damage to the left hemisphere could result in problems producing and/or understanding spoken language and loss of certain motor movements to the right side of the body, but it does not lead to paralysis throughout the entire body. Recognition of faces appears to reside primarily in the right hemisphere of the brain. The frontal lobe of the cerebral cortex is known to govern mood and personality.

5. **E.** An electroencephalograph (EEG) is the only procedure listed that measures electrical activity in the brain. An EEG records electrical activity emitted from neurons in the brain through electrodes placed on the scalp. MRIs provide detailed pictures of brain tissue by recording radio waves given off by brain tissue while a person lies in a powerful magnetic field. PET scans detect brain activity by measuring metabolic activity in the brain. CT scans use X-rays to take pictures of the skull and brain tissue. Lobotomies are actually a traditional form of surgery in which parts of the frontal lobe are removed in an attempt to placate or calm patients suffering from severe mood or behavioral disorders.

6. **D.** According to Erik Erikson, personality evolves across an entire life span. Erikson proposed eight psychosocial crises that occur from infancy to old age. Personality is influenced by the resolution of each of these crises. Each crisis represents conflicts between societal expectations and individual skills, abilities and competencies at a given stage of life. Thus, Erikson recognized the interplay of internal and external factors in influencing personality development throughout life. Though he recognized the influence of early childhood experiences on personality development, he also recognized that later experiences are as important as early experiences in shaping individual personality.

7. **B.** The American Psychological Association (APA) has set forth a number of guidelines that must be followed to ensure that human subjects are treated fairly and humanely in all research. Included in these guidelines are the following: (1) participants must be informed of what their participation entails; (2) participants may withdraw from the study at any time; (3) deception must be minimized, but if necessary, participants must be told of any deceptions immediately following participation; (4) participants responses must be kept anonymous and confidential. Participants do not have to be rewarded for their participation.

8. **D.** Sensory adaptation explains why you no longer notice the sound of the air conditioner running after you have been sitting in a room for 5 minutes. Our sensory receptors are designed to detect changes in stimulus energy. After a period of repeated stimulation from the same stimulus, the receptors diminish their responsiveness and no longer respond to the energy, making you unaware of the stimulus. This process is known as sensory adaptation.

9. **D.** Psychoactive drugs refer to drugs that cross the blood-brain barrier and affect the functioning of the central nervous system. Most psychoactive drugs exert their effects by altering the activity of neurotransmitters in the brain, not the actual number of neurons in the brain. Some psychoactive drugs are structurally similar to neurotransmitters and, thus, mimic their actions in the brain. Other psychoactive drugs either affect the release of neurotransmitters or the reuptake or breakdown of neurotransmitters within the brain. In all cases, the activity of neurotransmitters is either enhanced or disrupted.

10. **B.** The cerebral cortex can be broken down into several regions, or lobes, that are specialized for processing specific kinds of information. The temporal lobe, located on each side of the brain slightly above the ears, is responsible for processing auditory information. The occipital lobe, located at the rear of the brain, is responsible for processing visual information. Thus, the sight of the microwave stimulates the occipital lobe, whereas the sound of the microwave stimulates the temporal lobe. The other lobes of the brain include the parietal lobe (which is specialized for processing information about touch, temperature, pressure and pain) and the frontal lobe (which is involved in complex analysis and integration of information).

11. **A.** The GAS is a model that focuses on the physiological effects of stress on the body. The GAS outlines three sequential stages that are experienced in response to an initial stressor and its continued presence. The first stage, alarm reaction, involves a heightened sympathetic nervous system response or what some refer to as a fight or flight response. The decrease in immune system functioning does not come until the final stage, exhaustion, after the body has continued to fight off a chronic stressor. All the other options reflect psychological processes (for example, shock, confusion) and cognitive processes (for example, primary appraisal) that are not part of the GAS.

12. **B.** The dependent variable in an experiment is the variable believed to be affected by the independent variable. The dependent variable is not manipulated by the researcher in any way. The researcher merely measures each participant on the dependent variable following exposure to the independent variable to see whether the independent variable affected the dependent variable in any way. In this study, anxiety about aging is believed to be influenced by exposure to either older adults depicting positive aging or older adults depicting negative aging. The participants being tested are considered the sample in a study. The older adults depicting either positive or negative aging are qualities of the independent variable (the variable believed to affect the dependent variable).

13. **E.** Fundamental attribution error refers to the tendency for individuals to emphasize dispositional (personal) factors and ignore situational factors when explaining others' behaviors. This often leads to blame-the-victim thinking because of the emphasis on personal factors. Diffusion of responsibility refers to a weakened sense of personal responsibility to help a person in need when in the presence of many others who can also help. Deindividuation refers to a process in which the individual feels a sense of anonymity in a crowd of people as a result of being less likely to be noticed in a crowd. Moral relativism refers to an awareness that behaviors can be right or wrong depending on the circumstances surrounding the behavior. Low self-efficacy refers to a belief that one is incapable of performing or succeeding on a given task.

14. **B.** The brainstem comprises several structures that together control and regulate functions that are crucial for physical survival. The medulla is a structure within the brainstem that controls breathing, heart rate, blood pressure and swallowing. Other structures within the brainstem region include the pons, which plays a role in brain activity during sleep, and the reticular activating system (RAS), which plays a role in arousal and attention. The cerebellum, frontal lobes, cerebral cortex and limbic system are not directly responsible for monitoring or regulating basic bodily functions.

15. **C.** Behavioral psychologists emphasize the study of observable behaviors and do not believe that psychologists should study internal processes or factors that cannot be directly observed. Therefore, a behavioral psychologist interested in studying the effects of punishment on children's behavior is most likely to observe the reactions of children to instances of punishment. All the other options involve asking about internal thoughts or emotions and/or asking someone to report on behavior rather than observing the behavioral response directly.

16. **C.** Somatoform disorders refer to a group of disorders that involve complaints of physical symptoms that have no physiological or biological basis. Thus, the key feature or symptom of somatoform disorders is (**C**) physical complaints. The other options are distinguishing features of other groups of disorders or specific illnesses. Extreme anxiety is the primary feature of anxiety disorders. Manic behavior is a primary feature of bipolar disorder, formerly known as manic-depression. Psychotic episodes, hallucinations and delusions are all distinguishing features of schizophrenic disorders.

17. A. Gestalt psychologists argue that the brain organizes sensory input according to certain principles. Gestalt psychology is a field of psychology that outlines the principles by which the brain organizes sensory input (for example, principle of proximity, principle of similarity). According to Gestalt psychologists, the brain searches for patterns in incoming sensory data and organizes the incoming information according to basic principles. It was Gestalt psychologists who coined the phrase *the whole is more than the sum of its parts.*

18. A. Selective attention involves the ability to focus one's attention on a specific stimulus in the environment while filtering out other distracting stimuli. Thus, the basketball player who is able to ignore the sound of the crowd and the band while focusing on his coach's words during a timeout is utilizing selective attention. Divided attention refers to the ability to divide one's attention across more than one task. Dichotic listening tasks are a means of assessing one's ability to process two different messages being sent to each ear. Sustained attention refers to the ability to maintain one's attention over a period of time.

19. E. Longitudinal designs involve following the same group of people over time and assessing them on the variable of interest on multiple occasions. The researcher then compares the scores of individuals from one time to another to see whether scores change or remain the same. Cross-sectional designs involve assessing individuals from multiple age groups (for example, a group of 40-year-olds, 50-year-olds and 60-year-olds) on only one occasion, and then comparing the average scores of each age group. A cross-sequential design involves a combination of longitudinal and cross-sectional designs (taking multiple age groups and assessing them on multiple occasions). The case study approach is not the correct answer because it involves conducting a detailed analysis of a single individual. Naturalistic observation is a data collection technique in which one observes individuals in their natural environment without intruding in any way.

20. C. The nature-versus-nurture debate is one of the most fundamental issues in the field of psychology and in the field of developmental psychology. It reflects the age-old debate concerning whether behavior and development are the result of genetic/biological tendencies or environmental and life experiences. The nurture side of the debate argues for the importance of life experiences in contributing to behavior and development. Therefore, an individual who supports the nurture side of the debate is most likely to argue that life experiences play an important role in the development of mental illness. All the other options reflect the nature side of the debate, which focuses on the role of biological and/or genetic influences in behavior and development.

21. C. The serial position effect refers to the finding that individuals typically remember the first few and the last few words on a list well, but have difficulty remembering the words from the middle of a list. The other options refer to other memory processes and phenomena that do not directly relate to memory of words on lists. Retroactive interference occurs when new information interferes with the ability to recall previously learned information. Proactive interference occurs when previously learned information interferes with the ability to remember newly acquired information.

22. B. In the early 1900s, Spearman proposed the notion of a general intelligence, or g factor, in which he argued that a general underlying cognitive ability influences individual performance on all types of cognitive/intellectual tasks. According to this view, individuals should show similar levels of functioning on a variety of different types of tasks. In other words, if an individual scores high on a test of math skills, they should also score high on a test of verbal skills, memory skills and information-processing skills. Spearman's g factor says nothing about how intellectual skills change or remain the same across a life span. Therefore, whether an individual shows declines in intelligence during the late adult years and whether scores on IQ tests taken in infancy relate to scores on IQ tests in childhood and adolescence are unrelated to the notion of a g factor. The idea that individuals might show inconsistent scores across different intelligence tests is in direct opposition to the notion of a g factor.

23. B. Negative punishment involves the removal of a positive stimulus following a behavior to reduce the likelihood of the behavior occurring again. This is what the parent is doing when they take car privileges away from an adolescent who comes home past curfew. Positive punishment involves the presentation of an aversive or unpleasant stimulus (for example, yelling, assigning extra chores) to decrease the frequency of a behavior. Vicarious punishment involves changing one's behavior as a result of seeing someone else punished for a behavior. (Individuals are less likely to engage in a behavior that they see someone else punished for.) Negative reinforcement and positive reinforcement are incorrect because they serve to increase the frequency of a behavior occurring again.

24. **E.** Cognitive psychologists focus on thought processes and thought patterns (including beliefs, perceptions and biases) as important factors influencing personality. With respect to abnormal behavior, cognitive psychologists believe that negative thoughts (for example, I am a failure) and/or irrational thoughts (for example, I must always look perfect) contribute to mental illness and abnormal behavior. Thus, cognitive psychologists would argue that abnormal behavior results when an individual experiences irrational and/or negative thoughts. Biological psychologists would argue that abnormal behavior results from abnormal levels of neurotransmitters in certain regions of the brain and/or structural damage to the various regions of the brain. Psychoanalysts would argue that repressing tension and conflict in the unconscious is likely to lead to abnormal behavior. Humanistic psychologists argue that abnormal behavior results when individuals are unable to meet their psychological and social needs.

25. **A.** The SRRS is a measure of stress that focuses on the number of life changes and events one has experienced in recent months. The basic premise of the scale is that all life events, whether positive or negative, exert some degree of stress on individuals. Thus, Holmes and Rahe were the first to point out that stress can result from both positive and negative events in one's life. The notion that prolonged stress decreases the functioning of the immune system is the notion underlying the General Adaptation Syndrome (GAS), a model that outlines the physiological effects of stress on the body. The other options are findings from research examining the various factors that influence one's responses to stress, but are not principles underlying the development or use of the SRRS.

26. **E.** Many years ago, researchers identified various personality types that depict different approaches and responses to stressors in one's life. An individual with a Type A personality is described as intense, competitive, high-strung and hostile. In contrast, an individual with a Type B personality is described as laid-back, relaxed and relatively calm in the face of stressors. Research has also found that those with a Type A personality are at the highest risk for heart disease, heart attacks and strokes. Thus, compared to a Type A personality, individuals with a Type B personality are (**E**) more relaxed and laid back. They are *not* more likely to suffer a heart attack, they are *not* more emotional and volatile, they are *not* more likely to internalize stress, and they are *not* less likely to experience stress. (They just respond to stress differently than those with a Type A personality.)

27. **B.** Correlational research designs seek to determine whether a relationship exists between two or more variables and, if so, to identify the nature of that relationship. Correlational designs do not allow for the determination of cause-and-effect relationships primarily because they lack the stringent control found only in experimental designs. Correlational designs involve measuring participants on the variables of interest without any manipulation of variables, as one would in an experiment. Thus, **B** is the correct answer. Correlational designs do not require that one rely on self-report techniques or that one restrict their sample to a single individual. In fact, they are best conducted with a large group of individuals and can use any type of data collection necessary to gather information on the variables of interest. A correlational design also does not require that one use a double-blind design.

28. **C.** Expectancy effects occur when participants in a study behave in ways in which they believe they are expected to behave or when a researcher's expectations lead them to treat participants in a way that influences the behavior of participants in the ways expected. To avoid such problems, a researcher should use either a single-blind or a double-blind design. In a single-blind design, the researcher does not inform the participants of their membership in either the experimental or control group. This is the correct answer to this question. In a double-blind design, neither the participant nor the individual obtaining the measurements is aware of the individual's specific group membership. Striving to make the experimental and control groups as similar as possible, drawing a sample that represents the population one seeks to describe and using random assignment when putting participants into groups do not relate to expectancy effects but are issues of sample selection, generalization and experimental control. Obtaining informed consent is an ethical issue and is required in all studies involving human subjects, regardless of expectancy effects.

29. **A.** Psychologists who take a sociocultural perspective focus on broad social and cultural factors such as cultural values and beliefs, socialization practices, the media, and social norms and laws as important influences on human thought and behavior. In contrast, the psychoanalytic, cognitive and humanistic perspectives all focus on internal factors within an individual. The psychoanalytic perspective focuses on unconscious impulses and drives. The cognitive perspective focuses on thoughts, beliefs and perceptions. The humanistic perspective focuses on needs, desires and goals.

30. E. RET is a therapeutic approach developed by Albert Ellis, a cognitive psychologist/therapist. In line with the cognitive perspective on personality and abnormal behavior, this approach focuses on identifying negative and self-defeating thought patterns (I am a failure) believed to contribute to psychological problems. The other options focus on noncognitive factors (for example, early childhood experiences, external factors), which are not addressed by RET.

31. D. Self-actualization refers to a process by which individuals seek to reach their fullest potential or optimal level of functioning. The term was coined by humanistic psychologist Abraham Maslow, who argued that all human behavior is driven by needs, goals and desires. Self-actualization does *not* involve overcoming emotional or psychological problems. It is *not* a process whereby we become the person others want us to be. Self-actualization is *not* driven by genetic predispositions or by traits and characteristics inherited from parents. It is driven by the goals, needs and desires we set for ourselves throughout life.

32. E. *Tabula rasa,* meaning blank slate, is a term used by behavioral psychologists to imply that humans come into this world with no prior knowledge or tendencies and that behavior, knowledge and development are determined entirely by experience. This term is most consistent with an emphasis on experience in shaping behavior. It is in direct contrast to a biological perspective, a belief in genetic influences and the nature side of the nature-nurture debate (all of which emphasize internal and genetic influences as most important to human behavior and development).

33. B. Psychology is considered a scientific discipline because of the way in which it collects and analyzes data about behavior. As with other sciences, psychological research relies on the experimental method, which calls for the use of systematic and rigorous methods of data collection and analysis. The fact that psychology seeks to describe, explain and predict behavior; that it uses theory as a guide; that it studies behavior, thought and emotion; or that it relies on multiple perspectives to explain behavior does not make psychology a science. What makes psychology a science is the way it goes about studying behavior, thought and emotion.

34. E. Signal detection experiments test an individual's ability to correctly report the detection of stimuli when they are presented. False positives occur when an individual reports detection of a stimulus when nothing was presented. False negatives occur when an individual fails to report detection of a stimulus when one was presented. A miss is the same as a false negative. (The individual misses the stimulus when it is presented.) A correct rejection occurs when an individual correctly states that a stimulus was not presented. A hit is the detection of a stimulus when it is presented.

35. B. A correlation coefficient tells two things about the relationship between two variables: the strength of the relationship and the direction, or nature, of the relationship. The strength of the relationship is indicated by the absolute value of the number, with higher absolute values indicating a stronger relationship. Thus, –.73 represents the strongest correlation because it has the highest absolute value of all the numbers. The sign preceding the number indicates the direction or nature of the relationship, with a negative sign indicating a negative relationship (meaning that as scores on one variable increase, scores on the other variable decrease).

36. D. This question is asking about afterimages, which can be explained through the Opponent-Process theory of vision. Afterimages occur after an individual has looked at a stimulus for a period of time and then shifts their gaze away from the stimulus, only to see an afterimage of that stimulus. We know from research that afterimages produce an image in the color opposing the original color of the stimulus. (Red opposes green, blue opposes yellow, and black opposes white.) Thus, if you stare at a picture of a green flower for several seconds, and then shift your gaze to a blank white sheet of paper, you see an afterimage of a red flower.

37. D. Panic disorder is characterized by random and unpredictable periods of intense terror, apprehension and anxiety. Generalized anxiety disorder involves anxiety, but the anxiety is chronic and persistent instead of random and unpredictable. Obsessive-compulsive disorder involves anxiety that results from obtrusive and repetitive thoughts. Bipolar disorder is a mood disorder that involves fluctuations between extreme depression and mania. Conversion disorder is a somatoform disorder that involves loss of physical function(s) for which no underlying physiological cause can be identified.

38. D. The SRRS is a measure that assesses the amount of stress in one's life by calculating the number of life events or changes one has experienced in recent months. Numbers are assigned to each life event/change that represent LCUs—the degree of stress associated with each life event or change. LCUs are then summed to provide an index of the amount of stress one might be experiencing as a result of life events or changes. A great deal of research using the SRRS has found that LCUs are positively correlated with frequency of various illnesses. Thus, individuals with a high number of LCUs have been found to suffer more illnesses than those with a low number of LCUs.

39. B. The Gestalt principle of similarity states that the brain tends to group together stimuli that are alike. Thus, according to this principle, when an individual views the following figure, they are likely to report seeing a row of circles above a row of squares rather than four columns, each with a circle above a square. The report given by the individual is not consistent with the other principles listed: proximity (tendency to view stimuli that are close together as a group), closure (tendency to fill gaps in stimuli that are not complete), continuity (tendency to perceive stimuli as continuous and connected) and the figure-ground principle (tendency to sort stimuli into a central figure and background).

40. C. The notion that receptor cells in the eye function as antagonists is the basic premise of Opponent-Process theory. Opponent-Process theory argues that the receptor cells in the eye function in such a way that red opposes green, blue opposes yellow, and black opposes white. In other words, when red receptors activate, green receptors are inhibited; and when blue receptors activate, yellow receptors are inhibited. Trichromatic theory, previously known as the Young-Helmholtz theory, argues that only three types of color receptors exist in the eye (red, green and blue) and that different colors are represented by the varying degrees of activation of these three color receptors. Weber's law addresses difference thresholds in all the senses. Gestalt psychology does not address the functioning of receptor cells, but focuses on how the brain interprets and organizes incoming sensory information.

41. E. The myelin sheath is a fatty substance that coats the axons of many neurons in the central nervous system. The primary function of the myelin sheath is to speed neural transmission of impulses through the nervous system. The sheath has several gaps along the axon (called nodes of Ranvier). The electrical impulse is retriggered at each node along the axon, making impulses travel up to 100 times faster than impulses in axons without myelin. Thus, a primary symptom of Multiple Sclerosis, a condition in which the myelin sheath on neurons breaks down, is slower transmission of impulses throughout the nervous system leading to slower information processing and slower behavioral responses.

42. A. Individuals suffering from depression frequently show abnormal levels of serotonin in their brain. Serotonin is a neurotransmitter found heavily in the limbic and frontal regions of the brain and is known to play an important role in regulating mood, sleep, appetite and more. The other neurotransmitters listed are involved in other disorders, but are not implicated as major influences on depression. Abnormal levels of dopamine are associated with schizophrenia and Parkinson's disease. Abnormal levels of acetylcholine are associated with Alzheimer's disease. Abnormal levels of GABA are associated with a variety of anxiety disorders.

43. B. Diffusion of responsibility refers to a weakened sense of responsibility when in the presence of a group of people. The Asch effect is a phenomenon that also occurs in group situations, but involves the tendency of individuals to conform to group behaviors and/or judgments. Learned helplessness involves a pattern of not responding as a result of experiencing inescapable aversive stimuli or consistently failing to be rewarded for behavior. Low self-efficacy is a psychological phenomenon in which an individual believes they are incapable of succeeding on a task. Moral relativism refers to the awareness that behaviors can be right or wrong depending on the circumstances surrounding the behavior.

44. D. The somatic nervous system is a division of the peripheral nervous system that connects the brain to the various sensory systems and to all the muscles in the body. The somatic division consists of two sets of nerve fibers: sensory nerves that carry incoming sensory information to the brain and motor nerves that carry impulses from the brain to muscles and tendons in the body. Thus, an impaired somatic nervous system makes it difficult for individuals to sense the external environment and/or to make various motor/muscle responses. The autonomic nervous system connects the brain to internal organs and allows for all automatic and involuntary bodily processes such as heartbeat and fight-or-flight responses to stressful stimuli. The limbic system, in conjunction with the cerebral cortex, regulates emotional responses and control of emotions.

45. E. The Yerkes-Dodson law states that we perform at our best when we are experiencing a moderate level of arousal. According to this law, if an activity is overly arousing, overly challenging or extremely boring, our motivation is lowered significantly. The Yerkes-Dodson law does not address the influence of punishment or other external factors on motivation and behavior. Cognitive dissonance theory addresses the effects of discrepancies between thoughts/attitudes and behavior on motivation. Drive theory argues that we are motivated to maintain homeostasis in the body.

46. C. The RAS is a structure located in the brainstem region that plays a critical role in arousal, alertness and attention. When an individual is in an awake and active state, the RAS is highly active. When an individual is drowsy, not alert or asleep, the RAS reduces its activity. Thus, an individual who experiences problems with alertness, attention and sleep most likely has a problem with their RAS. The other structures listed are not directly involved in maintaining attention or alertness. The cerebellum coordinates fine motor movements. The hippocampus plays a critical role in learning and memory. The hypothalamus controls and regulates motivated behaviors and activities such as hunger, thirst and sexual behavior in addition to regulating many automatic bodily activities such as temperature and metabolism. The thalamus serves as a relay station directing all incoming information to the appropriate region of the brain for processing.

47. C. The sympathetic nervous system is most likely to become active when an individual is startled. It is a division of the peripheral nervous system that mobilizes the body in times of stress, danger or extreme emotional arousal. The activity of the sympathetic nervous system is responsible for the fight-or-flight response in which the pupils dilate, heart rate increases, breathing quickens and digestive processes slow. The sympathetic nervous system is not likely to become active when an individual is sleeping or when an individual is calm. Playing the piano and watching television require the activation of the somatic nervous system, which is involved in sensing the external environment and in moving.

48. C. The famous case of Phineas Gage illustrates the important role of the frontal lobes in governing mood and personality. Phineas Gage was a railroad worker who unfortunately had an iron rod shoot through his head and significantly damage his frontal lobe. Following the accident, Phineas could walk, talk and engage in most daily activities. However, he showed marked changes in his personality—he changed from a reliable, pleasant person prior to the accident to an irritable, impulsive, unreliable, moody and profane person after the accident.

49. B. Split-brain patients are individuals who have had their corpus callosum severed, most often as a result of severe epileptic seizures that spread throughout the brain. The corpus callosum is a bundle of nerve fibers that connects the left and right hemispheres of the brain, allowing communication between the two hemispheres. Severing the corpus callosum results in a left and right hemisphere that can no longer communicate with each other, hence the term *split-brain*.

50. A. The hippocampus plays an important role in two related processes: learning and memory. Specifically, the hippocampus is involved in processing and storing new information. Thus, damage to the hippocampus results in the inability of an individual to form new memories. Interestingly, the individual is likely to have no problem recalling past memories (those already stored in memory). Therefore, they should still be able to recognize family members and loved ones that they knew prior to the surgery, and they should still be able to produce meaningful speech (given that they could prior to the surgery). Also, aggressive behaviors and coordination of muscle movements should not be affected by damage to or removal of the hippocampus.

51. A. Shaping involves initially reinforcing approximations of a desired behavior, and then moving toward reinforcing only behavior that more closely approximate the desired behavior. When the desired behavior is achieved, only that specific behavior is reinforced. This is what the parent in this scenario is doing in trying to get their child to say "daddy." Counterconditioning involves the use of classical conditioning principles to condition an individual to make a new response to a stimulus. A token economy involves providing reinforcers that have no inherent value, but can be exchanged at a later time for real reinforcers. Systematic desensitization uses classical conditioning principles to eliminate fear responses to objects and stimuli in the environment.

52. C. According to the information-processing view of memory, information must be attended to and processed to be transferred and stored in long-term memory for later recall. The process of taking information into the system and processing it for storage is referred to as encoding. Thus, when an individual is unable to recall information because it was not attended to or processed, the forgetting is said to be due to encoding failure. Decay occurs when information fades from memory over time. Interference occurs when one piece of information interferes with the ability to recall another (usually similar) piece of information. Motivated forgetting and repression involve the process of memories being pushed out of conscious awareness, most likely because they are anxiety provoking or disturbing.

53. B. The reward circuits in the brain refer to neural pathways that, when stimulated, produce feelings of pleasure and euphoria. The reward circuits are found primarily in the limbic regions of the brain. None of the other systems or regions of the brain listed have reward or pleasure centers within them. The RAS is involved in attention, alertness and general arousal level, but not emotional arousal. The cerebellum monitors muscle movement and balance and helps to coordinate complex motor movements. The somatic and peripheral nervous systems are involved in sensory detection, motor movement and monitoring of bodily processes.

54. A. Self-efficacy refers to one's beliefs about their ability to perform various tasks. High self-efficacy implies a belief that one can perform tasks well; low self-efficacy implies a doubt about one's ability to perform tasks. Self-efficacy influences one's confidence level when performing a task, one's motivation to approach or avoid tasks and one's persistence on various tasks. High self-efficacy is associated with greater confidence, motivation to approach tasks and persistence in the face of difficulty. Thus, if Ashley has high self-efficacy, she has confidence in her ability to succeed on tasks.

55. B. The group to which researchers wish to generalize their findings in a research study is the population. The sample refers to the actual participants in a study. The experimental and control groups refer to specific groups in the study and, therefore, are not groups to which the researcher desires to generalize their findings. Rather, they desires to generalize findings from these groups to the broader population of interest.

56. E. REM stands for rapid eye movement, a primary feature of the REM stage of sleep. In addition to rapid eye movement, REM sleep is characterized by frequent dreaming and increased brain activity and heart rate. Muscle movement is largely inhibited during REM sleep, so much so that an individual is said to be in a state of partial sleep paralysis during this stage of sleep. Thus, all the options listed occur during REM sleep *except* increased muscle movement.

57. C. Systematic desensitization is a therapeutic technique based on classical conditioning used primarily to treat phobias. Systematic desensitization involves teaching an individual relaxation techniques to employ while they encounter a feared stimulus. After relaxation has been taught, the individual is gradually exposed to the feared stimulus in increments while employing the relaxation techniques. The goal is for the individual to learn to associate the previously feared stimulus with feelings of relaxation and comfort rather than fear and anxiety. Systematic desensitization is not typically used in the treatment of depression, schizophrenia, somatoform disorders or antisocial personality disorder.

58. A. Aversive conditioning is a specific form of classical conditioning in which an individual develops a dislike, or an aversion, for a previously neutral stimulus as a result of associating that neutral stimulus with a negative stimulus. In the question, Jesse has associated a previously neutral stimulus (the new restaurant) with a negative stimulus (becoming ill) and now has acquired an aversion for the restaurant. Systematic desensitization is a therapeutic technique to help rid people of irrational fears, but does not explain the acquisition of fears or aversions. Social learning and vicarious punishment involve changing one's behavior after watching someone else engage in a behavior that results in either positive or negative consequences. Operant conditioning involves changing the frequency of one's behavior based on the consequences that follow the behavior.

59. D. Codeine and heroin fall under the class of drugs known as opiates. Opiates are psychoactive drugs that act to suppress or reduce pain and are frequently used as analgesics during surgery or as pain suppressants following an injury. All the other options refer to other classes of drugs that exert different effects on the brain and body. Amphetamines fall under the general classification of stimulants, which serve to increase central and peripheral nervous system activity. Barbiturates, also known as sedatives, induce drowsiness and fall under the general class of depressants, which serve to inhibit or slow central nervous system activity.

60. A. A fixed-ratio schedule involves reinforcing an individual after a fixed number of behavioral responses. In the question, Patty is being reinforced (given $2) after she does the dishes five times, reflecting a fixed-ratio schedule. A variable-ratio schedule reinforces Patty after a random number of responses (for example, after five times, but then not again until after seven times). Variable- and fixed-interval schedules are based on time elapsed rather than number of responses (for example, Patty being reinforced at the end of the week or after a random interval of time, given that she has been doing the dishes throughout that time period). A continuous-reinforcement schedule involves reinforcing Patty every time she does the dishes.

61. C. An individual who suffers from sleep apnea awakens several times throughout the night. Sleep apnea is a sleep disorder in which an individual stops breathing at various times throughout the night and must awaken briefly to breathe. Those who find it difficult to fall asleep at night might suffer from insomnia, but not sleep apnea because sleep apnea is a problem that occurs with the regulation of breathing during sleep. Sleep talking and sleepwalking are referred to as somnambulism. Individuals who experience extreme sleepiness during the day and short onsets of REM sleep during waking activity suffer from narcolepsy.

62. A. Stimulants are psychoactive drugs that exert a number of effects on the central and peripheral nervous system, including enhanced central nervous system activity, increased alertness and arousal, increased energy, increased breathing, increased heart rate, increased blood pressure, suppressed appetite and reduced blood flow to the brain. Many stimulants (for example, cocaine, nicotine) create a sense of euphoria or pleasure in individuals as a result of their effects on reward pathways in the limbic system. Thus, stimulants do not generally induce sadness and depression.

63. A. A correlation coefficient indicates two things about a relationship between two variables: the strength of the relationship and the direction or nature of the relationship. The strength of the relationship is indicated by the absolute value of the number. Higher absolute values indicate a stronger relationship. The sign preceding the number indicates the direction or nature of the relationship. A positive sign indicates a positive relationship. A positive relationship means that the two variables are related in such a way that scores on the two variables move in the same direction. (As one goes up, the other goes up; or as one goes down, the other goes down.) Thus, if a researcher finds a correlation of +.85 between years of education and speed of typing, this indicates that individuals with more years of education are also fast typers. Correlational designs do not allow for the determination of cause-and-effect relationships because they lack the stringent control found only in experimental designs. Thus, the researcher cannot conclude that either variable causes the other to change.

64. E. Freud considered the superego to be an aspect of personality that demands we abide by moral principles. When the superego is strong, we behave morally and feel guilt when misbehaving. If the superego is weak, we feel little guilt or remorse after doing wrong. A weak superego does not lead to increased anxiety, depression or sadness, nor does it lead one to constantly doubt their skills and abilities. The superego is only involved in demanding moral behavior and causing feelings of guilt for wrongdoing.

65. B. Freud proposed three structures of personality: the id, ego, and superego. In his conceptualization, the id and superego are in constant conflict and directly oppose one another. The id operates according to the pleasure principle, seeking constant and immediate gratification. The superego operates according to the morality principle, demanding that an individual always behave in accordance with the rules and standards of society. The superego is often likened to a moral conscience. The purpose of the ego is to mediate the conflict between the id and superego. It is said to operate according to the reality principle—either finding an acceptable compromise that satisfies the drives of the id and superego or operating to repress the impulses and drives of the id.

66. **C.** Psychoanalytic theorists believe that psychological disorders are driven by unconscious and repressed impulses and conflicts. Thus, a psychoanalytic therapist would focus on identifying the unconscious forces that might underlie depression. Addressing negative and self-defeating thoughts would be the focus of a cognitive therapist. A biological psychologist or psychiatrist would focus on abnormalities in neurotransmitter levels. A humanistic therapist would focus on identifying the needs and goals that might drive depression. A sociocultural psychologist would focus on changing the socialization practices of a culture.

67. **B.** The graduate assistant has become a conditioned stimulus because Jill has been conditioned to feel anxious and nervous when encountering the assistant. The unconditioned stimulus is a quiz, which automatically elicits anxiety in Jill. The unconditioned response is the anxiety elicited by the unconditioned stimulus (a quiz). The conditioned response is the response that Jill now has to the graduate assistant (anxiety) after associating the graduate assistant with the unconditioned stimulus. The neutral stimulus is the graduate assistant prior to conditioning.

68. **B.** Ivan Pavlov discovered classical conditioning by accident when conducting experiments on the digestive processes of dogs. In his experiments, he ran into an unexpected event—the dogs began to salivate (triggering the digestive process) at the mere sight of the researcher, the sound of footsteps approaching and the sound of a bell. Pavlov went on to conduct additional studies in which he outlined the process and identified the elements of classical conditioning. Conditioned taste aversions were discovered later by other researchers interested in the applications of classical conditioning. Operant conditioning was discovered by B.F. Skinner. Social learning and vicarious learning were discovered by Albert Bandura.

69. **B.** Kara's dislike for hot dogs as a result of becoming ill after eating one is an example of taste aversive conditioning. In classical conditioning, individuals have been found to sometimes take a response learned to one stimulus and make that response to other stimuli (as Kara did with Bratwursts). This phenomenon is known as stimulus generalization. Stimulus discrimination involves the differentiation between various stimuli and actually prevents an individual from generalizing a learned response to all similar stimuli. Forward conditioning, trace conditioning and counterconditioning are all variants of classical conditioning that serve to condition responses in individuals.

70. **B.** The Skinner box was a contraption developed by Skinner that delivered reinforcers to animals following specific behavioral responses (for example, delivering a food pellet after the animal pressed a bar). The purpose of the Skinner box was to study the effects of reinforcement on animal behavior. This process relies on the principles of operant conditioning, which argues that behaviors can be strengthened or weakened through the use of reinforcers or punishers. Systematic desensitization, backward conditioning and classical conditioning are other forms of learning that do not rely on the principles of operant conditioning or the use of a Skinner box to deliver reinforcers or punishers.

71. **E.** Negative punishment involves the removal of a positive stimulus following a behavior to decrease the likelihood of the behavior occurring again. Dr. Black deducts points from students' grades (something they desire) to decrease student absences from class. Positive punishment involves the presentation of a negative stimulus (for example, extra work to do) to decrease a behavior. Reinforcement, whether positive or negative, always increases the likelihood of a behavior occurring again and, therefore, would not be used to decrease absenteeism.

72. **D.** A token economy involves providing an individual with small reinforcers following a behavior that in and of themselves have no inherent reinforcing value (such as stars on a chart). Their reinforcing value lies in the fact that they can later be exchanged for real reinforcers. A token economy is an application of the principles of operant conditioning and not classical conditioning. Vicarious reinforcement involves engaging in a behavior after seeing someone else reinforced for the behavior. Shaping is used if one desires to encourage an altogether new behavior. Partial reinforcement involves random or intermittent reinforcement of a behavior.

73. **C.** Learned helplessness is a phenomenon identified by Martin Seligman that tends to occur when efforts fail to bring about reward or consistently bring about punishment. According to Seligman, such circumstances can leave a person with a sense of no control that ultimately leads to feelings of helplessness (for example, nothing I do matters, there is no sense in trying). Seligman said nothing about extreme anxiety, latent learning or psychotic episodes.

74. C. Telegraphic speech is an early form of speech typically used by toddlers as they acquire language. It includes only the main elements of speech (much like a telegram) and leaves out verbs and auxiliaries. Cooing and babbling are prespeech behaviors shown in infancy that involve the production of vowel sounds (ooooh, aaaah) and the production of vowel-consonant combinations (dadada), respectively. Holophrastic speech involves the use of single words to imply a statement (for example, using only the word *light* to mean *turn the light on* or *turn the light off*) and is a form of speech that precedes telegraphic speech. Overextensions are errors made by young children in which they use a word too broadly (for example, using the word *daddy* to refer to all men).

75. D. Episodic memories refer to memories of personal experiences or episodes. Recalling whom we spoke to at a party over the weekend or what we did on our last birthday involves episodic memory. Semantic memory involves memory of facts and information about the world, such as naming the 50 states or the last five presidents of the United States. Procedural memories are memories for skills and habits, such as riding a bike or walking. Implicit memory refers to memories not intentionally learned and for which an individual has no conscious recollection. Flashbulb memories refer to clear and vivid memories of events that are especially meaningful and/or emotional.

76. E. Latent learning involves learning that is not displayed until a later point in time. (It lies latent or dormant for a period of time.) Shaping is a technique used to encourage altogether new behaviors and involves the application of operant conditioning principles. With the other forms of learning (instrumental learning, operant learning and acquisition), the change in behavior is more immediate.

77. C. Retroactive interference refers to the inability to recall an old piece of information (such as an old address) because newer information is interfering with its recall. In contrast, proactive interference occurs when an individual has difficulty remembering a new piece of information because previously learned information is interfering with its retrieval. The primacy, recency and serial position effects all refer to phenomena that occur when remembering lists. In general, each states how the position of the item in a list (whether it is at the beginning, end or middle) plays a role in how well that item can be remembered.

78. B. Divergent thinking refers to the ability to generate as many answers or solutions to a given problem as possible. Convergent thinking involves working toward a single solution or answer to a problem. Fluid intelligence involves the ability to see relationships between events and to process information efficiently and effectively. Deductive and inductive reasoning involve applying logic to analyze problems and draw conclusions.

79. D. Abraham Maslow argued that human behavior is motivated by a desire to attain certain needs including a need for self-actualization (a desire to reach one's optimal level of functioning). Psychoanalysts argue that behavior is motivated by unconscious forces and early childhood experiences. Cognitive dissonance theory argues that humans are motivated by a desire to maintain consistency between thoughts/attitudes and behavior. Drive theory argues that human behavior is motivated by a desire to maintain homeostasis within the body. No specific theory or perspective argues that humans are motivated by a desire to seek out challenging tasks.

80. C. The Wechsler Adult Intelligence Scale (WAIS) is an intelligence test that assesses two broad aspects of intelligence: verbal and nonverbal intelligence. It is *not* designed to measure emotional, social, experiential, contextual, musical or kinesthetic intelligence. It is also *not* employed as a measure of creativity or giftedness, though giftedness can be assessed to some degree using the WAIS.

81. D. The tip-of-the-tongue phenomenon is most likely a problem with retrieval of information from memory. The fact that people are sure they know someone's name, can often recall the first letter or a name close to the actual name they are trying to recall, and often remember the name at a later point all suggest that the name has been encoded and stored in memory. The problem lies in trying to trigger or cue the name to move from memory into conscious awareness.

82. E. Object permanence refers to the awareness that an object continues to exist despite it not being physically present to the senses. Thus, an infant who searches for a toy when it has been removed from view is showing signs of object permanence. Conservation refers to the awareness that objects remain the same despite changes in their physical appearance. Transformational thought refers to the ability to consider more than one aspect of a stimulus or situation simultaneously. Logical reasoning refers to the ability to apply logic to draw conclusions about events and situations encountered in the world.

83. **B.** In studies examining the capacity of short-term memory, George Miller discovered that on average, people can hold about seven items in memory at a time. The phrases *the magical number seven* and *seven plus or minus two* emerged from Miller's findings. The digit span task presented in the question has far more than seven items, so it is highly unlikely that individuals will remember all the items. Still, they are likely to remember more than two or four items. Miller's work suggests that the capacity of short-term memory is about seven items. It says nothing about which seven items in a list individuals will remember.

84. **C.** Recall memory requires that one retrieve information from memory without any cues or aids. Asking someone to list the four lobes of the brain is an assessment of recall memory. A test of recognition memory involves looking at an item(s) and determining whether one has encountered it before. A multiple-choice question is a test of recognition memory. A test of short-term memory involves asking someone to repeat an experience or list of words presented to them just seconds or minutes before. Implicit memory involves the unconscious recollection of material and is tested using priming tasks.

85. **E.** Kohlberg's postconventional level of moral reasoning involves a consideration of human rights and a belief in doing what is in the best interest of all humans. The preconventional level of reasoning focuses on oneself and the attainment of personal reward and/or avoidance of personal punishment. The conventional level of reasoning focuses on laws and rules and involves a belief that laws are set for a reason and must always be obeyed.

86. **C.** The Oedipal conflict occurs in boys during the genital stage of psychosexual development. According to Freud, the Oedipal complex involves a sexual desire for one's mother and animosity toward one's father. A focus on oral gratification occurs in infancy during the oral stage of psychosexual development. Repression of sexual desires into the unconscious is believed to occur during the latent stage of development. Direction of libidinal (sexual) energy toward peers occurs during the phallic stage of psychosexual development, which occurs in adolescence.

87. **B.** Projection involves attributing one's forbidden or negative thoughts to others as when a person who has desires to cheat on their spouse begins to accuse their spouse of cheating. Justifying one's actions with a socially acceptable excuse involves rationalization. Expressing extreme affection toward someone you hate is reaction formation. Discharging anger into a game of racquetball is displacement. Returning to a more childlike state following a negative experience is regression.

88. **D.** The ego is one of three personality structures proposed by Sigmund Freud. The ego is said to operate according to the reality principle—striving to find acceptable ways to behave that meet the impulsive and hedonistic desires of the id while at the same time satisfying the moral conscience of the superego. The id is a personality structure that operates at a completely unconscious level and strives to obtain immediate gratification. The superego is analogous to a moral conscience and leads to feelings of guilt and anxiety following misbehavior.

89. **C.** People with high self-esteem tend to engage in self-protective processes that serve to maintain or foster high levels of self-esteem. They do this by attributing failure to external factors and success to internal factors. People with low self-esteem and depressed individuals are more likely to attribute failure to internal factors and success to external factors.

90. **A.** Traits refer to aspects of personality that remain fairly stable across time and situations. Thus, traits do not fluctuate across time and situations. Traits are not determined primarily by external factors, but are believed to represent internal predispositions that remain fairly consistent despite changes in external factors. They are also not believed to evolve from early childhood experiences, but rather to be present at birth and remain fairly stable throughout one's life span.

91. **C.** Extroversion is a personality trait that refers to one's degree of sociability and outgoingness. Individuals who are highly extroverted tend to be sociable and enjoy social interactions and events. Those who are less extroverted (introverted) tend to be shy and to prefer solitary activities over social activities. Being open to new experiences and ways of thinking refers to the trait of openness. Showing instability in mood and emotion refers to the trait of neuroticism. Being easygoing and pleasant reflects the trait of agreeableness.

92. **D.** Individuals operating at the conventional level of moral reasoning are focused on laws and rules. They believe that laws should be followed at all times and that anyone who breaks the rules should be punished. Preconventional reasoning is focused on oneself and the avoidance of punishment and/or attainment of reward. Postconventional reasoning involves a focus on human rights and a belief that what is right is whatever is best for all individuals involved (even if it violates the law). Moral relativism and moral realism are *not* stages in Kohlberg's theory.

93. **E.** Projective tests are designed to gain insight into unconscious thoughts and desires. They involve the presentation of ambiguous stimuli to individuals who then provide an account of what they see in the stimulus. It is believed that the individual projects unconscious thoughts and desires onto their accounts of the stimuli. Objective tests come in many forms. Some are designed to determine the presence or absence of mental disorders (for example, the MMPI). Others are designed to classify individuals as high or low on personality traits (for example, NEO-PI). Aptitude tests assess one's potential for learning.

94. **E.** According to Erik Erikson, the late adults years are characterized by a psychosocial crisis called integrity versus despair. This final crisis involves a review of one's life experiences and achievements. To achieve integrity, one must accept the past and find meaning/purpose in life. A search for one's identity occurs during the adolescent years. A desire to help younger generations is part of the middle adult crisis, generativity versus stagnation. A need for control over one's life and a distancing of oneself from friends and family are *not* part of any of the eight psychosocial crises proposed by Erikson.

95. **C.** Formal operational thought refers to the final stage of thought proposed by Jean Piaget. This type of thought develops across the adolescent years and is characterized by abstract thinking, logical reasoning and hypothetical deductive reasoning. Presenting a pendulum to individuals and asking them to determine what influences the speed at which the pendulum swings is a test of formal operational thought. This task, called the pendulum problem and used by Piaget himself, requires hypothetical deductive reasoning. All the other tests are Piagetian tasks that assess other types of thought including conservation (**A**), perspective taking (**B**), object permanence (**D**) and classification skills (**E**).

96. **E.** Reliability refers to the capability of a test to produce consistent results. One way to determine the reliability of a test is to administer it to an individual on more than one occasion. Highly similar individual scores on different occasions provides evidence of a test's reliability. A test's availability and ease of use does not contribute to reliability. A test's capability to differentiate between individuals of varying degrees of intelligence and its degree of correlation with other tests of intelligence provide evidence of its validity.

97. **E.** Howard Garner proposed a theory of multiple intelligences in which he argued that at least seven types of intelligence exist: linguistic, logical-mathematical, spatial, bodily-kinesthetic, musical, interpersonal, intrapersonal and naturalistic. According to Gardner, these different types of intelligence are largely independent of one another. Therefore, it is possible for individuals to be high in one aspect of intelligence but low in another aspect. His theory of multiple intelligences also opposes the use of standardized achievement tests, arguing that they tend to focus on only linguistic and logical-mathematical intelligences and ignore other types of intelligence.

98. **B.** Dissociative fugue is a disorder that involves two primary features: a dissociation in the form of forgetting who one is and a fugue in the form of wandering away from one's home. Individuals who experience dissociative fugue might take on a completely new life with no recollection of who they are or how they got to where they are. Dissociative identity disorder differs from dissociative fugue in two ways: It involves the development of more than one personality in addition to one's original personality, and there is no fugue state or wandering from one's home. Conversion disorder is actually a somotoform disorder that involves the loss of a bodily function (for example, numbness in one's hand, loss of eyesight) with no underlying physiological cause. Delusions of grandeur and manic episodes do not involve a loss of identity or a fugue state as described in the question, but rather refer to an irrational sense of increased importance and significance (delusions of grandeur) and a state of extreme elation and high energy (manic episode).

99. **C.** The DSM-IV groups disorders into axes or classifications based on their primary symptoms. Some of the major classifications within the DSM-IV include mood disorders, somatoform disorders, anxiety disorders, personality disorders, dissociative disorders and schizophrenic disorders. The only pair that falls under the same general classification in the DSM-IV is conversion disorder and hypochondriasis, which are both somatoform disorders. Phobic disorder falls under the heading of anxiety disorders. Schizophrenia is a class of disorders itself that does not include phobic disorders. Dissociative identity disorder and dissociative fugue fall under the heading of dissociative disorders. Unipolar and bipolar disorder are both mood disorders. Post-traumatic stress disorder is an anxiety disorder.

100. **C.** Client-centered therapy is a therapeutic technique developed by Carl Rogers. Rogers believed that discrepancies in one's real and ideal self and unconditional positive regard by others contribute to personality and mental problems. As a result, he developed client-centered therapy, which focuses on providing individuals with an open and trusting environment in which they can reflect on who they are and develop more realistic (and positive) views of the self. The other options all reflect alternative therapeutic approaches. Delving into early childhood experiences and analyzing dreams for their latent content are both psychoanalytic therapies, often referred to as talk therapy and dream analysis, respectively. Changing maladaptive thought patterns is a focus of Rational Emotive Therapy (RET) and cognitive therapy. Extinguishing maladaptive behavior patterns is a technique used by behavioral therapists.

Free-Response Question #1—Explanation

Overall approach

- Be sure to answer all parts of the question.
- Note that you are being asked to explain to the company how to conduct the experiment, so word your answer to reflect this.
- Answer in complete sentences.
- Do not just list the steps needed to conduct a study; organize your response into a well-structured, coherent essay.

Key points to include

- The company has already identified the population of interest (older adults).
- They next have to identify and draw a sample from this population (a specific group of older adults).
- Participants should be randomly selected (to reduce sample bias) from the population.
- The final sample should approximate the population as closely as possible. (This allows for generalization to the broader population.)
- Define the independent and dependent variables in the study.
  - The independent variable is manipulated/varied directly by the researcher. (In this study, the independent variable is type of drug taken—either placebo or test drug.)
  - The dependent variable is the variable measured the same in all participants. (In this study, the dependent variable is performance on a memory task.)
- The researcher should randomly assign participants to either the experimental group or the control group. (This can be done by flipping a coin or by having the participant draw a card to determine which group the participant is in.)
- Random assignment to groups helps ensure that the two groups are equal in most respects and reduces the chance of group biases or differences.
- When group membership has been determined, the researcher should proceed with the experimental manipulation.
- The experimental group is the group that receives the special treatment—so, in this study, participants in the experimental group receive the new test drug.
- The control group is used as a comparison group—so, in this study, participants in the control group receive a placebo drug.
- At this point, the researcher would be wise to use a double-blind procedure to reduce the possibility of expectancy effects.
- Briefly define expectancy effects and describe how a double-blind study is implemented and how it reduces expectancy effects. (Participants do not know whether they receive a placebo or the experimental drug. Also, the individual assessing participants on the dependent variables does not know whether the individual is in the experimental or control group.)
- Following the experimental manipulation, the researcher tests each participant on the dependent variable. Be sure to address the hypothesis again at this point. (*Older adults who take the new test drug 1 hour prior to a memory test recall more words on a word recall task than those who take a placebo drug 1 hour prior to the memory test.*) Wait for 1 hour after ingesting the pill, then give each participant a list of words to remember.
- After a delay period, which should be the same length for all participants, test them for memory of the words.
- Test all participants on the memory test (regardless of group membership), and record their scores on the memory test.
- Compute the average score for the experimental group and the average score for the control group.

- Compare the average scores of the two groups to see whether they are significantly different. (This requires statistical analyses to test whether the difference is significant.)
- If a significant difference exists, identify which group scored better.
- If the experimental group scored significantly better than the control group on the memory test, the hypothesis is supported.

Free-Response Question #2—Explanation

Overall approach

- Be sure to answer all parts of the question.
- Answer in complete sentences; organize your response into a well-structured, coherent essay.
- Do not just list the steps involved in sensation and perception, but explain how an individual given this specific task senses and perceives the images.

Key points to include

First, you are being asked to describe how individuals sense the images and how they perceive the images.

- Begin with sensation, and address how individuals sense the images.
- Note that these are visual stimuli, involving the visual sense. Provide a brief description of the visual sense (for example, its sensory organs, its receptors and so on).
- Define sensation, and describe the processes involved in sensation (detection, conversion, transduction).
- Follow this with an explanation of how these processes are carried out in the task described in the question.
  - *Detection*: Sensory receptors in the eye detect light energy reflected from the images.
  - *Conversion*: Sensory receptors convert this energy into a neural impulse.
  - *Transduction*: The neural impulse is transmitted to the brain via the optic nerve.

Second, you are asked how the individual perceives the images.

- Define perception, and describe the processes involved in perception.
- Follow this with an explanation of how these processes are carried out in the task described in the question.
  - Information is sent to the occipital lobe for further processing.
  - In the occipital lobe, feature detections analyze and interpret specific features of the images (for example, slant, hue and so on).
  - At the same time, the brain compares the incoming information to information already stored in the brain to aid in the interpretation process.
  - As the brain analyzes and pieces together the specific features of the stimulus and compares these features to already stored information, it draws conclusions about the images.
  - Information is sent to the frontal lobe and the motor cortex, directing the individual to respond to the image.

Third, the question asks about the role of bottom-up and top-down processing in the analysis and interpretation of the images.

- Define each term, and explain how each is operating in this particular task.
  - Bottom-up processing involves analysis of incoming information about the specific features of the images; it relies on information coming directly from the stimulus.
  - Top-down processing involves the use of prior knowledge, mood, memories and so on to help process and interpret information. Thus, if an individual is familiar with any of the images, they might recognize them more quickly than unfamiliar images.